1 MONTH OF
FREE
READING

at
www.ForgottenBooks.com

By purchasing this book you are eligible for one month membership to ForgottenBooks.com, giving you unlimited access to our entire collection of over 1,000,000 titles via our web site and mobile apps.

To claim your free month visit:

www.forgottenbooks.com/free62428

ISBN 978-0-483-02319-2
PIBN 10062428

THE STENTOR.

VOLUME VI. OCTOBER 4, 1892. NUMBER 1.

PUBLISHED EVERY TWO WEEKS
BY THE

Lake Forest University Stentor Publishing Co.

BOARD OF EDITORS.

F. C. SHARON, '93................Managing Editor
R. H. CROZIER, '93..............Business Manager
S. B. HOPKINS, '93, }
N. H. BURDICK, '93, } ....Locals
L. N. ROSSITER, '93............ ....Alumni
B. R. MACHATTON, '95 ....Advertising

Terms—$1.50 per year. Single Copies—10c

————ADDRESS————

STENTOR PUBLISHING COMPANY,

LAKE FOREST, : : ILLINOIS.

Entered at the P. O. at Lake Forest, Ill., as second class matter.

THE STENTOR'S GREETING.

The STENTOR is again with you for '92-93, and in better shape than ever. It is on a firm financial basis, has an established reputation and is bound to succeed. Its advertising is of the best. We will repeat, however, for the benefit of new students that the STENTOR is not a literary magazine any more than a newspaper is, and simply aims to give the news of the school and town as pithily as possible. Therefore if you desire the *news* we ask your support and subscription.

A COLLEGE BUTTON.

Here we are one of the best colleges in the west, and without that necessary appendage, a college button. When we are away we have nothing to show where we are from except, perhaps, some streamers of ribbons flying in the wind, and one looks too much like a walking ribbon counter with these. A college button of gold and enamel can be purchased for from 75 cents to $2.50. It is a neat and very tasty ornament, and is something that none of us should be without. It is quite the thing at present, and we will not be "in it" if we don't procure a button.

JUST THE THING FOR MIDWINTER.

It may be somewhat early to mention indoor baseball, but the sooner a start is made in the right direction the better. There is no game like indoor baseball for winter. When the football season is over and we have turned to indoor sports, there is nothing that quite comes up to the aforesaid game.

Now here is the proposition! Organize a college team to play against a town nine. There could be no better place than the gymnasium for the contests to take place. We are all but assured that the town people will stand the expense of screening the windows; the floor can be cleared in a few minutes and there you are. An admission fee of perhaps ten cents could be charged for the big games, the proceeds to go into the athletic treasury. It would be a great novelty, the townspeople would be present, the students would turn out, the Ferry Hall girls would come and smile, and the fun would be immeasurable. Therefore let us have a team organized after football is over, enjoy ourselves, and leave a goodly balance in the athletic association's pocket.

WANTED--A UNIVERSITY SONG.

It is a sad fact, but nevertheless true that we have no distinctively Lake Forest College song. There are very few colleges now that have not, beside their war cry—the college yell—their hymn praising their dear old Alma Mater, a song which always will remain embalmed in the students memory, the strains and words of which will in after years bring tears to his eyes as the "good old days" pass dreamily before him, a song that is a slogan in victory, a solace in defeat. And yet here are we without such a necessary piece of music. True there is a piece of doggerel that goes under the name of the college song but both the words and music are puerile. It is granted that a college yell is absolutely necessary. Why then is not a college song just as indispensable. We claim that it is and are extremely desirous of seeing some genius in the University step forward with a song that will be worthy of us. In order to add an incentive the Stentor will offer two prizes of *five dollars* each, one for the best music, the other for the best words to the person or persons composing the best Lake Forest College song. All songs must be in the day before the Christmas Holidays and will be judged by a competent committee. The successful ballad will be published in the Stentor as will also the second best. Now we really mean what we say and this is an excellent chance for the poets and musicians to turn loose their muses. Think it over and let us hear from you. This is open to Alumni and townspeople as well as students.

Its a good maxim at the beginning of the year as well as any other time, boys, to stick to the truth. You win better in the end.

The Student's hand-book issued by the Y. M. C. A. is a very neat little pamphlet and contains valuable information for new students. The article by Doctor Haven is especially good and very practical.

THE NEW FEATURES.

As we strolled up to the campus on the opening day, several new features burst upon our enraptured view. First, a brilliant array of colors dazzled our eyes for a brief period, which we discovered on a nearer approach was our beloved college behind a new coat of many colors. Brown, yellow, green, drab, and white vied with each other in making the old building loom up. The sheds on the back side were removed and, as a member of the economics class remarked, "the value of the building was increased by taking part of it away." The old engine room is fitted up as a chemical laboratory. To the left in the ravine is the new steam plant which is to supply power and heat for all the buildings. A bridge across the ravine to the art building is also in the course of construction. Round by Principal Smith's are situated the buildings and campus of the new academy. One of the new dormitories is almost completed. It is of brick and contains very pleasant rooms. One of the cottages and Reid Memorial Hall are also under way. At present the academy is so full that the President's house is occupied as a dormitory. And it is said the end is not yet. We are but one of many who say "let the work proceed."

ORGANIZE A POLITICAL CLUB.

This is the presidential year and there is presumably great excitement and much speculation over the outcome of the election. Yet here we seem to have so many important things to watch, for fear the other society will get ahead, or so much studying (?), that a presidential election is but a secondary matter. At the present rate when we emerge into public life we will know as much about politics as the *average* mule and care as much. Let us be up and doing something. We represent partially "Young America." The issues of the present will affect us in the future, therefore let us study the subjects thoroughly and see whether we believe in Republicanism or Democracy, People's party or Prohibition. Organize a Republican club as other colleges have done. Organize a Democratic one—if you can. At any rate let's have a political club, arise out of our lethargy, and cast our vote sometime knowing why we vote as we do.

NOTES OF AN IDLER.
**
*

Did you ever notice the way boys receive letters? No? Well, having nothing to do lately, as our heading would indicate, we took our stand at the post-office one day and this is what *we* saw. Groups of boys are approaching from various Clubs and resorts to see what Uncle Sam's mail bag has brought them. The mail is not yet distributed, so into the office they all crowd and good naturedly chaff each other while awaiting their fate. "Bet you two to one you don't draw", "Oh, come off, I dont expect anything" (all the time hoping against hope that she did write.) "Well I'll be hanged, nothing but some confounded circular" "Say, swipes, your bill for box rent's all you get." "By George, if the old man has't sent my allowance, I'm in the consumme." Click, click, the window goes and the mail is open, "231, 416, 32, 56, 121" and on down the line it goes till all have received their portion. Now let us watch the most interesting proceeding. Here comes one fellow full tilt, down three steps at a time, his face beaming all over. He shoves a thick envelope into his coat and makes for his room. "Hello B— got a "square." What did she say about me, old man?" "She uses lots of stationary on you, B—." But B— is far away from the crowd now. He hangs onto the letter tightly. He knows almost what it says. It is too sacred to open any place but in his inner

sanctum. Thither we dare not follow. Then here comes the crowd. Beaming faces, disappointed faces, jolly faces, serious faces. We know the effect of each epistle. Heres comes the boy whose home writing consists of the following stereotyped message—"Dear Father. Am well. Please send me some funds, your loving son." There he goes waving his funds and thinking how he can best "blow it." This fellow who looks very sorrowful has probably just heard from pater to the effect that his last term's report has been received. This one with angry mien says under his breath that he "can't see why the Faculty had to go blab to the old man. He didn't flunk much more than the rest and as for those old *oil barrels* just wait till he gets a chance at some more." Then here's a group who didn't receive anything, who take especial delight in guying those who did, and who vote letter writing a nuisance and not "what its cracked up to be." Well lets go and see if we received anything —but stay—this is not all. Here comes a tall manly looking fellow, an upper-class man, and a shrinking homesick freshman. The former has folded up a long letter and replaced it in his pocket. He looks dreamily off into the distance and doesn't mind where he is going. He sees the old home, the dear old place, the loving faces, and reigning over all the sweet, dear, beloved mother who has penned those lines, who hopes and prays that her son will be a noble man. And he grows sad and thoughtful as he thinks that perhaps he doesn't think enough of home, and he wonders if the old home influence is being shaken off. He determines this shall not be, and walks briskly down the street strengthened by those loving sentences. And then the homesick lad, how he pores over those pages telling him how he is missed, how he wishes he was there, and yet how strong and happy he feels after he has read it, and feels that he *must* do something for them to be proud of. We turn away in a softened mood and thank heaven that "the mother" can do so much. Then we go up in a doubtful sort of way and tremulously ask if "there's anything for us." "Nothing." "Well I'm confoundedly glad they didn't write anyway, saves a fellow answering."

*
* *

We've often wondered why it is that good table manners are scarce as water in a desert in an ordinary college crowd. But why need we wonder? Men, especially American men, living to themselves in clubs, forget everything at meals, drop all manners they may have otherwise, and seem to be seized with an insane desire to see who can bolt his dinner first. Every way goes; shove it in with your knife, poke it down with your fork, toss it down in gulps and make sounds resembling a steam engine in full blast and then look up with an air of injured innocence that anyone should be annoyed. Manners that are so essential, that are so winning, that go such a way in helping one along, are often enough neglected, but table manners are almost tabooed by a majority at school. Surely of all places and of all things daintyness at table is the most pleasing, for where one is careful there, he is very apt to be careful everywhere. Cultivate therefore your table manners and when you are invited out you won't feel like "a stranger in a strange land."

*
* *

A youth approacheth our peaceful burg and is espied in the dim distance by two rival bands of warriors. The poor youth is swooped down upon and before he knows what has happened, is hustled off to "our society hall" by one band, while the other tribe soon after lugs him off to dinner at "our club." He is then made to understand that the "other society" is a set of chumps; they are dull and stupid, they don't know an oration from a debate, they—O, you play ball? Well, those other chumps *never* could play ball. One of their men accidentally caught a fly once—when his mouth was open —and they had a celebration and a war dance over it. Why, actually one of our men, when the score was two to nothing against us, knocked a fly to their center fielder and the short stop had to go out and wake him up. He then lost the ball coming in and our man actually made three home runs on it and won the game hands down. O! we're the stuff. Haven't we a fine hall?"

Soon after at "our club" he hears the following: "So those everlasting hoodoos showed you their hall? Well, such nerve. Why, half of it is old stuff fixed over. And said they could beat us playing ball? Why, the only thing they ever beat was a carpet, and they only half did that. And say, they're not in it with the girls! Naw! Would you believe it, every one of our fellows drew valentines last year and only one of their's did. He found out after he had written a passionate stanza to a fair "sem." that his brother sent it as a joke. The faculty think we're the people, too. Ever seen the gym? Our fellows are at the top of the heap there."

Soon after both parties leave the poor distracted youth to dream of home, but he cannot rest with his aching brow. He seeks the porch. He hears a member of "one society" greet a fellow from the "other society" thusly: "Hello, Swipes! how's your man." "O, we've got him suited." "O, come now, *we'll* get him *sure* Friday night." "Bet you won't." "All right, come over to the gym and I'll bowl you a game to see who gets him." And the poor, bewildered youth seeks his pillow and dreams that in his dilemma he joined the Aletheians and under their benign influence the troubled brow relaxes and he peacefully sleeps.

THE PENNANT WINNERS.

LAKE FOREST IS THE PROUD POSSESSOR OF THE BASEBALL RAG.

THE RECORDS OF THE MEN.

Lake Forest University tops the list of the colleges in the Western College Baseball League for 1892. The last game was played too late to give it more than a passing notice in the last STENTOR, and we now propose to give a full account.

The team that so successfully defended the name of the University began training last February under the captaincy of George William Ellis, '93. It was composed of the following men with their positions:

Catchers—William D. McNary, '93, and A. L. Zimmer, law.
Pitcher—George W. Ellis, '93.
First Base—Frederic C. Sharon, '93.
Second Base—William R. Dysart, '92.
Third Base—Frank E. Dewey, '96.
Short Stop—John A. Bloomingston, '94.
Left Field—Forest Grant, '96.
Center Field—Fred A. Hayner, '95.
Right Field—Harry Goodman, '94.
Substitutes—Dean Lewis, '95; H. A. Rumsey, '94.
Manager—Harry Goodman, '94.

William D. McNary was catcher for the

Academy team in '87-88, and played third base on the 'Varsity in '91. He went through the league season of '92 without an error.

George W. Ellis was class pitcher for '93 for the years '91 and '92, and in '91 also played center field on the 'Varsity. Last season as pitcher he held Beloit down to six hits, Evanston to five, and Champaign to five.

F. C. Sharon has played first base on the 'Varsity for three seasons, and also occupied the same position on his class team, '93.

W. R. Dysart played short stop for Macalester College in '91. Last season he occupied the position of second base on the 'Varsity and the '92 team.

Frank E. Dewey played left field on the Academy team for three seasons. Last season he played third base for the 'Varsity to a queen's taste.. He is known as a sure catch and a good batter.

John A. Bloomingston, "Our Bloomy," although small, gets there in shape around short stop's position, which he has occupied for two seasons, playing the same position on '94. His long willow bat generally connected at critical times.

Forest Grant is by far the best fielder in the league. He played third base on the 'Varsity in '90, but has played left field since then. He is the best base runner on the team and a good batter.

F. A. Hayner was Varsity pitcher in '91, and made quite a good record. Last season he guarded center-field perfectly and was a good batter.

Harry Goodman played short-stop for the 'Cad team of '90, which beat every " prep." school but Evanston High. Last season he played right-field and was also manager of the team. Dean Lewis was the class pitcher for '95. H. A. Ramsey played first for the 'Cads of '90, and the same for college '94.

To Ellis's superb pitching and general command of the team, and to Zimmer's coaching is due a large amount of the credit. It is the first time Lake Forest has had an undisputed champion team, and with su c a start will it be the last? The record of the league was as follows :

	Won.	Lost.	Per Cent.
Lake Forest	5	1	.866
Champaign	4	2	.666
Beloit	2	4	.333
Evanston	1	5	.166

The last game between Beloit and Champaign is undecided. We have put it to the credit of Champaign in the table.

The scores of the games were:

Lake Forest	10	Champaign	5
Lake Forest	6	Beloit (11 inings)	5
Lake Forest	6	Evanston	2
Lake Forest	0	Champaign	5
Lake Forest	9	Beloit	0
Lake Forest	9	Evanston	0
Champaign	5	Evanston	1
Champaign	9	Beloit	0
Champaign	6	Beloit	9
Beloit	7	Evanston	4

Second Beloit-Evanston game not played.

Such is the proud record of our last year's ball team, a team that lost but one game during the season. With such a captain and management as we had last season, we may be able to repeat the feat again next spring. Indoor base ball will be good practice for the eye and will keep the body in trim this winter. Honor to the ball team of '92, and may history repeat itself.

H. RIDER HAGGARD.

A CRITICISM OF HIS STYLE AND WORKS.

I offer no apology for taking up a theme from modern prose literature. In our essay work, whether for class or society, this wide field is almost entirely neglected. In some fields the ancient is too often all that is worthy of attention. But this cannot be said of literature.

Let us turn away, then, from the angels and archangels of Milton and Caedmon, from Chancer's " Crowing Chanticleer " and vulgar " Prioresse," from the painstaking and painful accuracy of Thucydides, from Wardsworth's "Blind Man," and the "Spirit Fierce and Bold," as well as from the "Ancient Mariner" who "Stoppeth One of Three," while we consider briefly the pathetic humanness of Haggard's novel "Beatrice," and the dread terrors of his "Cleopatra."

The works of Haggard are not classics. That is, they have not yet suffered the wear and tear of centuries; they have not been scoured and polished by the beating of the wings of time into that semblance, at least, of respectability possessed by the comedies and tragedies of Moliere and Shakespeare and the novels of Thackeray and Scott. Probably they never will be. They are lesser works than these.

Why, then, should they claim our attention? In the first place, the author's powers of imagining have never been surpassed. Excepting Edgar Allen Poe's prose tales, we know of no production revealing an imagination equal in range or power to that of the author of "King Solomon's Mines." Never has the English language been used, except by Haggard, to paint such scenes of gloom and desolation, of grandeur and sublimity. We present one example from the vision of Harmachis, the Egyptian, during his initiation into the mysteries of Isis. "And then I knew that things were not as things had been. The air around me began to stir, it rustled as the wings of eagles rustle; it took life. Bright eyes gazed upon me, strange whispers shook my soul. Upon the darkness were bars of lights. They changed and interchanged; they moved to and fro and wove mystic symbols that I could not read. Swifter and swifter flew the shuttle of the light; the symbols grouped, gathered, faded, gathered yet again, faster and still more fast, till my eyes could no more count them. Now I was afloat upon a sea of glory. It surged and rolled as the ocean rolls; it tossed me high, it brought me low. Glory was piled on glory, splendor heaped on splendor's head, and I rode above it all.

"Soon the lights began to pale in the roll-ing sea of air. Great shadows shot across it, lines of darkness pierced it and rushed together and my breast, till at length I only was a shape of flame set like a star on the bosom of immeasurable night. Bursts of awful music gathered from far away. Miles and miles away I heard them, thrilling faintly through the gloom. On they came, nearer and more near, louder and more loud, till they swept past, above, below, around me, swept on whirring pinions, terrifying and enchanting me. They floated by, ever growing fainter, till they died in space. Then others came, and no two were akin. Some rattled as ten thousand sistra shaken all to tune. Some rang from the brazen throats of unnumbered clarions. Some pealed with a loud, sweet chant of voices that were more than human. And some rolled along in the slow thunder of a million drums. They passed; their notes were lost in dying echoes; and the awful silence once more pressed in upon and overcame me."

In the second place, there is much about his literary style that merits no word but praise. His variety, for example, is apparently without limit. The expression "glory was piled on glory, splendor heaped on splendor's head" is a remarkable instance of the repetition of a thought in new words with emphasis rather than loss of force. He writes the commonplaces of ordinary social intercourse among all classes of men and the antique, accumulative modes of expression of the Egyptian priesthood with equal facility. The "Cleopatra" from beginning to end is extraordinary in its constant tension, every word in that which purports to be from the ancient papyrus is emphatic, and the effect of the whole is powerful beyond the conception of one who has not read it. The "Beatrice," on the other hand, is written for the most part in the simplest of styles, conversational, without tension, ordinary.

His use of alliteration is most careful, and the effect is always good. Not the accidental, meaningless recurrence of certain sounds, but intentional, onomatopoetic alliteration. This might well be studied with a view to mastery with the "Cleopatra" as a primer. The alliteration in "r" always expresses disaster, the overwhelming rush of the destroying elements being suggested by the rolling sound of the letter: "wreck and red ruin;" "hand in hand down the path of sin rushed Ruin and Remorse." The "d" is privative, the effect of the letter being to deaden the sound with which it is connected; "hearken to me now, who to-morrow may lie in the dumb dust, disempired and dishonored." The "f" suggests rapid motion, the quick, sharp sound of the letter being most noticeable: "he has fled fast and far." Such alliteration, if not used to excess or inconsistently, cannot fail to emphasize and please.

Another element of his style is its superlative force. We would scarcely have thought the English language capable of expressing all that he compels it to in places had we not read these novels. He absolutely startles us at times with the emphasis he gives to the conception on which he dwells. Love, the favorite theme of modern novelists, receives this comment from him in the "Beatrice":

"Now there was an end of hopes and fears; now Reason fell and Love usurped his throne, and at that royal coming Heaven threw wide her gates. O! sweetest and most dear; O! dearest and most sweet! Oh! to have lived to find this happy hour—oh!· in this hour to die! See, heaviness is behind us; see, now we are one. Blow, ye winds, blow out your stormy heart; we know the secret of your strength; you rush to your desire. Fall, deep waters of the sea, fall in thunder at the feet of Earth; we hear the music of your pleading.

"Earth and seas and winds, sing your great chant of love! heaven and space and time echo back the melody! For life has called to us the answer of this riddle. Heart to heart we sit, and lips to lips, and we are more

wise than Solomon, and richer than barbarian kings, for happiness is our slave.

"To this end were we born, and from all time predestinate. To this end do we live and die, in death to find completer unity. For here is that secret of the world which wise men seek and cannot find, and here, too, is the gate to Heaven."

There have, doubtless, been more rational comments on the tender passion, but surely none so grandly passionate, so superlatively egotistical, so original. Notice particularly the beauty, the originality, the force of the conception in the second paragraph of the quotation, where winds and waves are made to feel with man the power of "the little god."

But is there anything in this that will live? that will go down through the centuries to be read, and admired, and loved, more and more as time goes by? No, we answer, there is not. There is nothing in any of Haggard's novels that will either benefit or explain mankind. Did they do either of these things they would be extremely valuable, for in such a guise anything of use to man would be presented with the best possible chances.

But we find no indications of any attempt to do these things. None of the higher attributes of mankind receive any notice in these novels. There is no expression of a longing for higher and better things, only an over-active imagination conjuring up wonders that must attract for the moment and then leave behind them a feeling that you have been cheated. Expecting to read something of intrinsic value, you find nothing set before you but the productions of a power not only uncontrolled and uncontrolable, but, more than all, a power not backed up by any accurate knowledge of man, especially of man's higher nature.

Haggard suggests no thoughts that will tend to establish truth and religion in the minds of those who read. He is clearly not attempting to inculcate any moral principles.

In the conclusion of the "Cleopatra," Harmachis is made to speak of the Christian religion as but a revivification, after a long lapse of time, of the worship of the gods of old Egypt under new names. Osiris, Isis and Horus are the Holy Trinity and songs almost Christian in sentiment, in phraseology Egyptian, are sung to them during the progress of the story. The author rails at modern society in the love episode of Geoffrey and Beatrice, especially at the modern marriage compact in the wanton words of the "divine" Cleopatra, and is in general indifferent to the claims of morality and religion, all his religious characters being so overdrawn as to repel rather than attract, while a great majority of the population of his books make no pretensions to religion or morality.

We have not attempted to analyze the plots of the novels to which reference has been made, as this would have excluded all possibility of criticism in our limited space. But we have discovered and set forth in H. Rider Haggard great imagining power and wonderful rhetorical ability that, tempered and made use of by some noble conception, some deep truth demanding the attention of mankind for man's own bettering, would have been productive of a fame as great and an immortality as sure as any of the bards or philosophers of old can claim.

In the absence of this motive, however, there can be but one result—"Beatrice" and "Cleopatra" will be read only when we are in quest of a pleasure of the baser sort, or when we wish to discover and study the good points of one of England's most modern writers. When we want some lasting truth, some pure and noble sentiment, something to foster high ideals and aims, we will go as before to our time-tried heritage from the generations that have passed away.

S. B. H.

THE FOOT BALL SITUATION.

At present it is rather hard to determine who will make up the personnel of the '92 foot ball team that is to compete for the league championship. There are at present twenty-five candidates, who are working hard every evening under the leadership of N. B. W. Gallwey. The training at present consists of practicing tricks and playing against the second eleven for about half-an-hour, running around the grounds a few times, and topping off the whole by a shower bath in the Gym. The work will, of course, be increased as the days go on. At present we lack a heavy half-back. All the other positions are well filled. Champaign called her men back two weeks before school opened. They have all been in more or less training all summer, so that our hardest nut to crack will probably be our base ball rival, Champaign. Beloit, from all we hear, is not showing up very strongly this year. Many of her best men were '92 men and she has not yet filled their places. Evanston, also, according to report, is not in the best shape possible. Evanston never did take the stand in foot ball that she has in base ball, and this year, with two leagues, she will have a particularly hard row to hoe. Then, too, her schedule is against her. We reproduce it here. The reader cannot help but notice that she has too many hard games too close together.

Oct. 1.—At Evanston, practice game with Chicago Y. M. C. A.

Oct. 8.—At Albion, Mich., exhibition game with Albion college.

Oct. 12.—At Champaign, league game with U. of I.

Oct. 15.—At Evanston, league game with Beloit.

Oct. 19.—Exhibition with Chicago Athletic Club.

Oct. 22.—At Evanston, exhibition game with Albion College.

Oct. 29.—At Chicago, league game with U. of M.

Nov. 5.—At Madison, exhibition game with U. of W.

Nov. 7.—At Minneapolis, league game with U. of Minn.

Nov. 12.—At Lake Forest, league game with L. F. U.

Nov. 19.—At Chicago, league game with U. of Wis.

Here is the Champaign schedule :

The University of Illinois team will be seen in Chicago this season playing the Beloit College club Nov. 12.

The games arranged at Champaign are :

Oct. 12.— The Northwestern University.

Oct. 18.—Ann Arbor.

Nov. 5.—State University of Wisconsin.

Nov. 12 and 18.—The De Pauw team of Greencastle, Ind.

Thanksgiving day, the Lake Forest team.

If the Cornell College club comes west a game will be arranged with it.

The following games have been arranged outside :

Oct. 21.— Iowa College at Grinnell, Ia.

Oct. 22.—Iowa State University at Iowa city.

Oct. 24.—Nebraska State University at Lincoln, Neb.

Oct. 26.—Baker University at Baldwin, Kan.

Oct. 27.— State University at Lawrence, Kan.

Oct. 29.—Kansas City Athletic Club at Kansas City.

The following is our own schedule so far as made out :

At Lake Forest.—West Division H. S., Oct. 8.

At Lake Forest.—Chicago Y. M. C. A., Oct. 15.

At Milwaukee.—Univ. of Wisconsin, Oct. 22.

At Beloit.—Beloit College, Oct. 29.

At Chicago.—Chicago Univ., Nov. 5.

At Chicago.— Northwestern Univ., Nov. 12.

At Champaign.—University of Illinois, Nov. 24, Thanksgiving.

The men in training at present are :

Gallway, Woolsey, McNary, Williams, McGaughey, Flint, C. Durand, Hunt, Mac-Hatton, C. Everett, Thom, Henry, Marcotte, Nash, Rossiter, Sherman, D. Jackson, Yaggy, Rice, Hopkins.

The outlook, on the whole, is encouraging, and Manager Crozier and Captain Gallwey are leaving no stone unturned. Treasurer Mc-Gaughey is hustling on subscriptions. Every thing is lovely, and the pennant hangs high.

COLLEGE.

A dancing club in town will soon be started.

If you want your watch repaired, go to Buck, the jeweler, 134 Washington street, Waukegan.

The new red and black jerseys the foot ball men wear are very natty and present a gay appearance.

Spellman is running on a cash basis this year. No more will we receive the touching sentence " PLEASE REMIT, R. B. Spellman.

At the Lake Forest drug store your wants will be attended to promptly and carefully. Dr. Frenche's medicines are always pure and fresh.

The new electives this year are: Teacher's couse in latin, Prof. Stuart ; current politics, Prof. Halsey ; a senior course in physiology, Prof. Locy.

The very young cads have organized a football team, on which Cobb and Erskine are the stars. They practice very regularly and work hard.

The uniform, so to speak, of the senior class, to be worn only on great state occasions, is to be the conventional university cap and gown. Look out for them.

We are all glad to see Dave Williams on our football field and team again. He is a very strong runner, never misses a tackle and punts exceedingly hard.

Miss Humphries is the latest addition to the college.

N. H. Burdick blew in on a "half fare" a week since.

Albert Woelful, '93, was here the 26th on his way to John Hopkins'.

The football team will take along a couple of men to act as "rubbers" on their trip.

Misses Mabel Durand and Zaphine Humphrey attend Smith College this fall, and Miss Fales goes to Ogontz.

It is very probable that an athletic exhibition, similar to the one given last year, will be held in the Gym. this fall. It will probably be after the foot ball season.

The Interior, of Chicago, has made a special rate for the current school year to all students of L. F. U., and has appointed MacHatton special solicitor for Lake Forest.

Forsooth a young man Yclept Ellis,
Who last spring made all pitchers "jellis,"
Hied himself to Amherst
To have fun or "berst,"
But he's sorry he went, so they "tellis."

The senior class is glad to add to its roll the name of R. J. Dysart, brother of W. R. Dysart of '92. Mr. Dysart was half-back on the Macalester college foot ball team last year.

The poetry of Wordsworth was productive of numerous deep and interesting discussions, rhetorical and philosphical, between the senior class in literature and the professor in charge.

Students should remember that R. B. Spellman not only handles text-books, stationary, candies and toilet articles, but also acts as purchasing agent, going to Chicago every Saturday.

The elective class in surveying, has recently re-surveyed the foot ball field and the tennis courts. Other similar work is desired,

and will be done free of charge for the sake of practice.

It is said, *sub rosa* of course, that C. S. Davies, special, expects to become regular classical, and graduate with '93. We hope he will be successful, but advise him not to work too hard.

The tennis courts are in excellent shape now, and new tapes make playing more of a pleasure. David Fales was elected vice president in place of H. A. Rumsey. G. T. B. Davis will soon be around for "feefty cents."

The rhetoric and typography of the Y. M. C. A. hand book are hardly up to the standard this year, either of L. F. U. or of other universities. We would suggest a decided improvement in the issue for next year.

Why not re-organize that popular organization of last year, the Chess Club? There are a number of the new students who play the game, and interesting tournaments will be forthcoming if all can be induced to join the club.

The senior class expects to graduate with twenty-two members. Only two courses are represented, the classical and the Latin-scientific. The class will be much larger than any previous graduating class and about twice the average size.

Prof. Walter Smith reached here Sunday morning, the 25th, having been detained by broken machinery in the vessel. He was twenty-one days on the ocean, and thinks he prefers to teach '94 psychology rather than be on the sea another such period.

Last Thursday evening, the 28th, the Y. M. C. A. and the Y. W. C. A. gave its annual reception in the art institute. Like similar occasions of former years, a general good time was enjoyed by all, and THE STENTOR was pleased to note the *college* feeling above party feeling.

The September number of the University

of Chicago's *Quarterly Calendar* announces for the autumn quarter, to begin Oct. 1, a total of 175 courses. These are the revised announcements for the quarter, *i. e.* the requisite number of students have signed for these courses and all of them will be given this year.

Sept. 19th, Mrs. T. B. Durand gave a beautiful dancing party at her home. The floors were canvassed, and the conservatory and porch were thrown open to the dancers. The house was very prettily decorated, and Chinese lanters added to the effect. The music was from the city. The dancing continued to the " wee small hours."

The senior class met Sept. 22d and elected the following officer : President, R. H. Crozier ; Vice Pres., H. Marcotte ; secretary, Miss Williams ; treasurer, A. A. Hopkins ; Poet, Miss Taylor ; Historian, F. C. Sharon ; Prophet, Miss A. Adams. It was decided to adopt the cap and gown as the class costume. The class this year is unusually large, there being twenty-five members.

Ye ancient gag of funnel was played on several freshmen not long since. New men are always so positive that they can drop the penny in that they become indiscreet. A few also studied the 26th chapter of Numbers for the freshman Bible class. When you are a freshman, dear boy, hang back a little and let your fellow be the sucker. You will be fooled enough without tackling every buzz-saw that comes along.

Harry McElroy, manager of Dent's livery, in a drunken row with a coachman Sunday night, split open the coachman's head with a single-tree and then boarded the nine o'clock train for Chicago. He has not appeared since. The coachman was reported as dying, but he seems to be able to walk around and tell his woes. Our efficient marshall says he couldn't arrest McElroy because he didn't see the fight.—*Logic.*

The hand ball court is much used these bright fall days, and many exceedingly close and interesting contests take place there. There are a number of good players among the new students, but it is generally conceded that the senior class could win both in singles and doubles in a tournament. Such a tournament would be very interesting, however, and we would urge that the court be put in first-class shape and two tournaments contested before the season closes ; one for the older and one for the very young players, among whom are several very aggressive players.

A university indoor baseball team has been organized, with Forest Grant as captain, to play with the town people. A game last Saturday resulted in a victory for the town team to the tune of 13 to 8. The following men composed the university team : Grant, catcher and captain ; Nash, pitcher ; Parish, first base ; McNary, second base ; Lewis, third base ; Hamilton, short stop ; D. H. Jackson, left field ; Hughitt, middle field ; Gilliland, right field. The features of the game were the fielding of D. H. Jackson and the base running of Watson of the town team.

The Athenaean Society gave its semi-annual reception in their hall to new students Friday evening, the 23rd. The hall was very tastefully decorated and the members are much indebted to their Ferry Hall friends for their aid. The reception committee consisted of Miss Ripley and Messrs. Goodman, MacHatton and Sharon. The seminary was over in force and judging from first impressions Ferry Hall has no need to blush for its new invoice and the out look for '92-93 is indeed full of promise. This was the first reception of the season, and as such was intended to introduce the new students to Lake Forest life.

Next week our orator, Mr. A. A. Hopkins, contests at Champaign for the state oratorical prize, and may all the good luck possible attend him. Our opinion of the State Oratorial Association is not inclined to give the association "the swell-head." Far from it. When a man wins in this league his name happens to fall out of the hat first. It is a vile system of wire-pulling from the time one gets there till he starts to walk ties homeward. We don't wish to intimate that if Mr. Hopkins wins it will be on a toss up. Not in the least. But when three of our very best men have been counted out we cannot help but feel that there must be some deep scheming somewhere. But good luck to you, Hop, in your undertaking is the STENTOR's hearty wish.

The Executive Committee of the Athletic Association met in the President's room Monday evening, Sept. 26. The following delegates were present: Professor Harper, Goodman, MacHatton, Sharon, McGaughey, Flint, Warren, Everett, Crozier, Gallway. Professor Bridgman presided, The revised constitution of the new Illinois Inter-Collegiate Athletic Association was adopted, and it was decided to send three men to enter the track athletics at the face meet of said association. A training table is to be maintained at $5 a week for the football season, each man to pay $3 and the association $2 a week. It was also decided to purchase an athletic bulletin board and place it between the post-office and Proctor's, on which all scores and announcements would be made. The association will probably come out excellently as regards finances this year.

The Joint University Board of the Chicago Society for University Extension has changed its name to the Joint University Board for University Extension in the Northwest. Lake Forest University and the Northwestern University at Evanston have always submitted all applications received by them for university extension work to the board for its approval, while the other universities represented on the board have been accepting invitations to do such work and also soliciting work in the various states without consulting the board or the other universities. It was decided at the annual meeting of the board, held Sept. 24, Lake Forest University being represented by Prof. J. J. Halsey, that all the university extension work to be done by the universities represented on the board, be supervised by the board in order that all wasteful competition may be avoided. The representatives at the annual meeting were instructed to report this new plan as well as the change of name to their respective universities for approval. The following institutions were represented: Lake Forest, by Prof. J. J. Halsey; Northwestern, by President Rogers and Professors Young and Hatfield; Illinois, by Acting Regent Burrill and Professor Moss; Indiana, by President Coulter, Dr. Fellows and Professor Huffcutt; Wabash, by Professor Smith; Michigan, Wisconsin, DePauw and Beloit, by proxies. If all these institutions and Chicago University, which was not represented at the annual meeting, agree to the proposed board control of the university extension work of the northwest, the result will be a great university extension monopoly, controlled by the executive committee of the board, which will prevent all waste of time and money in competition, and greatly advance the cause of university extension in the four great states concerned. President Rogers, President Coulter and Acting Regent Burrill compose this important executive committee. President Rogers is also president of the new board and Mr. Raymond its secretary.

FERRY HALL.

Miss Ruth Smith, '92, was with us Sunday, Sept. 25.

Miss Ristine has been ill for several days, but is now better.

Red seems to be a favorite color this year among certain Sems.

Misses Vera Scott and Edna Smith spent Sunday in Lakeside.

Mrs. Congdon, of Oconto, visited her daughter Mildred last Saturday.

Miss Julia Ensign spent Sunday, Sept. 18th, with her sister, Miss Maggie Ensign.

Dr. W. K. Clement has returned to Ann Arbor, after a week's visit with friends here.

The serenade given the other evening did much towards raising the spirits of various melancholy damsels.

We are reminded that it is still leap year —Sem (most pleadingly) to college student— "Please ask for me."

The trunks were removed from the corridors the other day. Remarks concerning torn frocks are no longer in order.

The great expectations of the Sems concerning this year's football team will, no doubt, be gratified some sweet day by-and-by.

A mouse fully an inch and a half long was seen in one of the corridors recently. The girls evinced a sudden fondness for standing on chairs.

Valesi furnished music for the first seminary ball of the season, held Friday evening, the 30th, in the gym. Poor boys, you were not in it!

We have the Athenean Society to thank for a most delightful time Friday evening. By the way girls, *did'nt* those sofa pillows look natural?

The members of the new Physics class are beginning to have a settled conviction that they are likely at any moment to be dissolved into molecules.

A local thunder storm Thursday evening, in the third floor corridor disturbed many peaceful sleepers. The ducking was indefinitely postponed.

Miss Enid M. Smith, '90, who has been spending the summer with old friends in and around Chicago, will return to New York the first of October, to resume her study of music.

Etiquette in the extreme.—Dignified senior (at the head of table), " will you take tea?

New senior.—(carefully) " if you please.

D. senior.—" How do you take it?

N. Sen:—"If you please."

The new seniors and their newer privileges are objects of much interest and envy on the part of their less fortunate sisters, upon whom they are trying to impress the fact, startling and unique, that " value is that power " etc. Dear, dear, how we apples do swim.

Our juniors are evidently very progressive, for though it is yet early in the year, the class has been organized and received its privileges. The officers are as follows :

Miss Lucia E. Clark, President.

Miss Ristine, Vice President.

Miss Emma Parmenter, Secretary.

This is a large class of eighteen, and we hope they will show the same class spirit and purpose to enjoy and enable others to enjoy Ferry Hall life that the '93's do.

ACADEMY.

TRI KAPPA.

Mr. Roberts, who was unfortunate enough to go abroad this summer, has been quarantined, but is now out and among us again, happy as ever.

The Mitchell Hall pump has done some good-work for the last week or so, and several new boys have had an unlooked-for cold water bath.

Condon has been quite ill lately and much to his sorrow has not been able to attend recitations. He is now quite well again, and as bright and active as ever.

The choosing of new members by the academy societies took place on Wednesday, Sept. 24th. The first choice fell to Gamma Sigma, as she had less old members back than Tri Kappa.

At a meeting of Tri Kappa the following officers were elected for the ensuing term: President, N..W. Flint; vice-president, E. C. Yaggy; secretary, B. S. Cutler; treasurer, N. B. Hewitt. It was decided to appoint a critic for each meeting.

An Academy glee club has been formed under the direction of Prof. Dudley and bids fair to become a great success. The first call for volunteers was responded to by a large number of boys, many of whom have good voices and some musical ability.

We are glad to welcome a large number of new students in the Academy this year. It has been necessasy to turn the president's house into a dormitory to accommodate them until the new buildings are completed, which time we hope is not very far in the future.

The Academy will not be so well represented in this year's football team as it was in the team of last year, as most of our players have either graduated and gone elsewhere or entered the college. We will probably have quite a large representation on the second eleven.

Two new professors are here to lead us in the flowery (?) path of knowledge. Mr. David Williams, brother of our former teacher of mathematics succeeds him in that position, and Prof. Dudley fills the chair of science. We are glad to see both, and extend to them a hearty welcome.

A certain young gentleman made this remark at the Athenean reception: "The boys think they'll put me under the pump, but" (feeling of his muscle) "I don't *think* they will." This same youth was accordingly given an extra good soaking Monday night and has accordingly quit feeling of his muscle. M. K. B.

AMONG THE ALUMNI.

H. W. Bainton, formerly '93, spent Thursday Sept. 22 here.

J. Z. Johnson, '93, began his course at McCormick last week.

W. R. Dysart, '92, and W. B. Brewster, '92, are studying law at St. Paul, Minn.

W. E. Pratt and F. M. Skinner, both of '92, will make Lake Forest their home this fall.

M. McLeod, '92, spent Sunday, Sept. 25, at Lake Forest. He is at McCormick this year.

F. T. Radecke, '95, will spend the coming year on the staff of the Lake County *Post* at Waukegan.

T. S. Jackson, '89, who has been studying law in Chicago spent Sunday, Sept. 25, at Lake Forest.

W. D. McMillan, who was a member of '92 for two years, is in the grain business in Fort Worth, Texas.

C. A. Foss, a last year's special, is attending school in Galesville, Wis. "Tuck" is greatly missed this year.

W. S. Cargill, formerly of the '93d, has erected a house in La Crosse, Wis., and intends becoming a benedict next month.

A. M. Candee, '92, is at present superintendent of one of the departments in the Radford Iron and Pipe Works at Anniston, Ala.

George W. King, '93, is engaged in the pickle making business in Joliet. He manufactures exclusively the "Gilt Edge" brand. Give him a trial.

Miss Grace Beymer, '92; Miss Elizabeth Mason, '93, and Miss Enid Smith, Ferry Hall, '90, have been spending the summer at Highland Park, Ill.

E. F. Dodge, 91, spent part of his summer vacation at Chippewa Falls. He claims it was hard wood lumber that attracted him, but—we won't give our version.

Of '92, Messrs. E. F. Dodge, W. E. Danforth and W. H. Humiston have spent the summer in Chicago, and J. H. McVay has been sojourning at Neenah, Wis.

E. G. Wood, formerly with '92 here and graduating at Williams with '92, will this year hold down the Latin chair on the faculty of the academy at Woodstock, Ill.

George Horton Steele, '92, is monarch of all he can survey, headquarters at Milwaukee depot. "Georgie" occasionally "gets in the draught" and blows in to see his old friends.

G. W. Ellis, '93; Fred Ellis, '96; E. S. Cass, '93, and S. A. Goodale, '93, are at Amherst. Frank Dewey, '96, and H. A. Rumsey, '94, are at Williams, and W. G. Strong, '94, is at Cornell this fall.

B. Fay Mills, who has been conducting a very successful series of revival meetings in San Francisco this summer, was a former student here, and is now the only surviving member of the class of '79.

August 30, Miss Helen Goodsill, Ferry Hall, '86, and L. J. Davies, '88, were united in marriage at the bride's home in Hopkins, Wis. The couple have since left for China, where they will enter the mission field.

Alex S. Wilson, W. H. Matthews and G. W. Wright, all of '92, have spent the summer in Chicago, and this fall C. W. Irwin, E. S. Chaffee, M. McLeod and W. F. Love, all of the same class, will be added to their number as students of McCormick Seminary.

Herbert Manchester, formerly with '93, last year at Wesleyan, spent Wednesday and Thursday with us. He expects to enter the Chicago University this fall and for this purpose while among us he obtained the records of his Lake Forest work, which were very high and were given to him with a good "send off."

W. N. Halsey, '89, is making for himself an enviable reputation as an educator in Plattsmouth, Neb. He has been retained this year at an increased salary. The *Journal*, of that place, says: "Mr. Halsey is the best equipped principal the high school of this town has ever had, and no other place ought to be allowed to take him from this city without a contest."

Last June, at the home of the bride's parents in Lake Forest, Miss Juliet L. Rumsey, '81, and Grant Stroh, '89, were united in marriage by Dr. J. G. K. McClure. The maid of honor was Miss Lucy Rumsey, '92, and the bridesmaids were Miss Nellie Holt and Miss Minnie Rumsey, of Lake Forest, Miss Fannie Dresser, of Chicago, and Miss Laura Woodruf, of Louisville, Ky. The best man was Mr. Charles Stroh, and Aubrey Warren and H. A. Rumsey officiated as ushers. The decorations were, roses and a huge R and S of red and white roses formed a conspicuous part. One of the features was the wedding march, played on a harp.

As we looked over the new students in chapel the other morning, the thought came to us that it is seldom Lake Forest has welcomed as bright and fine looking a lot of new men. If we are good for anything in reading faces, Lake Forest has received an infusion of new life which will make itself felt in a raising of her already high scholarship, as well as in her social and moral life.

THE STENTOR.

VOLUME VI.   OCTOBER 11, 1892.   NUMBER 2.

PUBLISHED EVERY WEEK
BY THE
Lake Forest University Stentor Publishing Co.

BOARD OF EDITORS.

F. C. SHARON, '93 ....Managing Editor
R. H. CROZIER, '93 ....Business Manager
N. H. BURDICK, '93 }
S. B. HOPKINS, '93 } ....Locals
L. N. ROSSITER, '93 ....Alumni and Personal
B. R. MACHATTON, '95 ....Advertising

ASSOCIATE EDITORS.

HARRY GOODMAN, '94 ....Athletic Editor
FOREST GRANT, '96 ....Staff Artist
DAVID FALES, '96 ....Town

Terms—$1.50 per year. Single Copies—10c

————ADDRESS————
STENTOR PUBLISHING COMPANY,
LAKE FOREST,   :   :   ILLINOIS.

Entered at the P. O. at Lake Forest, Ill., as second-class matter.

AN EXAMPLE FOR FOOTBALL TEAMS.

The University of Minnesota is certainly progressive in more ways than one but in football she especially means business. We copy from the *Ariel* the football pledge and give it below: "I, the undersigned party hereby promise and agree on consideration of being placed on the football team of the University of Minnesota to abstain from the use of all tobacco and all intoxicating drinks, to board at such training table as the management sees fit to provide, to train in such a manner and to such an extent as the captain may direct, and to play at every practice game which is posted unless excused from such game by the captain in person. I further agree to forfeit five dollars or my place on the team if I break any of the above agreements." Comment on this is unnecessary. That such a contract will make a man more careful and energetic in his work is evident. Certainly he is in reality not more bound by it than by the laws of the captain in any other school, but the mere fact that one *signs* such a document makes him feel that he must do more conscientious work. We are thankful to say, however, that our team does not need such a pledge to keep them at work.

————

ARE WE TO HAVE A HOLIDAY OCT. 20?

The four hundredth anniversary of the discovery of our land is fast approaching, and with it the dedication of the World's Fair buildings in Chicago. The Governors of nearly all the States and Territories, the President of the United States, the chief men of the nation as well as the leading lights of foreign lands will be present, the affair will be unprecedented in granduer and something to be handed down to posterity. Here we are only twenty-eight miles from all this. Are we to be allowed to see these opening ceremonies or are we to be kept here those three days "so near and yet so far." It seems to us that the time of the students could not be better employed during that period than in seeing and hearing these great men speak, seeing the immense pageants and witnessing the impressive opening of such a stupendous thing as the World's Fair. This will come but once. We will not have another chance for four hundred years and there are precious few Methusalehs now.

Would'nt it be a wise step, if the Faculty have not already done it, to suspend recitations from Thursday the 20th through Friday and Saturday, to give the students and professors a chance to witness these ceremonies? Think it over, boys, you can see for yourself that such a display is going to be liberal education in itself. Petition the Faculty to suspend work during those days.

THE ORATORICAL ASSOCIATION.

A word as to the State Oratorical Association. The annual contest occurred at Champaign last Friday and according to all the best man won. But it seems to us, and it is the opinion of many, that it is foolishness for us to continue in such an association. What shall be done then? Do as Evanston has done in athletics, go up a peg and join a larger association. The colleges in the State league are all remote from us. We have very little in common with them and very seldom send much of a delegation. The association is now run in connection with athletics and everyone who has visited the annual meeting will admit that oratory holds a very subordinate place. The constitution is a loose-jointed affair; the judges are appointed by the college having the largest pull, and the whole thing seems to center on making money. Seldom have we seen or heard more awkward speaking than at the contests of '90 and '91. We do not claim that Lake Forest should have carried away first place in both contests, but we do say that the system now in vogue of appointing judges and the style of spread-eagle oratory that most of those colleges adopt are both opposed to the best oratory. Our man won the contest Friday last because he was so far ahead of anything else that a decision against him would have been a robbery. If we are not connected with the colleges in any way but this, we naturally do not have much to say in the appointment of judges. Then again, that "wire-pulling" of the worst kind is in common use can not be denied, and *all* these things tend against us. One who has never *heard* one of these contests has no opinions worth considering. There is no use speaking of athletics. The boys here know about the workings of that league as well as we. Why can not we join an association of colleges with which we are in closer contact? Have we not a better right to belong to the new athletic association of Ann Arbor, U. of W., etc., than Evanston, who has been tail-end in athletics in a smaller league for two seasons? Our record for scholarship "tops the heap" in the west. Why then have we not on equal right to ask for admission to a larger oratorical association? Are we to raise our reputation and make ourselves better known? Then join a larger league. Are we to spread abroad our fame as athletes? Then let us annex ourselves to colleges that will help us do this. Perhaps all do not realize what a tremendous change in athletics has come over us in the past two years, nor do they realize that with some incentive our orators would hustle those of any western school. Think this over, ye oratorical officers, and let us aspire higher.

THE NEW UNIVERSITY IS A HUSTLER.

That Chicago University has hustling abilities is certainly well displayed by the manner in which they are looking around for colors and a yell. The stars and stripes were flung to the breeze the other day and above them floated a yellow ribbon, the chosen color of the new school. The flower is golden-rod and the color is of that shade. Prof. Stagg had the boys hard at work several days practicing the yells that were submitted. Over fifty were tried, the favorite seeming to be "Chicago! Chicago! Chicago-go-go! Go it Chica-go it Chica-go it Chicago!" This is all very well, but wait for athletes. Its pretty hard to train in a city.

THE MUNICIPAL COLORS.

Chicago's municipal colors, terra cotta and white, which were made known through the *Tribune*, are certainly worthy of our great city. Prettier colors could not have been selected and Mr. Roewald is to be congratulated on his lucky hit. Why shouldn't every large city possess its colors just as every college does? Perhaps this will be the first step in that direction, and other cities will fall into line.

THE IDLER.

We strolled into the room of the Secy. of the Faculty not long since and were struck with astonishment at his appearance. Every particular hair on his head seemed pointed in every possible direction, his moustache seemed chewed off, his hands were clenched and his eyes had a savage gleam that boded evil. Ever and anon he would unclench and move small pasteboards over a large piece of paper resembling a checkerboard. The motions were rapid, the pasteboards were shifted from here to there, from there to here. At length he stopped. Then with an air born of desperation, made one last move. Evidently it did not do, for with a groan he swooned away in his chair. After restoring him we begged to know the cause of this change, for he looked much aged since the day before. Gazing at us intently he said in a sepulchral voice "I am arranging the schedule." With the cheerfulness and charity characteristic of us we offered to assist him. "Well, now," he said, "here we have eighteen hours to get into thirteen hours. Of course we can easily do it by adding a couple of hours to each day, making it twenty-six in all, and making Saturday a very short day. But there are objections to that. Now we can't put "International Gastronomy" at the same time as "Choctaw" because Tommy Jones takes both; we can't have Senior Geography at the same time as Junior Spelling because men elect them from both classes; we can't have Sophomore Athletics when the freshmen have "kindergarten" work because they must then occupy the same room; we can't have Senior Arithmetic and Junior Music at the *same* time because they must occupy different rooms and there is no other room to occupy; they can't have them at different hours because there are none; we can't put the Junior"—but we had fled. The schedule had muddled our head. We retired and fell into a troubled sleep dreaming that college chapel occurred at the same hour as football practice, that handball couldn't be played in the reading room because a recitation was to be held in the art building, that we had gone to the wrong recitations for a week and —oh, pshaw! we forget what we *didn't* dream!

***

One who visits our University town for the first time is struck at once with the great variety of restaurants and hotels, boarding houses and club houses, which burst on their enraptured view and make them think that here is where the student gets accommodations that remind him of the luxuriousness of the old Romans. Perhaps you are a stranger to our burg and have never viewed our unequaled "hasheries." Perhaps you are looking for a boarding place yourself. In that case let us be your guide. In such a variety our judgment is absolutely infallable. As you may know the students board in clubs. Beautiful clubhouses? Why there are several hundred people waiting now for clubs. There are so many beautiful houses waiting for occupancy that it is really difficult to choose. The people are so anxious to accommodate that they almost pay you for boarding with them. Restaurants? Everything under the sun that an epicure could want. Quick service and neat as a pin.

You see that building over there? Well that is *one* of the swell clubs here. It's a beauty. We reproduce it here:

THE EPICUREAN CLUBHOUSE.

As you see it is built in William the Conqueror style—you know with four walls and an excuse for a roof, and furnished in the style of Queen Sorachidoo of the Cannibal Islands. But that place is now occupied by the "Swells."

Now this place over here is noted for its beautiful furnishings and elegant table service. Come with me and look into the breakfast room. Does it not

make your mouth water? It is furnished in Queen Anne style (Anne Williams), although some of the chairs were once used by Mr. and Mrs. Noah. That table linen was used as a battle flag in the late war. You see many of those things are rare and valuable. But you haven't seen our hotel? That is the gem, the jewel of them all. This is it: It is built in the latest style—

which isn't out yet—its foundation is of imagination, the body is of airy nothing, and its furnishings are "out of sight." When you are up this way stop here some night. You'll get better accommodations than any other place in town.

WE ARE THE PEOPLE,

LAKE FOREST WINS IN ORATORY AND ATHLETICS.

Who said Lake Forest wasn't in it? Not those who were down at Champaign and saw us win everything we tried. Not much. Our turn was a long time in coming but it came at last and here is the result:—1st in the mile, 1st in the half, 2nd in the 100, 3rd in the 220, and 1st in the Oratrical contest. Thirteen points in athletics and the State representative to the Interstate contest with three men! Suppose we had sent down more. . Great Scott, don't mention it. We *might* have gotten everything. Friday morning L. N. Rossiter won the half-mile in a walk. To say the natives were surprised would be putting it mildly. In the afternoon he won the mile just as easily; Time, 4:59¼. This breaks the Intercollegiate record. The other colleges were so *sure*, that one had a camera ready to snap the Champaign winner, but somehow ."Lutie" came in ahead. A. O. Jackson was second in the 100 yards, and would have won the 220 but was forced to run the final *immediately* after his preliminary before he had recovered his wind.

Thursday evening occurred the annual banquet in the University building. All the delicacies of the season were served and the toasts given were especially taking. "The College Yell" was the subject which our delegate, S. B. Hopkins, responded to. Modesty forbids extended praise, but we are assured by outsiders that it was well up toward the top.

On Friday evening the oratorical contest was held in Walker opera house. That our orator did himself proud it is needless to state. He won easily. Although the noise and yelling outside would have disconcerted most orators he displayed nerve and coolness and held his audience despite the racket. The other speakers were only fair, although the Illinois orator who was second did quite well. Below is the program.

Orchestra.

Invocation...Rev. Wilder.

Oration....................................The Scholar as a Citizen.
W. C. Carter, U. of I.

Oration.................................Our Present Problem.
F. D. Finley, Monmouth.

Vocal solo—"For All Eternity"....................Macheroni.
Miss Gertrude Conn.
Violin obligato, Mr. John Beardsley.

Oration.....................,...Jeffersonism in American Politics
S. T. Burnett, Wesleyan.

Oration...................................Fanaticism and Reform.
F. S. Karaseka Knox College.

Oration........The English Bible: Its Study as a Classic in College
W. A. Stevenson, Illinois College,

Vocal Solo—"Tis not True"...........................Mattei
Wm. Frederickson.

Oration....................Man, Nature's Masterpiece.
S. A. Benson, Blackburn.

Oration..Cavour.
A. A. Hopkins, Lake Forest.

Orchestra.

Decision of Judges.

Here are the Marks:

	Cham.	Mon...	Wes....	Knox ..	Ill	Black...	L. F.
Thought							
Stryker	88-3	65-7	73-5	80-4	90-2	68-6	92-1
Seaming	68-4	98,5-3	99,1-1	98,5-3	99,1-1	99-2	99-2
Carter...	90-5	93-4	85-6	95-3	99-1	90-5	98-2
Delivery.							
Madden.	90-3	95-2	80-5	90-3	85-4	95-2	98-1
Reed....	85-4	80-5	70-7	75-6	95-2	90-3	100-1
Moore...	84-2	80-4	75-5	80-4	71-6	82-3	85-1

Hopkins 3 firsts in delivery, 1 first and 2 seconds in thought.

In the oratorical business meeting Lake Forest was given the option of having the contest next year or allowing Knox to take it, Lake Forest taking Knox's turn in '96. S. B. Hopkins was elected chairman of the credential committee. The officers for the association for the ensuing year are R. T. Barr, Champaign, President; I. R. Loar, Weslyan, Vice-President; T. W. Frackelton, Illinois college, Secretary and Treasurer; delegates to Inter-State contest, Ralph Pringle, Monmouth; E. P. Reece, Knox; G. W. King, Blackburn.

In the athletic association meeting Champaign was awarded the cup and then withdrew from the association, saying that their time hereafter would be devoted to base ball and foot ball. Champaign turned over the cup to the new secretary and treasurer. Finch of Weslyan was elected president.

NOTES.

The Lake Forest delegates and orator were entertained royally at Mr. Trevitt's on University Ave. The boys cannot thank them enough for their elegant treatment and are loud in their praises.

Champaign did not hold up her end very well as entertainers. There were no reception committees whatever, and the delegates headquarters were open only twenty minutes during the day. Everybody hustled for himself.

"Lutie" says the running track was "rank."

Champaign was rather unfair in the 220. There were five entries and two preliminaries of two runners each. The Champaign man was the fifth man. He did not run in the preliminaries and consequently was fresh in the finish.

Lake Forest as usual sustained her name for gentlemen.

The Zeta Epsilon Society gave a very pleasant reception in their hall last Thursday evening. The hall was prettily decorated and light refreshments served.

We noticed in Saturday's *Tribune* that a Miss Rhodes, of Waukegan, had made a great hit as a singer in her recent debut at the Lyric Theatre, in London.

COLLEGE.

THE WEEK'S AMUSEMEMTS.

AUDITORIUM—Sousa's Marine Band.
McVICKER'S—Crane in "The Senator."
COLUMBIA—"Alabama."
GRAND—Richard Mansfield in "The Scarlet Letter."
HOOLEY'S—"Imagination."

The most recent arrival in College Hall is Dean Lewis's furniture.

Rev. C. R. Burdick, of Oconto, Wis., was in town the fore part of last week.

A viaduct is being built at the crossing of the railroad and University Ave.

A benefit ball is advertised to occur at Healy's Opera House, on Friday evening, October 14th.

Don't forget your duty to the University Athletic Association. Subscribe all that you possibly can spare, and pay up promptly.

The Y. P. S. C. W. held its monthly business meeting last Monday evening in the missionary room in the tower of the church.

Rev. Mr. Dickey, of Detroit, led chapel last Friday and spoke before the University Club that evening on "The Scottish Church."

Mr. Frost and family, who occupied the Humphrey residence during the summer, and Mr. Hubbard and family, have returned to their winter residences in Chicago.

The date of the great Republican Rally is Oct. 24; the place the Auditorium. The best speakers in the nation will be present and also delegates from all Republican college clubs.

On the evening of the 30th Miss Horton, of Deerpath avenue, entertained at cards several members of the college faculty, some of the kindergarten teachers, and Mr. and Mrs. Townsend.

C. S. Davies entertained the senior class in literature last Wednesday with a very brilliant recitation. He was frequently interrupted by applause and Prof. Morris fairly beamed with delight.

The C. & N.-W. R'y is putting in the block system on its Milwaukee and Wisconsin divisions. The targets have been erected some time and the "triggers" are now being placed in position.

The ladies of the class of '95 will supply any "raven locks" that are dissatisfied with their present quarters, with another one. Foot-ball men a specialty. Send in your applications early and avoid the rush.

On Oct. 21st the members of the Athenaean Society will present in their hall a very interesting literary program. The prose and poetry of Bret Harte will be taken up and presented by means of selections and critical papers. A full and detailed program will appear in the next issue.

Spencer R. Smith, who filled for several years the chair now occupied by Prof. Morris, was in town with his wife last Wednesday to superintend the transfer of their household goods to the cars for removal to their new home. They have sold their property here, and will reside at Austin in order to be nearer Mr. Smith's place of business in Chicago, 84 La Salle.

The work of the various classes seems to be well under way. The recitation rooms are comfortably filled. The usual excuses for flunking are rapidly being learned by new students, and the most approved and time-tested methods of "bluffing" are being acquired as rapidly as could be expected. At the same time, much hard and earnest work is being done and enviable records are being made.

One thing which has been a detriment to the University is in the profuse aid given to students. This charity has ceased to be considered as such in many instances and has become to be looked upon as a right. The faculty have made a move in the right direction in refusing any aid whatsoever to those who do not keep their grade to the passing mark.

Overheard on the tennis courts: "If 'practice makes perfect,' Coolige will be a tennis player sometime." "'Double A' puts more balls into 'the drink' than any two men. He averages four a set." "Don't you think Dave Fales plays splendidly." "I wish Marcotte, for variety's sake would get a 'Lawford' down occasionally." "Don't you care, he may sometime, and in the meantime he's 'awfully amoosin'.'"

The Trustees of the University met on Tuesday of last week. Reports from the different departments showed the institution to be in the best possible condition. Eighty-six thousand dollars has been raised for building since May. Prof. Drummond, of Scotland, was offered the presidency but declined, saying that he was not open to an invitation to leave Scotland. Two other men were mentioned and Dr. McPherson was empowered to interview them.

Ex-President Roberts attended a meeting of educators in Chicago, Tuesday afternoon of last week, whose purpose was the taking of such action as would insure educational interests. a proper exhibit at the World's Fair next year. As a result of this agitation 170,-000 square feet have been guaranteed for this purpose by the Columbian officials. For some reason unknown to us, Dr. Roberts did not give us the pleasure of looking into his pleasant, rubicund face.

The students in the south end of College Hall were favored with the most exquisite serenade of the season last Tuesday evening. Four beautiful maidens, with mellifluous locks and honey-colored voices, gave a variety performance under one of our noble oaks, while the leaves rang with tumultuous applause and the winds soughed through the students in the windows. The last act was a spirited rendition of that most appreciated melodrama— "they skipped by the light of the moon." Come again, girls!

A meeting of "students interested in the organization of a Republican club" was called immediately after chapel Tuesday morning. Mr. Grant called the meeting to order and Mr. Sharon was elected chairman. On motion of Mr. Hopkins, a committee consisting of two seniors and one from each of the classes, was appointed by the chairman, as follows: S. B. Hopkins, W. N. McKee, W. A. Bishop, B. R. MacHatton, M. Woolsey. This committee is to draw up a constitution, provide for discussions, and nominate permanent officers.

The plowing up of Deerpath avenue near the railroad is accomplished only with great difficulty. One man takes hold of the plow-handles which immediately "go into committee of the whole" to handle him as roughly as possible; two men sit on the beam and try to find out by experience which can jump the higher from a sitting position whenever the plow strikes a rocd; and four others with reins in their hands guide the faltering footsteps of the eight fleet steeds—six horses and two mugwumps—that furnish the motive power for the whole apparatus. We all hate to see the streets torn up, but the improvement will doubtless repay us for all inconveniences and violation of the artistic sense during paving.

Prof. Halsey's recitation room in the Art Institute has been fitted up as a special reading room for the elective class in current events—the largest elective in the history of the University.

A fine, substantial table of white pine and poplar has been put in and loaded down with such standard magazines as the *Contemporary Review*, the *Nineteenth Century*, the *Fortnightly Review*, the *Review of Reviews*, *Current History*, etc. Prof. Halsey also makes clippings from various papers not on the table or in the college reading room, and distributes these, classified and arranged on heavy paper, among the 36 members of the class, to be read and returned. Half as many keys as members of the class have been given out, the order being "pick out a 'chum' and get a key between you!"

"Souvenir Echoes of the Princeton Township High School, 1867-1892," is the title of a book received by the University librarian and placed in the reading room. It contains a very detailed history of the school from its inception to the present time, the names of all the teachers, all the commencement programs, histories of all the classes and many of the valedictories and other addresses. Principal Smith, of our Academy, was assistant principal at Princeton in '76-'77 and principal in '77-'78. Our students will be interested in a fine portrait of him in the "Echoes." There is a fine steel engraving of Wm. Cullen Bryant, who delivered an address to the class of '71 and splendid cuts of the building and the various rooms. The book would be a credit to any college, and Princeton, Ill., may well be proud of the work of her high school.

Among the periodicals in the reading room may be found the *Herald, Tribune, North American Review, The Forum, The Arena, Popular Science Monthly, Puck, Judge, Life, Harvard Lampoon, Fliegende Blatter, Harper's Weekly, Frank Leslie's, London News, Black and White, Century Magazine, Harper's Monthly, Cosmopolitan, New England Magazine, Outing, Atlantic Monthly, Youth's Companion, Art Magazine, Sun and Shade, Scientific American* and *Supplement*, in addition to numerous other publications. For humorous literature alone $100 has been expended. It would seem that in view of the fact that so much more money than usual has been appropriated for the reading room there might be an absence of the species of vandalism which manifests itself in a mutilation of the matter placed there for the free use of all. Besides being unmanly, it is dishonest to take clippings from papers and magazines belonging to another. It is extremely exasperating to look for an article much needed and to find it gone. A word to the wise, etc.

The suggestion in the last number of the STENTOR relative to the Chess Club was taken up and the club is now ready for another year's work. The first meeting was held Wednesday afternoon in the library, with Mr. Linn in the chair. Many of the last year's difficulties will be obviated by the new "plan of campaign" which has been adopted. Instead of requiring all games to be played at regular meetings of the club, a time schedule will be made out, each player meeting each other player a certain number of times and being allowed to play his games any where and at any convenient time during the week to which they are assigned. The result of each term's games will be tabulated and published in the STENTOR as soon as all have been played. The following are the club's officers for the year '92-'93: Mr. Linn, pres.; N. H. Burdick, vice-pres.; E. H. McNeal, sec'y and treas.; Dr. Seely, Mr. Linn and A. B. Burdick, executive com. Profs. Dudley and Agar, Messrs. Rogers, C. G. Smith and S. B. Hopkins will probably join the club this year, and it is hoped that many other players will also enroll themselves and apply for games.

ATHLETICS.

Fred Hayner, '95, who played right end on last year's foot ball eleven, and did creditable work in centre field on the base ball team, spent a couple of days last week at Lake Forest.

We are advised from Amherst that both Ellis and Goodale are doing good work back of the line. In a game with the Agricultural College the playing of our "Toot" was mentioned as a special feature.

Of the three big eastern colleges, Yale, Harvard and Princeton, Yale seems to be the weakest. Harvard is showing up the strongest in practice, with Princeton not far behind. Our old friend, Joe Flint, on account of an injury received in a recent practice game, is retired for a time. He is trying for tackle this year, Bartels playing left half-back.

The announcement of the death of Carl Bothne, who took a post-graduate course at Williams last fall, and attracted universal attention by his phenomenal work on the eleven, will be received with genuine regret by all Lake Forest men, among whom he had many friends. He was sick only a short time and died of typhoid fever in Chicago about three months ago. Great things were expected of him at Yale this year, both in foot-ball and on the crew.

Of the base ball outlook it is hard to say. Base ball affairs always look dubious for us in the fall, more so perhaps this year than ever before. Of last year's team but four have returned to college, and the positions of pitcher, second base, third base, short stop and centre field are open to competition. Practice games should be played in the fall to bring out material so that some estimate of our chances may be formed. Let those who make any pretentions in the base ball line lay aside their modesty and come forward. We need you. Hard practice and attention to work will accomplish great things. The manager and captain for the ensuing year have not as yet been elected.

Another week has gone by and the football outlook is still favorable. We are somewhat hampered by the weakness of the second eleven, so that it is hard to draw any conclusions as to the real strength of the team. We are weak behind the line and the accident to full-back Williams renders us more so. The accident was an unfortunate affair. It seems that after punting the ball it hit an opposing player, and bounding back struck Williams in the eye. We are assured, however, that the injury is not serious, but will necessitate his retirement from the field for a time. MacHatton does good work. He is a fearless rusher and plucky when tackled, but is perhaps a little slow. Nash is rather too light for a half-back and lacks the necessary nerve in guarding. Of the rest of the team it is unnecessary to speak individually. The line is strong and in last year's form. We miss Hayner on the end, but Everett is doing conscientious work, and will develop into a strong player. We hear that Hayner will be out this week for the year.

FERRY HALL.

The Misses Chaffee are attending school at the Elgin Academy.

LOST—One white straw hat. Finder will please tie to Larned's pier. Owner will secure it in the dark.

Harp playing by Miss Messenger was thoroughly enjoyed by the Ferry Hall folk, one morning last week.

It was late, but greetings still seemed in order, for through the midnight air rang out the cheery words—"Hello, girls."

If you notice soon you may be able to recognize a Senior by the pin she wears. It is a purple pansy—class colors, purple and white.

In response to a suggestion of some of the girls, each inmate of Ferry Hall paid a small sum towards purchasing some dishes which can be used at feasts, spreads and other entertainments given by the girls. [Great Scott, boys, they use *dishes* at a feast!]

For the Question Box:—Does the Ferry Hall Laundry buy starch by the car load, or support an independent manufactory?

The Seniors elected officers not long since, and Miss McWilliams, Miss McCord and Miss Johnson carry the respective honors of president, secretary and treasurer.

There is no telephone communication at the Sem., but one may easily believe that a goodly number are under the impression that there is, from the number of "Hello's" that one hears in the halls.

Miss Ruth Smith, '92, entertained at luncheon in Wimetka last Saturday, the following Ferry Hallites: Misses Alice Conger, Jeannette Kennedy, Tina Kennedy, Mildred Lyon, Ada Barker, Bessie McWilliams, Grace McCord, Ida Kehl, Dora Franklin, Theo. Kane.

Overheard at a reception, and given as an illustration of the advancement of the 19th century girl—-Sem. (over her left shoulder with infinite scorn) "Do you think *you* could protect anybody?" Cad (squelched) "Whe-e-e-w!" And he went out and wept bitterly and voted against protection.

A few of the Sem. girls were fortunate enough to enjoy the luncheon which Miss Elsie Webster gave for Miss Enid Smith, Saturday, October 1st. The party consisted of Miss Ensign and Miss Beth Mason, of Chicago, Misses Bessie McWilliams, Mildred Lyon and Jean Steel, of Ferry Hall.

The Sem. Juniors and College Seniors were bewildered recently upon receiving the following unique invitations:—

"Ye Spinsters will be glad to greet thee,
    And ye object is to feast ye.
    At ye hour of nine they'll be
    In ye Art Room thee to see."
Are they still wondering?
[Yes. At least *some* of the *College Seniors*

are wondering—why they didn't "stand in.—ED.]

While pursuing her housewifely duties on Sunday one of the college girls had the unmeasurable misfortune to decapitate one of her long-tried and fully-trusted friends—"Beelee Jap." Friends in this world are few and the sounds of mourning and remorse awakened sympathy in the hearts of fourth floor residents. The verdict of the coroner's jury is "death by accident." The remains have been embalmed, and are on exhibition in room 345, where the funeral services will be held Wednesday, Oct. 12th. Miss Jean Steel fills the unenviable position of chief mourner and has our heartfelt sympathies. Let the Jap R. I. P.

Society life at Ferry Hall opened with a very successful ball in the Gym. Friday evening, September 13th. The grand march at 7:30 was led by Madam de Kerstad and Miss Lucy Smith and was followed by sixteen delightful dances to the music of Valesi's orchestra. The artistic costumes of the girls were "fearfully and wonderfully made"—in a day. The scene was perfect, being marred by no manly forms. [S. grapes.] A number of the old girls, as well as guests from the city and town participated. Among the number were the Misses Mae Barnard, Ruth Smith, Julia Moss, Elsie Larned, Hattie Durand, Mame Pratt, Mrs. Welton and Miss Nightingale. Light refreshments were served at nine and at ten the Gym. was deserted (not from choice, but necessity.) Many thanks are due the girls of the "second floor corridor" for this jolly good time.

ACADEMY.

TRI KAPPA.

The tennis courts are in great demand these pleasant days.

Mr. Newcomb enjoyed a visit from his father last week.

Both societies held their first literary meetings on Wednesday, Oct. 5.

The Tri Kappa banquet hall is being painted in anticipation of next spring.

It is reported that Hatch has been chasing Sems lately. It's dangerous work, Hatch, don't try it.

Much to the pleasure of Mitchell Hall boarders "Professor" Everett has returned to his accustomed place at their tables.

We wonder if Mr. Roberts really thinks that Parysatis was the son of Dareios, as he solemnly affirmed in Anabasis class the other day.

Prof. Jack has exchanged places with Prof. Mendel, taking charge of Academia, while Mr. Mendel assumes authority in the President's House.

"Sport" Williams has commenced playing foot ball. His first efforts were made against Flint, a poor man to begin with, but fortunately he escaped with a few pieces left.

Mitchell Hall has a great abundance of musical talent this year and when it is all let loose life is well-nigh a misery there. If any one is in need of a little of this, just call around. We give it away.

Why not revive the Academy orchestra. True, many of last year's members have left, but their places can be filled by new boys who play instruments. It will be very useful to the Academy, and with enough practice ean be made a success. Then with a glee club and an orchestra we can indeed "vie with Gabriel while he sings."

GAMMA SIGMA.

"Willie" Hughitt, '99, is with us again.

Mr. Joe Rogers when asked his favorite fruit, replied, " Dates."

The "Cad" will be represented on the foot ball team by Chas. Durand, Nott Flint and Prof. Williams.

Many of the "Cads" expect to attend the dedication of the World's Columbian Exposition, which is to be held October 21.

Gamma Sigma was favored on the 5th inst. with a vocal solo by Prof. Dudley, and also a piano solo by Sigfried Gruenstein. They were both appreciated by all.

The following are the officers of the Gamma Sigma Society for the ensuing term: President, W. R. Cheever; vice-president, T. W. Harvey, Jr.; secretary, E. W. Everett; treasurer, E. M. Breckenridge.

AMONG THE ALUMNI.

J. E. Carver, '96, is traveling in Pennsylvania.

Joe Montelius, '95, is traveling in Europe this fall.

Miss Carrie Griffin, '89, is teaching in Springfield, Ohio,

F. G. Conger, '89, is studying medicine in Pittsburg, Pa.

"Jerry" Smith, '91, is insuring people in La Crosse, Wis.

W. U. Halbert, '96, expects to teach during the coming year.

J. H. McVay, '91, has resumed his studies in Rush Medical College.

Louis Linnell, once of the Academy, spent Friday, September 30, here.

J. F. McNary, Academy '94, is with the Remington Typewriter Company in Milwaukee.

F. C. Albrecht, '96, will spend the fall at his home in Piper City, Ill.

P. W. Linebarger, '91, is Spanish secretary to Hobart C. Taylor, in Chicago.

J. D. Russell, once with '93, is now married and holding a good position in Evansville, Ind.

Keyes Becker, '89, has left Elgin and is now telegraph editor on the leading paper in Ogden, Utah.

Miss Anna Davies, '89, is taking a post-graduate course in the new Chicago University.

Sartell Prentice, Jr., '91, is taking the middle year of his theological course at Princeton Seminary.

Miss Charlotte Underwood, once with '92, is this year teaching in the Racine, Wis., public school.

Charles Foss, '93, is reported to be training for the foot ball team at Gales College in Galesville, Wis. "Jack" also edits the college paper at that place.

A. E. Platz and W. B. Medary, both of Academy '95, are this fall working in a tannery in La Crosse, Wis.

E. M. Wilson, '89, is, on account of poor health, compelled to remain at his home in Hopkinton, Iowa, this fall.

Miss Florence Griffen, once with '91, is teaching in the primary department of the Red Stone Academy, in Uniontown, Pa.

J. D. Pope, once a student here, is running for state senator from Saline county, Neb. Mr. Pope has already served one term and has won much credit for himself. His home is at Friend, Neb.

C. A. C. 10; EVANSTON 0.

CHICAGO, Ill., Oct. 8. (Special). Owing to some misunderstanding the game between C. A. C. and Lake Forest was not played, Evanston playing in our stead. At 3:30 the teams lined up as follows:

C. A. C.	POSITIONS.	EVANSTON.
Sager.	Left end.	Oberne,
Rafferty.	Left tackle.	Van Doosen.
Remington.	Left guard.	McClusky.
Thomas.	Centre.	Pierce.
D. Remington.	Right guard.	Clark.
Malley.	Right tackle.	Culver.
Lewis.	Right end.	Oates.
Crawford.	Quarter.	Deering.
Smith.	L. Half back.	Kennicott.
McNary.	R. Half back.	Noyes.
Marcotte.	Full back.	Young.

It was not until the second half that points were made. By several good rushes on Malley's part and by the running of Smith the ball was forced over the line. Crawford tried for goal but missed. The second touch down was the same story, Malley carrying off the honors. Harding, who had taken Marcotte's place, kicked the goal. Five minutes remained with the ball in Evanston's possession. Noyes punted dangerously near the C. A. C.'s goal, the 'Varsity's still holding the ball. The call of time robbed them of a possible touch down.

NOTES OF THE GAME.

King and Shirra were among the interested spectators at the game.

"Slugging" was freely indulged in by both sides, Kennicott having his nose broken. He had to retire.

The punting of Noyes, the tackling of McClusky and the rushes of Malley and Smith were the features of the game.

Noyes makes a splendid captain. He punts well, tackles strong and sure and at the same time puts energy into his men.

Lake Forest may learn a lesson from this game. If we intend to beat Evanston it means persistent work. N. W. U. is showing up in good form and under the captaincy of Noyes will make it hot for all comers.

THE STENTOR.

VOLUME VI.   OCTOBER 18, 1892.   NUMBER 3.

PUBLISHED EVERY WEEK

BY THE

Lake Forest University Stentor Publishing Co.

BOARD OF EDITORS.

F. C. SHARON, '93 ....Managing Editor
R. H. CROZIER, '93 ....Business Manager
N. H. BURDICK, '93 ⎰ ....Locals
S. B. HOPKINS, '93 ⎱
L. N. ROSSITER, '93 ....Alumni and Personal
B. R. MacHATTON, '95 ....:..............Advertising

ASSOCIATE EDITORS.

HARRY GOODMAN, '94 ....Athletic Editor
FOREST GRANT, '96 ....,............Staff Artist
DAVID FALES, '96............................Town

Terms—$1.50 per year. Single Copies—10c

————ADDRESS————

STENTOR PUBLISHING COMPANY,

LAKE FOREST,   :   :   ILLINOIS.

Entered at the P. O. at Lake Forest, Ill., as second-class matter.

CHAPEL REFORM.

It is simply outrageous the way the students leave chapel after morning prayers. A stranger would think the building was on fire or a small sized riot was in progress if he were to appear in the hall just as chapel was over. Everyone is squeezing and pushing and climbing over his neighbor in vain efforts to be the first one out. The students are none too dignified during prayers, but when, as the last word is spoken, this undignified scramble takes place, it makes the whole thing *absolutely ludicrous.* It seems to us that this is the last place that such an exhibition should be made. In other schools precedence is given to the upper classes. The exercises are made more impressive. The only proper way in going out would be to have the Faculty file out first; the young ladies next; the Seniors next, the Juniors next, then the Sophomores, and Freshmen last. It is no more than right that this order should be observed. The idea of a lot of Freshmen crowding out Seniors or Juniors is ridiculous and in any other school would be checked immediately by the students themselves. There is no use talking, there will be no order until class lines are drawn a little closer and chapel will continue to end in a bedlam until some plan something like the one proposed, be adopted.

THE INDOOR BALL SCHEME.

That members of the Faculty could possibly find any excuse for not allowing the boys to invite the townspeople to play indoor ball with them is indeed a marvel and something that the students cannot understand. In the first place the gymnasium is for the pleasure of the students. A great number have not the time to give to a regular gymnasium course and would not take it if they had. The Athletic Association is in need of money. The students bring forward this scheme for the purpose of furnishing amusement and the same time putting more money into the Athletic treasury. In order to get up interest the townspeople are asked to participate. *Then* permission is absolutely refused, on the ground that it will gradually lead to the townspeople using the gym. for their own use. Now here are a few reasons indorsed *by every student* why the townspeople should be allowed to join us in these games. In the first place the feeling between town and college has always been very cordial, and the town has certainly assisted the college more than it returns. The townspeople have supported the college athletics, their field days, their entertainments most liberally and have certainly made the students feel at home in their houses. If the townspeople are debarred from this it will certainly antagonize them to a certain extent, they would be justified in withdrawing their support and *where* would athletics land? At the bottom of the sea with McGinty. It is granted that Evanston or any visiting school could play against us in the gym. Do we owe anything to Evanston? No, and yet they can play. Do we owe anything to the town? Ask yourself and see if you can answer " No." The townspeople are allowed to play on our campus. Why aren't they driven off if such strict rules are to be drawn? How often do we ask that they be allowed to play with us? *Once a week.* Think of it, only twenty times during the year, and then only when students are there also. The games would take immensely and the treasury of the Athletic Association would flourish. It means more money and less subscriptions. It interferes with *nothing*. The gym. is lighted up and heated at night and not more than two or three are there at any time after seven o'clock. This an innovation but is there any law against progression? How any objection to this plan could be raised is a thing that strikes the students dumb with astonishment.

THAT WONDERFUL CUP.

At the last meeting of the Intercollegiate Athletic Association of this state, Champaign withdrew, saying they had won the trophy and could gracefully retire. Before this last meeting the championship cup had been held by Champaign and every year there would be a fight over who owned *that cup.* Champaign claimed it and supported her claim by hanging onto it. Knox claimed it and had it proclaimed in the newspapers that she owned it, although Champaign had it. For aught we know the other colleges may have believed they owned it. Suffice it to say, Champaign won and held it three straight years. This year, according to the constitution, she gave a new cup to the association. By her retiring, the cup would, of course, go to the secretary of the league to be competed for next year. What does Knox do now but come forward and blandly say that the new cup is hers and she means to have it! Such unlimited nerve is rarely displayed. How she will get it remains to be seen. And so the old annual "scrap" is at hand and Knox and Champaign "quill-drivers" will lavishingly spread ink supporting their views. Champaign saw fit to withdraw and yet we remain! This is a strange world.

IT'S THE GENTLEMAN WHO WINS.

Lake Forest has always had a splendid reputation for the gentlemen she has sent out to every collegiate gathering. The last meeting at Champaign was no exception. Entertainers asked for the Lake Forest boys and would take no others. The ball team had been down in the spring and left a good impression, so that the people knew what kind of boys they were getting when Lake Forest went down this last time. We rest assured too that our representatives upheld us well in this respect. This reputation for gentlemanliness we should always strive to maintain. It is one of the greatest compliments that a stranger can pay and we should show our appreciation by remaining up to the top notch and winning a still more enviable name. It may be very smart to act rowdyish when away but it loses you the respect of the people whom you most need. Remember this, boys, and let "Lake Forest" always be a synonym for "gentlemen."

THE NEW YERKES TELESCOPE.

Chicago University is certainly getting everything she wants. Last week Mr. Yerkes came forward and offered to have made the largest and finest telescope in the world, regardless of expense. The glasses are each to cost $55,000, the mountings $60,000, and the dome $50,000. This means a great deal for Chicago. It means that her name will go abroad with the fame of her telescope. The largest and finest telescope in the world is indeed something to be proud of. Chicago University will be known all over the civilized earth as the home of this great instrument and it will be the greatest of the many important features that will bring Chicago University before all people. What does this mean to Lake Forest? It means that she must hustle to keep her place and if we are to cope with this new rival, students and all must put their shoulder to the wheel and push old L. F. U. ahead of everything in the West.

THE PRESIDENTIAL SITUATION AT LAKE FOREST.

At the present moment the students and friends of Lake Forest University are looking forward with eager expectation to the appointment of a permanent president. This same interested look has been directed towards the College for now nearly six months, and it is still uncertain as to when, and in what form our expectations shall be converted into reality. Naturally, the students feel some anxiety regarding the situation.

While the question is still open it may not be out of place for THE STENTOR to speak of some of the qualifications the President ought to possess; for we belive that any suggestions that may contribute to the selection of the right man will be welcomed by Trustees and Faculty.

To our mind, the President ought to be the man whose presence or absence in the college community would make more difference than that of any other man connected with the school. He should not be simply the chief officer of the College, but should be the one who represents the university life in its completest sense, and, also, the one who is incessantly active in co-ordinating the varied interests of the institution, both educational and material. Upon him devolves attention to symmetry in the educational work, the representation of the institution to the public, the increase in its attendance, and also its material equipment.

It is everywhere conceded that the president should possess the qualifications of the man of business, but it should also be borne in mind that a college president is *pre-eminently* the director of an educational system, and his qualifications for that part of his work are of paramount importance.

The lack of attention to this fundamental qualification in selecting a president has given to more than one college a chief officer, who, although strong in other lines, was not sufficiently in touch with the educational world to shape the work of his college with intelligence or to form a plan for its substantial growth. It is not enough that the president should be a very good man, or a man of broad intellectual grasp.

He is called upon to either inaugurate plans or to approve of those given by others for the growth of his college, and also to represent to his board the *real* needs and the aims of the institution. Upon his representations in these matters hangs the welfare of the school. It is he alone who has the ear of the board and if his conceptions of the aims and needs are inadequate or faulty, the institution suffers.

The importance of the president's being in touch with his work from the professional side is clear. Chosen from some other profession he is at a great disadvantage. For, although he may be professionally equipped in his own line, he may be obliged to figure as an amateur in educational matters, with some of his most important duties lying entirely outside his range of thinking.

No man can do the work of a physician without having studied medicine professionally, and it is equally true, that no man can give an adequate administration to a college to-day (although assigned to the position) without knowing the educational work of the day, and what is required in the sphere of higher education.

The work of the presidential office is very different from what it was fifteen years ago. During that time the work of higher education has rapidly shaped itself into a profession with its technical side and in the present period of transition and unusual activity the interests of this institution should be under a professionally trained president.

Let the new president for Lake Forest be by all means chosen from the ranks of educators.

It is sometimes spoken of in a congratulatory way that the college will run itself, and that there is no immediate need for a president. To substantiate the view the fact is pointed out that, this year the old students return and that new ones are attracted to the college. It is much to the credit of the Faculty that this is the case. Former students, by their own statements, return merely to be under the instruction of their old teachers in the face of the fact that the presidential chair is vacant, and there is, also, an increased confidence in the teaching force of the college. This is a good basis for the work of the president, who, in nearly all institutions of learning, is recognized as the one who, along with his other administrative work, is to give particulrr attention to increasing the attendance of students.

It is our conviction that the interests particularly of the college will suffer even under the best of temporary management. It cannot run itself any more than a business can.

Both Ferry Hall and the Academy are well officered, and the prosperity and growth of these departments is dependant upon the management of their respective principals. Now, the college, which is the head of the schools in Lake Forest, needs a chief officer even more than one of these lower departments. The results of the work of the competent college president will show, first, in the college, and then in the whole system of schools here; for, he stands first in the same relation to the college as the principals do to Ferry Hall and the Academy; and in addition is the councellor of the principal and the director of all the educational work here.

The chief thing to be desired at the present moment is competent direction in the shape of a president who can form a coherent educational plan and unite it to the general plan for the development of the institution. No one will undertake to form such a plan except a permanent head who expects to develop the same through a series of years, and the institution has much to lose while it is waiting to be put into this line of definite growth. W. A. L.

COLLEGE.

Are "melons at eleven" the best food for football men?

"Say, professor, have you seen my wife around here anywhere?"

Mr. Reinhardt, of Academy Hall, was quite ill several days last week.

Many of the boys were "personally conducted" to the outer air tne night of the Sem. reception.

The junior class in literature has arrived at that time "whan that Aprile with his showres swoote," etc.

Mrs. Tabor has returned to her home here after an extended summer tour in England and on the continent.

Harry Thom, of the elective class in surveying, has been assisting Mr. Lee during the past week. Practice makes perfect.

A. A. Hopkins, the winner of the contest at Champaign, favored the senior class in oratory with his oration on Cavour last Tuesday.

Two tardy Tri Kappas took their tardy time-tellers to K. S. Buck, the Waukegan time-tinker, and he taught them to tell the time without trying twice or thrice.

Mr. Learned died last Friday at his home in Lake Forest of typhoid fever. The funeral was held Monday. The deceased was connected with Reid, Murdoch & Co.

Verne Ray of the cad. in attempting to vault the horse in the gym. a few days ago, broke his arm but is doing nicely.

The room formerly occupied by R. S. Spellman for the college book store is being built over into a fire and burglar proof vault for the university's valuables.

The lightning-rod down the east side of the college building went with the old coal sheds. Our roof-climbers will now have to ascend to the belfry from the inside or by the corner rods in front.

The "old G. P." resumed its gastronomic operations as a club last Monday, at Mrs. DesRochers'. The following new members came in: W. Smith, Dysart, Grant, C. G. Smith, and J. Jones.

H. C. Durand's ferocious dog has frightened "Tiny," "Dory," and several other timid seniors almost into convulsions recently. It is at least eight inches high and accompanies our benefactor wherever he goes.

Carroll Erskine, who fell through the roof of the new boiler house to the floor, twenty feet below, escaping dislocation or fracture of the thigh as by a miracle, is able to walk about some with the assistance of a walking stick.

The new rule of the scholarship committee in regard to conditions is causing some of those take-it-easy-and-forget-about-it students to rouse themselves from their somnolent states and see if it strikes them. Better look this thing up.

New drains were put in last week to conduct tne rain-water from the roof of the college building around the south end to the pond near the gym. Frye is to be commended for the rapidity with which the work was accomplished. The next thing in order might be some new pipes from the roofs to the drains.

Do not miss the magnificent pyrotechnic displays next Friday night. They will occur in Washington, Lincoln and Garfield Parks and each will be an exact co uterpart of the other. Several carloads of fireworks will be burned in each place.

The Germania Verein is to be reorganized. This is a society for social and literary purposes in which German is spoken exclusively. Those wishing to join should hand their names to Miss Liese, of the Sophomore class, who will furnish full particulars.

Its still leap year and the girls are showing their appreciation of it by serenading the college youths. Last Friday evening a party of sems made "music in the air" till the boys had to adjourn society to show *their* appreciation. You are always welcome, girls, and songs about "tunnels." are just the thing.

Reginald the sem. driver, left his "fiery steeds" untied alongside the depot platform last Tuesday. They took fright, as untied horses always do, and dashed madly along towards Blackler's. Here they took the sidewalk and drew the heavy wagon along the narrow walk with great precision, until they were finally stopped at the new railroad bridge. C. S. Daves viewed the inspiring sight from his front steps.

The appropriations of the trustees together with funds obtained from other sources for the purchase of literary material for the library amount to about $2,000. This is an increase over the money available for the same purpose last year.

Messrs. Goodman, McNary, and Bishop laid the student's request for a Columbian vacation before the faculty at the regular weekly meeting last Tuesday. The result was the granting of Thursday and Friday, Oct. 20 and 21, to the students, that all may attend the magnificent Chicago ceremonies.

Alexis Claremont, the mail carrier from Green Bay, Wis., to Chicago sixty years ago, has recently made a pedestrian trip over his old route. He passed through here Friday morning. He is a short and slight man with snow white hair. He wore his old buck-skin suit, consisting of a long coat and trousers and Indian moccassins. His old mail sack was strapped to his back. He is making the trip as a contribution to the Columbus celebration.

"Build the finest and largest telescope in the world and get every adjunct to make the observatory the most complete anywhere. I'll pay the bill." So said Chas. T. Yerkes to President Harper, of the Chicago University. Alvan G. Clark, the maker of the Lick lenses, has the contract for the making of the lenses for this new telescope. This lens is to be forty-five inches in diameter, just eleven inches greater than the Lick glass. Lick will be thoroughly li—, whipped.

The delegates to Champaign reported to the Oratorical Association last Thursday that Lake Forest would be allowed to transfer the contest for '93 to Knox College, in which case it will come here in '96. The association, by a unanimous vote, decided to take this course. We will, therefore, take a pleasant jaunt to Galesburg next year, instead of working ourselves to death in a vain endeavor to feed and shelter the orators and athletes of the other colleges in our over-hoteled (?) burg.

The freshman class now has the most complete class organization in college. The plan in vogue in congress has been adopted, and a committee selected for each smallest detail of work. It remains to be seen whether this scheme will facilitate or complicate the transaction of business. There are four committees of five: Colors, Miss Linnell, chairman; social, Hopkins, chairman; yell, Rogers, chairman; motto, Thomas, chairman. A financial committee of three is presided over by T. M. Hopkins.

The reception given during the first two weeks by the Athenaean Society and the Y. M. C. A., so thoroughly prepared the way for the Sem. reception Thursday night that no time was lost in preliminaries. Everybody seemed to know just where he or she was wanted, and each moment was utilized. The most popular resort was beneath the gigantic palms in "Madam's room." Delicious refreshments were served, and soon after—that terrible bell! We cannot thank Dr. and Mrs. Seeley enough for their hospitality. Mr. Little, of McCormick Seminary, who visited Mr. Crozier, was among those received. The boys anxiously say "next."

The chess club games, so far as have been played, are as follows: Dr. Seely, 2, Prof. Eager, 1; Wilson, 3, Parish, 0. The other games scheduled for this week have not as yet been played. The schedule for the week Oct. 17-22 is as follows: Dr. Seely vs. Prof. Dudley; Prof. Eager vs. J. A. Linn; N. H. Burdick vs. W. E. Ruston; A. B. Burdick vs. E. H. McNeal; S. B. Hopkins vs. G. L. Wilson; A. A. Hopkins vs. C. O. Parish; J. S. Lee vs. C. G. Smith; Rogers vs. W. D. McNary. There seems to be considerable interest taken in the game and better results are hoped for this year than were realized last.

The republican students had a meeting last Wednesday to perfect their campaign organization. A constitution was reported from committee as follows: The organization shall be called the Students' Republican Club of Lake Forest University; its object shall be to educate the students in the principles of the Republican party; that a meeting shall be held once a week, the first to be held on Monday, Oct. 17th. The officers for '92 are: A. A. Hopkins, president; B. R. MacHatton, vice-president; Forest Grant, secretary and treasurer; F. C. Sharon, W. N. McKee and Warren Everett, executive committee. Some talented campaign speakers will address the boys, and in case the Art Institute can be secured all will be invited to come and hear them.

ECHOES OF THE CONTEST.

The U. of I. Athletic Association gave a ball in the Walker Opera House on the night of the inter-collegiate reception and banquet. May L. F. U. never have so many students that the oratorical and athletic associations will clash and get up rival entertainments.

The athletic delegates wish to express in this way their great gratitude to Ed. Craig of Champaign, secretary and treasurer of the association, for numerous kindnesses shown them.

We have heard several say that Findley of Monmouth, or Karasch of Knox, should have taken second instead of the Illinois College orator; but no one, to our knowlege, even thought of objecting to the awarding of first place to A. A. Hopkins.

The Lake Forest delegates were well and carefully "ticketed," receiving complimentary tickets to the banquet, to the ball, to the contest, and to all the athletic games. They were also much sought after by wire-pulling delegates and cannot complain of neglect in any respect.

The Chicago and New Orleans limited took three of the Lake Forest delegates from Chicago to Champaign on Thursday afternoon. The towns of Danforth and Harvey brought to our mind "our Dan," and the M. H. pump. The train tore madly through the extensive farm lands about Doran's Crossing, but kindly pulled up near a saloon kept by F. T. Radecke at one of the minor towns.

U. of I. won so easily in the athletic games that they were less interesting than they might have been if more closely contested. A credit of 102 points were to her credit at the close, the next higest number being 20. The lowest score made by any college which was represented in the game at all was 12, made by Illinois College. Lake Forest, with only two contestants on the field, come home with 13 points to her credit—a record to be proud of.

ATHLETICS.

We played the Chicago Y. M. C. A. Saturday, Oct. 15, and play Madison in Milwaukee, Oct. 22.

Bunge, captain and center rush of the Beloits, resigned from his place on account of lameness. This cripples Beloit somewhat.

In the meeting of the Athletic Association Friday evening last, Professor Harper, Grant and W. Everett were appointed a committee of three to have charge of and be responsible for the gym. while being used for indoor base ball.

. It is quite likely that Ellis will not play with Amherst this fall. He says the work is too hard and takes up every minute of his time. Goodale has secured a position on the team. It is rumored about that Ellis will return to Lake Forest this year.

If the foot-ball men do not develop into giants of strength it will not be because they don't get enough to eat. As a starter for breakfast each one has a raw egg; then comes oatmeal without cream, a pound apiece of mutton chop or steak, and coffee three times a week. For dinner, three-quarters of a pound of rare roast beef per man, boiled potatoes without dressing, sliced tomatoes, all kinds of fruits, coffee three times a week and ginger ale. For supper, four boiled eggs, cold roast beef, toast, fruit in abundance, and one cup of tea every night. Some of the men after putting away about a ton of victuals a day, actually have the nerve to come around to the manager's room about 10 p. m. and say they are hungry.

Each succeeding day witnesses an improvement in the foot ball team. We are glad to see Williams again in his old position behind the line. When once started Williams is a hard man to stop and is by all odds the best ground-gainer on the team. His punting is not up to his usual standard, due probably to the fact that he had to retire for a week. It is to be hoped, however, that he will soon resume his old form. MacHatton still plays a strong game and leads one to expect great things of him. Dickinson has been playing right half-back in very creditable style. He is comparatively new at the game but displays a great deal of agility and pluck. Hayner will return this week. This may alter things somewhat, Hayner and Everett playing the ends and McNary half-back. It would be a good move. Everyone knows McNary's playing abilities and while he would be missed in the line yet the strength added to the backs would more than make up for it. Flint, Hunt, McGaughey and Woolsey are men hard to pass. A general criticism to be made is that the boys are careless about off-side plays and foul tackles. This could be remedied in a measure by having a referee and umpire in every practice game played with the second team. There are plenty of fellows here who would be glad to act in that capacity. On the whole we have reason to be proud of our team, and we wish the boys every possible success.

ECHOES FROM THE GYM.

Why not set aside one day in the week for visitors? Last year they came in unexpectedly at all times, much to the discomfort of many.

Arrangements are being made to have several exhibitions this year, similar to the one given last spring. These will preserve the interest and give the boys something to work for.

Classes in the gym. will be organized the first week in November. They will begin with light gymnastics until the muscles have been strengthened, then the heavier work will be introduced.

As no arrangement has as yet been made in regard to lockers, we suggest the following plan: Let the University give the Athletic Association the privilege of putting in lockers at its own expense. These lockers can be rented to the boys for 50 cents a year or term, and besides paying for themselves, would add a little something to the Association treasury.

The time is now drawing near when the students will look to the gymnasium for their pleasure and exercise. Would it not be advisable to quote a little from Instructor Everett in regard to the use of the gym? He says, "Many believe the gymnasium a place where one learns to perform tricks and to become a circus actor. But these ideas have been exploded by the recent strides taken in physical culture. If the new student would gain benefit from the gymnasium he must join the classes and take *regular* exercise." This is good, wholesome advise and should be followed.

FERRY HALL.

THE RISING BELL.

In the morning, tolling early,
Sounds the dreaded rising bell.
Hark! the servant gaily ringing,
Ringing to your rest, a knell.

And you think when rudely wakened,
Of some friend in mystic lore,
While the maid goes gaily ringing,
Ringing at your chamber door.

O, that bell that breaks your slumber,
Sounding on the morning air!
Shake your fist and mutter grimly
"Ring it, ring it, if you dare."

Still she goes on blithely ringing,
Waking all the sleepers sound,
Ringing yet, an hour too early,
Ringing in her daily round.

If you wish one little dreamlet,
For a moment and no more,
Comes the goblin of the morning,
Ringing, ringing ever more.

(ONE OF THE OLD GIRLS).

We had almost forgotten the existence of the "little green chair in the office,"—in fact we think many of the new girls had perhaps never heard of it, until this week, when it has seemed to resume it's old popularity.

Mr. Holt's last year's Sunday school class were kindly entertained by him at a dinner given Tuesday, October the eleventh, in honor of Miss Kehl, who is spending a short time with us. The favored young ladies were the Misses McCord, McWilliams, Lyon, Sizer and Kenaga.

Although no telephones are found in Ferry Hall, certain apartments are connected by a tic-tac, and when anything of importance, like the bon-fire of October 8th, occurs, those who are still in dreamland are awakened by a "tapping, tapping, gentle tapping" on the chamber window.

Monday morning at chapel the girls were delighted when Dr. Seeley announced that Mrs. Hester had kindly consented to sing for them. The authorities perhaps do not realize how much it means to the girls to go to their work with bright faces and pleasant feelings; and nothing is more conducive to such results than Mrs. Hester's singing, as was demonstrated by the hearty applause with which she was greeted.

Miss Helen Lyman '90, was married Tuesday evening, Oct. 11th, to Mr. Howard Greer, Jr., of Edgewater. The ceremony was performed in the Union Park Congregational church by Dr. Noble. The church as well as the bride's home at 200 Ashland Bd., where the reception was held, was decorated in pink and green. The bride's gown was of rich white satin, trimmed with duchesse point lace. The veil of tulle fell to the hem of her train. The bouquet was of bride roses. The wedding is pronounced one of the prettiest of the season, and Mr. and Mrs. Greer have our sincerest congratulations.

Dr. and Mrs. Seeley, assisted by a reception committee of Mrs. Hester, Misses Robinson, Smith and Searles, received their friends in the parlors of Ferry Hall Thursday evening. It was a gay scene—pretty girls, happy smiling young men (except when "the other fellow" talked to *her* the whole evening), and tastefully arranged rooms. The parlors were decorated in autumn leaves and smilax, but perhaps the prettiest as well as the most popular place was the north recitation room, which under the supervision of Madame Kerstad, was turned into a perfect bower of autumn leaves and roses. A number of old friends who still have Ferry Hall interests at heart graced the occasion, Misses Rhoda Clark '92, and Maude Baker, Messrs. Geo. Steel, Geo. Wright '92, and Wm. Danforth '91, who bobs up serenely on such occasions, but is none the less welcome. The warning bell rang out at ten, and very gradually the numbers thinned out. Mrs. Seeley as hostess-in-chief was charming in a heavy red silk trimmed with jet. Her cordial greeting to every one is heartily appreciated. Miss Robinson in light blue silk with ribbon trimmings, and Mrs. Hester in a rich dress of black velvet, lace and jet did equal honors to the occasion. In fact, it was a good time and we settle down to work again with renewed interests.

· The ambition of the Seniors to make this year the pleasantest in the history of Ferry Hall, was made evident by their very successful feast given Friday evening, October the seventh. Promptly at nine o'clock, they received their guests in the art room, which was artistically decorated. The tables were uniquely arranged in the form of a cross and very tastefully adorned with smilax flowers and ribbons. In place of souvenirs, cards tied with the class colors and bearing a quotation, portraying the characteristic of some one of the girls, were found at each place. The feast which was served in very dainty and tempting courses was pleasantly brought to a close by a few remarks from the president and a short impromptu program, consisting of music and recitations. After several familiar songs, good nights were said and we separated, knowing each other better for the pleasant evening spent together. The following was among the numerous quaint acceptances:

To ye kind, sweet invitation
Of ye spinsters young and fair,
For a feast in ye old art room,
Far up the winding stairs,
Miss Barker, of the Juniors
To enjoy this pleasure rare,
In reply would say, " I thankee,"
And certainly will be there.

ACADEMY.

TRI KAPPA.

Since his walk last week Hall says he has no use for the "Sem."

· To say we are glad Thursday and Friday are to be holidays would be putting it mildly.

Tri Kappa extends her heartiest congratulations to Mr. Hopkins on his well-earned victory.

Kimball and "General" are practising a new duet entitled "Home, Sweet Home," which they will soon present to the public.

At a meeting of the Senior class Mr. N. W. Flint was elected president and a committee was appointed to draw up a constitution.

Prof. Mendel enjoyed a stay in the city on Tuesday night, attending the banquet given to the Faculty of the new Chicago University.

Almost all the Academy Seniors attended the reception given by Dr. and Mrs. Seeley Thursday night and it was pronounced a very pleasant affair.

Prof. Palmer has a number of models of Roman implements of war in the Latin room. They are probably the only ones of their kind in the country, and for this reason they have an additional interest to us. They consist of Ballista, Onager, Falx Muralis, a movable tower and a battering ram. It is well worth the time of anyone to go in and see them.

GAMMA SIGMA.

The "Cads" all favor the organization of a political club.

The "Cad" glee club have organized and officers will be elected next meeting.

The Mitchell Hall boys welcome Prof. Mendel to their "festive board" (?).

The Senior class spent a very pleasant evening last Thursday at the reception given by Dr. and Mrs. Seeley at Ferry Hall.

The "Cads" believe cleanliness in next to Godliness, and are all glad to see the tank ready for use.

Mr. Forbes—"They tell me there is enough energy in Niagara Falls to run the universe. Is that right, Professor?"

The old members are glad to see the new ones so prompt in ordering society pins. You can show your loyalty in no better way.

We all enjoyed the talk on Alfred Tennyson that Principal Smith gave us last Monday in chapel. We hope to hear more of the same order.

The algebra class was treated with a shower-bath last Thursday morning by the bursting of a water pipe on the floor above. No damage was done.

School will be closed Thursday and Friday of this week, and most of the "Cads" will spend the time in the city. Why not include Saturday, which is a very short day?

AMONG THE ALUMNI.

Alex S. Wilson, '92, visited friends here on Thursday last.

Clarence Royce, Academy '92, is in the Milwaukee Business College.

Miss Hallie Hall, Ferry Hall, '92, spent Sunday, Oct. 9, here.

H. E. House, ex-'94, now of McCormick Seminary, spent Sunday, Oct. 9, here.

G. W. King, ex-'92, of Joliet, visited friends here on Sunday, Oct. 9.

Paul Scofield, Academy '93, is this year in his father's lumber office, in Marinette, Wis.

Mr. L. J. Buck, Academy '94, is in the butter and egg business in Cobden, Ill.

A. C. Davison, Academy '95, now has a good position in the advertising department of the Chicago *Tribune*.

L. Z. Johnson, ex-'93, now of McCormick Seminary, paid his old classmates a flying visit Sunday, Oct. 9.

Miss Jane S. Wilson, '88, is again this year teaching in the Ossining Seminary, in Sing Sing, N. Y.

It is rumored that both W. B. Brewster, '92, and W. R. Dysart, '92, will shortly enter McCormick Seminary.

Miss Helen Lyman, Ferry Hall '90, was married to Mr. Horace Greer, in Chicago last Tuesday.

E. S. Cass, '93, G. W. Ellis, '93, and F. C. Ellis, '96, have all joined the Chi Psi's at Amherst.

Miss Alice Hoyman, an old Ferry Hall girl, is making a specialty of vocal training at her home in Clarence, Ill.

Misses Daisy and Blanche Wiser, who were at Ferry Hall last year, are now at their home in Chicago, under a private tutor.

Miss Lilian Robinson, a former Ferry Hall girl, is spending the fall in New York City. Her address is 71 East 128th St.

Mr. Shirra, Academy '93, is the general collector for the Edison Electric Co., at Chicago. Mr. Shirra was pitcher on the 'Varsity ball team during the year 1889-90, and was quite a good athlete.

LAKE FOREST, 26; Y. M. C. A., 6.

The game of football between Lake Forest and the Chicago Y. M. C. A. took place last Saturday on the university athletic field. In spite of our best efforts we could not keep them from scoring. We were somewhat handicapped by the absence of Captain Gallwey and MacHatton. At 3:30 the teams lined up as follows:

LAKE FOREST.	POSITION.	Y. M. C. A.
Hayner.	Right end.	Bainer.
Dickinson.	Right tackle.	Diener.
Flint.	Right guard.	Wikel.
Hunt.	Centre.	Penfield.
Woolsey	Left guard.	Claflin.
McGaughey.	Left tackle.	Zaramba.
McNary.	Left end.	Buell.
Durand.	Quarter.	Paige.
Everett.	R. Half back.	Sunday.
Jackson.	L. Half back.	Ford.
Williams.	Full back.	Marcotte.

First half. L. F. had the ball. On a wedge 15 yards were gained. Jackson went around end for 28 yards more. Everett went through for 7 yards and McNary took the ball around the right end and made a touch down in 4 minutes. Williams kicked the goal. It was now the Y. M. C. A. ball, and having lost it on a fumble the 'Varsity's pushed toward the Y. M. C. A. goal, Jackson taking ball around end for the second touch-down. Williams kicked the goal. Score, L. F. 12; Y. M. C. A. 0. After the ball had passed from one side to another on 4 down the 'Varsity pushed it to within 2 yards of the Y. M. C. A. goal, where they lost the ball on a fumble, but so strong was our line that it succeeded in forcing the Y. M. C. A. team through their own goal, thus scoring a safety. The ball was brought to the 25 yard line, and as soon as it was touched to the ground by the Y. M. C. A. center Everett fell on it. The ball was passed to Jackson who, by a run of 27 yards around the right end, scored another touch down. Williams failed to kick the goal. This ended the first half. Score, L. F. 18; Y. M. C. A., 0.

Second half. On a wedge Y. M. C. A. made 20 yards. On their failure to score the necessary 5 yards on 4 downs the ball went to L. F. by several good rushes on the part of McNary, Jackson and Williams the ball was again forced over the line, McNary scoring the touch down. Williams failed to kick the goal. On the wedge Y. M. C. A. made 35 yards. The rushes of Sunday and Ford were irresistible, Ford carrying the ball over the line. Paige kicked the goal. At this point Hayner, who is not yet in training, retired in favor of Rogers. The 'Varsity's made 10 yards on a wedge but lost the ball through fumbling. After the Y. M. C. A. had gained 10 yards McGaughey secured the ball in a scrimmage and with a clear field scored another touch down after a long run of 70 yards. Williams failed to kick the goal. From this on until time was called the ball was kept pretty well in the center. Final score, L. F. 26, Y. M. C. A. 6. Umpire, Campbell; referee, Nyce.

NOTES OF THE GAME.

In the absence of the Y. M. C. A. full back Marcotte played that position for the visitors.

The features of the game were the tackling of Hayner, Sunday and Zaramba, the rushes of Williams and McNary, the gains by Jackson, and Durand's interference.

On account of a sore finger Diener had to retire in favor of Raaaoch.

There were six off-side plays, three by McNary, one each by Hayner, Everett and Penfield. The men should be more careful about this as it materially aided the Y. M. C. A. in scoring.

MacHatton and Gallwey were both laid off. The former on account of a sore knee and the latter because of other duties.

EVANSTON, 36; BELOIT, 0.

The game Saturday between Evanston and Beloit was a very monotonous exhibition of poor defensive play by the Evanston line and worse fumbling by the Beloit full-back. Evanston's first touch-down was made from the center, without losing the ball, in about four minutes. All the others were much alike, Beloit starting with the ball at the centre and working it down the field by the magnificent rushes of Atkinson and some good end runs by Bradley, till they reached the 25-yard line. Then somebody, usually the full-back, would fumble the ball and let Evanston fall on it. A punt of 30-40 yards by Noyes was so much clear gain on account of the wretched work of Baldwin and the good end work of Oberne and Stebbings.

After one or two kicks, the end runs of Noyes and Kennicott and the bucking of Sheppard and Culver soon scored a touch-down. Only once was the ball dangerously near the Evanston goal, when some one interfered with one of Noyes' kicks, the ball being downed only two yards from the line. A run of 10 yards by Noyes around one end, followed by

20 yards around the other end by Kennicott, took the ball out of danger. Then Noyes punted again, and so on.

The line up was as follows:

EVANSTON.	POSITION.	BELOIT.
Sheppard.	Full back.	Baldwin.
Noyes (Capt.)	R. Half back.	Bradley.
Kennicott.	L. Half back.	Atkinson (Capt.)
Griffith.	Quarter back.	Parr.
Stebbings.	Right end.	Kennedy.
Culver.	Right tackle.	Buck.
Clark.	Right guard.	Song.
Pierce.	Centre.	Short.
McClusky.	Left guard.	Dwight.
Van Dooser.	Left tackle.	Martin.
Oberne.	Left end.	Holmes.

NOTES OF THE GAME.

Parr, Beloit's veteran quarter-back, says he's played his last game of foot-ball.

The work of Atkinson is simply marvelous, even the Evanston crowd cheering his terrific rushes.

Craig, ex-Cornell, and Parr, ex-Lehigh, acted as referee and umpire and seemed to give perfect satisfaction to all.

Beloit's regular right end, colored, and regular right half-back, were detained at Beloit by the college Faculty on account of "unsatisfactory scholarship."

The beautiful new grand stand at the south end of the grounds, was dedicated with impressive ceremonies, between the halves. Evanston having already scored 18 points, everybody was happy and a great deal of enthusiasm was let loose.

The second game of indoor base ball between the town and the 'Varsity was played in the gym. Saturday evening. The town team was again victorious, winning by a score of 18 to 15. There is enough good material in the College and Academy for a winning team, but the fellows must learn to hustle and must not get rattled so easily. Grant did some splendid base running for the 'Varsity. The score by innings:

```
Town ............. 2  5  0  0  0  0  5  4  2—18
Varsity .......... 1  3  1  3  1  3  1  0  2—15
```

Sunday evening, about 6:30, the house formerly occupied by Spencer Smith, but now owned and occupied by Mrs. L. E. Platt, was burned to the ground. The fire started in a back shed and was caused by tipping over a lamp. All of Mrs. Platt's furs, pictures, and books were destroyed, but most of the furniture was saved. The total loss was about $6,000; insurance, $3,000. Some kind of fire department is sadly needed. A garden hose would have put out the fire at first.

THE STENTOR.

VOLUME VI.   OCTOBER 25, 1892.   NUMBER 4.

PUBLISHED EVERY WEEK
BY THE
Lake Forest University Stentor Publishing Co.

BOARD OF EDITORS.

F. C. SHARON, '93............Managing Editor
R. H. CROZIER, '93............Business Manager
N. H. BURDICK, '93 ⎫
S. B. HOPKINS, '93 ⎭ ....Locals
L. N. ROSSITER, '93..........Alumni and Personal
B. R. MacHATTON, '95................Advertising

ASSOCIATE EDITORS.

HARRY GOODMAN, '94..............Athletic Editor
FOREST GRANT, '96................Staff Artist
DAVID FALES, '96....................Town

Terms—$1.50 per year. Single Copies—10c

————ADDRESS————

STENTOR PUBLISHING COMPANY,
LAKE FOREST, : : ILLINOIS.

Entered at the P. O. at Lake Forest, Ill., as second-class matter.

A DRAMATIC CLUB.

As everyone knows, as soon as the football season is over we drop into a sort of lethargy and the dull season is made duller still by our seeming lack of interest in everything. It is the custom of colleges now-a-days to have a dramatic club, an organization which is as peculiarly characteristic of a school as is a glee club. This club gives during the winter several plays or comic operas, and besides furnishing a vast amount of fun for all concerned, rakes in many shekels and develops one's talents in a dramatic line to a great extent. Why not organize such a club here? There is without doubt much latent talent here in our midst that only needs bringing out to make its owner famous. We will not assert that we have an Edwin Booth, a Richard Mansfield, or a Joe Jefferson, but we *may* possess one, who knows? We are sure Prof. Booth would heartily endorse such a scheme and would aid the venture. Several students have gone from here to Princeton and became members of the Princeton dramatic club the same year. We are possessed of a good stage, a splendid hall, good ante-rooms, good scenery, all the properties needed for college plays. Lastly, we hope there are none so narrow in this school as to assert that the drama is something so immoral as not to be countenanced. If such there be, we do not care to become acquainted. What say you, students, shall we branch out or tread the old time-worn rut of precedence?

A NEW READING ROOM.

Are we never to have a new reading room? It seems to us that the present excuse for a room becomes worse every year. It is dirty, the tables are rickety, the benches are usually broken, and it is entirely too small. We were promised a new reading room when the Art Institute was built. Can we not have it now? There is a room over there next to the one used by Prof. Halsey which would make a splendid reading room. It would require a very small outlay of money to convert it into a beautiful modern reading room. There is a grate in the room and large windows, just what are needed to make an ideal place to read in. The only things to be purchased would be racks for the papers. The present room is not only gloomy, but cold and cheerless. Not only this, but it is situated in such a place that every class at the end of every hour pours into it yelling and whooping and kicking over the benches so that no one can enjoy reading in such a place. Moreover, we are sure the young ladies will side with us in this. There is so much rowdyism in the present reading room that it is rarely one sees a young lady venture in. In the art building we could have comparative quiet, and as soon as the ravine is bridged, which will not be long, it will not be out of one's way in the least. With a room in such a place those who go there will go to *read* and not to prevent others from reading.

AWAKE FROM YOUR LETHARGY.

The organization of the Republican club has awakened a small amount of enthusiasm and the great rally at the Auditorium last night has aroused a little more, but there are many fellows in the college who dont seem to care a straw who is elected, or whether the government becomes a kingdom to-morrow, or what happens anywhere so they get their three meals a day. Such a state is deplorable. What kind of men will such people become? What kind of *citizens* will such a crowd make? What a selfish, indifferent policy to

pursue! Do these students imagine that it was such men who threw off the British yoke? Do they think for a moment that such men put down the Rebellion? Do they think such men established this grand republic and keep it where it is now? They should cease such vain imaginings. While the nation is not in such imminent danger as it was in the times mentioned, still it is being thrown onto the shoulders of the young men and if they are indifferent and ignorant of government who shall say what will happen? It is the young American that the world is looking up and greater things are expected of him than of his father. If he fails—imagine for yourself the result. Therefore, if you wish to have a place in the world take some interest in your country's welfare. A fellow who does nothing at school but pore over books continually is not recognized as part of a college. A man who does nothing but work for his own selfish interest is not looked on as part of his country. There *ought* to be such a thing as clean politics, if there is not, and it is the duty of every young man to do his part in raising politics to a higher plane.

THE IDLER.

The student who did not attend some of the exercises in the city last week missed something for which he will pine in vain. Besides missing the beautiful pageats he did not experience that thrill of enthusiasm that came over every one with one spark of patriotism in them and made them thankful that they were Americans; he did not realize that we have an army of which we need not be ashamed; he did see the greatest crowd that Chicago has ever held, nor did he have the breath squeezed out of him in a vain endeavor to walk in the streets. We were jostled, stepped on, squeezed, slugged, and managed to get into everything that was going, but we wouldn't have missed it, not we.

⁎

Did you ever watch a football crank? If you never have, take our advice, retire to a sufficient distance, procure a pair of opera glasses and gaze upon him. We ask you to retire to a safe distance because *we* were so unfortunate as to stand near one last week. When the crank appears on the field he is as quiet and docile as others of the same genus. He even talks rationally and to all *appearances* is in his right mind. After such a review we plucked up courage enough to stand near one of these creatures. But, heaven preserve us, at that moment the game began! At first the crank is restless and prowls around like a caged hyena. Then someone gets the ball and starts down the field. The crank rouses into action. He lets out a small yelp and charges down the field with the team, waving his hat wildly and running square into some poor fellow, knocking him endways. Then the other team gets the ball. Back again he charges like a wild bull, draws up in front of you, waves his arms against your nose, steps on your toes, and yells in your ear "Whash ma'er wish us." Then the two teams line up and push back and forth. The crank yells, he whoops, he chews his fingers, he says "Shoot the umpire," or "that's the stuff;" he thumps you on the back and yelps "Wasn't that

a corker?" He pounds his cane on your feet and "begs pardon, didn't know you were there;" he bets they won't score; he says it is the best game he ever saw; he tells the football men they are "stars;" he warns the referee that another of those decisions loses his job; he says to everyone, "get out of my way." Just then somebody on the other side makes a touch-down. The crank throws away his hat, pulls his hair, raves, foams at the mouth, and when time is called, collapses, and is carried off the field. He is tenderly cared for, and recovers in time for the next game. Such is his life. Don't be a football crank, but watch one in a big game.

THE POLITICAL SITUATION.

A FEW REMARKS THAT EVERY STUDENT SHOULD READ.

In a few weeks it will be decided at the polls whether the government for the next four years is to be in the hands of Mr. Harrison or Mr. Cleveland. If the choice lay merely between these two contestants it might be very difficult for an independent voter to decide how to vote, for both men as presidents have given the country most excellent administrations. The one blemish upon the personal policy of Cleveland was the outrageous turning over to the tender mercies of Adlai Stevenson of so many postmasters to be slaughtered, in sad defiance of all civil-service reform principles. The one dark blot upon that of Harrison has been, and is, the scandal of the Pension Bureau, and the retention at its head of Green B. Raum.

Admitting these exceptions, both administrations have been patriotic, business-like, and as clean as politics is ever likely to allow administrations to become. Both are men of sincere conviction and of personally good political intention. But back of them lie the two great parties, and alongside of them, when in harness, works the co-ordinate branch of our government—Congress. We all desire to know, not only what Harrison or Cleveland intends, but also what a supporting or opposing Congress will be likely to do. To the personality of the man must be added the policy of his party, if we would make our guesses probable, although the two candidates are not influenced by party pressure in equal degree. Where lie the differences of the parties? On the silver heresy they are at one in their orthodoxy; on the treatment of the election question in the south their variance is only apparent; as regards "the new navy" and our foreign policy their action has been continuous under rival administrations. The tariff is the great rock of offense upon which public opinion has split; and here is the issue at the polls next month: Shall the "high protective" policy, as expressed in the McKinley bill, continue to prevail, or shall "tariff reform" bring a return to more moderate duties? Many thoughtful Republicans are leaning the latter way, despite the charming naivetté with which Mr. McKinley and the New York *Tribune* eliminate from a practical world all causes of present prosperity except the McKinley tariff. The former discovers in the rise in price of American wheat abroad the influence of the McKinley tariff, but says naught about the shrinkage of the English crop twenty-three per cent. The latter with ferocious joy depicts the wide-spread distress in the tin-plate districts of Wales as a result of the McKinley tariff, but draws no inference from the over-production in that industry, which is shown to have been long continued by the very press comments which the *Tribune* cites approvingly. It is really too bad that the simple truth, which every college Senior recognizes, that so long as the prosperity of this new and only partially developed continent is due to manifold causes, no one phenomenon of its industrial life can make or mar its onward progress, never gets a hearing in a campaign newspaper or a campaign speech. What the people should be shown plainly is whether or no the increased cost of living, which a "high tariff" policy entails upon sixty-five millions of consumers for the benefit of a small favored class, is in the long run for the benefit of the whole nation. If so, let us accept it gladly.

J. J. HALSEY.

FRIDAY EVENING, Oct. 21, 1892.
DEAR STENTOR:

I did not notice your account of the fire which resulted in an almost total loss of our house and furniture, until to-day, (Friday, Oct. 21st,) or should have written you sooner and asked you to correct some of the statements contained in the paragraph.

The fire started in the laundry in rear of the kitchen but was not caused by tipping over a lamp as you state. The origin of the fire is a mystery as there was no lamp or stove in the room and no combustibles of any kind that we know of. But a very small part of our furniture was saved and that in such a broken up condition as to be nearly worthless and so making the total loss nearer $10,000 than $6,000, with an insurance on house and furniture of $4,000. Mrs. Platt and myself desire through the columns of your paper to acknowledge gratefully the very many kindnesses extended to us by the people of Lake Forest during and since the fire. We cannot express in words the gratitude we feel, but will ever pray that no such calamity may befall any of them.

Sorrowfully yours,   L. C. PLATT.

COLLEGE.

S. B. Hopkins' young brother visited him last Thursday and Friday.

W. D. McNary visited his parents in Milwaukee during the recess.

Earnest Glen Wood, '92, made his parents a flying visit Thursday and Friday.

Mrs. Warren and family have moved into the city and are residing on the North Side.

The pine blocks for paving Deerpath avenue have arrived, and the work is progressing rapidly.

It is reported that E. Smith Cass, '93, is to sing first tenor on the Amherst Glee Club. If such is the case we congratulate you, Eddie.

Work in all departments was suspended Thursday morning and the trains carried a goodly number of our students to view the great civic parade.

The football team remained in town during the recess and practiced every day. A few went in Thursday noon to see the parade but all were *positively forbidden* to stir out of the place Friday.

The Republican club met last Monday evening in the chapel and was addressed by A. A. Hopkins. Mr. Fales was expected but did not arrive. There will be some good speakers present at the meetings this week and next.

The Rev. Grant Stroh preached at the Sixth Presbyterian Church, corner of Oak and Vincennes avenues, Sunday the 16th. The Sixth Church is Dr. Worcester's old pastorate and has a large and wealthy congregation.

We notice in a last week's *Tribune* the death of Robert Reid, of Cincinnati, on Tuesday the 11th. Mr. Reid was well known in Lake Forest, having lived there some length of time up to about three years ago. He was a prominent church member.

The discipline committee held a matinee last Tuesday afternoon. Admission by invitation only. Attraction, several students in a spectacular production of "Wild Bill, the Chapel Skipper, or five absences to account for." Music by the Faculty. Ten students occupied private boxes.

Last Monday '95 and '96 in a joint meeting decided that the cads were becoming entirely too fly and that it was their duty to inform them so and warn them not to carry canes on the streets. A proclamation in red ink to that effect was accordingly posted and there has been "blood on the moon" ever since. The cads have ordered an extra supply of canes, the sophs and freshies have been eating raw meat for a week and thus it goes.

The lectures which are given to the Lake Forest people under the auspices of the literary societies are always en-

tertainments of the highest order. In
introducing Prof. Alexander Forbes to
the people of Lake Forest the Athenaean Society feels confident that this
reputation will be fully maintained.
Mr. Forbes is a pleasing speaker,
witty, pathetic, eloquent, as occasion
demands, and never fails to please. His
subject is "Elements of Individual
Character," and will be delivered at
the Art Institute Building Thursday at
8 o'clock p. m.

Scene—The shore of a wild, lonely
lake. Dramatis Personae—five hunt-
ers—dead shots—three dignified professors, one townsman, two students.
They are pursuing the wily duck. They
have not enjoyed the best of luck, and
are wending their way homeward when
—"Hush, hist, look in there gentlemen,
do you see those objects sailing around
on the water?" and then comes one
of the profs pushing through, all excitement. "Let me get at them, let me at
them. I can slay them easily." The
rest fall back. Tremblingly a shell is
inserted, the gun cocked and bang,
bang, it rings out on the clear air. The
ducks are as serene and calm as a June
morning. Once more rings out the
trusty gun and once more the ducks
seem to look on in mild surprise. The
hunter becomes nervous, turns pale and
exclaims, "Great heavens, am I shooting blank cartridge, or have I lost my
eye as a shot." But with this comes a
resolve to get those ducks or die in the
effort. He creeps up on hands and
knees, and pours enough shot in them
to kill a cow. But there they are. A
thought strikes him. He must have
killed them so beautifully that they
must have died instantly without a

wiggle. He rushes out and grasps
them. Heaven preserve us! they were
wooden. And then the wood rang with
merry laughter, he saw his mistake and
its the Doctor's turn now to "set 'em
up."

At the Y. M. C. A. football game the
ticket sellers met with expressions of
some dissatisfaction directed at the
management for charging admission
upon the ground that it was not a
league game, that he had subscribed to
the athletic association or, in some
instances, that last year's *base* ball
tickets held good. Neither the plea
that it was an exhibition game nor that
the base ball tickets hold good is
worthy an answer. It costs as much to
carry a Y. M. C. A. team from Chicago
to Lake Forest as it would a league
team.

To the Athletic Association subscriber we owe a word. The subscription
solicited goes into the general treasury,
from which not only foot ball but base
ball and track athletics draw. Now
foot ball receives only a proportional
part of each subscription and any fair
minded student can, at the expense of
a little graphite and paper, easily com-
pute an estimate of expenses required
to carry a team of sixteen men through
an eight week season, making excur-
sions to Milwaukee, Beloit, Champaign,
Chicago, not to speak of the additional
expense of providing uniforms, shoes,
and bandages, besides seventeen dollars
per week for the sustanance of the
training table.

The expensive part of the season is
still before us and it behooves us to get
every cent possible.

There is to be but one more game played on our campus this season and we are sure that any student possessing a millegram of college patriotism will not begrudge *fifty cents* to witness the season's play on the Lake Forest field and that no one will attempt to assume the role of "deadhead". when Northwestern meets us November 12th.

ROBT. H. CROZIER, Manager.

FESTIVITY BRIEFS.

"Coffee" says that McKinley recognized him and bowed.

Most of the boys occupied prominent positions "on the curb."

A great number of Ferry Hall girls viewed the pageant from Giles' in the Masonic Temple.

Probably a larger crowd went in to view the fireworks than to see any other one attraction.

Burdick, as the STENTOR representative, was a prominent figure in the World's Fair grounds on Friday. He was busy interviewing most of the notables.

Messrs. MacHatton and MacGaughey "bucked the line" for several yards on Madison and State streets. They, however, ran into a "cop" who forced them back to the 25-yard line.

FERRY HALL.

Miss Grace E. Taylor of Washington, D. C., was the guest of Miss Alice Conger several days this week.

The girls who serenaded last week Friday were pleasantly surprised by a lovely box of candy from the boys in the president's house.

We are glad to welcome back to our number Miss Byrd Huddart, who has been spending the summer in Europe.

Miss Eva Bouton acted as bridesmaid last week at the marriage of Miss Cora Riedle to Dr. William C. Bouton at 5837 Washington Ave.

The girls who took advantage of the opportunity offered for viewing the World's Fair parade from the Masonic Temple are much indebted to Mr. Giles for his kindness.

The Ferry Hall Primer—Here is a duck. This is a wooden duck. This is the wooden duck at which Dr. Seeley shot. There is a live duck. This is the live duck at which Dr. Seeley did *not* shoot.

First Sem.—"Yes, he has an awfully nice face. He could go through the world on his face."

Second Sem:—"Well, I'd want a man who would go through the world on something beside his cheek."

Last Thursday evening the gymnasium was party to a scene at which its old eyes opened in wonder. It was transformed into a gipsey camp and the Aletheians did the honors attired in "the costume of their tribe," but judging from some of the costumes displayed by the gentlemen their tribes must have existed in prehistoric times. The singing, the gymnastics and the pantomimes given by the gentlemen were highly appreciated. Taffy pulling occupied the latter part of the evening and everybody had a good time.

Mrs. Helen R. Geaves '79 writes us from Chicago: "My life since leaving school has been a very happy one, but at the same time so uneventful, that the outline can hardly prove exciting. Many ambitious plans and a pleasant social life filled the first four years. Then came the fullfillment of one plan in two years of school teaching. In 1886, why, "they married, and lived happy ever after"—with special emphasis on the "happy." This is the sum and substance of my record. There should be hair breadth and stirring adventures perhaps, and yet I am not sorry that those have been left to someone else."

CUPID AT SCHOOL.

AN ARGUMENT FOR CO-EDUCATION.

Young Cupid was his mother's joy,
  A child of most bewitching looks;
And yet he was a naughty boy,
  Because he would not mind his books.
Some things he studied well, 'tis true,
  For what he knew he got by heart,
And learned to practice all he knew;
  So every body called him smart.

Co-education came in vogue—
  The new idea pleased him well.
"Now, lads and lasses," lisped the rogue,
  "I'll teach you how to love a spell."
Such words as "dear," "divinest maid,"
  My "angel," "sweet heart," darling," "dove."
The school soon learned—they even played
  With letters—letters learned to love.

The teacher taught the "Rule of Three;"
  They asked was there no "Rule of Two."
She said, "Oh no! that could not be,"
  But Cupid said there was, he knew.

Geography seemed pastime gay;
  The lads found "Nancy," "Charlotte," "Ann;"
The maidens soon found "Lover's Bay,"
  Then "Heart's Content,"—the "Isle of Man."
Dull grammar grew as sweet as song.
  That nouns have gender all could see,
That adjectives to nouns belong,
  And nouns and certain verbs agree.

"This verb is active," whispered John;
  "I love, dear Jane—this tells the truth."
Blushing, she pointed further on:
  "Passive, for you are loved, dear youth."
"I would be loved," hummed Mabel J.
  "Ah! that's the mood," spoke Tommy S

(Surprising her) "And if I may,
  I'll call you 'sweet heart'—may I?"
      "Yes."

"If I were loved," sighed Mary Gold,—
  "You are!" cried Alf, "I do declare!
I'm only waiting to be told
  To parse 'am loved'—Oh, may I, fair?"

Of course he might! how could she be
  So cruel as to tell him "nay?"
So Cupid danced for very glee,
  While grew the school from day to day.

O naughty Cupid! thus to fool
  Your mother Venus, throned above,
And, while she boasts you love your school,
  Bewitching all the school with love.

ACADEMY.

GAMMA SIGMA.

Thornton has had his hair cut.

Do we carry canes? Well, I guess, yes.

Alexander is on the sick list. The doctors are baffled.

Franklin visited with his parents in the city over Sunday.

"Harry" Bellamy, an old Cad., was out to the football game last Saturday.

Oh where, Oh where are my privileges gone?—words and music by Joe Rogers.

Kickbush's voice has gone in training for center rush on the second eleven.

Wouldn't it be a good idea to get up a game between Gamma Sigma and Tri Kappa?

We would like to ask the Tri Kappa correspondent where the "Tri Kappa banquet hall" is.

We would like to know how it is that Prof. Burnap sees everybody who goes down to the lake or to the Sem.

It was quite amusing to see "Wild Bill" from Denver guarding the household effects at the fire Sunday night. He had a "Nichol" plated revolver in his hand.

It now looks as though the Cad. will be represented by at least two more men on the football team, Dickinson and Coe Everett. The latter made a gain every time he got the ball against the Y. M. C. A.

The Cad. was thrown into a fever on Tuesday of last week by the proclamation from the college in regard to our carrying canes. A mass meeting was held and it was decided that we would carry sticks to a man. The question now is, will anyone prevent us?

MADISON 10; LAKE FOREST 6.

MILWAUKEE, Oct. 22. (*Special.*) The game here to-day resulted in a victory for Madison, but the contest was a fight to the finish. The teams were evenly matched and the interest was maintained throughout. Without any disparagement to the Wisconsin boys it is safe to say that they won the game through luck. It was one of those games which delight a lover of the sport as no 'slugging" was indulged in. At 3:30 the line-up was as follows:

LAKE FOREST.	POSITION.	MADISON.
Hayner,	Right end.	McGovern,
Gallwey,	Right tackle.	Silerwood,
Flint,	Right guard.	Jacobs,
Hunt,	Centre.	Kull,
Woolsey,	Left guard.	Kreushaw,
McGaughey,	Left tackle.	Francis,
McNary,	Left end.	Richards,
Durand,	Quarter.	Lyman,
Jackson,	R. half back.	Thiele,
MacHatton,	L. half back.	Karel,
Williams,	Full back.	Dillon.

First half. L. F. won the toss and took the ball. On their failure to gain the necessary 5 yards Madison took possession. It was the same story with them and then Williams gave an exhibition of how the game should be played, he making 15 yards on three downs. Then came the catastrophe. L. F. fumbled and Karel pouncing on the pigskin scored the first touch-down after a run of 40 yards. Thiele kicked the goal. Score, Madison 6, L. F. o. L. F. started in with a wedge and made 15 yards, but by fumbling lost the ball again. Madison pushed dangerously near our goal, but so strong was our line that they could not score. Through the sprints of Jackson and McNary and the perfect bucking of Williams the ball was taken to the middle of the field and was soon in Madison territory. When within 25 yards of the goal Williams made a try for a drop kick over the post, but missed it by a hair. This ended the first half. Score, Madison 6, L. F. o.

Second half. Wisconsin gained nothing on the V, and lost the ball to McGaughey on a fumble. Then L. F. showed her mettle. Williams gained 11 yards by bucking the centre, and McNary by a superb run of 30 yards carried the ball to within 2 yards of Madison's goal, but stumbled and fell. Williams was forced over the line and kicked the goal. Score, L. F. 6, Madison 6.

Madison started in determined to win. Thiele gained 25 yards around the end. Karel made 5 more through the centre, but lost it on a fumble. L. F. could not gain the required 5 yards, and Thiele made a touch-down after a run of 10 yards. He failed to kick the goal. Score, Madison 10, L. F. 6. The remainder of the game while exciting was unproductive of results. The ball was first at one goal, then at the other, L. F. making vain endeavors to push it over the line. When time was called the ball was in Madison territory. Final score, Madison 10, L. F. 6.

Umpire, Nyce.

Referee, M. Addison.

NOTES OF THE GAME.

Next Saturday we play our first championship game with Beloit at Beloit.

MacHatton played in hard luck. He played strong, but whenever his number was called there was no hole for him to go through, consequently he did not gain much ground.

The features of the game were the playing of Thiele and Karel, the tackling of Jacobs and Durand, the runs of Jackson and McNary, the bucking of Williams and L. F's interference.

Financially the game was not a success. Madison attended to the arrangements, but let it be said to the credit of her managers that it could not have been done better. Every detail showed carefulness on their part. Everyone knew of the game but for some reason or other did not care to attend.

Lake Forest has gained a great deal of experience. We are weak at centre and extremely careless about fumbling and off side playing. Off side plays are inexcusable and the exercise of a little care would soon remedy the fault. Generally speaking, however, the team is as strong as last year and will do credit to the high position Lake Forest has taken in athletics.

The contest was one of the cleanest ever seen. The Madison boys showed themselves to have the true gentlemanly instinct, and resorted to no mean tricks. While the fact remains that we were beaten, still it is a satisfaction to feel that it was done honestly, and administered by worthy opponents. We wish Madison all possible success in the future.

LATE NEWS

Don't forget the lecture Thursday evening by Mr. Forbes.

Dr. Hursh has returned from the east and is at his old quarters.

Rev. Mr. Hall will occupy the pulpit of the Presbyterian Church next Sunday.

The football team goes to Beloit next Saturday and we hope we can record a victory.

"Free Masonry" was quite lucidly discussed at the Young People's Meeting Sunday.

To-day was the last day you could register. If you haven't done it, you have yourself to blame.

W. R. Nash and Charles Durand remained in Milwaukee over Sunday, the guests of Mrs. Dewey.

Charley Smith donned a soldier's uniform last week and did duty with his Iowa company at the parades.

The actual paving of Deerpath Avenue has begun. The cedar blocks do not look to be of very good quality, nor is the street wide enough, but it is better than no paving at all.

The Republican club, thirty strong, attended the great rally at the Auditorium last night. Seats were reserved for them in the main balcony and the club was quite an important factor in the noise part of the meeting.

THE STENTOR.

VOLUME VI. NOVEMBER 1, 1892. NUMBER 5.

· PUBLISHED EVERY WEEK

BY THE

Lake Forest University Stentor Publishing Co.

BOARD OF EDITORS.

F. C. SHARON, '93................Managing Editor
R. H. CROZIER, '93..............Business Manager
N. H. BURDICK, '93 ⎱ ....Locals
S. B. HOPKINS, '93 ⎰
L. N. ROSSITER, '93..........Alumni and Personal
B. R. MacHATTON, '95..................Advertising

ASSOCIATE EDITORS.

HARRY GOODMAN, '94...............Athletic Editor
FOREST GRANT, '96....................Staff Artist
DAVID FALES, '96..........................Town

Terms—$1.50 per year. Single Copies — 10c

————ADDRESS————

STENTOR PUBLISHING COMPANY,

LAKE FOREST, . : : ILLINOIS.

Entered at the P. O. at Lake Forest, Ill., as second-class matter.

WHO IS TO BLAME?

At present there is absolutely no steam running through the registers in the Art building and no steam in the Gymnasium until after 4 o'clock in the afternoon. It is said that *someone* is trying to economize and begins by cutting down our steam supply. The students desire to enter a most hearty protest against this way of doing business. Sometimes the Art building is so cold that recitations have to be transferred to the College building. Again, no hot water in the gym. till after four. What is the use of opening that building at all if it is not heated?

Now, who is to blame for all this? Who is it that has such power and control that they can shut off the steam whenever it pleases his gracious majesty? Last year in the college if one man said we could have steam, we had it; if he wasn't in the right mood, we didn't have it. The boys have few enough comforts without being deprived of heat, and at least, if no better accommodations can be furnished, let them keep warm.

THE PROGRESS OF FOOTBALL.

It is wonderful to note the advance of the great modern game of football and see it each year becoming more than ever the representative college sport. A few years ago it consisted of a slugging match from beginning to end, in which most of the new men were badly laid out. Broken noses, staved-in ribs, broken collar bones, and mashed faces were the rule, not the exception. Look at the game now. It has advanced until the science displayed is simply marvelous. No longer are there any " accidents" to speak of. Entire games are played in which no one receives a scratch. Strength and endurance are still required, but brute strength and force no longer hold sway and win games. Science is what tells. True, some men are hurt occasionally now, but most from accidental causes, as in other games. Slugging is dis-

countenanced and the team that in-
dulges in it, soon becomes ostracized.
The game is occupying a higher plane
than ever before, and is destined to go
still higher. It is one of the few games
in which new plays can constantly be
made. There is no end to the combinations that can be formed, and it requires a good head to figure them out.
However, such exhibitions as occurred
in Lincoln, Neb., recently, between
Champaign and Nebraska Universities,
will do nothing toward raising the
sport. A few years ago some of the
eastern colleges alone played the game
and possessed elevens. Now every
college in the country, every high
school has its team. Naturally the east
has held undisputed sway, but of late
years the west has been steadily creeping up, and when the game is as old in
the west as it is now in the east, we can
easily turn the tables on our eastern
friends and give them a taste of their
own medicine. There is no possible
reason why such a thing should not
happen. Ann Arbor showed the east
that baseball can be played as well in
the west as anywhere. Chicago is
already demonstrating that she can
hold her own in the east, although with
practically no training. A few years
more of system and work and the proud
title of "Champions" will be carried
west along with everything else that
represents energy and pluck.

WHY NOT ORGANIZE A NEWSPAPER LEAGUE?

At present we are connected with
adjacent colleges in athletics of all
kinds and in oratory. Why would it

not be a good scheme for these adjacent
colleges to form a college newspaper
league, a sort of college associated
press for the furtherance of college
journalism. The college newspaper or
periodical has taken a step forward in
the last few years. It aims more than
ever now to imitate the great Metro-
politan journals in obtaining *news* and
in advancing new ideas. There is at
present a Western college press association but it hardly fills the bill. What
we all need is more intimate connection,
a more direct exchange of news with
each other and to be constantly forming plans, not for the furtherance of
the interests of one paper, but the
raising of college journalism in general.
If Madison, Beloit, Evanston, Champaign, Chicago University and Lake
Forest would combine and form an
association not merely to meet once a
year and discuss questions but by discussing live questions *the whole year* to
arouse a lasting interest in college
journalism, it would begin a new era.
We would suggest that if such an association be formed, an executive board
consisting of one man from each college
be appointed whose duty it shall be to
look up questions of vital importance
to all, to obtain articles from leading
journalists, in fact to act as an associated press.

Why should the college newspaper
confine itself to its own college merely,
or to an occasional oration, or articles
on the greatness of Cæsar? Let college
men discuss subjects of the present,
subjects in which the world is interested.
They must become interested in such
questions when out of school, why not
allow and promote discussions by col-

lege students on questions of the day? Get them interested before they are out of school, and college journalism will be doing more for them than it is at present. Another thing, such an association would form a newspaper fraternity. Editors visiting other schools, or desiring to, would be received by the local newspaper men and made to feel at home; would be shown every attention, in fact, would feel a pleasure and pride in being connected by such ties. There is the advantageous side in a social way, as there is in a business way. Of course it need not be confined to the schools mentioned. There are excellent college papers published by Minnesota, Knox, and Illinois colleges, if they are not too far distant for such a close connection as is proposed. How say you, brethren of the quill, shall we combine?

THE DEATH OF MRS. HARRISON.

All colleges and all college students will sympathize and mourn with President Harrison in his great loss and bereavement. Mr. Harrison was himself a college student and no class of people should give him more profound and sincere expression of sympathy than the student body of the country. Lake forest wishes to be among the first to offer the most heartfelt loyalty and sympathy in this, his hour of trial.

SURPRISES LAID IN WAIT.

STORIES OF WHITELAW REID, BAYARD TAYLOR AND A DAPPER CLERK.

An old New York newspaper man told a story to a few of us at the Chicago Press Club the other day that has the merit of never having been in print, and it is a good one on Whitelaw Reid, candidate for vice-president.

"I can vouch for the truth of the story," said the narrator, "because the managing editor of the New York *Tribune* told it to me. We were warm personal friends and he told me the story in confidence, so I will not mention any names.

"It was a few years ago, soon after Whitelaw Reid had assumed active control of the New York *Tribune*. My friend had just been installed as managing editor and he was not familiar with Mr. Reid's handwriting.

"About once every three days my friend used to receive a batch of editorials from the editorial rooms to be read by the copy-readers and sent up to the composing room. These editorials were always written in a peculiar hand, and my friend took a dislike to them. He, however, came to the conclusion that they were weak, inane things, and it was common talk along Newspaper Row that those particular editorials were hurting the paper. But the stuff kept coming in regularly, and at last the managing editor became so exasperated that he determined to go to Mr. Reid and complain that one of the editorial writers was getting up such infernal rot that it was hurting the paper.

"My friend had the talk with Mr. Reid.

"Said Mr. Reid; 'You have no idea who it is that writes the stuff?'

"'No, I can't say. The copy is sent by messenger regularly from the editorial rooms. All I know is that it is poor stuff nobody but a fool would write. As managing editor my reputation is at stake, and I determined to speak to you about it personally.'

"'Have you any of the copy with you?' asked Mr. Reid.

"My friend had come loaded and he took some of the editorials, just as they had been written, from his pocket for Mr. Reid to peruse.

"'So you think these editorials are weak?' asked Mr. Reid.

"'Yes, I must say I do, and all the newspaper men in town are covertly laughing at the *Tribune*,' seid the managing editor.

"'Well,' remarked Mr. Reid slowly, 'I wrote that stuff.'

"My friend was nearly paralyzed. He had made a fearful blunder and he began to apologise.

"'No, you needn't make any excuses,' Mr. Reid hastened to say. 'If those editorials are rot, as the boys say and you say, why it is time I had a rest for a while.'

"It was fully six months before Whitelaw Reid wrote another line for the *Tribune*.

.

I met Louis Kindt, the scene painter, at the Schiller Theatre a few evenings ago and he related to me a funny experience he once had with Bayard Taylor.

"I was coming down the river from Minneapolis in one of the old fashioned steam boats several years ago," said Mr. Kindt. "We had not steamed far down the river towards La Crosse before I fell into conversation with one of my fellow passengers. He seemed very much of a gentleman and spoke German so fluently that I thought he must be a countryman of mine, although he did not look like a German. We became so well acquainted in the course of an hour or two that I asked him to go down into the cabin with me and have a bottle of wine. He accepted my invitation. In all our conversation he did not mention his business or name, and I did not feel like inquiring because he was such a gentleman that I had a delicacy about asking what he had not given voluntarily. When our boat steamed into La Crosse we found a big crowd standing on the wharf. They were cheering and waving handkerchiefs at our boat. I asked my new friend if he knew what it meant. He smiled and said he did not. At length I caught the name of Bayard Taylor from the crowd and then I knew that Bayard Taylor, who was then traveling in this country, must be on board, and that it was he whom they were cheering. I said to my friend:

"'Now if Bayard Taylor is on board, why havn't I seen him? I must have his autograph.'

"My companion smiled, and taking a pencil from his pocket he said:

"'If you will kindly let me have your card, I think I can give you the autograph of Bayard Taylor.'

"When I recovered from my astonishment I took out my card and obtained my desire. I do not know whether the joke was on me or on the author of 'Views Afoot.'"

.

It is not always safe to judge a man by his clothes, as an incident I met with in a broker's office the other day testifies. A certain office in the Board of Trade building is occupied by a speculator whose name many of you would recognize as prominent if it were mentioned. The broker was once a country lad, and is still a farmer's son. although the dapper young clerk who sits in the outer office of the broker did not know it.

While I was in the office last week waiting to see the broker, an elderly man came in and asked to see him. The old man was evidently a farmer. His coat was a trifle seedy. He wore an old straw hat and there were milk stains on his boots. The clerk sized him up and made some joking remark to the type-writer girl about "hayseed," in an aside that the old man could not help hearing.

"Did you say that Mr. R—— was out?" asked the old gentleman of the dapper clerk.

"No, he's not out," snapped the clerk, "but he's busy in his private office, and you'll have to wait like other people. Don't you see that there are three or four waiting to see him?"

"Will he be occupied long?', queried the olk man again, after waiting a few minutes.

"I have no means of knowing. I'm not paid for keeping track of what goes on in his mind," replied the clerk. And the type-writer girl looked as if she thought it was a good joke.

A moment later the broker came out of his pritate office for some papers. He incidentally caught sight of the old man, dropped the papers and said: "You here, father? Why, step into the office. I wasn't expecting you till to-morrow."

The dapper young clerk is wondering when he had better look for another situation. W. E. D., '91.

COLLEGE.

AMUSEMENTS FOR THE WEEK.

AUDITORIUM—Theodore Thomas, Saturday night.
McVICKER's—Keene in Shakespearean repertoire.
GRAND—Dickson in "Incog."
SCHILLER—"Gloriana."
HOOLEY's—The latest comedy, "Friends."
COLUMBIA—Miss McHenry.

The STENTOR sympathizes with Mr. Waldo in the loss of his sister.

"Hi-ho-ha! Boom-cis-bah! Harrison-Fifer! Rah-rah-rah! Lake Forest!"

The Senior orations came in thick last Tuesday. At least four were handed in.

The Chicago *Times* became a 1-cent paper last week. For its merits, consult Mr. Crozier.

J. A. Linn and A. B. Burdick heard Keene in "Richard III." on his opening night at McVicker's.

Several of the boys were at the Schiller during the recess. They report "Gloriana" as immense.

It is rumored that "Cat" met somebody at the Palmer House while he was dedicating the World's Fair.

Several of the students attended the games at the Second Regiment Armory Saturday night, to see "Lutie" run in the mile.

The "fancy dress ball" at Ferry Hall Saturday night was "out of sight"—completely so, as far as the boys were concerned.

Several of the *Tribune's* souvenirs of the World's Columbian Exposition are to be seen on the boys' walls. They are decidedly ornamental.

During his absence attending the state Y. M. C. A. state convention, R. B. Spellman left his "cash basis" in charge of Messrs. Marsh and Vance.

Arrangements have been perfected whereby Dr. Edward Pick will, during the year, deliver a course of lectures upon the subject of "Memory."

The *Inter Ocean* building, lavishly decorated with festoons of red, white and blue electric lights, was one of the prettiest night sights in Chicago during dedication week.

For some iron-clad red-tape, read the faculty's new regulations concerning the making up of conditions. We now have tabulated rules concerning absences and conditions—what next ?

Rev. Mr. Williams, who has been engaged for the last twenty-five years in missionary work in the north of China, near the Great Wall, addressed the students in chapel Friday morning.

Prof. French, of the Chicago Art Institute, delivered a lecture before the Lake Forest Art Institute on the "Innocency of Vision" Thursday evening last. This was the first meeting of the club for the present year.

We notice by Friday's *Tribune* the marriage of Miss Anita Wakem and Roy Johnston at the Church of the Ascension, Chicago. Mr. Johnston was well known here and has many friends who congratulate him and wish him joy.

Who said Lake Forest boys cyuld not yell? Twenty-four of us caused the following to appear in the *Tribune's* account of the rally, October 24: "One hundred students from Lake Forest University occupied seats in the main balcony," etc.

Tuesday, Oct. 25th, was the 92nd anniversary of Thomas Babington Macauley, "the nimrod of literary criticism." This is the gentleman who, when four years old, replied to a condolence, "Thank you, madam, the agony has abated." The senior class on Wednesday discussed his essay on the "Comic Dramatists of the Restoration."

A wagon load of books belonging to Prof. Harper's department were removed from College Hall to the Art Institute last week. Prof. Harper's working material is now all in the latter building.

The beauties of Frye's uew smoke consumer (?) can be best appreciated about firing-up time in the evening. The "Chicago smoke nuisance" cannot compare with the Lake Forest heating apparatus when the smoke consumer is in active operation.

A notice was read after the college chapel exercises that handball must not be played at the south end of the college building. None of the *college* students have played there this year, and in the light of this fact, the reading of such a notice to them seemed very strange.

The massive new (?) iron doors for the fire and burglar vault just put in the basement of College Hall, arrived last week. They are billed from Burnstein & Co., of South Canal Street. It may be economy to buy old rusty iron doors to protect our valuables, but we fail to see it.

The Republican Club of the University is to hold a big rally next Thursday evening in the Art Institute building, at which A. T. Lester, of Springoeld, and Mr. Partridge, of Waukegan, will address them. There will be music beside the "speakin'" and every one is invited to attend.

The Lake Forest correspondent of the *College Life*, Emporia, Kas., thinks Illinois students are slow and uninteresting. He was disappointed that the audience which greeted the orators at the state contest were not provided with tin horns, cow-bells, "kazoos," etc., as is the custom in wild and wooly Kansas. Sorry, but that isn't our style.

The following students claiming residence on Lake Forest have placed their names upon the register of voters, and will cast their ballots in this place: N. A. Burdick, C. E. Cleveland, W. F. Curry, C. S. Davies, A. Haberli, S. B. Hopkins, W. D. McNary, and

N. McKee, J. A. McGaughey, L. N. Rossiter, and W. R. Nash. Others will register to-day (Tuesday).

We understund that the Freshmen of Lake Forest took D. I. Jones, late of '94, and held him under a pump for some time. Perhaps, by this time, Dave realizes the mistake he made in leaving the College of Emporia.— *College Life.*

Not so. Dave has not been under the pump, nor does he admit that he made a mistake in leaving Emporia.

The first number of the second volume of the *University Extension Journal,* containing the announcements of the joint University Board for University Extension for the coming year, is on the reading room table. Of interest to Lake Forest are the following announcements:

AMERICAN HISTORY.

Prof. J. J. Halsey, A. M., Lake Forest. *A*—History of American Parties, 6 Lectures. *B*—The Growth of our Constitution by Interpretation, 6 lectures."

" BIOLOGY.

Prof. Wm. A. Socy, M. S., Lake Forest. *A*—The Simpler Animals and their Relation to the Higher Forms, 6 lectures. *B*—The Physiology of the Nervous System, 6 lectures."

" ART.

Walter C. Larned, A. B., L. L. B., Lake Forest. Some Great Masters of Art from the Renaissance to our own time, 6 lectures."

" CLASS INSTRUCTION.

In addition to the regular courses of University Extension lectnres outlined above, the institutions co-operating in the Joint University Board offer to give in any convenient locality courses of regular instruction, to be conducted by professors and instructors of the colleges."

Among the names of those who have "signified a willingness to undertake a certain amount of class instructions," are those of Prof. Emil Mendel, M. A., German, French, Italian or Spanish; Prof. William S. Burnap, A. B., Greek and History.

Dr. Haven is having a large addition built to his residence on Washington Avenue.

Prof. Halsey was obliged to omit meeting his classes the latter part of the week on account of illness.

We wonder what has become of the street sprinkler. At no time during the summer have the streets been in sorer need of sprinkling than now. The dust is suffocating.

W. E. Danforth informs us that James Foraker has converted him from Democracy to Republicanism and he now talks protection tariff as glibly as Mr. Foraker himself. "Billy" is always surprising his friends.

In connection with an article on the architects of the " White City," in Jackson Park, the current *Harper's Monthly* presents an admirable half-tone likeness of Henry Ives Cobb, architect of the Fish and Fisheries Building.

Mr. Winston's new residence between Mr. Dwight's and Ferry Hall, is so neatly completed that its magnigcent proportions can be observed. It will be one of the most beautiful and convenient of the Lake Forest residences.

The Athenaean society voted to postpone its lecture by Mr. Forbes from Thursday to Tuesday evening on account of the arrangements which the Art Institute had made for a lecture for Thursday evening and which could not well be changed.

Among the new additions to the library we mention the following as being of special value: Lord Lytton's works, three volumes; the works of Holmes, thirteen volumes; Burrough, eight volumes; Chas. Kingsley, eight volumes; Lowell, eleven volumes; Whittier, seven volumes; W. D. Howells, four volumes; Marion Crawford, four volumes. There are also three bound volumes of " Poet Lore." The works of Holmes, Lowell and Whittier are in the celebrated Riverside edition.

It would seem as if certain of the younger students of the Academy were under the impression that the rules of the gymnasium committee of the frculty did not apply to them.

There is a rule which reads: "Bathers must not dry themselves in the dressing rooms." Every evening when the football teams come in off the field they find that either there is a young deluge on the dressing room floors, or that from five to a dozen small fry from the Academy, wet as drowned rats, have pre-empted the aforesaid rooms and are, with sublimest disregard of authority, wringing out their wet bathing suits on the floors. This should be stopped.

In the Athenæan Hall, Friday evening, the society and a number of visitors from Ferry Hall and the town, thoroughly enjoyed the presentation of the works of Bret Harte through selections and brief papers. The following is the program:

PART I.

Biographical Sketch,	. . .	N. H. Burdick.
Prose Selections,	. . .	{ E. H. McNeal. { H. Goodman.
Paper—Bret Harte's Prose,	. .	F. C. Sharon.

PART II.

Music,	. . . . .	Pratt, Sharon, Fales.

POETICAL SELECTIONS.

John Burns of Gettysburg,	.	B. R. MacHatton.
Ramon,	. . . .	J. A. McGaughey.
The Heathen Chinee,	. . .	C. W. Sherman.
Paper—Bret Harte's Poetry,	.	S. B. Hopkins.

ATHLETICS.

Results of the foot ball games last week were as follows:

At Lafayette—Purdue, 24; U. of M., 0.
At Lincoln, Neb.—U. of N., 8; U. of I., 0.
At Boston—Harvard, 28; C. A. C., 0.
At Princeton—Princeton, 40; Man. Athletic C., 0.
At New Haven—Yale, 50; Springfield Y.M.C.A., 0.
At Philadelphia—U. of P., 8; Lafayette, 6.
At Lawrence, Kas.—U. of K., 28; U. of I., 4.

We play Stagg's Chicago University team at Chicago next Saturday.

At a meeting of the base ball team held last Thursday night, W. D. McNary '93 was elected captain for the ensuing year. Those present were Sharon, McNary, Grant, Hayner, Lewis and Goodman. Training will begin sometime in January.

Again misfortune has overtaken us in the shape of injuires to Williams and Durand. Williams has a sore shoulder and Durand's knee is in such shape that he will not be able to play for another week. It is needless to say that both were very much missed in Saturday's game. The team continues to do fair work, but there is still room for great improvement.

In the first place nothing can be accomplished in twenty-five minutes, the time usually given to practice. *The men must come out earlier.* There is no excuse whatever for starting play later than 4:30. Capt. Gallwey's reason for changing McGaughey from tackle to guard is not easy to perceive. McGaughey is certainly a fine tackle and played well in that capacity. Now at this stage of the game he is to be broken into a new position. Much dissatisfaction is expressed over the change and we hope it will not be long before we see him at his old place. Flint is a little slow, and it is a noticeable fact that whenever a man is bucking the line he usually does it alone. The play should be more concentrated. Taken on the whole the team has improved somewhat but have yet many things to learn.

FERRY HALL.

Miss Brett enjoyed a visit from her father two weeks ago.

Who saw Gov. Fifer thrown from his horse Thursday, the 21st? Ask E. J. S.

Miss Sue Flack, '88, after a pleasant summer in the South, is again at her home in Quincy, Ill.

Miss Jean Smith, '92, is visiting her sister, Mrs. Selby Vance, '85, at the latter's home, Girard, Kas.

Miss Elizabeth Howes, of Clinton, Iowa, is spending several days with Misses Margaret Conger and Edith J. Smith.

The girls who attended the Athenæan special meeting Friday evening, may justly consider themselves fortunate.

Miss Whitney and Miss Vrymen, neices of Dr. Seeley, from New York State, are spending a few days with Dr. and Mrs. Seeley.

We hope Prof. Eager was not discouraged by the clamor for "more music" when he played for us to dance Thursday evening, for we want him to play again.

Miss Hays spent vacation week at home on account of illness. During her absence the *other* college girls had the pleasure of entertaining Mr. Coffman, of the *Interior.*

Found! a stemless rose,
Pale pink. If he chose
The owner might call
At Ferry Hall.

THE STENTOR.

9

Miss Hays gave a spread last Monday evening, and never did eyes and mouths open wider than at the sight of the cake and—water.

From the interesting accounts of the gypsy part, the girls who were at home at the time wish they had been here. The boys' suits were wonderful to behold. They wore cuffs on their ankles, pretzels for breast-pins, paint and powder for complexions, and—O my, the ingenuity of man!

Friday's *Tribune* contains an account of a reception given by Mr. and Mrs. W. W. Shaw, 251 Ashland Boulevard, in honor of Mr. and Mrs. Robert Shaw, who have just returned from their wedding trip. Mrs. Shaw, formerly Miss Bessie Harland, was a well known Ferry Hall girl.

Last Friday night the Gym. was literally filled with girls, who, dancing, rejoiced in the fact that Prof. Eager was playing music which "the *other* girls" did not know. Though we've had the pleasure several times of Prof. Eager's music in chapel, this is the first treat of the kind in the Gym., but we hope it is only a beginner. We are always ready to listen to the professor play, whether in the Gym., chapel, or wherever it is.

Mrs. Hester spent Saturday and Sunday, Oct. 15 and 16, at her old home, Bloomington, Ind., as the guest of Judge and Mrs. Miers. We copy the following from the Bloomington *Telephone:* "Like all persons upon whom Nature has bestowed rare gifts in song, Mrs. Hester possesses in a marked degree, the amiability and equable temper, and charming manner, as well as attractive personality, of all specially favored prima-donnas. And yet notwithstanding her high rank as a musician, and her distinguished appearance, there are many traces remaining upon the sunny countenance which remind us of the bright little school-girl so well known here a few years ago among her acquaintances as 'Jessie Henderson.' She has come here at the special instance of her friend, Mrs. Miers, and the ladies having in charge the concert to-night to assist in beautifying the cemetery in which rest the remains of so many of her beloved kindred."

ACADEMY.

TRI KAPPA.

Mr. Scott favored his old friends in the Academy with a visit last week.

There is much "wailing and gnashing of teeth" now, as the reports have been read.

Saturday afternoon restriction hours have been resumed by the faculty much to the sorrow of the students.

Academy boys are glad to note the progress being made in the new buildings and are watching them with a great deal of interest.

Mr. Gruenstein was suddenly called home on account of the death of his sister last week. Our heartiest sympathy goes with him on his sad journey homeward.

We were all made happy the other morning by the announcement that a change would be made in the singing-books used in chapel. The new ones are a great improvement.

Several students have come since the members were chosen by the two societies and as a consequence they belong to neither. This should be attended to at once.

The poetic genius of the members of the Rhetoric class have been given an opportunity to show itself lately. Many of the boys distinguished themselves by producing some very good poetry.

Charley Durand injured his knee quite severely in a practice game Monday and it will be necessary for him to keep quiet for a while. Prof. Williams is also disabled as he hurt his shoulder in the game with Madison.

GAMMA SIGMA.

Can any one tell us where Baker got that laugh?

Two new members for the Cad this week—Wiley and Noble.

Have you seen Warren Everett's moustache? It's a dead ringer for Prof. Phillips'.

The Mitchell-Hall foot ball eleven has organized with Jos. Rogers as captain.

Prof. Williams returned from the foot ball game at Milwaukee in pretty bad shape.

Now boys, do not feel hard towards Alonzo Kimball for playing "Home, Sweet Home," it is his hobby, or else it is all he knows.

The Academy Glee Club is progressing in every particular. The double quartette is also doing good work.

What is this world coming to? There wasn't a sick man in Mitchell-Hall last Wednesday or Thursday.

Mathew Mills was visited by his father and sister last Thursday.

The executive committee of the Gamma Sigma this term is Forbes and Whitney.

Now that the cane affair is hushed up let the Academy again join hands with the college and pull together.

If Kimball keeps up his present rate of improvement we expect to find him as bucking-half on the 'Varsity eleven next fall.

Prof. Jack (in 3rd English.) "Now I may have a wife and love her dearly—yet." He is still wondering what made the class laugh.

Wouldn't it be a good idea for the two societies to have a joint debate on the issues of the day? Last year we had joint meetings frequently, why not have them this year?

LAKE FOREST 22; BELOIT 0.

The Lake Forest league season opened at Beloit, Oct. 29. The teams lined up as follows:

BELOIT.	POSITION.	LAKE FOREST.
Bunge.	Centre.	Hunt.
Hinkley.	Right guard.	Flint.
Short.	Right tackle.	Gallwey, Capt.
Warner	Right end.	Hayner.
Dwight.	Left guard.	Thom.
Martin.	Left tackle.	Woolsey.
Holmes.	Left end.	McNary.
Bradley.	Quarter.	Rogers.
Baldwin.	Right half.	Jackson.
Willard.	Left half.	MacHatton.
Athinson, Capt.	Full.	Marcotte.

Umpire, Goldsberry. Referee, Pratt.

Lake Forest won the toss and took the ball. The first play consisted in McNary's taking the ball around the end for a touch-down in 15 seconds. Marcotte failed at goal. Lake Forest, 4; Beloit, 0.

Beloit took the ball and gained five yards on a V. but were forced back four yards where Woolsey came out of the scrimmage with the ball. By good work Beloit forced L. F. to surrender the ball after four downs. L. F. then rallied and took the "pig" on the fourth down. MacHatton bucked the line for 10 and 5 yards and then McNary made a run of 40 yards and scored the second touch-down of the game. Marcotte goaled. Lake Forest 10; Beloit 0.

Beloit gained nothing on V. but kicked, aided by the wind, to the L. F. 15 yard line. At this point Jackson exhibited superior play, guarded by Rogers, McNary and Thom he made a flying excursion to Beloit's goal, but Mr. Pratt's understanding of the game was such that the touch-down was not allowed. Beloit fumbled the ball and Hayner fell upon it. L. F. failed to advance in four downs and Atkinson bucked for 5 and 3 yards. Bradley tried the end but was tackled by Thom. Beloit dropped the ball. Flint and MacHatton went through the line for 10 yards a piece and Jackson made a detour of the end for 15 yards and a touch-down. Marcotte kicked goal. L. F. 16; Beloit 0.

Second half.—Beloit took the ball and advanced it seven yards; Baldwin was sent against the line but gained nothing. Then one of the prettiest plays of the game occurred. The ball was passed to Atkinson to make another of his telling rushes upon the line when Gallwey broke through and tackled fully fifteen yards from the snap-back. Willard of Beloit was injured and Keith was substituted. Lake Forest now gained good ground and forced the ball to within 2 yards of Beloit's goal but could not advance, and Beloit took the ball on four downs. Atkinson now began heavy bucking through the guard and advanced 15 yards, but lost most of the ground by a break through and tackle by Woolsey. Atkinson then made a long punt which was received on the bound by Jackson, who again made a touch-down after a long run, guarded by Hayner, MacHatton and Woolsey. Gallwey kicked goal. Lake Forest 22; Beloit 0.

After a gain of 10 yards on the V Beloit assumed the aggressive, plunging through the line with the ball in Atkinson's possession, which, together with an off-side play landed the pigskin on L. F.'s 10-yard line. L. F. gained the ball on a fumble and by a series of brilliant plays by MacHatton, Hayner, Jackson and Flint, the ball was carried to the midway territory, where it remained until time was called.

NOTES OF THE GAME.

The Beloit's play a clean, gentlemanly game and a very good one when consideration is taken of the adverse faculty legislation.

To make a success as a referee Mr. Pratt should bury partiality and invest 10 cents in a football manual.

The play of the substitutes was superfine; Rogers at quarter, Marcotte at full, and Dickinson at the carriage showing up in especially good form.

Atkinson did superb work—as Gallwey remarked, "Whenever Beloit advanced it was done by Atkinson's bucking, and when they advanced again it was when Atkinson bucked, and so on."

Ruby red and black were worn by a number of Lake Forest lady admirers.

THE STENTOR.

VOLUME VI.   NOVEMBER 8, 1892.   NUMBER 6.

Extra Edition, Wednesday, Nov. 9, 4 a. m.

HARRISON	CLEVELAND
	X

THE WAY THE DOUBTFUL STATES WENT:

............................New York..*36000*

............................Indiana......*1500*

Dem................Illinois......*10000*

............,...........Connecticut...*2000*

............................W. Virginia...*1500*

............................Wisconsin......*1000*

Weaver carried Nebraska & Oregon

A blue mark will be found under the name of the winning candidate.

We claim a scoop on every other college paper in the world, and even the Chicago papers circulating in Lake Forest.

MANY students cast their first ballots Tuesday. How did they vote, with their fathers or with their convictions?

ARE the students going to take the subject of a new reading room in hand, or are we to go on in the old way using the old rattle-trap now dignified by that name for our periodicals. If the boys themselves would use a little effort we could accomplish something.

A GREAT deal is said among the students and a large amount of grumbling is indulged in in regard to the slowness of the trustees or the difficulty of obtaining requests. Let us examine the matter closely. We do not wish to defend the trustees in all things, but right here let it be said that too much is left to them. *The boys do not do enough themselves.* We want our ball-ground improved. How do we expect it done? Do we look to see the trustees have a force of men put at work and have everything fixed up in shape in short order? Perhaps we do. Perhaps they should do it. But that is not the point. The fact remains that the grounds *must* be put in order, not that they *should* be. We can hardly blame the trustees who have so many things to look after, if they can not comply with some of the wishes of the students, when the students themselves show no interest. The fact is the boys here expect too much. We are too dependent. How did Champaign get her splendid ball grounds? *The students made it.* How can we get a new reading room, get our ball grounds fixed up, get a hundred things we want? *Hustle, depend on no one, get them ourselves.* That is the way things are obtained in this world. "The Lord helps those who help themselves." The trustees would be only too glad to see us manifest a spirit of willingness to help things along. Then let us cease vainly wishing for things and be up and doing for ourselves. It will be surprising to see how much the students can accomplish.

THERE is one thing that the trustees seem to be overlooking. No one more worthy or better fitted for the place could have been chosen for temporary president than Doctor McClure. The trustees made a wise selection. He nas done more than was expected of him, he has more than filled the place. But all this has not been accomplished without the most arduous labor on his part; the most earnest thought and effort, and the people of the town, together with the students, feel that that the trustees are putting too much on Dr. McClure, and that he will in consequence overwork himself. The duties incumbent upon him as pastor here are in themselves arduous and ordinarily enough for one man. But it is felt that the trustees are thrusting too much on him. Dr. McClure is a man who will never half do a thing. There are few men who could perform so admirably the duties of both positions as he has done. If he would accept the presidency, none would rejoice more sincerely than the students, but if he feels that his sphere is more in the church, the trustees and all should see that his duties are lightened as soon as possible. We learn too that Dr. McClure is giving his services *gratuitously*. All the more reason that the trustees should look carefully into this matter and see that in the future he is not burdened to such a degree as he has been. We do not offer this as advice. We merely voice the sentiments of the townspeople.

Now that the campaign is over there is no use dropping politics and disbanding our Republican club. The avowed purpose of the club is to instruct students in Republican principles. How can we do this in three or four weeks? Has any member of the club learned any new points since becoming a member? It is hardly possible that they should. Let us therefore retain our organization and carry out our project, viz, to instruct in Republican principles. It is the only place where members of the two societies meet for discussion. Let them lay aside partisan feeling for a while and discuss political subjects as citizens of the United States, not as members of societies. A good scheme would be, after a proper test had been made, to choose four debaters and have a big public political debate in the Art building some time this winter. It would keep the interest up and would be the best drill in the world.

THE IDLER.

If you happen to be near the gymnasium some evening after foot-ball practice, drop in and watch the team undergo the "rubbing down" process. If you are unacquainted with this proceeding we will explain that every evening after the team is through practicing the members are hustled into the gymnasium, put under a cold shower bath and then rubbed down in the latest approved style by the "rubber." After having his breath taken away and finding his heart in his throat by being put under the cold shower, the footballist is taken in charge by a man who looks harmless enough, and yet before he is through you have decided he is a double-dyed villian picking a fight. He first rubs the youth with a heavy towel as if the prime object was to peel off his skin. Being satisfied this won't come off he begins to jerk the poor fellow's joints. He twists and pulls and cracks and yet they do not break. Then he grabs the muscles and attempts to tear them off the limbs; then he slaps the patient, pounds him on the chest, beats him on the legs, thumps him in the back and has a regular all round circus with him. Then he gives him a final pound, a final jerk, a final rub and the victim pulls his remains together and retires, clothed — in thought. But when he reappears he looks rosy and bright and says he wouldn't miss it for the world. The two "rubbers" and physicians have everything in their mysterious satchels from a spool of thread to a bale of cotton, from vaseline and Jo-he to Hood's Sarsaparilla and Red Cross Cough drops. The team under their care is thriving and they deserve all credit for their work.

* *
*

Professor Booth has been showing us how to place our feet when we get up to speak our "piece." He says, and so do the rules of delsarte, that there is a vast amount of expression in feet. We have been ruminating lately and have come to the conclusion that delsarte is right. We have examined our own feet carefully, and viewed in certain positions and in certain lights they certainly do express something, just what, 'tis hard to decide. However, in looking about, we have seen some pedal extremities that puzzle us. We can not say definitely what emotion or how much strength, or what they do express. Therefore, we appeal to the professor. Now here are a pair of feet we saw

performing this act last week. Do they express strength? Does the size of the shoe show anything? Does it mean that the gentleman possessing these extremities is under an intense mental strain, or has some intense physical force been applied from behind? We confess we are in the dark. But let us turn to this pair. We would

suggest that their position signified confusion or repose. The owner is evidently struggling with "Casibianca" or "Gladicus to the Sparticators." Notice their breadth. This suggests a good foundation, a person not easily *moved*.

What does this suggest? The top one evidently shows that its owner is trying to catch the last suburban train.

Its mate, if reproduced would be on the next page. The other pair tell a simple story of perfect repose. "Dey belongs to a cullud gent an' he's happy as a big sunflowah." But our last one, taken from "high life," shows eminent satisfaction."Me pawnts are cweased, me shoes are polished, me necktie is stwaight, what moah can I awsk." Oh, yes, feet are expressive. We shall hereafter study them with avidity.

THE NEW IMPROVEMENTS.

Lake Forest is being improved to an extent never known before and the end is not yet, so we hear. If the improvements now being considered by the council are carried into effect we will have an ideal little city.

The paving, for which the streets have of late been torn up, is the result of long and careful deliberation on the part of the council. Many have said it was the wrong kind of pavement, that it is not being laid right, or that it will not last. Let these persons rest assured that the council has fully weighed these questions and the road when finished will be a credit to our city, On the east side of the track the paving is of cedar blocks. It will be a continuous roadway starting from the south end of the depot and thence running to the Seminary bridge, via the church and H. C. Durand's; skipping the road in front of the Seminary, it will go past Mr. Yaggy's and Prin. Smith's; then turning west at Mr. Reid's corner will run directly to the new sub-way under the railroad. The contract calls for the pavement to be finished December 1st. However, it will hardly be accomplished so soon. On the west side of the track the main street from the sub-way to the north end of the station will be paved with macadam. The cost of the whole road will be in the neighborhood of $50,000.

The new sub-way under the railroad opposite Mr. Anderson's residence is being built by the railroad at a cost of $5,000. The town pays the few hundred dollars for the excavations.

And next we will have electric lights. The contract has not yet been let, but several plans have been favorably discussed by the council. Foremost among them is the following: The wires are to run from the plant along the principal streets. In order to prevent accidents and get them out of the way they will be encased in tubes and placed underground, beneath the paving. Along streets not much used they will he strung on poles. Arc lamps will be used and will be hung from poles, not swinging from wires as in Highland Park. The city council is looking at this favorably and we will advise you further anon.

Along the lake shore near Buckingham's a new road has been cut and is splendidly macadamized. A new bridge has also been built for it. On the ground where the old road ran, Mr. Byron Smith will build a magnificent mansion. There is more coming yet. Wait and see.

HOW THEY VOTED.

A STENTOR reporter has made a canvass of the college with a view to ascertaining the political convictions of the students. We have only space to give the opinions of the leading men, but it is evident that there is a strong Republican majority in the school.

A. Haberli: "I shall vote the Prohibition ticket. While I do not expect that this party will win in several years I do think that to vote the Prohibition ticket is the only way to make the great parties feel our strength and insert a Prohibition plank in their platforms."

A. P. Bourns: "I am going home to vote for Harrison."

R. H. Crozier: "I shall vote for Harrison. I think reciprocity is the true solution of the tariff problem."

C. S. Davies: "I shall vote the national Democratic ticket and the local Prohibition."

W. N. McKee: "I shall vote for Harrison. I believe in a tariff for the protection of American industries."

R. B. Spellman: "I am a Prohibitionist. I do not think that the tariff issues are to be compared in importance to the liquor question. I have not looked into the wildcat currency question."

C. D. Thomas: "Neither party's platform suits me. I don't want the repeal of the ten per cent tax on state bank issues, and I don't believe in Republican protective tariff."

B. R. MacHatton: "Harrison every time."

S. B. Hopkins: "I shall vote for protective tariff and honest money."

H. Goodman: "I am a Democrat. I believe protective tariff iniquitous. I do not believe in robbing the laboring man to stuff the pockets of the monopolist."

N. H. Burdick: "I am a Republican and shall vote for no repeal of the tax on state bank issues."

A. A. Hopkins: "The Republican party and Harrison first, last and all the time."

W. R. Nash: "My first vote will go for Harrison, Fifer and the rest of the crowd."

W. D. McNary: "I shall vote the Republican ticket. I am opposed to Democratic free trade and wildcat money."

F. C. Sharon: "So far as I have studied the situation, I believe in Republican principles, but I would like to see suffrage on an educational basis."

Forest Grant: "Harrison's my man."

COLLEGE.

AMUSEMENTS FOR THE WEEK.

AUDITORIUM—Theodore Thomas, Saturday night.
McVICKER'S—"By Proxy."
GRAND—Roland Reed.
SCHILLER—Lottie Collins—"Ta-ra-Boom-de-aye."
HOOLEY'S—"Across the Potomac."
COLUMBIA—James T. Powers.

A few scattering snow-flakes Friday reminded us that winter is near.

The soda fountain at the drug store has ceased to "fizz" for the season.

The following men went home to vote: Grant, McKee, Henry, Bird and Sweezey.

Seven special police were sworn in to prevent the boys from moving Lake Forest into the lake Hallowe'en evening.

The "G. P." club has transferred its headquarters to F. H. Anderman's where the boys will be more pleasantly located.

A. A. Hopkins spoke on Republican issues at Waukegan last evening. A delegation from the Republican Club accompanied him.

Lake Forest offered three special attractions Thursday evening—the Republican rally, the missionary library social and the University Club.

Bill of fare at Ferry Hall Tuesday morning last week: Roast chicken, fried chicken, boiled chicken, boiled eggs, fried and poached eggs, etc., etc.

Spellman has athletic goods. Candies received fresh every week.

Dr. French keeps medicines, pure and fresh. Prescriptions put up carefully and promptly.

Buck, the Waukegan jeweler, has a fine line of souvenir rings for gifts. Anything in the line of jewelry can be found there.

The "Kasten and Quinn Athletic Combination" gave an axhibition of sparring, wrestling, etc., at Healey's Opera House, Tuesday evening, the 8th inst.

It may be of interest to the Alumni to know that city water has been placed in College Hall, Academy Hall and Ferry Hall, and is in the new buildings.

Geo. F. Walles, of La Porte, Ind., formerly in the Academy, is at present at home engaged with his father in the wholesale grain business, forming one of the largest grain firms in La Porte.

The University Club met at Prof. Locy's Thursday evening. The evening was devoted to a very dignified observance of Hallowe'en myth, consisting of readings, papers and songs bearing upon the customs of the day.

Hallowe'en was observed with appropriate ceremonies by the students. Contrary to usual custom the M. O. T. A. did not perform, but a few of the boys managed to entertain Doctor and the Sems. for a while until the chickens, etc., could be introduced.

The new Young People's Missionary Library was formally dedicated Thursday evening. Reading by Prof. Booth, vocal selections by a quartette from McCormick Seminary, lemon ice and cake, and a surprisingly large (?) number of the dear Sems., were the principal attractions.

In its issue of October 11th the STENTOR contained an item saying that Dr. Roberts had been in Chicago and had failed to visit Lake Forest. We gleaned our information from a leader in the Chicago *Evening Post*. Dr. Roberts wishes it stated that the item in question is a mistake, for he has not been in Chicago this fall. Furthermore, he says that when he does come to Chicago he will certainly visit us. We are glad to make the correction, as we did not like to feel that our former president would so slight us.

The first and last big rally was held by the Republican Club in the Art Institute last Thursday evening. The meeting was addressed by Hon. A. T. Lester, of Springfield, and Mr. Heydecker, of Waukegan. President Hopkins called the meeting to order, and in a short address told of the origin of the club and its object. Mr. Rumsey then surprised the club very agreeably by presenting them with a flag, the gift of Lake Forest citizens. The Hon. A. T. Lester then made the principal address, and aroused great enthusiasm. Mr. Heidecker, also spoke. Just before the close the club passed formal resolutions of thanks to Mr. Rumsey and the other citizens of Lake Forest who contributed toward the club's new flag.

TOWN TOPICS.

Mr. L. W. Yaggy, who has been planting apples on his farm in Kansas, has returned.

Mrs. C. K. Giles left Friday for a two weeks visit with her daughter, Miss Mabel Giles, who is at Ogontz.

Mr. and Mrs. Grant Stroh left last week for Del Norte, where Mr. Stroh will take a position as pastor of the First Presbyterian church.

Mrs. Schearer has been visiting with her mother, Mr. Joseph Durand. Her sisters, Miss Nellie and Miss Florence Durand, will accompany her on her return east.

The Executive Committee of the Lake Forest Art Institute has decided that the principal subject for the season shall be the "World's Columbian Exposition." The following is a list of the lectures to be delivered this winter:

1. The Innocency of Vision,.....Mr. French, of Chicago
2. Velazques,........................Mr. W. C. Larned
3. Columbus,...............................Mrs. Ferry
4. Philosophy of Art,...............Prof. Walter Smith
5. History of Fairs,......................Prof. McNeill
6. The Cliff Dwellers,.............Mr. L. Scudder, Jr
7. Architecture of the Fair,....Major Jennny, of Chicago
8. Sculpture of the Fair,....Mr. Lorado Taft, of Chicago

In addition there will probably be a paper from Mr. Tomlins, of Chicago, on " The Music of the Fair," and another paper from Mrs. Alice Freeman Palmer, Dean of the Woman's Department of the Chicago University. There will also be one or two musical evenings. The first meeting of the Art Institute was last Thursday at Mr. Larned's, when Mr. W. M. R. French delivered the lecture, " The Innocency of Vision."

ATHLETICS.

We play Evanston next Saturday at Lake Forest. A hot contest is anticipated.

Work in the Gym. has begun in earnest. Classes were organized last Monday and will continue through the winter.

Woolsey is playing a strong game. He tackles hard and invariably breaks through the opponent's line. Moreover, he is very prompt.

Durand's recent illness does not seem to have interfered with his playing. He is putting up his usual game at quarter and inspires confidence by his brainy methods.

Of the "scrubs," Capt. Marcotte, C. Thom, Kimball and Richards are carrying off the honors. All the men are to be commended for their faithfulness, and as a means of promoting the interests of the 'Varsity team they are indispensable.

The enthusiasm over indoor ball seems to be flagging. It should be revived. At this time of year it is good practice for 'Varsity base ball men. It makes them active and concentrates their attention on the play, important elements in base ball. If not already done, a good captain should be elected, the team organized, and let everyone take a hand in promoting the interest.

We are glad to see most of our cripples back in their respective positions. Capt. Gallwey is still suffering with a lame foot, but expects to be around in a day or two. McNary's ankle is not entirely healed, but with his customary pluck "Mac" insists on playing. As a team,

the boys are doing good work. There is a marked improvement in concentrated play and interference, and individual playing is sacrificed for the general work. Wet weather has interfered somewhat with daily practice, yet the criticism concerning the lateness of starting play is still pat. If the men would make it their business at 4 o'clock to rush to the gymnasium, and get into their uniforms, there will be no reason whatsoever for the 'Varsities and "scrubs" lining-up later than 4:20. In the future let each man attend to this and there will be no cause for further complaint.

FERRY HALL

Miss Humphrey has been ill for the past week.

Henceforth good-nights will be exchanged *outside* the door.

Miss Grace Linnell has had the pleasure of a visit from her mother during the past week.

Some of the College girls attended the political meeting given by the Zeta Epsilon society last Friday evening.

First College boy—"What do you think of Miss ——?" Second College boy—"O, she's the kind of a girl that would work a fellow like me."

The '92 Lake Forest-McCormick boys and a few Lake Forest girls were very pleasantly entertained at the home of Miss May Stowell, in the city, Saturday eve, Oct. 29.

Only three favored Sems. were permitted to go to the church sociable Thursday evening. The permission was granted them because they obediently kept their rooms Hallowe'en.

We would advise the gentlemen
Who, to young ladies, by a friend,
Merely *verbal* invites send,
Not to try the same again.

Now in the chapel Monday morn, the Doctor rose and said,
" There is to be no play to-night, though Hallowe'en it be,
For in the German, Saturday, enough of fun you had,
No more of foolish jest and sport will be endured by me."
With warning glance each to her bestest friend turned round about,
And said, " The Doctor'll catch you,
Ef you don't watch out!"
The rainy night at last came round, and with it came the boys;
They built a bonfire, blew their horns, and made a fearful noise.
The Doctor in their midst was jovial and gay;
And for the barrels that they burned, he didn't make them pay.
Meanwhile a few courageous youths fled to the chapel quick,
And heaped the chairs of the Faculty with many a bright red brick.
Then came the cry of the cautious girls from all the windows out,
" The Doctor'll catch you,
Ef you don't watch out!"

A little later in the house the girls forgot the rule,
A noisy hall, a pillow fight, quite roused the entire
    school;
But they, alas, were thwarted in their little schemes
    so bright,
The next day came the "hauling," loss of privileges,
    a fight.
And this is what they say, indeed they cared the
   ·   most about,
That Doctor Seeley caught them,
    'Cause they didn't watch out!''

  The Seniors are going to entertain to-night,
    What is it going to be?
A feast with its dainties, and table so bright,
    A party, a concert, a tea?
But we are told to wait and see,
    It will commence at eight,
And at that hour the chapel was filled,
    And woe to those coming late.

When all were seated and quiet as mice,
    The piano gave forth the old strains,
To which many a girl's heart hath wildly throbbed,
    As she thought of the "set" of her train.
Then came sweet Mildred and Donald,
    She in her robe of gleaming white,
He with his proud and stately bearing
    Reminded one of ye old-time knight.

Behind them came another couple,
    Bessie and Harold as every one knew;
She with her face all wreathed in blushes,
    He so loyal, honest and true.
Bridesmaids and groomsmen, looking so splendid,
    Ushers too, to show you your seat,
But he who attracted our latest attention
    Was the charming young minister,
Tall, slim and neat
Such a brilliant success will not soon be forgotten,
    And all will join me I know,
In wishing a bright and prosperous future ·
    As our sweet buds into full blossoms grow.

Down in the Gym. at Ferry Hall
    Last Saturday a ball was given,
I think it opened with a march gay,
    The giddy hour was seven.
A German the affair was called,
    (Though why, I don't pretend to say,
In fact, I've often wished to know
    Wherein the Teutonism lay.)

At all events 'twas a success,
    What more is ever asked at balls?
No dearth of partners there,
    A fact whose blissful novelty appalls.
Such gallantry was there displayed,
    'Twas really touching, I declare;
No fans were spoiled, no demis torn,
    But all was right side up with care.

And what was stranger still, each girl
    Declared upon her roomward way:
"Oh, wasn't it the mostest fun!"
    And not, " I wish I'd stayed away."
Though boys are mighty nice to know,
    I'd like to teach a moral here,
That under dire compulsion, girls
    Can do without them for a year.

      Mrs. E. J. Bowes now counts among her joys
      Two happy, bouncing baby boys.

ACADEMY.

GAMMA SIGMA.

Wanted—Good excuses for not attending Gym. classes.

Gamma Sigma again has first choice of the newest members.

The reports were read in chapel Wednesday a. m. General " Kick " is now in order.

Some of the new fellows are aching for another pumping. Just for one warm evening!

Edgar Owsley visited here over Sunday. We were all glad to see " Weasel " up and around again.

Joe Rogers was quite ill last Wednesday. No one seems to know "eggs-actly" where he was failing.

Heineman resigned his position as manager of the Mitchell Hall foot ball eleven in favor of Lyman Bournique.

At last an Academy foot ball team has been organized with Chas. Durand as manager, and E. W. Everett as captain. Its success is assured.

Hall's recitation in Physics goes something like this: " The what, professor? Oh! yes, it's a, it's a, oh, I've got it mixed with something else."

Prof. Jack's brief talk on Tennyson in the Gamma Sigma society was enjoyed very much. We look forward with much pleasure to the promised talk on Tennyson before the whole 'Cad.

Quite a number of Cads attended the foot ball game in Chicago last Saturday. We sincerely hope that the idea that the Cads intend to withdraw from the College in athletics is dispelled.

Last Saturday the first of a series of receptions by the Faculty was given in the main room from 2 to 5 p. m. The costumes were most dazzling. Everyone agrees that Levering attired in a beautiful orange and black sweater, was the lion of the day, although Hall and McDonnell both looked very pretty. Prof. Burnap's solo on the bell was well rendered.

TRI KAPPA.

Gymnasium classes have taken up their work for the winter.

We are glad to see Durand and Williams on the field again.

Prof. Mendel's World's Fair sandwiches are the wonder of the 'Cad.

Forbes was kept indoors by a short illness last week, but is around now and attending classes.

Quite a number of Academy Republicans attended the rally at the Art Institute Thursday evening.

" Those who have no singing books will please stay away from classes until supplied with one."

The political views of Cross have been made known to the public. He will probably favor the Republican club with a speech before long.

Heineman's latest is a lame foot which he says he received in a foot ball game. Thid did not prevent his walk on the lake shore, though, the other afternoon.

An Academy eleven has been formed with Warren Everett as captain. There is no reason why it should not be an excellent team, as there is plenty of good material. However, they are beginning a little late and will have that to contend with.

The Academy foot ball eleven defeated Mitchell Hall by a score of 16 to o last Wednesday. This same M. H. team, or rather part of it, was not allowed by the Faculty to go to Waukegan to play a game they had arranged for. The reason is one of the greatest mysteries of the day.

AMONG THE ALUMNI.

W. D. Curtis, ex-'95, is now ushering in the Auditorium.

H. W. Millar, ex-'93, is now at Deer Lodge, Mont.

J. H. McVay, '91, spent a few hours here lately.

Miss Agnes Brown, '92, is now teaching in Racine, Wis.

Miss Marion Whittimore, who last year attended Ferry Hall, is now at Oberlin.

A. C. Wenban, '85, is practicing law in Chicago, and occasionally in the Lake County courts in Waukegan.

Charles Russel, Academy '90, is now surveying for the Chicago & North-Western railroad, at Racine, Wis.

A. T. Osgood, formerly of the Academy, is now associated with his father in the hardwood lumber business in Chicago.

Fred P. Kellogg, Academy '95, half-back on last year's 'Varsity foot ball team is now with an Art company in St. Louis, Mo.

J. A. Mitchell, ex-'92, is now on the road traveling for a large Chicago house with the expectation of soon entering McCormick.

C. Joyce, Rush Medical, who caught on our base ball team in the spring of '90, is now practicing medicine in Ogden, Utah.

The Rev. G. D. Heuver, '87, of Milwaukee, Wis., spent last Wednesday here. Mr. Heuver is now occupying the pulpit of the Perseverance Presbyterian Church of that city.

C. A. Frick, Academy '90, was in town on Saturday, Oct. 22. Mr. Frick is now in business in Cobden, Ill., and was present at the World's Fair Dedication exercises in Chicago.

Miss Blanche Loveridge, ex-'93, and now of Chicago University, delivered a lecture on "Assyrian Sculpture," before a large audience in one of the big Chicago churches recently.

Herbert G. Alward, who last year refereed the Madison-Lake Forest foot ball game, and who is now playing with the Chicago Athletic Club in the east, graduated from the Academy here with the class of '85. While in the Academy Mr. Alward pitched on the 'Varsity base ball team, and was the best all-round athlete in the school.

IT WAS A TIE GAME.

LAKE FOREST 18; CHICAGO UNIVERSITY 18.

CHICAGO, Nov. 5. — (*Special.*) — The game here to-day was one of the most exciting and best played contests ever seen on a foot-ball field. For one hour the teams surged back and forth with now and then a brilliant run and honors were easy. The STENTOR wishes to congratulate Mr. Stagg and his team on their honest and clean methods. Both teams played like Trojans but slugging was conspicuously absent. The line up was as follows:

LAKE FOREST.	POSITION.	CHICAGO.
McNary.	Left end.	Conover.
Woolsey.	Left tackle.	Brenman.
McGaughey.	Left guard.	Smith.
Hunt.	Centre.	Rulkoeter.
Flint.	Right guard.	Knapp.
Gallwey.	Right tackle.	Wyant.
Hayner.	Right end.	Chase.
Durand.	Quarter.	Raycroft.
Jackson.	L. Half back.	McGillivary.
MacHatton.	R. Half back.	Stagg.
Williams.	Full back.	Rapp.

Referee—McCord. Umpire—Heywood.

First Half. L. F. won the toss and took the ball. On the wedge Jackson by a beautiful run scored a touch-down in 10 seconds. Williams kicked the goal. Score L. F. 6; Chicago 0.

Chicago tried the wedge and made 35 yards. Stagg carrying the leather 5 yards. More were made when L. F. secured the leather on a fumble. Successive rushes by MacHatton and Jackson, Williams' punt of 25 yards carried the ball back to the center of the field where it was lost to Chicago. Here Chicago did some good playing. They pushed and squirmed until the ball was on L. F.'s 10 yard line. Twice they tried our tackle for a gain but to no avail. The third time Stagg was sent through the center as though shot from a cannon, scoring Chicago's first touch-down. McGillivary kicked an easy goal. Score L.F. 6; Chicago 6.

The ball was now passed from one to the other on 4 downs but L. F. finally carried it to within 2 yards of Chicago's goal. Here Capt. Gallwey must have been taken with a temporary fit of insanity for instead of using the turtle crawl or sending a man through the line for an easy touch-down he sent Williams around the end and the ball and game slipped from our hands. Stagg, McGillivary and Rapp carried the ball to the center, when by a clever criss-cross from Stagg to McGillivary another touch-down, was scored by Chicago. McGillivary kicked goal. Four minutes remained and L. F. secured another touch-down just as time was called. MacHatton, Jackson and Hayner carrying off the honors. Williams kicked goal. Score L. F. 12; Chicago 12.

Second Half. Chicago gained 10 yards on the first wedge, but lost the ball to L. F. on four downs. Mac-Hatton worked the center for 5 yards, Williams the end for 3 yards, McNary for 4 yards, Hayner for 5 yards and Jackson for 5 yards more, when the ball was lost on four downs, but quickly regained. Mc-Nary, Hayner and Jackson carried the ball to the 10-yard line, when the mighty MacHatton, breaking through the Chicago line, scored another touch-down. Williams kicked a difficult goal. Score, Lake Forest 18; Chicago 12.

On the wedge Chicago made 17 yards and in a short time were dangerously near L. F's goal. Capt. Gallwey fell on the ball in a scrimmage, and the pig-skin was soon at the center again. L. F. was covering Chicago territory, but lost the ball on four downs. It was at this point that the calamity came. The crowd, in its excitement had crowded on to the field, and Mc-Gillivary becoming mixed with the spectators so that it was impossible to stop him, scored the last touch-down of the game, after a run of 70 yards. He kicked an easy goal. Score, L. F. 18; Chicago 18.

Three minutes were left, and Lake Forest started in to win. Jackson, MacHatton, and Hayner carried the ball to the Chicago's 20-yard line, just as time was called. Final score, L. F. 18; Chicago 18.

NOTES OF THE GAME.

Mr. Stagg expressed himself as being pleased with Lake Forest's playing. Such a gentlemanly athlete cannot fail to exert a good influence on western athletics and we trust that in the future Chicago may meet with all possible success.

The features of the game were the rushes by Stagg, MacHatton and Woolsey, the running of McGillivary, Jackson and Hayner, and the goal kicking of McGillivary and Williams.

Durand's interference and tackling were superb. As a quarter-back, Charlie has few equals.

The chief criticism to be made of Lake Forest' play is the fact that they watch the man instead of the ball. They seemed to be in mortal dread of Stagg and their best efforts were centered towards stopping him to the exclusion of every one else. Through this fault Chicago gained a great deal of unearned ground.

On account of the weakness of McNary's ankle, Everett played left end the last part of the game.

The *Tribune* said a youthful prodigy by the name of Jackson dodged the Chicago line so dexterously that they wondered "where he was at."

Touch-downs—MacHatton and McGillivary each 2; Stagg and Jackson each 1.

Goals—Williams and McGillivary each 3.

THE STENTOR.

VOLUME VI.   NOVEMBER 15, 1892.   NUMBER 7.

PUBLISHED EVERY WEEK
BY THE
Lake Forest University Stentor Publishing Co.

BOARD OF EDITORS.

F. C. SHARON, '93................Managing Editor
R. H. CROZIER, '93..............Business Manager
N. H. BURDICK, '93 }
S. B. HOPKINS, '93 } ....Locals
L. N. ROSSITER, '93...........Alumni and Personal
B. R. MacHATTON, '95.................Advertising

ASSOCIATE EDITORS.

HARRY GOODMAN, '94..............Athletic Editor
FOREST GRANT, '96 ....Staff Artist
DAVID FALES, '96...........................Town

Terms—$1.50 per year.   Single Copies—10c

————ADDRESS————
STENTOR PUBLISHING COMPANY,
LAKE FOREST,   :   :   ILLINOIS.

Entered at the P. O. at Lake Forest, Ill., as second-class matter.

WHAT caused the overwhelming political landslide?   Could it have been the Republican College League?

WE are not surprised at anything now.   We really expect the Prohibition Party to carry Chicago next election.

MR. LESTER said there were 80,000 young men in this state who cast their first votes last Tuesday.   From the result we should say that about 79,975 of these same young men made crosses for Cleveland.   The rest of them helped carry Lake Forest for Harrison.

BECAUSE Harrison was defeated is no reason why the Republican club should disband.   In fact it is just the reason why it should continue its work and train up the next generation in the way it should go.   The STENTOR suggestion regarding debates should be looked into and next campaign we will turn out orators that can talk intelligibly on everything from the tariff to socialism and free trade.

THERE should be some better arrangement made in regard to our oratory. It is an injustice to Prof. Booth as well as the students.   No no can teach much oratory seeing his classes one hour a week only.   No student can learn anything or obtain any drill the way it is managed at present.   If the trustees would allow us to have drill throughout the week with the Professor we would be duly thankful.

"THE King is dead.   Long live the King."   The campaign is over and our king has been defeated.   It behooves us now as American citizens to transfer our allegiance to the king who won.   It is not hard to accept Grover Cleveland nor do we believe that absolute ruin will be the result of a few years democratic rule.   But, oh my, what a bitter pill Adlai and Altgeld are to swallow! One a Mossback, the other a Socialist. However we understand it is not good policy to call hard names so we refrain. We will not be like the Irishman "Agin the government whatever it is."   A

great many Lake Forest college men
are weeping and gnashing their teeth
over the result, but we ought at least to
accept it as philosophically as Harrison
does, say we didn't get enough votes,
settle down to study and—see that it
doesn't happen again.

THE STENTOR has received many compliments on its report of the election
last week and perhaps it would be of
interest to some to know how it was
done. In the first place as can be
readily seen everything was printed
beforehand but the result and returns
given. The papers were received in
the evening and by ten o'clock were all
addressed and sorted into districts. In
the meantime two members of the
board were in Chicago stationed at the
headquarters. At one o'clock our first
dispatch from them declared positively
that Cleveland was elected. The papers
were run over and a blue mark made
in everyone under the name of Cleveland. At 3:15 A. M. came the final dispatch with the exact figures on the
states as given out at the headquarters.
Then came the work. Six men with
pen and ink filled in the spaces with the
figures as rapidly as their fingers could
work. By 4:50 the last one was ready,
the men were divided into squads of
two each and a certain district mapped
out for each squad. By 6:45 Wednesday morning the STENTORS had been
delivered to every subscriber in town,
college, cad, and seminary. Then the
weary editors sought their pillows satisfied with the night's work.

"SOMETHING ROTTEN IN DENMARK."

Not only in Denmark but here in
Lake Forest there is something

sadly in need of repairs and that something is the management of this institution. We have as yet no President and
if ever one was needed, this is the place
that is in the direst need. The way
the buildings are heated and lighted at
the sweet will of one person is simply
outrageous. There is no milder way of
expressing it. The heat is turned off
in the college building very early every
night and sometimes is disconnected at
seven or eight o'clock. The art building is half the time filled with smoke
and there is no heat. It never seems
to occur to this grand high potentate to
send any steam to the gymnasium
before 4:30 or 5 o'clock in the evening.
The gymnasium is opened at 1 o'clock,
but it is *economy* to hold off the steam
till 5. In the meantime no one can
use the building. The other evening
the gas machine gave out and refused
to work. Wilson, the janitor, says it is
not his fault. He does his best as all
the boys know. If all did as well there
would be no kicking. But back of
Wilson there is Frye and back of Frye
—well is one man who is responsible
for this state of affairs. One evening
the students roast, another evening they
freeze. It is an extremely healthful
scheme, one that is calculated to build
a man up and enable him to do his
college work well. We would like to
see a time in this place when everything went along smoothly. When
things were not controlled arbitralily
by one man who is practicing false
economy, when some kind of a system
is adopted and adhered to. We do not
ask for new buildings. We merely
ask for regular heat, light, and decent
management. When that blessed time
arrives the students will require a
special Thanksgiving vacation.

TENNYSON'S POETRY.

A CRITICISM OF THE LATE POET-LAUREATE.

Tennyson is pre-eminently a lyric poet. The word lyric is used here in a broad sense, to include the antique studies (like " Œnone" and " Demeter "), the English idyls in blank verse (like " Godiva " and " Aylmer's Field "), and the dramatic monologues (like " St. Simeon Stylites " and " Sir John Oldcastle "). The laureate's lyrical efforts embrace an extensive range of subjects and a wide variety of metres. Not having naturally the rhythmical facility of Shelley or Byron, he conquered the technical difficulties of his art by painstaking labor. In this field, Tennyson made himself a master. But, not realizing his limitations or not content with the glory of being a great lyrist, he ambitiously essayed to enter fields where supremacy was for him impossible. In the epic and the drama, he achieved only partial success. It is, therefore, as a lyric poet that Tennyson is chiefly known and will be remembered.

" In Memoriam " and " Maud " are merely collections of lyrics. The songs in " The Princess " and some of the little melodies scattered through his idyls and dramas will go far toward insuring the perpetuity of his fame when the works themselves shall have been forgotten.

The " Idyls of the King " have been called an epic. When arranged in their true order, these romantic stories supply a tolerably clear account of a succession of events more or less related. They trace the rise and fall of the mythic Round Table. There is material enough for an epic in the deeds of King Arthur and his knights, but Tennyson's mind is not cast in the heroic mould requisite to sing of battles. To write an Arthuriad in this age would be a colossal undertaking—quite beyond the powers of any modern poet. The Arthurian idyls occupied the laureate's attention during many years. From the pains bestowed upon them and their elaborate design, it would

seem that he intended these idyls to be a monumental work. Such they cannot be, owing to their unevenness of merit and their want of coherent structure. They are idyllic, not epic, in tone and character. A minstrel must live among heroes and be a man of action, in order to write a popular epic. At times there is something of the Homeric spirit in Tennyson's lines, but it is not sustained. The main interest of these poems lies not in the historical fidelity of the pictures of legendary or medieval Britain, for they portray the life of the Victorian era; it is rather in the melodious cadences of the verse, in the artistic beauty of the word-painting, and in the spiritual teaching which permeates and transfigures them.

Tennyson's dramas are lyrical in spirit, if not in form. They are not adapted to the stage of to-day, being deficient in theatrical effects which tell. The historic trilogy—as Dr. Van Dyke calls " Harold," " Becket," and " Queen Mary "—affords a better example of the right use of genius than do the Arthurian romaunts. " Harold " is valuable from a historical standpoint, but it it is rather tame poetry. "Becket" and " Queen Mary " are both noble poems. They are destined to become classical, and will be ranked not far below Shakspeare's historical plays. " Becket" is the laureate's dramatic masterpiece. It surpasses all his other extended works in strength and passion. This splendid tragedy deserves a wider recognition not only from lovers of Tennyson, but from all admirers of virile and sonorous blank verse. His other plays--" The Falcon, " " The Cup," " The Promise of May," and " The Foresters" —are comparative failures. The play-wright's instinct is absent, although here and there are flashes of poetic fire.

There are two views of Tennyson. It is the fashion among some of his admirers to praise him lavishly and indiscriminately. They call him the greatest poet of the century—which is equivalent to placing him next to Shakspeare and Milton. Full credit can be given to Alfred Tennyson as a renowned singer, without bringing him into competition with his distinguished brother-bards. Another age must settle his position in the poetic hierarchy of England.

By some critics Tennyson is regarded as more of a literary artist than poet. He has written much that is admirable, and much that can be described as polished mediocrity. A great deal of his poetry is open to criticism. It is labored, and lacking in sustained force and elevation. His felicities are often such as only the cultivated few can appreciate. Ordinary people would enjoy less of refinement and more of vigor. His subtleties and mannerisms are carried to excess, and detract from the value of some of his writings. All of his longer productions show the varying character of his work, by turns superb and weak. It is too often pretty rather than substantial. Yearly the elements make havoc with an immense mass of brilliant metrical foliage, and a considerable portion of Tennyson's will wither " with the process of the suns." Much, too, is enduring.

Tennyson is, assuredly, not to be classed with the world-poets—the few chosen ones who reared majestic edifices of thought like the *Iliad*, or the *Divina Comedia*, or *Paradise Lost*, or *Faust*. Not one of those who suffered for poetry's sake, and whose words are graven into the heart of civilized humanity, he sang so sweetly and did so much to brighten and to dignify the life of mortals that his name must long remain a household word wherever the Saxon tongue is spoken. He is more than a skillful versifier or literary artist. His poetical performances won for him the lasting distinction of being a genuine bard. Such incomparable lyrics as " Break, break, break," "The Bugle Song," and " Crossing the Bar," prove Alfred Tennyson to be a singer by right divine—one whose fame is immortal.

EUGENE PARSONS.

A special train was run from Chicago to Lake Forest by the Athletic Association to accommodate the city departments and the Evanston students who wished to attend the game Saturday.

COLLEGE.

AMUSEMENTS FOR THE WEEK.

AUDITORIUM—Gilmore's Band.
McVICKER'S—"By Proxy."
GRAND—Roland Reed.
HOOLEY'S—"Across the Potomac."
COLUMBIA—James T. Powers.
CHICAGO—Mrs. Brown Potter in " Therese."

Snow fell quite industriously for a few minutes Friday morning.

J. A. Mcgaughey, '96, went home to vote. But Harrison wasn't elected.

What has become of the movement toward organizing a students' fire company?

Remember that W. E. Ruston is agent for Spalding's athletic goods. Prices the lowest.

The pond near the gymnasium was covered with thin ice Thursday afternoon. Get your skates ready.

If you are a friend of the STENTOR and have any news don't be bashful about telling one of the local editors.

Thanksgiving recess begins one week from to-morrow (Wednesday) and lasts until the following Monday afternoon.

The exuberance of Goodman, Thom, Rogers and Chaffee since the announcement of Cleveland's victory is well nigh irrepressible.

Let each one lay aside all party spirit and join forces and see if we cannot get better reading-room facilities. It can be done.

The Seniors, under Prof. Halsey's efficient direction, are now discussing the great question, "Protection or free trade, which?"

At a meeting of the directors of the Athletic Association Harry Goodman was unanimously elected manager of the base ball team for the season of 1893.

The foot ball game that was to have been played at Champaign on Thanksgiving Day will be played in Lake Forest on the same day.

Before the election several Republican students wore large badges of "American tin plate". On Wednesday morning Rogers came down from Waukegan wearing a piece of "free English tin" about a foot in diameter.

Rossiter appeared among us only at night for a while on account of injuries received to his face while wrestling with the station platform. He tripped on his long overcoat and nearly fell under an approaching train.

Great excitement broke loose among the Academy students Thursday night over a report that Harrison had been elected after all. They gave the yell of the Republican club and manifested their joy in other uproarious ways.

A reform has been instituted in the appearance of the programs posted upon the societies' bulletin boards. Instead of the slovenly scrawls that were wont to meet the eye there are now neatly lettered and written announcements.

The literary societies were never in a more flourishing condition than at present. The membership list in each is comfortably filled and the general character of the work is above that of former years. At least so say the alumni who occasionally visit us.

Is there any reason why the recitation rooms in the Art Building should be deprived of steam and become so cold that it is a serious risk to sit through a recitation? Is it a good way to build up the University to shut the steam off from the dormitories and compel the inmates to shiver with the cold or go to bed to keep warm? If we are going to do good work, personal comfort is most essential. If this is to be denied us let us know and we will find a remedy.

The Freshmen class and a number of Sems. were received at Miss Marie Skinner's Thursday evening. About 7 o'clock the Sophomores went out to waylay the fellows on their way to the Seminary. They stood around and shivered until 8:30 without seeing a Freshman, man or woman. In the morning they learned that all had gone to the party at the early hour of 6 p. m., which they call an indication of cowardice! Rather an indication of Sophomore slowness, as we see it.

The Sophomores appeared Tuesday crowned with mortar boards and brindled yellow tassels, whereat the festive Freshmen took offense and, ere the sun had thrice risen and set, became custodians of several of the insigniæ of Sopomorial dignity. Just here let us say that class "scraps" should never become boyish fights. It is becoming unfashionable to indulge in hazing and Lake Forest should not be unfashionable.

There is by far too much apathy among the students with regard to college needs. With our present laboratory, astronomical, reading-room and other facilities the college man who will indifferently sit down, fold his hands and do nothing, lacks not only spirit, but loyalty. A vigorous effort on the part of the students toward one object, and, upon the attainment of that, toward another, would result in achieving the desired ends and would shortly build up an institution which would be a lasting monument to their energy and perseverance. At present our observatory consists of a brass tube, with a magnifying glass at each end, mounted on three legs. Our apology for a physical laboratory is a standing disgrace. Our reading-room is little better than a hotel bar-room in a Prohibition town. We sadly need club-houses. And so we might go on through the list. The man who starts a movement that will result in obtaining any one of these things will make a lasting and enviable reputation for himself. Who will start it?

W. E. Danforth is rapidly winning laurels as a press reporter. Upon the occasion of Wayne MacVeagh's speech in Central Music Hall, the orders given by the editor of the

Tribune were to detail the best man on the
force to attend.   Danforth was the choice.
Concerning his work the *Evening Post* had
the following to say editorially:

"A FINE REPORT.

"The thanks of the entire community, but
especially of the Democratic campaign committee, are due to the *Tribune* for its comprehensive, accurate and altogether scholarly report in Sunday's paper of the tariff reform
speech delivered by Wayne MacVeagh on
Saturday night in Central Music Hall.   This
speech must be considered altogether the most
dignified and significant utterance heard in
Chicago during this campaign.   It drew
together one of the most noteworthy audiences
ever seen anywhere in any campaign.   The
Tribune's report was worthy of both the
speech and the audience.   It omitted nothing,
nor set down aught in malice or extenuation.
Of many thousand examples of the *Tribune's*
skill in faithful graphic reporting it was easily
the finest."

TOWN TOPICS.

Mr. Granger Farwell has taken a house in
Lake Forest and will spent the winter here.

Mrs. Duncan has been visiting with her
mother, Mrs. Learned, and will probably remain here some time.

At prayer meeting last Wednesday evening,
there was an election of an elder to succeed
Mr. Simon Reed, and of two deacons. Dr.
Haven was elected elder, and Mr. Harry
Durand and Mr. J. Frank Rumsey deacons.

Mrs. James Hubbard gave the fourth of her
series of lectures at Mrs. Yaggy's, Wednesday
the 9th.   The topic for the course is the
"Women Educators of the United States," and
"Lucretia Mott" was the subject for last Wednesday.

The total vote cast in Lake Forest on election day amounted to 351, which is only a
medium vote. Neither candidate for president
had a majority; the largest number of votes
cast for any individual was for W. G. Rainey,
who received over two-thirds of the Lake
Forest vote. The following is the vote of

Shields township for the different candidates:
Harrison, 159; Cleveland, 152; Bidwell, 27;
Weaver, 3; Coon, 165; Smith, 142; Ragan, 167;
Coe, 148; Heydecker, 114; Rainey, 223;
Knight, 177; Foley, 147; Lee, 174; Wester-
field, 141.

FERRY HALL.

Eleven of Miss Georgia Bennett's friends
surprised her with a birthday supper Wednesday.

As a result of the national vote Tuesday
Prof. Eager gave the Senior table a splendid
treat from Kinsley's.

Misses Myrtle Titus, Lucia Clark, and
Rubie Adams left Thursday morning for
Galesburg, at which place the state convention
of the Y. W. C. A. is being held.

Misses Jessie Phillips, Alice Spies, Clara
Stephenson, and Nellie Fleshiem, of Menominee, Wis., who are attending the N. W. University, spent Tuesday evening with Misses
Bird, Parmenter, Wells and Somerville.

Don't let the gentlemen students think that
they can manopolize the glory due the L. F.
voters, for Tuesday an electoral vote was
taken in Room B. Harrison won the day—
103 to 19. We only wish this mimic election
were real.

Friday, Nov. 4th, the Seniors gave a dumb
concert in the gymnasium. It was thoroughly
enjoyed by the large audience present.
Prominent features of the evening were the
ease with which the musicians appeared on the
stage, and their enthusiasm in the various parts
they took. Their costumes were a marvel,
each original and individual in its design, except for the one point of likeness that the
gowns all fell in graceful Grecian folds.

SOME LINES ON HALLOWE'EN.

READ AT THE UNIVERSITY CLUB BY F. R. R.

Oh! banks and braes o' bonny Doon
Ye've much to answer for,
Ye've given us logic by the ream,
And ministers galore,

Carlyle, oatmeal, and Paisley's Shawls
Scotch mist and more I wean
But, never such a luckless gift
As that o' Hallowe'en.

Long Syne upon thy purple hills
The Fathers built their fires
This blessed night, a flame for Gods
Lit up by high desires,
While all along the Rhine they saw
The brochen spray arise,
And heard with shivering delight
The Lorelie's harmonies.

But Sam O'Shanter takes a flip
And Hans his lager beer
And in the dusk o' Hallowe'en
Familiar shapes grow queer.
Belike the moonlight fell athwart
A silver leech, which seemed
A dainty lady, and one saw
The form of which he dreamed.

Or mad sprites of Johannes Nacht
Come back to play with frost
And on the Northern Maiden's cheek
Their rose of summer tossed,
And if with patience three times three
The maiden said her rune
The image in her tender heart
Walked near her, neath the moon.

And if Jack found a barley sack
Too stout and let it fall
Of course Jean told the neighbor wives
The Brownie's did it all,
Old time played his Promethean trick,
He plays it now and then,
And stole the altar fire of Gods
To craze the wits of men.

He played it well on newer shores,
From where the Hudson sees
The horsemen follow Ichabod
'Mong Autumn's wraithlike trees,
To where our great lake's border lands
New border legend weave,
Goblin and Fairy spread their spells
"And practice to deceive"

They practice in philosophers
Until it almost seems
That Berkeley may have had its jests
And Schopenhauer his dreams
Since wise men of the West forsooth
Build fires to mark the spot
Where squirrels learn philosophy
And where wild ducks are shot.

There canny Scot with Clausmen meet
To sing as Scotchmen sing
To give us many a jest and quirk
And ca't a Highland fling,
While other laddies having found
Neath tub-waves dunk and dim
The precious apples, now alas!
Seek Eve's who're "in the Swim."

And Scientist and Theologue
Lay side by side their nuts,
And watch the hard shells crank and split
Along the ember'd ruts,

Till through some open door there sweeps
A freshening breeze, and lo!
The kernels linger side by side,
The shells up chimney go.

Lake Forest hath its goblin charms
For dames of Ferry Hall
Who wander forth when stars are out
Can find no path at all.
The naughty imps mislead her
Whichever way she strays
Knowing these ladies are unused
To any crooked ways.

And when a grave Professor sends
From famous college shelves
Its books of lore to these same dames
These same mischievous elves
Change parchment into paper
And names writ large in fame
By magic—we'll be *Clement*
To Rider Haggard's name.

But holy church through all the year
Doth keep the balance even
And gives us after nights of earth
The better days of heaven
'Gainst roses of her Mardi Gros
Ash Wednesday sets her rue,
And after a night with imp and sprite
All Saint's Day dawneth true.

We have lowered the fires of our Altar pyres
To the homes aud haunts of men
But ever the holy spiral smoke
Climbs up to the clouds again
By the hour and the power of Hallowe'en,
Away with pious plaints
To-night we are happy and naughty folk
Tomorrow we're—All Saints!

ACADEMY.

GAMMA SIGMA.

Come, "Warren and Alonzo," get out your wheel-barrows.

Levering is sick, but people are disposed to think it is a "Guy."

The Faculty are doing all in their power to make the Glee club a success.

Quite a number of Cads. had friends out here to see the foot ball game.

They say that "General" was very much taken with the Waukegan girls.

Matthew Mills is at home and quite sick. We hope to see him back soon.

Cross thinks that the people of the country made a great mistake in electing Cleveland. His views are identical with Joe Medill's. He sees nothing but strikes, bloodshed, etc., ahead.

Thanks to Prof. Mendel for the boys getting off to go to Waukegan to play foot ball.

"Stay in your room Sunday nights and think of home, and don't go out except by special permission."

Forbes—" O, Hall!"
Hall—" What is it?"
Forbes—" Got any trade-lasts for me?"

Prof. Smith is still quite confident that the beginning of next term will find us in the new buildings. We hope he will not be disappointed, but ———

TRI KAPPA.

Thornton was visited by his mother last week.

We are glad to see Stearns and Smith around again after their illness.

All the old students were glad to see Moriette, one of last year's "Cads," who paid us a flying visit a week or so ago.

Many of the Academy students went to Chicago to see the game with Stagg's team, and all lustily cheered the good playing of Lake Forest.

The orchestra held a meeting right after Glee club Tuesday evening, when some important business was transacted. We are glad to see it revived and wish it the best success.

Letters for Kimball postmarked Hyde Park come very frequently, and the letters which leave Mitchell Hall addressed to the same place are also very numerous. We wonder what it all means?

Hall is happy now that Cleveland is elected, and the Republicans in the Academy will be obliged to take a back seat. We hope, though, that the Democrats will follow the wise advice given by Prof. Burnap in chapel.

Mitchell Hall's foot ball eleven came off victorious in a game with Waukegan last Wednesday by a score of 12 to 0. They made a remarkably good showing considering the

practice they have had, and many good plays were made. "General" accompanied the team with his voice. Prof. Mendel also went up with the boys and acted as referee of the game.

AMONG THE ALUMNI.

H. M. Giles, Academy '93, of Waukegan, is working in Chicago at present.

J. L. Taylor, Academy '88, is still in business in Libertyville, this state.

A. B. Mitchell, Academy '91, and E. C. Crawford, Academy '93, are both at the Chicago College of Dental Surgery.

J. M. Humiston, '95, and R. V. Erskine, Academy, '91, are both working for the Towle Silver Company on State Street, Chicago.

Alexander McFerran, '96, has been visiting friends in Ohio this fall and has just returned. He says he intends to rejoin his class here next term.

Of our old students, the following were a few of those seen at the Lake Forest–Chicago University foot ball game Saturday, Nov. 5: Of the Academy; Messrs. Busse, Rising, Owsly, Crawford, Shirra, Duggan, Mitchell. Of the College; Messrs. Eakins, '93, Jerolman, '93, Wright, '92, Pratt, '92, Manchester, '93, and J. Z. Johnston, '93.

A large size cut of B. Fay Mills, '79, evangelist, adorns the front page of the *Interior* of Nov. 4, 1892. Late reports give more and more praise to Mr. Mills, who is certainly earning glory for himself and his Alma Mater in his work among the lower classes in California.

IT WAS A WATERLOO!

THE RUBY RED AND BLACK GOES UNDER
BEFORE THE WEARERS OF THE ROYAL
PURPLE—THE CONTEST ONE-SIDED.

Last Saturday dawned bright and fair. When the day closed Lake Forest students were sick at heart. Their mighty foot ball team had been defeated and what made it harder to bear is the fact that the drubbing was administered by Evanston. At no stage was Lake Forest in the game but were clearly out-played and out-generaled. Evanston came up with about 300 supporters and Rush medical, the Dental school, and McCormick Theological Seminary were all represented. The crowd was a good natured one and by far the largest ever seen on the Athletic field, numbering about 1200, of which one-third were ladies. Tin horns and other instruments of torture were in abundance, giving forth the most heart-rending noises. A special train of eight coaches was run from Chicago for the accomodation of the departments in the city. After kicking the ball around in order to get warmed up, at 3:15 the two teams lined up as follows:

EVANSTON.	POSITION.	LAKE FOREST.
Oberne	Left end.	McNary
Van Doosen	Left tackle.	Woolsey
Wilson	Left guard.	McGaughey
Pierce	Centre.	Hunt
McClusky	Right guard.	Flint
Culver	Right tackle.	Gallwey
Oates	Right end.	Hayner
Griffith	Quarter back.	Durand
Kennicott	L. Half back.	Jackson
Noyes	R. Half back.	MacHatton
Sheppard	Full back.	Williams

THE TALE OF WOE.

First half—Lake Forest won the toss and chose the ball, N. W. taking the west goal. On the wedge L. F. made 12 yds., Durand carrying the ball. Hayner lost 3 yds., but MacHatton recovered 2 of them. With 6 yards to gain, Williams punted 30 yds. and N. W. secured the ball. Kennicott made 25 yards around the end, to which Noyes added 3 yards; Kennicott gained 8 yards more, dropped the ball, and in the opinion of everyone except the

umpire, McGaughey fairly downed it. Noyes made 3 yards and was brought down by a good tackle by MacHatton. N. W. pushed steadily toward L. F.'s goal and were presented with 11 yards by the umpire on an alleged foul tackle by Gallwey. When within 10 yards of a touch-down N. W. could find no opening in L. F's line and lost the ball on 4 downs. Jackson ran 10 yds. around the end; MacHatton shot through N. W.'s line and what might have terminated in a brilliant run, was stopped by his dropping the ball after a gain of 10 yds. N. W.'s ball; Noyes made 8 yds, and when the ball was passed to Kennicott, by a magnificent tackle Hayner stopped him before he was able to start. L. F. secured the ball on a foul. Williams made 7 yds. Durand lost 3 on a fumble, and Williams in attempting to punt lost 6 yds. It was now N. W.'s ball for keeps and Noyes was pushed over the line 15 minutes after the call of time. He kicked an easy goal. Score, N. W. 6; L. F. o.

L. F. made 11 yds. on the wedge, but could advance the ball but 3 yds. more on 3 downs when it was passed to Williams. He punted 12 yds. and Sheppard pounced on the pigskin outside the line. N. W. tried the criss-cross from Kennicott to Noyes, but lost 5 yards on Hayner's fine tackle. MacHatton stopped Noyes before he had a chance to run. Noyes attempted a punt, but failed, McGaughey making a fine catch. L. F. failing to make the 5 yards on 4 downs, Williams tried a goal from the field, but it proved disastrous, as 30 yards were lost. From now on N. W. kept the ball and by successive rushes by ther backs the leather was taken over the line, Noyes scoring the touchdown. He kicked goal just as time was called. Score, N. W. 12; L. F. o.

Second Half—N. W. made 11 yards on a V but lost the ball on a fumble. McNary, Woolsey and MacHatton gained 20 yards but the ball was lost on 4 downs. The teams surged back and forth, first one side taking the ball and then the other. However N.W.'s stalwarts proved too strong for L. F.'s line to hold and breaking down everything before them, Evanston pushed Capt. Noyes over the line for the third touch-down. He kicked a difficult goal. Score N. W. 18; L. F. o.

But. 10 minutes remained and L. F. made frantic but futile endeavor to score. Twice the ball was near Evanston goal when the ball was lost either on four downs or by fumbling. Darkness was creeping over the field and when time was called the ball was in L. F. territory. Final score N. W. 18; L. F. o.

Umpire, Goldsberry. Referee, Williams.

NOTES OF THE GAME.

Williams took Kennicott's place in the second half owing to the injury sustained to the latter's ankle.

Gallwey was hurt in the second half but pluckily finished the game.

Northwestern did not "slug" as much as was expected. Their team work is excellent, and their trio of backs are hard to beat. Capt. Noyes deserves a great deal of credit, as he has certainly turned out one of the best elevens in the west.

It was a conspicuous fact that the right side of our line, Hayner excepted, was an easy mark for Evanston rushers. Hayner covered himself with glory by his excellent tackles. Our center was lamentably weak, and if we intend to beat Champaign Thanksgiving day, the team must be shaken up considerably.

The features of the game were the tackling of Hayner, MacHatton, Noyes and VanDoosen, the rushes of Noyes, Kennicott and MacHatton, Durand's interferance and the general team work of Evanston.

For some reason or other Capt. Gallwey was badly rattled. At times his judgment of plays to be made was a little off. For instance, with the score 6 to o against us, the ball within 10 yards of Evanston's goal and 4 yards to make he gives the signal for Williams to try a goal from the field.

On account of the shortness of the time 30 minute halves were played.

Williams and Jackson were suffering from injuries received in practice so that they did not put up their usual game.

SATURDAY'S GAMES.

At New York. Yale 28, U. of P. o.
At Ithaca. Cornell 44. Mass. Techs. 12.
At Lafayette. Purdue 63. I. U. o.
At Cleveland. Cleve. A. C. 26, D. A. C. o.
At Crawfordsville. Wabash 12, R. P. I. o.
At Toledo. Ann Arbor 18, Chicago U. 10.
At St. Louis. Iowa U. 30, Wash. U. o.

LATE NEWS.

The 'Varsity indoor base ball team defeated the town nine Saturday evening in the Gym. by a score of 11 to 9. This is the boys' second victory. Sharon is an improvement on first. Rossiter's fielding was a feature of the game, but he should play with the 'Varsity. Grant, Nash and Yaggy did some very heavy batting. This is the way it went:

'Varsity..............1 1 1 0 1 1 3 0 3—11
Town,................2 3 0 2 0 1 0 0 1— 9

A second game of five innings also resulted in favor of the 'Varsity nine by a score of 8 to 5.

Did you ever see the girl who did not enjoy a nice present at Xmas? Spellman is giving one-quarter off from list price on Albums, Plush Goods, etc.

Prof. Halsey will open the University Extension season at the Madison street Y. M. C. A., on Friday evening with a lecture on " The Rule of the Federalists, 1789-1801." This is the first of a course of six lectures on " The History of American Parties." Prof. Halsey has perfect command of this and all kindred subjects.

On the first Friday evening after the Thanksgiving recess, the works of Edgar Allan Poe will be considered by the Athenæan Society through selections and critical papers.

Cold weather is coming and with it much fun on the ice. Don't use an old worn out skate but give your order to Spellman for a new pair.

THE STENTOR.

VOLUME VI.   NOVEMBER 22, 1892.   NUMBER 8.

PUBLISHED EVERY WEEK
BY THE
Lake Forest University Stentor Publishing Co.

BOARD OF EDITORS.

F. C. SHARON, '93.................Managing Editor
R. H. CROZIER, '93..............Business Manager
N. H. BURDICK, '93 }
S. B. HOPKINS, '93 } ....Locals
L. N. ROSSITER, '93...........Alumni and Personal
B. R. MacHATTON, '95.................Advertising

ASSOCIATE EDITORS.

HARRY GOODMAN, '94··············Athletic Editor
FOREST GRANT, '96.....................Staff Artist
DAVID FALES, '96..........................Town

Terms—$1.50 per year. Single Copies—10c

————ADDRESS————
STENTOR PUBLISHING COMPANY,
LAKE FOREST,   :   :   ILLINOIS.

Entered at the P. O. at Lake Forest, Ill., as second-class matter.

THAT CHICAGO ALUMNI CLUB.

A year or so ago certain of our Alumni residing in Chicago conceived the idea of organizing in that city a Lake Forest Alumni Club. The object was primarily, as we understand it, to keep the boys together after graduation as much as possible and in so doing to keep up the interest in their alma mater. For this purpose rooms were to be rented and a headquarters established so that old students coming to the city might have a rendezvous and obtain information as to their old college mates. For some reason this scheme seems to have fallen through and we hear nothing more of it. In some ways perhaps it was impracticable, but taken as a whole it was a worthy venture and one which not only the Alumni but the Faculty and undergraduates should further. The advantages that would accrue to us from such an association are obvious. In the first place we are behind all other western colleges in not having a Chicago club ; secondly, no persons have such power for a University's good as its Alumni; thirdly, it will preserve the old ties and friendships formed in school; and lastly, it will bring us before the public more and add to our name and fame. Every student who graduates here will like to feel that he does not necessarily cut himself off from his old friends and acquaintances when he leaves college. Such an association would be of especial value the coming year as the World's Fair will bring together a large number of the old students from all over the country. Will the Alumni take this in hand? We think we can promise the undergraduate support.

THE INFLUENCE OF THE COLLEGE IN THE TOWN.

A great deal has been said and written about the great influence for good the town exerts over the students and how much is done for them by the townspeople, This is all true, we do owe them a great deal and should show our appreciation by our acts. But at the same time is there not something to be said on the other side? Do the students return nothing to the towns-people? We think they do and can readily demonstrate it. There has been a great change in the town as well as the school in the last few years. It has progressed, old fogyism has been thrown off, and it has in all things kept pace with the university. The town has progressed not alone because of a real estate "boom" but because the needs of the University demanded that improvements should be made. The town depends on the college for its news, it depends to a large extent on the University for its entertainments and the students are making its name famous. Lake Forest without the University would be known only as a suburb of Chicago and its great beauty would be comparatively unknown. As it is however it has become known as a University town and advances in cele-brity as does the college. The athletic teams that represent us on other college fields make a reputation not only for their college but for the town. The various teams that visit here carry away a good impression not alone of the University but of the town. The members of the Faculty, most of them interested in university extension, become known as residents of Lake Forest. Princeton is celebrated not as a large city but as a college town. The University makes it. So is it and so will it be with Lake Forest. The bright men and women turned into the world from here will make a lasting name and fame for our University and in so doing will spread abroad the beauties of our little city. Give us time. Princeton, New Haven, Cambridge have had col-leges over two hundred years; we have had one only twenty. Give us time, and Lake Forest will yet be known as the site of the best University in the Great West.

THE THANKSGIVING SEASON.

It would seem at first thought as if we were the creditor this year, as if we could sit back and say we have no cause to be thankful, The election didn't suit most of us, the recent foot ball game didn't suit any of us and yet —stop and think. We *are* thankful it is no worse. We are glad Beloit didn't beat us and that Belva Lockwood wasn't elected. We are happy when we realize that we won the State Ora-torical prize. We heave a sigh of satis-faction when we think of the base ball pennant, and we look with pleasure on our new buildings. But, seriously speak-ing, we should be devoutly thankful this year. We have in the various de-partments a cleaner, more earnest, more energetic set of men than ever before; they are placing the University on a higher plane; they will make their Alma Mater proud of them. We have a Faculty in touch with the students and up to the times; we have a town which is unsurpassed for a university site and whose people are in full accord and sympathy with us. The World's Fair is within hailing distance; the fin-est city in the world is at our beck and call. But looking at it more generally, education has lately taken strides of a perfectly marvelous order, university extension is making an opportunity for everyone, and not many years will have drifted into the past before life will be on a higher basis and consequently on a more Christian plane. So when we sit down to our Thanksgiving turkey we can look back on our past year with pleasure and return sincere thanks for the progress made.

The STENTOR heartily endorses Prof. Thomas' remarks on the conduct of the students in chapel. The students make it too much of a jollification meeting. Studying and newspaper reading is carried on in the room as if it were a public reading room. We devote a very small amount of each day for chapel exercises and it seems rather strange that we can not face our Maker for a few moments in a serious, devout manner. We hope the Peofessor's words will not be sown on stony ground.

FALTERING STORY OF SANDY McLAIN.

It was a Thanksgiving Day that might have been the happiest of all, but it ended so mournfully for everything that was dear to Sandy McLain.

In his palmy days Sandy was one of the brightest men on the staff of the morning *Flopper*. Meet him once and you would never forget him. Long, slim, a trifle stoop-shouldered, with a bullet shaped head atop of his long neck, red hair closely cropped, long ears, smooth face, big watery eyes under shaggy sandy brows, prominent Roman nose, wide stretch of face between mouth and nose, fluctuating lips—these were a few of the features that made up Sandy's unique personality.

He always spoke in a slow, measured tone, his face breaking into a sad sort of smile often

as he spoke. Every sentence he uttered was droll. He never expressed himself as any one else would. And his writings were even funnier than his speech. He could turn out a column on a common-place subject that would make you laugh and cry by turns. Everybody admitted Sandy's worth, for he had as good a heart as he had a peculiar head. However, a condition was always put upon an estimate of Sandy. He loved red liquor. He was none of your stingy fellows, but was the kind of a man to go up to the bar and ask every one in the room to take something, the bar-tender included.

It was the same old story. Never a kindly, generous heart rum-sodden but what the poor brain succumbs. Sandy's love for red-liquor caused his fall. He began to neglect his work. When he was sent out on an assignment by the city editor he whiled away his time with the boys at Jim McGarry's saloon and trusted his wits to invent a story where his facts were lacking. He grew so irregular that once or twice he fell down on his assignments,—got drunk and the paper was scooped in consequence.

True Sandy was valuable to the paper when sober, but his lucid minutes were becoming few and far between. Every person in the office from the boy that carried copy to the elevator man marked the course of his fall with sorrow. Sandy's brilliant career, sun-lit as it had been, was merging into the dark clouds, into a night that was black and starless.

One evening Sandy was sent out to get the facts of a burglary on the West side.

"We must have a good story, Sandy," said the city editor. "Don't drink anything and get your copy in early."

"Yes, sir; yes, sir," said Sandy gaily.

Outside the office Sandy met a friend. Of course they had to take a drink. When that was down, B——n of the morning *Blow-hard* dropped into Jim McGarry's and that meant another round.

"Make it a little rye," said Sandy.

While that was going down Col. Mongrelly,

the fencing master, came in. Sandy and his companions must sit down at a table and sample some Private Stock. It was several rounds of Private Stock, and soon Sandy, who always had a good foundation on hand, was maudlin. How about the burglary? It never enters Sandy's head after the first drink.

The paper waited and waited for Sandy's copy but it never came. It was too late to send another man, and the paper went to press without Sandy's story.

The next morning every paper in town except the *Flopper* had a first page story on burglary. The *Flopper* was scooped again through Sandy's love for red-liquor. It was two much for the *Flopper*.

Sandy lost his job.

Not everyone knew that Sandy had one of the sweetest and most loving little wives that ever suffered from a weak man's folly. She and Sandy lived on a back street over on the North Side. But the boys on the *Flopper* and the city editor found it out and were sorry for her the next day when the timid, frail creature came down to the office to plead for Sandy and beg that he might be taken back. Sandy wouldn't do so any more. Sandy meant to do his best.

Yes, the city editor knew Sandy meant well, but there had been scores of promises before. No, Sandy couldn't be trusted any more.

The elevator man said he saw tears trickle down behind her veil as she was going away.

Some of the boys thought the paper ought to pension Sandy off, in his weakness, but others said he couldn't keep from spending the money.

Fall came on. Sandy couldn't get a job on any of the papers. He gained a meager pitt ance by writing specials now and then. It was hard lines for his faithful and sorely tried wife.

Thanksgiving Day Sandy came to himself. His nobler nature asserted itself. There would be a Thanksgiving dinner, and more dinners after that, and the wife would not wear that poor, pinched look. Sandy made up his mind that he and red liquor would never meet again.

He told the wife so. She smiled through her tears. But he had told her so many, many times before. Still she trusted him.

He went down to the office of the *Flopper* and told the city editor that he had reformed.

The city editor laughed.

"Do you mean it, Sandy."

"Yes, sir, I do. For the sake of my wife try me once more!"

Sandy had never spoken like that before. He was too earnest even to be droll.

"I'll try you once more, Sandy."

Chauncy Diffuse of New York was to be in the city that night to address the Confederate League Club. It was necessary to send a man out to Hyde Park to catch him on the train as he came in and interview him regarding the strike among the employes of the New York Central railway. Once in the city Chauncy Diffuse would be a difficult man to get hold of. So the city editor gave Sandy the assignment and sent him out to Hyde Park to meet Chauncy Diffuse in his private car.

"The train will probably slow up at Hyde Park, Sandy," said the city editor, and you will have to look lively to catch it. Get a good story and don't miss the train."

Sandy gave a strong promise and started out with a light heart and a clearer brain than he had possessed for many a day. For half an hour he waited at Hyde Park station. It was a cold, disagreeable morning with a driving sleet and a hailstorm blowing from the West. Buttoning his well-worn coat more tightly Sandy waited.

Soon a whistle sound told of the approaching train. In it came, flying over the rails.

"It must stop," said Sandy to himself, "but it's coming in almighty fast."

Would it stop? No. Down came the train with never a slow-up.

Sandy's brain worked as fast as the drive-wheels of the coming engine and his mind was made up to catch the train and get an interview at all hazards. If he missed it the city editor would think he had broken his promise.

The engine rushed by. One car passed;

two cars; the third came, and next to it the private car of Chauncy Diffuse.

Sandy made a leap.

He failed to grip the car-rail. His foot slipped and down under the merciless wheels went Sandy.' A brakeman on the platform had seen his effort and his fall. The train was brought to a stand-still and backed up to where Sandy was lying with both legs severed near the knee. Tenderly the trainmen, at the bidding of the big-hearted Chauncy Diffuse himself, bore poor Sandy, bleeding and mangled, into the great man's private car. A telegram was sent to the next station to have a surgeon in waiting ready to board the train.

They unbuttoned Sandy's coat and the re-porter's star on his vest told them who Sandy was and what was his mission.

His life was almost gone.

When the surgeon came aboard at the next stop he said that he could do nothing for the man.

*   *   *   *   *   *   *·

The passengers standing by saw that Sandy was whispering. With ears close to his lips they listened. Only a few disconnected, flut-teringly whispered words could be gathered.

"Tell—them," trembled the lips, "was sober—best—I could."

There was only a tremor of the lips. The sentence was never finished.

As the train rumbled into the city Sandy McLain's soul went home. He had turned in his copy, brilliant and faltering as it had been by turns, to the great Editor-in-Chief of the Universe; and his story will be printed in the Newspaperman's Edition of the Book of Life.

WILLIAM E. DANFORTH.

The sidewalks about town are a menace to the pedestrian's limbs. Holes, rotten boards, unnailed boards and no boards at all are by far too abundant. To walk from the College to the post-office after dark requires great care and magnificent nerve. Repairs should be made before the city has to settle a bill for a sprained ankle or something worse.

COLLEGE.

AMUSEMENTS FOR THE WEEK.

AUDITORIUM—Theodore Thomas,—Saturday night.
McVICKER'S—"Miss Roarer."
GRAND—Hoyt's "A Texas Steer."
HOOLEY'S—Joseph Murphy.
COLUMBIA—Lillian Russell.
SCHILLER—Chas. Frohman's Comedians.
CHICAGO—Mrs. Brown Potter in "Therese."

Thanksgiving.

Roast turkey.

Cranberry sauce and celery.

Mince pie, candy, nuts and the doctor.

Has anyone seen the missing Soph. mortar boards ?

L. E. Zimmerman and G. W. King were with us last week.

The term Musical Recital, of Ferry Hall, will occur Thursday evening, Dec. 15th.

E. U. Graff and C. O. Parish have trans-ferred from the 19th Century Club to the Grand Pacific Club.

Did you ever see the girl who did not enjoy a nice present at Xmas? Spellman is giving one-quarter off from the list price on Albums, Plush Goods, etc.

The week of prayer for colleges has just closed. The attendance has been fairly good and the interest has been well sustained. Meet-ings were held every evening.

The usual Thanksgiving dinner at Ferry Hall will not occur this year. Owing to the foot ball game in the afternoon it has been thought best to make a change. Instead, guests invited by the young ladies will be en-tertained in the evening by a cobweb party, refreshments, etc.

OUR PRESENT READING ROOM.

Dr. and Mrs. Haven are boarding at the G. P. Club this week.

W. D. McNary has been elected captain of the Senior class foot ball team.

It is reported that "Our Harry" is to play quarter-back for '94, and "Sherm-dear" for '96.

The classes in chemistry will begin work in the new laboratory immediately after the Thanksgiving recess.

Jim, the barber, has discharged his silver-tongued German assistant and now does all his tonsorial work himself.

The cedar block pavement on Deerpath Avenue, is completed as far as the ravine just east of the Art Institute.

Two copies of the London *Times* (weekly) and one of the New York *Herald* (daily) are now on the table in the Current Politics reading room.

"All de push" went to Evanston Saturday to see the Northwestern-Wisconsin game.

Nothing is more delightful after work than a good skate upon the ice. A good pair of skates adds much to the enjoyment. Order a new pair of W. E. Ruston.

The Midnight Club is at last to name itself. The above name was given it by outsiders to deride its early breakfast hour. It is now to be styled the Auditorium.

The University Club met at the Manse Thursday evening. Prof. Eagar supplied the music and Dr. Seely read an instructive and interesting paper on Herbart, a German philosopher and pedagogue.

"Sport" and "Redda" appeared Thursday in bran new mortar-board. The devotion with which they keep in sight of them at all times is touching in the extreme. It is reported that they sleep in them, but we don't believe it.

The Athenæn members of the class of '92 have presented the society with their photographs arranged in a neat group in a massive oaken frame. F. M. Skinner made a pleasant presentation speech Friday night and N. H. Burdick responded for the society.

The Seniors who are taking the teachers course in Latin were formed into a class in Caesar last Wednesday, and J. A. Linn conducted a recitation in the third book of the Gallic War. He makes a splendid "professor" and the Seniors know lots of Latin, too.

Our foot ball manager in his wide correspondence has received appellations which are unique to say the least. Here are a few:—Rozier, Crozure, Goldzier, Corice, Croziar, Courier. If the season were longer there is no telling what others could be added to this list.

The Y. M. C. A. treasurer's book shows that twenty-seven men have not yet settled their term dues. It is not much trouble for each of these twenty-seven men to find the treasurer and settle. But it is just twenty-seven times as much work for him to hunt up the twenty-seven delinquents. P. S.—The above is a gentle hint.

The Sem. bridge has been condemned. The old structure, the trysting place of lads and lassies for years, has outlived its usefulness and must go. Barricades have been erected at each approach and red lights displayed by night. Here is a chance for some genius to win immortal fame by writing a suitable epitaph.

How delightful Saturday seemed without the dreadful bore of chapel to break up the morning for us! Some, however, wandered around disconsolately, utterly unable to accustom themselves to the absence of the wonted exercises; yet no reform instituted by the Faculty this year has given such general satisfaction to all as this one.

Prof. John J. Halsey lectured on "The Rise of the Democratic Party," at the Farwell Hall University Extension Center, No. 148 Madison street, Friday evening. This was one of a series of lectures on "The History of American Political Parties," which Prof. Halsey commenced one week ago Friday evening. The course is largely attended. The subjects for the four remaining lectures are: Nov. 25, "The Rise of the Whigs;" Dec. 2, "The Rise of the Republican Party;" Dec. 9, "The Triumph of the Republican Party;" Dec. 16, "The Epoch of the Centennials."

What will the comet do? Astronomers tell us that only by a million miles and eight hours is a collision avoided. Sunday, Nov. 27, we will pass through the tail of the wanderer. On the highest authority we are assured that nothing but a beautiful phenomenon will ensue. This is the famous comet of Biela, discovered Feb. 27, 1826.

The Seniors have too many essays. At least that is the verdict of the class. There is one due in elective Philosophy, two in Literature, and one oration. A committee has been appointed to see if a reduction in number cannot be effected. A committee has also been appointed to confer with the Faculty and see if a change cannot be made in the Commencement program. The class does not wish to inflict thirty orations upon the public.

The chemical laboratory will soon be completed. The old boiler room in the basement has been cut in two by a partition. One division is a toilet room, the other is for the laboratory. Six desks, with drawers and lockers, accomodating six students each have been put in and fitted with gas and water. Just in front of each worker will be two shelves for reagent bottles. While the laboratory is limited in size, it will afford ample accomodation for present needs, and, while not expensively finished, will present all necessary conveniences. Now for a better physical laboratory.

Saturday's chapel exercises have been abolished. At its meeting Tuesday evening the Faculty took the wise action of relegating this ancient, custom, burdensome alike to teachers, and students, to antiquity. At its same meeting the red tape fiend again broke loose in the inauguration of a new rule relative to absences. Hereafter students of the Senior class desiring absence-from-town permits will apply to Prof. Halsey, Juniors to Prof. Dawson, Sophomores to Prof. Thomas, and Freshmen to Prof. McNeil. The time is not far distant when an attorney to interpret the Code of College Laws will become an indispensable adjunct in order that students may have time to study.

The attendance at the Art Institute is increasing. The last meeting was at the residence of Mr. Chapin. After the election of several to membership the following program was listened to by an appreciative audience, the music being rendered by the Tomaso Mandolin Orchestra, of Chicago, to harp accompaniment:—

Music, Dansa Carateristica,   .   .   .   *Marenco.*
Music, La Media Noche,   .   .   .   *Francis.*
Paper, Velasquez and His Work, illustrated, *W.C.Larned.*
Music, Spanish Patrol,   .   .   .   *Tobani.*
Music, La Paloma,   .   .   .   *Zradier.*

The music was all Spanish. After the program the usual refreshments were served and the remainder of the evening devoted to social intercourse.

Another invoice of new books has been added to the library. The most valuable works are: " The Nature and Elements of Poetry," recently published as a series of papers in the *Century*, by Edward Clarence Stedman; " Elements of Logic," by James H. Hysop, Ph. D., who was formerly a teacher in our own Academy, now of Columbia College; " The Spirit of Modern Philosophy," by Josiah Royce, Ph. D., of Harvard; " The Speech of Monkeys," by R. L. Gardner, who has made a special study of the means of communication between animals; a very fine work; " The Dialogues of Plato, translated," 5 vols., by B. Jowett, M. A., of Oxford; " Lectures on the Origin and Growth of Religion," 9 vols.

now in the library and several more to be added, belonging to the " Hibbert Lectures," series of 1887, by A. H. Sayce, of Oxford; and lastly, an "Index to the Periodicals of the World." The University library is rapidly becoming a very valuable collection.

" There's a trunk at East Chicago Avenue Police Station containing $600 worth of wedding presents, and there it will stay until Mr. and Mrs. Roy Johnston return from their honeymoon," says last Thursday's *Tribune*. Roy Johnston, many of our readers will remember, was a Lake Forest man. Oct. 27th he married Miss Anita Wakem, a Chicago young lady. Their wedding presents were very valuable, one set of solid silverware being worth $2000. This was packed in a special trunk. Mr. Johnston had another trunk very similar in outward appearance to the first one. In the second one was packed wearing apparel valued at $600. Both trunks, after the wedding, were removed to the house of the bride's parents. Shortly before the bridal pair left for their wedding tour an expressman presented a written order purporting to come from Roy Johnston to Mr. Wakem for the " peculiarly shaped trunk." By mistake the less valuable trunk was delivered. Soon Johnston himself turned up and denied the order. The expressman, finding that he had not the trunk he was after, returned to get it, was detained, arrested, and compelled to deliver his first prize to the officers, who placed it where it now is and where it will remain until Mr. and Mrs. Johnston return.

TOWN TOPICS.

Mr. E. S. Wells has returned to his Lake Forest home for the winter.

Mr. L. C. Platt has determined not to build on the site of his burnt house, and has sold his Lake Forest property. Mr. Platt and family will, for the present, reside in Highland Park.

Mr. Carter H. Fitzhugh will spend the winter in his Chicago home on Bellevue place. Mr. Fitzhugh will build opposite Blair Lodge in the near future.

The paving, which according to contract was to be finished by Dec. 1st, will not be completed this winter. The blocks will be laid to the culvert between Mr. Henry Durand's and the Art Institute, by the end of this week, after that the work will be left until spring. Lake Foresters may therefore look forward to another muddy, slushy winter, and the City council are to blame for not starting the paving sooner.

SIGNIFICANT OF THANKSGIVING.

ATHLETICS.

We wish to correct the mistake in the last edition of the STENTOR which spoke of Gallwey's having made a foul tackle. It should have been given to McNary.

Class games will soon be in order and lively sport is anticipated. The different teams are getting in shape and will show up evenly matched. Grant is captain of '96, MacHatton of '95, Thom of '94 and McNary of '93.

The men must watch the ball instead of individual players. This criticism has been made before but it cannot be repeated too often. Great harm results therefrom, as was clearly proven in both the Chicago and Evanston games.

The depression among the boys owing to last Saturday's defeat, is fast disappearing. The team has gone to work with a will, determined to beat Champaign at all hazards. The new rule of the Faculty excusing foot ball men from 3 o'clock recitation is a good one, though it comes a trifle late.

Work in the Gym. progresses smoothly. The boys are fast learning to handle themselves with agility. Would it not be a good scheme to have an Athletic entertainment this term? Instructor Everett is heartily in favor of it, and under his able supervision, success is assured. The question should be agitated.

A game was played last Wednesday between the Academy team and Evanston Township High School in which the former was victorous by a score of 16 to 0. Durand made the first touch-down eight minutes after the call of time and kicked an easy goal. He quickly followed it up with another, scoring a second goal. In the second half E. T. H. S. were forced through their own goal scoring a safety for L. F. A. The ball was brought to the 25 yard line where C. Everett securing it, made a third touch-down. Durand failed at goal. The running of Durand, the tackling of Richards, Dickinson, Rogers and Yaggy, and the general team work of L. F. A. were the features. The High School team was clearly out-classed. L. F. A. lined up as follows: Richards, l. e.; Dickinson, l. t.; E. W. Everett, l. g.; Harvey, c.; Williams, r. g.; Bodle, r. t.; Yaggy, r. e.; Rogers, q.; C. S. Everett, r. h.; Durand, l. h.; Flint, f.

The time is fast approaching when we must turn our attention to base ball. Training should be begun earlier than heretofore because so much new material needs development. A sliding cage and batting net are very essential, as we have learned by past experience. Grant of last year's team was the only man who knew how to steal a base, and the defeats suffered in former years may be in part attributed to lack of good base-runners. Strict discipline should be maintained and for such maintenance Capt. McNary will not be found wanting. A ball team has no place for men dilatory in practice. We made a reputation in base ball last year, let us sustain it this year. Nash, Hayner and Lewis are candidates for pitcher. McNary will probably catch. Sharon will play 1st base, Goodman is going to try for 2nd base and Grant will play his old position again. Everyone has a chance, so let us get to work with a will.

FERRY HALL.

Miss Howard, of Marion, Iowa, visited Marshall last week.

Miss Humphrey has been compelled to leave college because of ill-health.

It is rumored that Miss Ada Barker will spend the winter in California.

Miss Oberne gave a spread last Saturday eve. in honor of Miss Tilford, ex-'93.

Last Friday evening Mrs. Ferry read before the girls a very interesting paper entitled " The Dull Girl."

Mr. Kennedy, of Rib Lake, Wis., spent Thursday with his daughter at Ferry Hall and his son at Academia.

Miss Mildred Congdon enjoyed a visit from her sister, Miss Congdon, of Oconto, Wis., on Sunday, Nov. 13th.

Mrs. Thos. Beckwith, '79, died Sep. 25th of typhoid fever, at her home, Sterling, Ill. She leaves a husband and three children.

A very enjoyable affair was the five o'clock tea given Thursday by the Seniors to the Seminary Faculty and Dr. and Mrs. McClure. The class colors were the scheme of decoration, and was carried out in purple and white chrysanthumums.

Last week Wednesday, the Juniors and Seniors, and a favored few, received the following unique invitation: " My mama wants to know if your mama will let you come to my party?" signed Birdie Huddart and Muriel Cosby. Of course all the dear girls were there with their dolls, and looking just too sweet. The young hostesses received their guests in the Art room. The time was spent in playing children's games, and during the evening dainty and appropriate refreshments were served. At an early hour the little dears went home, each made happy by the gift of a doll and a stick of candy.

ACADEMY.

TRI KAPPA.

Forbes is again confined to his room on account of sickness. He is having hard luck.

We are sorry to say that Mills, who was taken sick while home, will not return again this fall.

Gruenstein's anarchistic sentiments are beginning to show themselves, and his advice to new students is not the best.

The choosing of members lately arrived took place Friday morning. Gamma Sigma having first choice Mr. Bournique was her first choice and Mr. Rice Tri Kappa's.

We, the undersigned, request that Mr. Cutler hereafter refrain from pounding on that much abused piano in Mitchell Hall.

M. H. BOARDERS.

The latest arrival at the Academy has had a piece of misfortune which almost breaks Condon's record. On the very day he arrived he fell down a terrace and broke a tendon in his leg. He will be confined to his room for a couple of weeks, after which he can be about with the aid of crutches.

What's the matter with the Cad. foot ball eleven? The first game played goes down on the list as won, and what makes it still better is that it was over a team from Evanston. A large number from the Seminary, College and Academy watched the game and tin horn resounded on all sides.

Hudson was severely injured while going up to Waukegan the other day. His foot was caught in a cattle-guard while the train was moving very rapidly and his leg was broken in two places. It was a very serious accident and one which should teach all to be more careful while on a moving train.

GAMMA SIGMA.

Please pass the Alexander.

Fisher, Cad. '94, is attending Miami college.

Condon has privileges. (Paste this in your hat).

We regret to hear that Matt. Mills will not be back.

The Second English class is again out of restrictions.

Nichols—" Say, old man, did you see that tackle I made to-day?"

Can any one tell us what makes Bournique late to supper every day?

Mr. Harvey McAlister Keithe intends going south to spend the winter.

Kimball spent Sunday at home. He says the breweries are still doing an immense business.

Alfred Smith, a new student, has been laid up from an accident he received the first day he arrived.

Prof. Smith has something pleasant to announce to the two societies after Thankgiving. What CAN it be?

Hall (in Physics): "Professor, if an irresistable force hits an immovable object, what action will it produce?"

A junior Mitchell Hall team has been organized with Hope Rogers captain, and R. Bruce Glover manager.

Jos. Rogers received a very bad injury in last Wednesday's game. It is feared he can play no more this season.

AMONG THE ALUMNI.

Josiah Sutton, '91, spent Sunday, Nov. 13 here.

J. E. Duggan, Academy '93, is collecting for the Chicago Telephone Co. in Chicago.

W. H. Money, Academy '87, is with Markley, Alling & Co., on Lake street, Chicago.

John D. Pope, '80, was re-elected state senator of Nebraska, at the recent election.

Abbott Davison, Academy '95, has gone on the stage as a member of the Henshaw and Feeley Combination.

Hawley W. Claflin, an old Academy student, is playing the role of tragedian. He is with the Clay Clement Company.

Sartell Prentice, Jr. '91, now at Princeton Theological Seminary, is just recovering from a severe attack of typhoid fever.

LATE NEWS.

Mr. Anderson's store was entered Friday night and robbed of a small sum.

Miss May Stowell, ex-'95, of Chicago, spent Saturday and Sunday in Lake Forest. Her many friends were very glad to see her again.

The Mitchell Hall foot ball team defeated the Harvard School Saturday afternoon by a score of 14 to 4. The tackling of Whitney, Yaggy, and Dickinson and the long gains of Co. Everett were features.

The 'Varsity indoor base ball team overwhelmingly defeated the town team in the Gym. Saturday night, the score being 26 to 8, made as follows;

'Varsity................1 12 0 1 6 0 0 3 3—26
Town................0 2 0 2 0 3 0 0 1— 8

The features of the game were Grant's two home runs, the way Sharon caught fouls and pop-ups, Charlie Durand's sure hitting, and Nash's one-handed catch.

Two foot ball teams composed of the younger Cads. and captained by Erskine and Hewitt played a tie game last week that was full of interest and good foot ball playing. They played one hour without intermission, and each side scored a touch-down and goal, Erskine and P. Cobb carrying off the honors. Erskine runs the more strongly, while Cobb does some exceedingly clever dodging.

MADISON 26; EVANSTON 6.

A fair-sized crowd went out to the Athletic ground at Evanston last Saturday to see their pets downed by Madison. The day was cold and uncomfortable and the game too one-sided to be interesting. Wisconsin played " horse " with Evanston. They ran around the ends and plowed through the line at will. The score hardly tells the story of the game. Evanston gains were made mostly by punting aided by a high wind. Madison's interference was superb. Noyes, on account of alleged injuries retired from the game in order to relieve himself of the blame for the disgraceful defeat. It is a conspicuous fact that after his retirement Evanston scored its first and only touch-down. Deering, who succeeded the mighty Yale substitute, far outplayed him. It would be hard to ascribe the glory of the victory to individual Madison men as all showed up in magnificent form. The playing of Thiele however was especially noticeable. Evanstonians are in mourning over the defeat, as they were so confident of victory.

OTHER GAMES OF THE WEEK.

At Springfield.   Yale, 6; Harvard, 0.
At Chicago.   U. of I., 10; Chicago U.; 0.
At Williamstown.   Amherst, 60; Williams, 0.
At New York.   Cornell, 16; M. A. C., 0.
At Lafayette.   Purdue, 38; Chicago U., 0.
At Bethlehem.   Lehigh, 15; Lafayette, 6.
At Crawfordville.   Wabash, 36; I. U., 24.
At Ann Arbor.   Ann Arbor, 22; Oberlin, 18.

THE STENTOR.

VOLUME VI. DECEMBER 6, 1892. NUMBER 9.

PUBLISHED EVERY WEEK
BY THE
Lake Forest University Stentor Publishing Co.

BOARD OF EDITORS.

F. C. SHARON, '93................Managing Editor
R. H. CROZIER, '93...............Business Manager
N. H. BURDICK, '93 }
S. B. HOPKINS, '93 } ....Locals
L. N. ROSSITER, '93...........Alumni and Personal
B. R. MACHATTON, '95.............Advertising

ASSOCIATE EDITORS.

HARRY GOODMAN, '94...............Athletic Editor
FOREST GRANT, '96....................Staff Artist
DAVID FALES, '96..........................Town

Terms—$1.50 per year. Single Copies—10c

————ADDRESS————
STENTOR PUBLISHING COMPANY,
LAKE FOREST, : : ILLINOIS.

Entered at the P. O. at Lake Forest, Ill., as second-class matter.

AT present the case of Dr. Briggs and Union Seminary is exciting the religious world to a considerable degree. It is with much pleasure, therefore, that we call attention to the able article on that subject by Prof. Thomas. Prof. Thomas is a profound student of religious matters, and his opinions are given high regard.

LESSONS LEARNED.

The foot ball season is a thing of the past, and as usual we can see our mistakes and learn new lessons from experience that the team has had hard luck everyone will admit. Circumstances have had a great deal to do with it and it hardly seems as if the boys had had a fair chance. But still, let us look it over. The team this year has had more done for it than any team of any kind has ever had here. The board at the training table was advanced to five dollars; rubbers and surgeons were provided; a good gymnasium was near at hand with all conveniences; everyone contributed freely to the fund. Certainly no complaint can be made by the team of their treatment. If the students could leave out the Evanston game they would have no complaint either. But it was that last straw that broke the camel's back. Many complaints have been heard of the boys' lack of practice before that game, of the captain's mismanagement, of the big-head over the Beloit game, of a hundred things that will float about. However these may be, it is not our pleasure to criticise. The team finished second, which is very creditable. If there were mistakes they will not be repeated another season. The management cannot have too high praise, and the captain and his assistants certainly did the best they could under the circumstances. However, the lessons learned by the season's work will benefit the Association and enable it to correct mistakes in the future.

THOSE FACULTY LECTURES.

The lectures delivered last year by

members of the Faculty and Mr. Larned and which formed such a desirable part of our entertainments, will not be given this year *unless*, as we are informed, the students take more interest in them themselves. We can hardly blame the Faculty for this condition because some of last year's lectures were miserably attended. But the students can not afford to let such a chance slip by. We need the lectures and we should see that our part is done. Last year it was an experiment and of course everything did not run as smoothly as could be desired. This year however we could profit by experience. The lectures might be in regard to the World's Fair or on educational topics. But it is sufficient to say that unless the students rouse themselves and petition the faculty expressly, we will go on, like the brook, forever, before we will get those lectures.

PERSONAL JOURNALISM.

Until personal journalism is exterminated from our college papers, the college press will never take a position of importance in the newspaper world. By personal journalism of course we mean violent attacks on other papers and colleges, slanderous statements and accusations such as mar our daily papers at present. We know whereof we speak for in days past we confess our guilt in this regard. Such work lowers the tone of a paper and makes it lose its dignity. It is never the result of sober thought. Rather the outcropping of envy and malice. It is a relief to pick up a college paper and see an impartial account of some game or contest. The defeated team always raises a tremendous howl and really lowers itself by not giving its opponents credit for good play. Of course there are two sides to every question but college journals should especially strive to present their own side in as calm and argumentative a way as possible. We say *especially* because college youth as a general thing are as hot-headed and combustible material as one can find. Again, this constant bickering is what is keeping college journals apart. And it is this standing aloof from each other that keeps college journalism from advancing. Some radical change must come some day and some one must start it. We propose hereafter eliminating all such objectionable matter from our paper.

UNION SEMINARY AND THE PRESBYTERIAN CHURCH.

I have been asked to state briefly the present relations between Union Theological Seminary and the General Assembly of the Presbyterian Church. In order that these relations may be clearly understood, it is necessary to trace to some extent the history of the Seminary. It was organized in 1836, the year preceding the violent separation of the church into the two branches, Old School and New. The doctrinal controversies which preceded and attended this separation led to its organization. Its founders were members of the New School party, who designed "to provide a Theological Seminary which may commend itself to men of moderate views, who desire to live free from party strife, and to stand aloof from all extremes of doctrine or of practice." In 1839 it was incorparated by the legislature of the State of New York, and its control vested in a body of directors, twenty-eight in number, half of whom are clergymen and half laymen, and who are required to subscribe to the Westminster Confession of Faith and Form of Government. It was thus, while loyal to the Presbyterian Church, entirely free from all ecclesiastical supervision. In this respect it differed from Princeton and Alleghany, which by the nature of their organization were and are subject to the General Assembly. This state of absolute independence continued for thirty-four years until the reunion of the two branches of the Presbyterian Church in 1870. Then, in order to secure for those Seminaries under ecclesiastical control the privilege of electing their own professors, the Assembly retaining only a veto power, Union gave unto the Assembly this same veto power over herself. In the warmth of generous feeling attending the reunion it was natural that strict constitutional and legal questions should not be severely and solicitously regarded, although it is said that at the time the Assembly suggested to the directors of the Seminary the importance of so changing its charter that this voluntary subjection to ecclesiastical control should become part of its organic law. This, however, was never done; and it is only since the question concerning Dr. Briggs has arisen that attention has been directed to the character of the relationship between the Seminary and the Assembly existing since the reunion.

As is well known, Dr. Briggs, having been a professor in the Seminary since 1876, was transferred in 1890 from the chair of Hebrew to that of Biblical Theology. When the report of the transfer came regularly before the General Assembly it was decisively vetoed, on the ground of his doctrinal unsoundness, and that, in spite of the fact that he had not yet been declared unsound by any ecclesiastical tribunal. Union Seminary refused to recognize the rightfulness of this veto, claiming that the power could be exercised only at the election of a new professor and not at the transfer of one already a member of the faculty to a new position. This led to a more careful consideration of the character of the agreement and it has been, not perhaps discovered, but more clearly discerned, that the agreement was constitutionally null and void from the beginning, that the directors of the Seminary could not legally abdicate their rights and lay aside their chartered powers. This is the decision of competent jurists whose opinions have been solicited. These affirm that according to the laws of the State of New York the Seminary would subject itself "to the hazard of a forfeiture by judicial decree of its corporate existence" should the directors give it over to the control of any other body.

In view of this fact, therefore, the directors on the 13th of October last, rescinded the action of 1870, and restored the Seminary to its former status of freedom from ecclesiastical control, affirming at the same time "the undiminished loyalty of Union Seminary to the doctrine and government of the Presbyterian Church." That this affirmation is sincere and without reserve no one who knows the character of the men who make it will for an instant doubt.

This action of the directors has, of course, been widely and severely criticised, and mainly by those who hold that doctrinal errors can only be avoided by the direct control of ecclesiastical bodies, and that questions of scriptural truth and fact can rightly be determined by the authoritative decision of such bodies. History, however, disproves this position. Church assemblies are quite as liable to error as those more select bodies who usually compose the directorate and faculties of our higher educational institutions. In so far as delicate questions of scholarship are concerned and the bearings of newly ascertained facts, the latter are far less liable to err. This would seem to be stating only the barest of truisms. But it is not merely disregarded but directly disputed. Ecclesiastical supervision is claimed to be the only safeguard. It really, however, guards not infrequently neither truth nor justice. In large assemblies of even Christian men party cries are raised, party prejudices excited, party zeal inflamed, unreasoning fears aroused, and great questions, demanding prolonged and careful investigation and a special training for their settlement, are too often arbitrarially decided in haste and passion by the mere voice of numbers, many of whom are utterly incompetent to make such decision. In these decisions men of great piety and learning have been deprived of ministerial and professorial standing and their character as teachers clouded. Happily in these days mere ecclesiastical authority is being less and less regarded. Truth and fact are considered by an increasing number quite beyond its determination. It would seem to be clear then that all of our higher schools, which are, or ought to be, engaged not only in teaching but in the wider process of investigation, should be free from ecclesiastical control. There is no sphere, not even that of Biblical history and interpretation, in which all facts have been discovered and all truths determined. These things, therefore, should be left in the hands that are alone competent. There they must and will be left sooner or later. Mere authority can only interfere to embitter controversy and delay the universal acceptance of the truth.   M. BROSS THOMAS.

SOME QUESTIONS ASKED.

A POST ELECTION PAPER.

LAKE FOREST, Nov. 29, '92.
To the Editor of the "Stentor."

In a late issue of the STENTOR, there was an article by Professor Halsey, upon "The Political Situation," in which he mentioned the tariff as the "great rock of offense upon which public opinion has split," and the professor also said: "With charming *naivette*, Mr. McKinley and the New York *Tribune* eliminate from a practical world all causes of present prosperity, except the McKinley tariff. * * * Mr. McKinley discovers in the rise in price of American wheat abroad, the influence of the McKinley tariff, but says naught about the shrinkage of the English crop twenty-three per cent." The professor also stated that

the "New York *Tribune* depicts with ferocious joy the widespread distress in the tinplate districts of Wales, as a result of the McKinley tariff, but draws no inference from the overproduction in that industry."

Will you kindly allow me to say to the readers of the STENTOR, what all know who have read or heard his speeches or are acquainted with him,—that Gov. McKinley is not a petifogger, but an educated, scholarly gentleman, of sterling principle and character, who states his views and facts, accurately, fairly, and carefully.

Will Professor Halsey kindly quote from speeches of his, taken from authentic sources, any expressions that justify the foregoing interpretations. Again, will the professor quote from the New York *Tribune* what can be, by any interpretation, considered as "depicting with ferocious joy the widespread distress," etc.

I do not of course intimate that Prof. Halsey has knowingly or intentionally misrepresented Major McKinley or Whitelaw Reid; but the "simple truth" is what we wish in "clean politics," and I am not alone in wishing to see these expressions, or quotations, and the authority therefor.

It would be interesting, also if Prof. Halsey will state, in detail, a few articles, upon which there is a "high protection," why it is high, what it should be to be considered "moderate" and what the effect of a change to the moderate would be; also, if the "Mills" bill, which the Ex-Confederate Chieftain Mills, with the assistance of the Democracy and the South, sought to push through Congress is better, and if so, in what particulars, for the purpose of revenue or for the interests of all the people than the McKinley bill.

Will Prof. Halsey "plainly show" upon what article or articles, there has been an "increased cost of living," entailed upon "sixty-five millions," and give a few examples of "the small favored class," who are thus benefitted at the expense of the myriads mentioned.

Please give simple specifications, that we may see exactly to what the general statement refers.

The great mass of Republican voters believe, as a matter of principle, that the system of protection is, by long experience, shown to be the best for every American citizen, whether workingman, clerk, manufacturer, merchant, or college professor, and we are, therefore, patriotic enough to advocate and sustain it by every honorable method, and we also believe that the safest men to govern this beloved land and control affairs, are those who stood by our banner our constitution and our country, rather than those who fired upon our flag, and sought our destruction; we considered the issue, in the late election, of far greater importance than the mere choice between two men and the little question of offices.

We preferred to see at the head of our nation such a Christian man as Gen. Harrison with his associates, nearly all men of the highest character.

May I add that nearly all the friends of Lake Forest college, I think, rejoiced to hear that a great majority of the students cast their first vote for the grand principles of the Republican party, and we regret to hear that, in this noble act, they had the example or encouragement of only a very few of their honored and excellent instructors in other branches of learning. Yours truly,

N. D. PRATT.

———

One of the neatest publications we have seen lately and one which every Lake Forester should own is a book of Lake Forest views published by William Herbert Baker, 358 Dearborn Street, Chicago. There are seventeen full page views, photogravures, comprising the Northwestern Station, Academy, College Campus, President's House, College, Gymnasium, Art Institute, the Church, Ferry Hall, College Residences, Farwell's Pond, View from the Bluffs, Bluffs from the Beach, and street scene. The photogravure work is very fine and as a souvenir of Lake Forest it is unsurpassed.

COLLEGE.

AMUSEMENTS FOR THE WEEK.

AUDITORIUM—Theodore Thomas,—Saturday night.
MCVICKER'S—Joseph Jefferson.
GRAND—"Yon Yonson."
HOOLEY'S—"Niobe."
COLUMBIA—"Men and Women."
SCHILLER—Chas. Frohman's Comedians.
CHICAGO—Modjeska:

———

The foot ball team traveled, in the aggregate, 11,000 miles.

For anything in the line of tooth brushes, go to French the druggist.

The Sems., duly escorted by teachers, visited the scene of the wreck Thursday afternoon.

Mounted slate blackboards have been placed in the Greek and Latin recitation rooms in the Art Building.

The comet failed to keep its date—like the Champaign foot ball team—and still old mother earth revolves serenly.

Buck, the Waukegan jeweler, repairs watches for the students. His work is first-class.

Prof. Halsey's class in current politics now have access to the New York *Herald*, which may be found upon the class reading room table.

B. R. MacHatton was detained at home beyond the Thanksgiving recess by a painful abcess on his elbow, the result of an injury received on the foot ball field.

Many of the students and townspeople hung around the wreck all day to see the unusual sight of replacing a six wheel, 67-ton locomotive upon the track. At six o'clock their patience was rewarded when the helpless monster was once more enthroned monarch of the road.

The Sem. bridge is not to be removed and replaced with a handsome new structure, but simply patched up and allowed to continue indefinitely its vocation of " trysting place," etc.

Nash has turned over the stewardship of the G. P. club to MacHatton who was at the training table until Thanksgiving. The club now boards nineteen men besides the steward.

Cold weather is coming and with it much fun on the ice. Don't use an old, worn-out skate, but give you order to Spellman for a new pair.

Upon the breaking up of the training club, McNary, MacHatton and Woolsey went to the G. P.; Marcotte, Hunt and Hayner to the Nineteenth Century; T. M. Hopkins to Academia, and Thom to the Midnight. The Academy representatives now dine at Mitchell Hall and Academia.

Several of the Lake Forest alumni met in the Law School Wednesday evening, Nov. 30th, and appointed a committee on constitution for an association of the Lake Forest alumni in Chicago and vicinity. They adjourned to meet at same place Dec .14th, at 7 o'clock. Every alumnus should be present at next meeting.

The "aprons" of two members of the Senior class in chemistry are at present engaged in travelling about the country for their health. Purchased in the city, they were placed in a valise for convenient carriage, but, unfortunately, each thought the other would see to the valise and it proceeded northward into Wisconsin, not having since been heard from.

The Senior class in English Literature has been considering the four great English novelists—Scott, Thackeray, Eliot, Dickens,—by means of individual essays on special topics in the favorite novels of each author. The essay of Miss Annie Adams was especially well received. The rest of the term will be devoted to the late poet-laureate, Alfred Tennyson.

The formation of the new Joint University Board for University Extension in the Northwest, of which Pres. Rogers is president, and Mr. Raymond secretary, was announced in the STENTOR of Oct. 1st, and a list of lectures to be given by Lake Forest talent was printed in the issue of Nov. 1st. In compiling this list, the name of Prof. McNeill, astronomy, six lectures, was accidentally omitted.

A meeting of those interested in indoor base ball was held last week and arrangements were made for a regular team. Forest Grant was elected captain, and it was decided that all games should begin promptly at half past seven. The captain will, some time during each week, post a list of those whom he wants for the next Saturday night's game. He should be enthusiastically supported by all lovers of the sport.

" G. Willie " Wright, '92, now at McCormick Seminary, is one of " Two College Students on Hazing," representing Lake Forest and Cornell in the *Interior* of Nov. 24th. He gives a concise history of the decline of hazing here and expresses himself as preferring " an evening's hazing " to the constant pounding and guying of a student at all times and in all places. He says that much good has been done by hazing and thinks that in its milder form, the practical joke, it will be in vogue to some extent " as long as time lasts." The article is exceedingly well written and sound as to facts and opinions.

Seniors and Sophomores were alike glad to begin work in the new chemical laboratory last week, but it seems too bad that those in charge should think such iron-clad " rules and regulations " as those now in force necessary in dealing with *college* students. Should not Seniors and Sophomores be trusted to pay for articles broken by them and not compelled to deposit a large sum with the sub-treasurer each term? And think of fining Seniors and Sophomores twenty-five cents for each and every misdemeanor! Such rules betoken a lamentable lack of confidence in the students on the part of the professor to say the least.

The former classmates and friends of G. I. Scofield, " Sco," as he was familiarly called, for a time with '93, will read with regret the following from the *Oconto County Reporter*, Wis.:

We regret to announce that George, eldest son of Major and Mrs. E. Scofield, is very sick, and his symptoms have not been as encouraging as his many friends would desire. A celebrated physician from Milwaukee arrived Wednesday night, and after a diagnosis expressed hope for recovery of the patient.

Since writing the above we learn that the attending physicians have given up hope and that his death is a question of a few days only.

We clip the following from the *Daily Palo Alto*, Leland Stanford, Jr., University, Cal., issue of Nov. 18th:

The STENTOR, of the Lake Forest University, is one of the college papers of the United States that has a little push and energy in its management. At 4 A. M. on Nov. 9th they issued a special edition giving the results of the election, and the result of the count of doubtful states. This gave the news to the people of Lake Forest several hours before the Chicago papers arrived. To-morrow the *Daily Palo Alto* will give three-minute bulletins of the Harvard-Yale foot ball game which takes place at Springfield. Such schemes as these ought to be appreciated by the students, as they require push and cash to carry them out.

The Athenæan " Poe Evening " was thoroughly enjoyed by the members and a number of the society's friends from Ferry Hall, the Academy, and the town. The following program was rendered:

Character Sketch of Poe   .   B. R. MacHatton.
" The Raven,"   .   .   .   Prof. E. M. Booth.
Violin Solo,   .   .   .   Chas. Goodman.
        Accompained by Siegfried Gruenstein.
" Ulalume,"   .   .   .   .   David Files.
Review of Poetry,   .   .   .   A. O. Jackson.
Essay Prose,   .   .   .   J. A. Linn.
Vocal Solo,   .   .   .   Miss Brett.
        Accompanied by Miss Sizer.
" The Masque of the Red Death,"   .   D. H. Jackson.
" The Devil in the Belfry,"   .   .   Forest Grant.
Narrative Prose,   .   .   .   N. H. Burdick.

Prof. Booth is at his best in " The Raven," and also in " The Bells," which he gave as an encore. It is a genuine treat to hear Prof. Booth declaim, and we all wish we could do it oftener.

From the " Minutes of the Synod of Wisconsin," October 13-17, we make the following extracts from the report of the visiting committee to Lake Forest University:

" Lake Forest University, since the resignation of Dr. Roberts last spring, has been without a permanent president. The position is being filled, however, very acceptably for the time being by Rev. James G. K. McClure, D. D.

Many improvements have been made during the year which will add greatly to the accommodations of the students. * * * It was feared that on account of the resignation of Dr. Roberts, and the vacancy he left being still unfilled by a permanent president, there would be a falling off in the number of students. We are glad to say that such fears were not realized, in that the number of students enrolled for the fall term is larger than ever before. * * * In view then of the great usefulness and success of Lake Forest in the past; its present prosperous condition and far-reaching influence; its promise for still greater power for good in the future, it is the conviction of your committee that the Synod of Wisconsin should make Lake Forest University the center of our higher educational interests."

All the delightful features of a cane rush were furnished free with the Freshmen-Sophomore "scrap" Wednesday night. The upper hand was with the Sophomores from the start; it was their fight. The first act was the capture of Mr. Sherman as he issued from the Athenæan Hall. His lusty yells of " '96, '96," soon brought his classmates on the scene, and as they appeared they were tackled by the Sophs., tied hand and foot and tumbled unceremoniously into room 50, an empty room on the top floor. All the Freshmen in the building were disposed of in this fashion (as were also Grant and Sherman) except " Gentleman " Jones and " Garibaldi " Vance. The latter was told by sympathetic outsiders to get to the town Freshmen as quickly as possible and bring them into the action. He soon returned with five besides himself. These bound the guard at the foot of the stairs, stowed him away under the stairway, and then ran to the aid of their classmen. All were stopped in the hall except one, who broke into room 50 brandishing a knife and crying, "I have a knife." One of the Sophomore guards said excitedly, "let me take it quick to cut this man loose," and threw it far out into the night. But someone was loose and soon had all the Freshman muscle untied. Then, neglecting to tie up the '95 guards which would have won them the fight, they burst out into the hall. Then began the cane-rush like proceedings, resulting in a clear case of victory for '95, though '96 fought with desperation and to exhaustion.

At 6:25 Thursday morning fast freight No. 182, south bound, collided with passenger No. 38 at the switch just north of the depot, derailing and wrecking freight engine No. 826, passenger engine No. 606, five freight cars, one combination passenger and baggage coach, and breaking the knee, crushing the ankle and cutting the face of the fireman, Thomas Kelly, of the freight engine.

The freight was several hours behind time and was running at thirty-five miles an hour. A dense fog was prevailing at the time and prevented Engineer Moody, of the freight, from seeing the passenger until too late. The passenger was just pulling off the switch when the big 67-ton freight engine dashed into the combination car, throwing it from its trucks, and struck the tank of the passenger engine, breaking the coupling and carrying both it and the engine to the platform shed. The freight cars piled themselves promiscuously along both tracks, smashing the switch, crossing gates and platform to smithereens. Fireman Kelly was in the act of putting coal into the furnace when the crash came, and, without waiting to see the effect, dropped his shovel and jumped, sustaining injuries which caused him the loss of his leg. The engineer did not have time to jump and escaped without a scratch. No one else was hurt. The engineer of the passenger shut off the steam, turned on the air, and with his fireman jumped before the crash and escaped.

The tracks were not cleared until 3:30 p.m., and after the morning trains, which transferred passengers, baggage, express and mails around the wreck, each returning whence it came, all through trains were sent *via* Wisconsin and Kenosha divisions to Kenosha, where they again took the main line. Very little delay was experienced by suburbanites in getting to business. The lass will probably not exceed $8,000.

TOWN TOPICS.

Mr. Hobert Chatfield Taylor, whose summer home is in Lake Forest, has changed his last name to Chatfield-Taylor.

Mr. E. F. Chapin and family have returned from the East. Mr. Chapin went to Brooklyn, Mass., to spend Thanksgiving at the old homestead.

The Art Institute met last Tuesday at the house of Mr. Holt. Mrs. Ferry gave a lecture on Columbus, and Prof. Eager rendered some very enjoyable piano selections.

The district school house on the road to Ft. Sheridan is being rebuilt, to be finished by Christmas. The building was burned last August, and for some time it was thought that the fire had been the scene of a murder.

Mr. E. S. Wells, Sr., who was one of the first settlers of Lake Forest, is soon to marry a Mrs. Hinton, of Lee, Mass. Mr. Wells has always been an earnest friend of the students. The STENTOR gives him its sincere good wishes for his future happiness.

For several years the trustees of the church have been talking of enlarging the present seating capacity of the church. Nothing definite, however, was done until last week, when Architect Cobb came up to look at the church and to consult with the board of trustees. Mr. Cobb will immediately submit plans to the board.

The fair held at Mrs. Watson's new home last Thursday turned out a great success. Beautiful fancy work of all kinds was sold immediately and in another room ice cream, coffee and candy were dispensed. Towards the last the remaining articles were sold with a rush at auction, with Mr. Calvin Durand as auctioneer. The proceeds will go to the free kindergarten.

FERRY HALL

Miss Edna Smith, because of needed rest, will not return until January.

Miss Marie Ensign is compelled to give up work for a time on account of trouble with her eyes.

All the guests at the Athenæan Society on Friday last, enjoyed the program very much.

Miss Ada Mathis, a former student, spent the Thanksgiving vacation with her sister, Miss Lily.

Uriah Heap was discussed in a very satisfactory manner by Miss Annie Adams in Literature on Nov. 30th.

Several Lake Forest students attended an orange party given by Miss May Stowell at her home, on Nov. 25th.

The Aletheians introduced a new feature in their program Friday evening,—that of tableaux from Shakespeare.

An example of the brilliancy shown at the Sem. breakfast table: " O, girls, did you see the sun-set rise this morning? "

In the dress line the city dealers have a rival at 218. All those who wish ready made garments of lowest price and latest style please call.

Miss Agnes Brown, '92, Miss Christy McKenzie and Miss Bessie Beach visited Lake Forest during the Thanksgiving vacation.

The Senior College girls and a number of the Chicago Theological students were very pleasantly entertained at the home of the Misses Adams on Thanksgiving.

Mrs. Seeley was very pleasantly surprised Monday by the arrival of her brother, Mr. Franz Hesse, from Germany. Mr. Hesse will make his home in Chicago, having a position with H. C. & C. Durand.

Festive Sem (to Faculty): " Well now, what would you do in my place? "

Faculty: " I think were I in your position—"

Festive Sem. (interrupting): " But you wouldn't be in my position, for you wouldn't be in it."

The Thanksgiving vacation was a festive season with us. Many of the girls went home or spent the time with friends, but about forty thought (and rightly) that they saw a good time ahead if they remained here. Rules were removed with the exception of callers from dawn till twilight, (the time being limited to the evening) and the courtesy of letting Doctor know when we wished to be out in the evening. Unfortunate.y some one forgot, causing us all to suffer, as Doctor one day put us under the regular rules, to remind us his word was still law. Dr. and Mrs. Hester and Prof. Eager spent Thursday with Dr. and Mrs. Seeley. In the evening the cob-web party— but we are modest—if it was a success we leave some one else to tell of it. Friday a candy pull, and Saturday a chestnut party in the Gym. On the whole we had a splendid vacation, and wish it might have continued till December 21st, instead of bringing us so soon face to face with reviews and examinations. Why not adopt the ninety per cent. plan for all regular students? Where would the specials be then?

Why isn't there as much enthusiasm shown in athletic sports among the girls as the boys? To be sure we can't play foot ball, nevertheless had we one in our gymnasium we would use it to advantage. Then, too, we *need* two or three medicine balls of light weight, so we can have games as well as simple practice. Will not some kind friend remember that the season for gifts is near? Exercise is always good, but how much better if it is pleasure as well as work! Last year we worked at a disadvantage, as the regular classes met just before the evening study hour. This year work is arranged so we have an afternoon hour, and while we feel this is a gain, we still believe that the work is not given its proper place. Why is the excuse of absence from the gym. always, " We haven't time," " We can't practice here and take outdoor exercise too, without slighting our lessons?. " Because a student fills—no, *crowds* her time with other studies. Why not recognize in the course of study in the catalogue the amount of time required for this work, as well as that for mathematics, languages, or any other subject?

ACADEMY.

Mr. Hunting, a professor in Berea College, Kentucky, paid us a visit last week.

We should like to advise that the clock by which the college bell is rung be set according to the correct time.

Glover's illness last week prevented his attending recitations for a few days but he is able to be around now.

Prof. and Mrs. Smith extended a very kind invitation to those who stayed here Thanksgiving to dine with them on that day.

It was very noticeable that several of the boys had unusually fine shines on their shoes just before Thanksgiving. Some new boys must have been at work.

Mr. Holt has very kindly offered to renew the prizes for the contest between the two societies this year. It will probably be held in the chapel of the new Reid Hall.

The prospects for an Academy library are beginning to look very bright and several liberal donations have been received for it from gentlemen interested in the work of the Academy.

AMONG THE ALUMNI.

Geo. M. Entriken '80, is married and is at Omaha, Neb., with the Wabash R. R. Co.

Herbert H. Hyde '84, is one of the owners of the Fredonia Linseed Oil and Paint Co., in Fredonia, Kan.

E. G. Wood '92, now teaching at Woodstock, Ill., spent the Thanksgiving vacation with his parents here.

Keyes Becker '89, of Ogden, Utah, is contemplating becoming interested in a $150,000 irrigation ditch on the Jainer river, Utah.

Elmer Stearns '80, is with the Kern County Land Co., of California, and is just at present taking a pleasure trip through the far West.

Miss Blanche Loveridge '93, who was com-pleting her course at the new Chicago University has on account of ill health left and gone to the Wisconsin pineries.

W. F. Lewis '90, has received a call to the Presbyterian church at Wilmington, Del., and he will take charge there the 1st of next April. This is the church where Dr. W. C. Roberts, ex-president of L. F. U. held his first pastorate.

LATE NEWS.

Warren Everett, instructor in the gymnasium yesterday resigned his position and will leave school on account of his father's illness. Everyone is sorry to lose Everett as he made himself exceedingly popular while here.

A close and exciting ten-inning game of indoor base ball was played Saturday night in the Gym. between the 'Varsity and the town team. The game was won by the 'Varsity by heavy batting in the tenth inning, as follows:

Town........... 4 1 0 3 2 2 0 0 2 0—14
'Varsity .... 1 0 4 2 0 2 4 1 0 4—18

A novel entertainment in the shape of an old-fashioned " Spellin' School," will be given by the Y. M. C. A. the coming Thursday evening in Ferry Hall Chapel. A social in the parlors will constitute the afterpart. The admission is twenty-five cents, proceeds to go to the Association.

The Academy foot ball team added another victory Saturday afternoon at Douglas Park, Chicago, by defeating a team composed of graduates of the West Division High School team by the score of 20 to 4. The result of the game is due to the fine team work of the "Cads." Their center plays were irresistible and the High Schoolers could figure no way in which to stop the " fall in " play.

The Students' Bureau of Correspondence for the purpose of opposing secret societies was organized Saturday at the Sherman House. There were present twenty-three delegates from Wheaton College, Chicago Theological Seminary, Naperville Academy, Evangelical Lutheran Theological Seminary and Lake Forest. R. B. Spellman was elected President for the ensuing year. We are sorry to see Lake Forest lower herself by joining such an organization with such colleges.

THE STENTOR.

VOLUME VI.   DECEMBER 13, 1892.   NUMBER 10.

PUBLISHED EVERY WEEK

BY THE

Lake Forest University Stentor Publishing Co.

BOARD OF EDITORS.

F. C. SHARON, '93...............Managing Editor
R. H. CROZIER, '93...............Business Manager
N. H. BURDICK, '93 }
S. B. HOPKINS, '93 } ....Locals
L. N. ROSSITER, '93...........Alumni and Personal
B. R. MACHATTON, '95.................Advertising

ASSOCIATE EDITORS.

HARRY GOODMAN, '94...............Athletic Editor
FOREST GRANT, '96.....................Staff Artist
DAVID FALES, '96...........................Town

Terms—$1.50 per year. Single Copies — 10c

———ADDRESS———

STENTOR PUBLISHING COMPANY,

LAKE FOREST, : : ILLINOIS.

Entered at the P. O. at Lake Forest, Ill., as second-class matter.

THE ENLARGEMENT OF THE CHURCH.

No one thing that has been done for some time will be received with such satisfaction as the contemplated enlargement of the church. For some time there has been great dissatisfaction among the students about the pews in church. The gallery is totally inadequate for them. The Academy is given one side and the college boys are expected to crowd into half of the other side. For some unexplained reason the college girls occupy one whole side. There are seldom empty pews downstairs. So there you are. College students pay their $1.25 apiece to stand up. However this has been, the trustees are fully awake to the fact that the church must be enlarged, and have now definite plans. If some arrangement could be made so that the upper classes could have the pews downstairs it would prove a popular measure. The gallery is not an especially desirable place and classes should be given seats elsewhere according to order.

A NEW EDUCATION.

The Chicago Theological Seminary has opened a new field in an educational way and has, in rather a novel manner, adopted a new method which will to a certain extent revolutionize education. It is *people* with which ministers have to deal; it is people that they have to teach; and it is people they must save. Can a minister who does not understand people, save them? The Faculty of the Chicago Seminary says *not*, and so will all thinking men. Therefore, they propose establishing a school, or rather a post, in the very slums of the city, where students are to study human nature and learn in what way individuals can best be appealed to. It is a great step in advance and one which can not fail to make a deep impression on the thinking public. It brings this question before us: Why should such an education be confined to theological students? Literary students, law students, medical students have to deal with men, with all classes and conditions of human beings. When we enter business or the professions we must face every one. Why should we not all become students of human nature? If more people would study and could see the world's misery and happiness, its hopes and fears, its struggles and triumphs as they really *are*, instead of learning the theories, there would not be so much anarchism abroad in the land. Men would become more in touch with human affairs and the world would become sweeter to all.

EXAMINATIONS AGAIN.

The discussions concerning examinations are old and hackneyed and yet with each approaching examination week we can not but feel that something about the system might be bettered. By substituting the words "excellent, good, and passed" for "passed with honor and passed" the Faculty are approaching the high school. If a change is to be made why is it not made with an idea to getting the best work out of a student. Excuse from examinations those students above a a certain per cent. and make all those below this take the "exams." Such a system would naturally stimulate the student during the term and make class work much more valuable. In their zeal to get out of examinations the students would work very hard during the term and the purpose of the class-room would be accomplished. As it is now, however, class-room work is more or less neglected during the term

and a general "cram up" for the examination takes place a few nights before. The pernicious system of cramming would be done away with and we would have good, honest, *real work*. Certainly everyone would strive harder to be ranked above the certain per cent. We think some such scheme will sometime come up; bright minds will see the possibilities and it will become a college law.

DO WE WANT FRATERNITIES?

THE PROS AND CONS EXPRESSED BRIEFLY BY FACULTY AND STUDENTS.

There has always been a feeling, more or less strong, cherished for Fraternities in this institution. Fraternities are prohibited by the charter of the University, but this might be changed if the desire became universal. From time to time attempts have been made to arouse enthusiasm on the subject, but just as often has it died out. Recently, however, the meeting of the Student's Bureau of Correspondence in Chicago for the purpose of opposing secret organizations, has again brought the subject before our minds. In order to present the subject fairly the STENTOR has asked representative men to express their views. They are given below. Whether Lake Forest needs Fraternities now or whether she can support them, are open questions; but of one thing we are sure: Lake Forest is not opposed to them, nor does she wish to be ranked with colleges which are opposed. If the college is strong enough we would say, let us have Fraternities. If not we can wait.

***

THE FACULTY.

It does not seem fair for a fair-minded man to take an extreme position on either side of the question about which you ask an expression of opinion, for the arguments both pro and con are many and strong. To barely state these arguments and then try to deduce a logical conclusion would carry one far beyond the bounds of your request; therefore, let me briefly express the conclusions which my own experience has brought me to, premising that I am myself a loyal Fraternity man.

The secrecy of college Fraternities seems to me quite innocent, though I think any effort to carry their influence beyond college life, as in politics or society, is undemocratic and to be condemned. It is said that the decision between two candidates for the presidency of an important eastern college turned in favor of one of them because of Fraternity influence in the board of trustees.

In large institutions the Fraternities give opportunities for social intercourse which would not be possible without them; yet at Cornell the Fraternity is put above the college, and at Harvard society rivalries have sometimes injured athletics. In both large and small colleges Fraternities are fatal to literary societies.

In small colleges like ours I am inclined to think Fraternities undesirable, because we could not get the best ones, because, by reason of firmness, rivalries would be personal rather than general, and, chiefly, because the wearing of a Fraternity pin is likely to add to a man's conceit, and conceit, or an inability to properly estimate one's self, is one of the chief drawbacks of the student in a small college. In other words, all that tends to diminish friction between man and man, as a preparation for the world, should be discouraged.

Let me add that while I have never sounded very much the praises of Princeton, I have the most unqualified admiration for the magnificent record of her two great debating societies, which in solid work and real dignity surpass any Fraternities in the country.

Yours respectfully,
WALTER R. BRIDGMAN.

_

PROF. HALSEY said: "Personally, I have no objection to Fraternities. I am a society man myself, having been a Beta in Chicago University. However, I think we are hardly prepared for them yet, as the college is not large enough. My policy has always been to fall in with the students' desires where they are not absolutely harmful. Therefore, when we are a little larger I say let them come if the students so desire. In regard to this Student's Bureau of Correspondence, to my mind it is about as useless as the Prohibition party is to-day."

_

PROF. BURNAP said: "I haven't time to write. I'm a Fraternity man myself and would be prejudiced. I don't want to see Fraternities in Lake Forest yet, because the college isn't strong enough to get good ones."

_

PROF. STEVENS said: "I do not believe in having the professors write for the college papers. I am a Fraternity man. I think Fraternities are of more advantage to men after leaving college than while in. They help him to positions which he could not otherwise attain. There is a great deal in the argument that Lake Forest is not at present strong enough to get a good Fraternity, even if the trustees were not opposed to them. I do not know how I should feel, personally, about having my own Fraternity introduced here."

_

THE STUDENTS.

Membership in a good chapter of a good Fraternity is a privilege and a help. Membership in a poor chapter of a good or poor Fraternity is a misfortune and a curse. The company of fellows, mutually congenial, each with a high idea of life and a high purpose in life, is a stimulus and inspiration; it deposes egotism and exalts altruism; it corrects faults and strengthens virtues; it vanquishes all tendencies to irresolution and inconstancy and promotes ambition and perseverance. This is the *ideal* chapter; those which have not such a goal before them, have no claim to recognition.

Membership in a Fraternity of high standard insures cordial recognition wherever there are college men; it is an introduction into the friendship and the homes of your "brethren;" it broadens and deepens one's interests. Fraternities formed on the basis I have mentioned, do not engender strife with other Fraternities; their members are *loyal* but *not* narrowminded, and other Frats receive their just dues. Happy is the college which has *such* Fraternities; none other should be tolerated.

WILLIAM N. McKEE, '93.

₊

I desire to correct the item in last week's issue concerning the Student's Bureau of Correspondence. The Bureau was organized some two years ago, and its purpose is "to work in promoting inquiry and disseminating information in respect to secret organizations." This work is carried on almost exclusively by correspondence. I went not as a delegate from Lake Forest, for I had no authority so to do, but as an individual.

Personally, according to my present knowledge, I am opposed to all secret organizations, and have gone into this, an unprejudiced seeker after truth, and am open to convictions.

The requirements of a secret organization narrow a man's field of usefulness, and, if a Christian man, he binds himself to do to his fellow-members no more than he might do to all mankind.   R. B. SPELLMAN.

₊

Never having had the opportunity of observing the practical workings of a Fraternity my opinion must necessarily be based upon theory only.

The Fraternity offers opportunities for the cultivation of the social side of college life which are, as a general thing, not to be found in literary societies because of the large membership of the latter.

The Fraternity serves as the strongest kind of a link to bind alumni to their Alma Mater.

Any action which tends to exterminate Fraternities from American colleges is too pain-

fully similar to that of the backwoodsman who was sore because of some fancied slight by the authorities of the World's Fair. He would " Get a few of the fellers together and boycott the whole consarn."

In regard to introducing the Fraternity here in Lake Forest, I think that the argument that the college is at present not strong enough to get a good one should be final.

N. H. BURDICK, '93.

₊

I would like to see Fraternities introduced in Lake Forest, provided good ones could be secured. There is no question but that as a means for promoting interest in college affairs they are vastly superior to literary societies. If a Fraternity man is striving for honors of any sort, whether it be in scholarship or athletics, he is seconded by all his fellows; whereas in a literary society a man under like circumstances generally works alone. It is claimed by some the Fraternities breed immorality, but, although it may be true in some cases, it is due to flaws in character of the individuals composing the Fraternity and is not a valid argument against the Fraternity idea. Let them find a home here.

HARRY GOODMAN.

₊

Some days since the Chicago papers chronicled the proceedings of the initial meeting of " The Students' Bureau of Correspondence," an organization which is to utterly blot from the face of the earth and the memory of man that most direful of all human and Satanic creations—the secret society.

" The Bureau " has decreed that the Mason must bury his trowel; that the day of rest has come to the Ancient Order of United Workmen; that the Redmen must be converted into negroes; that the Modern Woodmen must come out of theForest; that the Odd Fellows must cease being so unique; that " taps " have been sounded upon the G. A. R. for the last time; and that the College Fraternity goat will be duly hanged at the next unlocking of the "Bureau."

We will attempt to place a small-sized taper of enlightenment upon the basswood cover of the "Bureau."

We wish to speak only of the College Fraternity.

Anti-College Fraternity cranks have existed since "time was." Of the genus crank the anti-Fraternity species is the most inexcusably diabolically cranky crank; he is a fungus growth upon the symmetrically developed tree of college life; he exists in two species—the uninformed and the "sore-head."

The "uninformed" is the man who is in attendance at a college where Fraternities do not exist. He has never come into active contact with their workings, neither does he understand their functions nor methods, yet being impressed that it is his duty to say something and knowing not what else to say he assumes them to be the college department of the lower regions and promptly condemns them.

The "sore-head" is he who attends a Fraterniy college, but upon whom no Frat. bestows the honor of a "spike." This man, wishing to join, but being unable to do so, often sees evils in the system which he must expose. Now this man finds others who are opposed to Fraternities, not because of any intrinsic fault, but chiefly because they have not been deemed worthy of membership.

There is no one quite so inconsistent as this anti-Frat. crank. Let this man be "spiked" by a Fraternity man and he can not consent quickly enough; he is willing to sustain the severest shocks from the most powerfully developed goat if he is but permitted to have his name inscribed upon the chapter roll, and to taste the sweets of "Grecian" culture.

The "secrets" of a Fraternity are such in name only; everyone knows the object of the Fraternity, and even its Greek motto and awful ritual are not always sacred to the initiated.

The benefits of a college Fraternity are manifold. The chapter is composed of men of kindred minds and aspirations. Care is taken that the members are developed symmetrically. The Fraternity is the patron of letters, oratory, society and religion.

The old-time arguments against these institutions are exploded. "By their fruits ye shall know then." When we recall that Pres. Harrison, Secretary Foster, Pres. Ballentine of Oberlin, Moderator Young of the General Assembly, our own Dr. Roberts, and a host of other men of marked integrity have been, and are, loyal Fraternity men, we may at least conclude that not all college Fraternity men are totally depraved knaves.

R. H. C. '93.

COLLEGE.

AMUSEMENTS FOR THE WEEK.

AUDITORIUM—Theodore Thomas,—Saturday night.
SCHILLER—" Mr. Wilkinson's Widows."
McVICKER's—"Glen-da-Lough."
CHICAGO—Modjeska.
GRAND—"Yon Yonson."
HOOLEY's—"Niobe."
COLUMBIA—"Jane."

The "Spelling Match" netted about $55.

The term closes Wednesday noon, the 21st.

Christmas and New Year's fall on Sunday.

And still those Y. M. C. A. dues are not all paid.

For anything in the line of tooth-brushes, go to French the druggist.

It is reported that the Freshmen still owe the janitor for that barrel of water.

Gymnasium suits and shoes on hand. Best quality at lowest prices. W. E. Ruston.

Next Friday evening the literary societies of the college elect officers for the winter term.

The C. & N. W. Ry. is now heating its passenger cars by steam from the locomotive.

W. D. McNary is at his home in Milwaukee, having been called thither by his mother's illness.

Mr. Ruston has two foot ball suits in stock which are for sale at a bargain. Now is the time to get a good outfit for next season.

Both Minnesota and Wisconsin are advocating the dropping of Northwestern from the foot ball league. They want Chicago in her place.

Dr. Pick delivered a lecture on " Memory " in the college chapel Monday, the 5th, at 4:30 p. m. The lecture was quite instructive and well received.

Old Chris, on his annual tour of inspection, has made the jewelry store of K. S. Buck, Waukegan, the depository of many of his most beautiful gems.

Examinations begin Thursday. We make this announcement in order that the nervous shock may not be too great when you see certain ones study. They are "cramming."

The Christmas numbers of the periodicals have been placed in the reading-room. *Harper's Magazine*, *Puck* and *Judge* are perhaps the most attractive, each in its own line.

It gives us great joy to state that since our last issue G. I. Scofield has passed the crisis of his illness and the attending physicians have said that there is now a strong probability of his recovery.

The Societies received communications from the Faculty last week to the effect that but *one* open meeting a term could be given and that only then could young ladies attend. They are striving very hard to tie us up with red tape.

The method of reporting the standing of the students has suffered still another change. The first grade, passed with honor, has been divided into two, excellent and good. This is a step back towards the old order, when a grade was given each individual.

The Sophs. "did" the Freshmen. And now any evening you happen to be in the college building just take a look in the Sophs.' rooms. You will find in most of them from four to eight of them dressed in foot ball suits, with water, *et cetera*, expecting a Freshman raid.

It's been going the rounds of the college press. It's the same old thing, but we ask your forgiveness, brace our anatomy, and attempt it. "A Freshman knows everything; he has explored the universe. A—Sophomore —has the—wisdom—;" the effort is too much. We are not equal to it.

For high grade imported and domestic furnishings we refer our readers to Schuster, 66 Adams St., Chicago. Line comprises beautiful novelties in scarfings, mufflers, nightrobes, shirts, canes and umbrellas. A hint to your friends that "Schuster's" is the best place for suitable presents will be wise.

The subject of the Union Missionary meeting of the Y. M. C. A. last Tuesday was our favorite, Persia, where our missionary is working. Mr. McNeal read a carefully prepared paper on "Mohammedanism in Persia," and Mr. Spellman read a very interesting letter from Mrs. Wilson, our missionary.

Apropos of some recent fatherly advice from the Faculty to certain individuals:

A little boy, a little smoke,
A little roll between;
A little grave, a little stone:
".Our Darling."—Nicotine.
—*Star*.

The spelling-match for the benefit of the Y M. C. A. was a decided success. Everybody had a delightful time, and the debt of the Association was entirely wiped out. The first match, between Ferry Hall and the Academy, was won by Mr. Flint of the Academy, and the second, between the college and the town, by Mrs. Principal Smith of the town, Mrs. Smith easily defeating Mr. Flint in the finals and winning first prize. In the pronounciation match, which was conducted on a very unique plan, Mrs. Ferry and Mr. McNeal carried off the honors. Prof. Eager delighted the audience with two instrumental numbers, and after it all, in spite of the lateness of the hour, Dr. Seeley invited everybody to the parlors for an informal social. The Y. M. C. A. is to be congratulated on its marked success.

Scene, the Thursday afternoon matinee, under the auspices of the discipline committee. Attraction, "Skips, or Why We Cut Chapel," a farce, by the students' stock company.

G. L. W——n. "I didn't like to ask for an excuse for the boys guyed me so."

Prof. M. B. T——s. "What is the rule in such cases made and provided, Professor?"   -

Prof. M——l. "In Vol. XXII., Chapter 65, Section 14, pp. 4567 of the Codified Laws, Rules, Regulations and Suggestions, of Lake Forest University, edition 1891-2, I find, "All absences unexcused above five, shall go over to the account of the next term."

The Trustees have passed the following resolutions:—

"Whereas, since our last meeting Mr. Jacob Beidler, our honored trustee and our generous benefactor has completed the house built by him for occupancy by the Jacob Beidler, Professor of the Physical Sciences and has handed it over to the University for use. We desire to make special acknowledgment of this gift and to express our hearty gratitude to him for this valuable addition to the University property. The house is large, commodious, convenient and beautiful. It has been built with great care and at large outlay. Mr. Beider has spared no expense in material and in labor to make the house worthy of the name of his beloved son John Beidler, who, born December 16, 1859, died July 22, 1881, as he was entering upon his strong, young manhood.

The Trustees believe that this beautiful and useful building will be a memorial that in his son's name will long bless the world.

In recording this special expression of gratitude to Mr. Beidler the Trustees desire to make mention of Mr. Beidler's devoted interest to the University, continued through so many years, and of the repeated gifts, amounting to $90,000 which have done so much to lay permanent and broad foundations for an Institution whose one purpose is to be good.

TOWN TOPICS.

Mr. and Mrs. Dennison have been visiting at Mr. Charles Durand's.

The marriage of Mr. E. S. Wells, whose engagement was announced in the last STENTOR, takes place to-day, Tuesday, at Springfield, Ill.

Mr. F. E. Hinckley and family will shortly return to their home in Lake Forest. Mr. Hinckley has sold his Chicago home, with a view to residing permanently in Lake Forest.

The funeral services of Mrs. Robinson, the mother of Mrs. Fauntleroy, took place Friday morning at Mr. Fauntleroy's. The interment was at Graceland Cemetery. Mrs. Robinson died very suddenly of heart disease, Tuesday, December 6, while engaged in conversation.

The burning of Mr. Wm. Henry Smith's house, west of the track, again emphasizes the need of an organized fire-department. The buiding, which Mr. Smith had bought but a short time previously was a total loss, the insurance being little or nothing. Mr. Smith will probably rebuild next spring.

At the last meeting of the city council, the mayor was ordered to appoint a committee of citizens to look into the question of fire protection for the city of Lake Forest. It is to be hoped that this committee, encouraged by the willing support which the students have offered, will at least make it *possible* for Lake Forest to have protection against fire.

Lake Forest was well represented at the Columbian Bazaar which was held last week at the palatial home of Mrs. Potter Palmer.

Mrs. F. C. Farwell had charge of the booth of Turkey, and among those who assisted her appear the names of Mrs. Shirley V. Martin and Miss Julia Day. Among the others there, who either live in Lake Forest or make Lake Forest their home for a part of the year, were: Mrs. Larned, Mrs. Moss, Mrs. W. H. Hubbard, Miss Warren, Miss Day and Miss Poole.

WE MAY GET THE TELESCOPE.

It may surprise some of the STENTOR readers to learn that the great Yerkes telescope may possibly come to Lake Forest. When it was learned that the telescope could not be located in or around Chicago on account of the smoke and impure atmosphere, various schemes were suggested, one of which was that an island for the telescope should be built in the lake. Several real estate speculators offered inducements for it to be located in the respective towns in which they were interested, the most favorable of which were Morgan Park and Hinsdale. But Pres. Harper, of Chicago University, thought that Lake Forest was the place for the instrument, for two reasons: 1st. The high situation of Lake Forest, which also renders it entirely free from all the soot and dirt of Chicago. 2nd. It would be near an educational institution. In accord with this wish, Pres. Harper, about a week ago, asked Dr. McClure if it would be possible for the telescope to come to Lake Forest.

Since then, the citizens have signified not only their willingness but their desire to give the Chicago University their choice of Lake Forest property, with the exception of the Lake Forest park. This park would be entirely spoiled by the great buildings.

Thus it may readily be seen how near Lake Forest is to getting the great telescope. About 20 acres of land is necessary for the building and its appurtenances. The main building, which contains the great telescope, will be 125 feet square and 100 feet high, while there will be several smaller, although large telescopes in buildings round about. Of course there will be other buildings for the professors and astronomers. The cost of the whole plant, including the telescope, will be $500,000.

The telescope, which will have a lens 40 inches in diameter,—4 inches larger than the Lick telescope, and with 25 per cent. more magnifying power—will be 75 feet long, and its dome will be 80 feet in diameter. The machinery will be operated by electricity.

FERRY HALL

Mr. S——m's headquarters are in the oak chair in the hall.

Mrs. Greenlees, nee Lizzie Smith, has gone to her home in Australia.

Some of the College girls enjoyed the pleasure of hearing Joe Jefferson in Rip Van Winkle.

Miss Zona Gale, of Portage, Wis., also of U. of W., '94, was the guest of Miss Rogers a short time ago.

Miss Helen Decker is at her home in Evansville, Ind., continuing her study of vocal and instrumental music.

We are glad to learn that Mrs. Thornton has returned to her home at Amherst, Mass., very much improved in health.

Miss Charlotte Liese was called home Dec. 8th, because of the dangerous illness of her grandmother. Miss Liese has the sympathy of all the girls.

Miss Francis Patrick, '92, who has been with her brother in Duluth, Minn., the past three months, was with us Wednesday and Thursday. She has now returned to her home in Marengo, Ill.

The Faculty sent a notice to the Aletheians a short time ago informing them that the other two College Societies are permitted to have open meetings but *once* a term and *only* on such occasions are the young ladies allowed to go above the first floor of the College. The girls, accordingly, sent word to Prof. Locy that they had been forbidden going to his recitation room. Prof. Locy took the responsibility on himself of permitting them to go and before recitation began the Prof. made the remark, " Faculty's mistake, Faculty's treat."

Refreshing table talk in the Sem.:
First Sem.—" Is the exam. list posted yet?"
" No, not yet."
First Sem.—" When will it be?"
" Next Monday, probably."
First Sem.—" Oh de-ear-r! Not till *then!* I know I shall have to stay till the very last for that old Latin, and then I can't get home till *Wednesday night.*"
Second Sem.—" Where do you live?"
First Sem.—" In Clinton. I wish I was a Senior or Junior."
Senior—" Don't you though! I'm going home Saturday (if I get out of Economics.)
Second Sem.—" What happens if we don't pass?"
" Another examination in three weeks."
Second Sem.—" I know I shall have to study all vacation and go through all this again at the end of three weeks."
First Sem.—" Are they *very* hard? Do you think they'll be worse than the reviews?"
Third Sem.—" How many questions will they give us?"
" Probably ten or more."
Third Sem.—" We only have five or six in the reviews. Oh! Did you have the impromptu pun in Latin class to-day?"
First Sem.—" No."
Third Sem.—" Why one of the girls thought ' non ' was a new word, and Miss T. innocently remarked, ' No, we haven't met it in the text before, but we've *known* it for some time.' "
First Sem.—" O, yes, I did notice it. Well, I don't care if I do flunk in exams., I'm *not* going to cram. Oh, say, when will you study History? Isn't it awful! Sixty pages for to-

morrow! I'm going to get permission to stay up later to-night. I *must.* I *never* can get through if I don't."
Second Sem.—" It's just awful to have to work this way. I hope the exams. won't be so very hard."
Voice from the far end of the table—"What are you talking about? Oh! the examinations. I know they'll be awful, just awful."

AMONG THE ALUMNI.

H. E. House, ex-'94, spent Sunday Dec. 3rd, here.

Archie Davison, Academy '95, was in town on Dec. 3rd.

T. S. Jackson, '89, of the Chicago bar spent Sunday the 3rd here.

F. M. Skinner, '92, is now on the staff of the Chicago *Daily News.*

G. H. Steele, '91, from Milwaukee, make a flying visit here Monday evening, Dec. 4th.

The Rev. Enos P. Baker, '82, and wife have on account of Mr. Baker's ill health moved from Santa Monica, Cal., to Golden, Colo. Mrs. Baker, formerly Miss Carrie Ordway, graduated here in the same class with Mr. Baker and both are now actively engaged in mission work at the above address. Mr. Baker is a frequent editorial correspondent of the *Worker*, a Presbyterian mission paper published in Philadelphia, Pa.

Victor Hugo's works in French, a splendid edition on heavy paper, in large type, were placed in the library recently. There are thirty volumes, as follows: *Poesis*, sixteen volumes; *Roman*, nine volumes; and *Drame*, five volumes. Also, *Essays and Reviews*, by E. P. Whipple, two volumes; *Studies in Literature, 1789 1877*, by Edward Dowden; and *Black Beauty* and *Geo. T. Angell's Autobiography*, from the American Humane Education Society.

THE CHESS CLUB.

The standing of the members of the Chess Club participating in the tournament was as follows on Saturday evening, December 3rd:

	NAMES	PLAYED.	WON.	LOST.	PER CT.
1	{ Linn	15	15	0	1.000
	{ Lee	3	3	0	1.000
3	Wilson	7	6	1	.857
4	A. B. Burdick	15	12	3	.800
5	N. H. Burdick	15	11	4	.733
6	McNeal	21	13	8	.619
7	McNary	12	7	5	.584
8	C. G. Smith	17	9	8	.529
9	Dr. Seeley	14	6½	7½	.464
10	S. B. Hopkins	13	6	7	.462
11	Prof. Dudley	18	3½	6½	.350
12	{ Ruston	15	5	10	.333
	{ A. A. Hopkins	3	1	2	.333
14	Rossiter	12	2	10	.167
15	Sherman	18	1	17	.055
16	Rogers	12	0	12	.000

THE STENTOR.

VOLUME VI.   DECEMBER 20, 1892.   NUMBER 11.

PUBLISHED EVERY WEEK

BY THE

Lake Forest University Stentor Publishing Co.

BOARD OF EDITORS.

F. C. SHARON, '93 . . . . Managing Editor
R. H. CROZIER, '93 . . . . Business Manager
N. H. BURDICK, '93 } . . . . Locals
S. B. HOPKINS, '93 }
L. N. ROSSITER, '93 . . . . Alumni and Personal
B. R. MACHATTON, '95 . . . . Advertising

ASSOCIATE EDITORS.

HARRY GOODMAN, '94 . . . . Athletic Editor
FOREST GRANT, '96 . . . . Staff Artist
DAVID FALES, '96 . . . . Town

Terms—$1.50 per year. Single Copies—10c

————ADDRESS————

STENTOR PUBLISHING COMPANY,

LAKE FOREST, :   :   ILLINOIS.

Entered at the P. O. at Lake Forest, Ill., as second-class matter.

A MERRY CHRISTMAS.

Not a student but feels at this time of year a longing for home and a fond desire to skip examinations and hie him hence. The student probably enjoys the Christmas season to a greater extent than any other species of the human race. The world at large is becoming more intimate with college life. The Glee clubs, foot ball teams, dramatic clubs, etc., that go forth from the Universities now are looked upon as necessary adjuncts of the holiday season. The college student enjoys his brief vacation at Christmas to the utmost and no one begrudges it to him

except some old fogies who have never seen a college. Christmas to a student means not merely the stocking-hanging and the exchange of gifts. It means a release from study, a change of companions and of life for a time. Variety is the spice of life. So no wonder he enjoys it. Sophomores and Freshmen when they reach home will talk grandly of battles and vaguely hint at wonderful feats and larks, but forgive them, dear reader, it is merely their way and they will get over it. Wish them all a Merry Christmas as the STENTOR wishes you one.

THE SOCIETIES' OPEN MEETINGS.

There is a decree of the Faculty stating that each Society can have but one open meeting a term. An "open meeting" means one at which the Society throws open its doors to the general public and offers a special program as a specimen of its work. The two societies in the college have been in the habit for some time of having one or two special features in their programs occasionally and inviting *special* guests among whom are usually some young ladies. Under no circumstances can these be called open meetings. The Faculty have lately confounded these meetings and have decreed that open meetings can be held but once a term and the young ladies can attend that meeting only. We wish to be guided by the Faculty in certain things but we cannot see what right they have to dictate to the societies as to the times when guests may be invited, or as to the guests who may be invited. There is nothing that stimulates a society to good work like the presence of outsiders. Again the societies are not merely literary organizations. Since fraternities are denied us they are *social* as well. And why should they not invite young ladies? It is casting a slight on them as well as on the society to say they can not be invited. The societies have obeyed the Faculty's behests when they ought to be obeyed but the rules are becoming altogether to stringent and approach the high school in dignity. We sadly need a president.

THOSE GYMNASIUM THIEVES.

The Chicago highwaymen are not abroad in Lake Forest but our own Gymnasium is becoming worse than Chicago's thoroughfares. All this year it has been apparent that a very expert system of thievery has been going on in the Gym. and things are coming to such a pass that something should be done. Numbers of the boys have had money taken from their clothes in the dressing rooms when they were upstairs or in the tank. A member of a visiting foot ball team lost five dollars in that way. It is so now that it is not safe to leave anything for a few minutes, and the latest is, that some overcoats have been stolen! How the thief or thieves have managed to withhold their identity so completely is a mystery. It seems to us that very little effort is made either on the part of the students themselves to stop this work. It is getting to be a serious matter and one which will work an injury to the schools. The students should take some action.

THE COLLEGE GREEK PLAY.

We notice that Beloit Sophomores gave the annual Greek play last week in their new science hall. The play was "Alkestis" and was splendidly rendered in English, the translation being made by the performers. The costuming was said to be very true to life. We see accounts every year of plays given in the eastern colleges, also in Ann Arbor, in Madison, in Beloit, and they are given well too. Why shouldn't Lake Forest have her Greek or Latin play with the rest of them? We have excellent Greek scholars here, a splendid professor and everything for staging a play. Something of the kind was contemplated a few years ago. What has become of it? Not only would it stimulate a love for the classics but would arouse interest in the drama and show us the extent of our talent. Let the Sophomore class turn its attention from "scraps" and win immortal fame by introducing this custom.

Students are hardly to blame entirely for the destruction of the reading room table. It had fought a good fight and simply died of old age. From expressions heard students will do nothing toward a new University reading room,

TO RETRIEVE A FELON.

"Tomorrow will be Christmas but it does not seem so. I couldn't bear the thought of staying up if it wasn't for your being here too, Ellery."

Vincent Cole, the speaker, was one of two young men who were spending the Christmas recess at the old college building in Baymouth while every one else had gone home to Christmas joys.

Vincent Cole was staying it out in Baymouth not because he had no home, but because that home was closed to all its former happiness. His mother had died before he came to college, and only two months before that Christmas Eve his father had passed beyond the grave. Vincent had no near relatives, and there were no others to whom he cared to go.

Ellery Channing was supposed to be staying at Baymouth during the recess from choice. I say supposed, for in reality no one knew much about Ellery's affairs. He had come to Baymouth with entrance papers from a high school in New York. He seemed to have plenty of money to meet his bills, and although the faculty had questioned him somewhat as to his antecedents he had never said much. His face was a recommendation owing to its frank and open look, and his entrance papers recorded an excellent standing at the New York school. The young man had made a good record at college from the start. There had been no further questions asked.

Vincent Cole and Ellery had fallen together as room-mates by one of those chances that no one ever attempts to explain. All through Vincent's troubles over the death of his father Ellery proved himself a friend that Vincent could have ill dispensed with. The lives of the two young men had become linked together, but even in their intimacy Ellery had never uttered a syllable to Vincent about his own life previous to his coming to Baymouth. Vincent respected his friend too much ever to ask any questions. People at Baymouth recognized in Ellery a straight-forward, earnest

fellow of bright mind and noble character. He was not only a leader in his classes but also on the athletic field and in the general life of the college. Modest but manly, his worth was its own voucher. Vincent Cole was less a leader in athletics, but in other respects he was as popular as Ellery Channing. The two young men were always pointed out as among Baymouth's best fellows.

"Well," said Ellery, in response to his companion's remarks, "there will be a good many little hearts gladdened to-night by old Santa Claus. You and I can imagine ourselves back in the sixes and sevens and be happy in forgetting."

"I would like to be back in the old Santa Claus days in reality, but Santa Claus is a myth, and all the good things seem in danger of becoming relegated to the same category. There seems sometimes to be little left that is really true in this big world. In our youth there were so many bright and beautiful Santa Clauses—good deacons that later experiences proved to be painfully bad, pretty Sunday-school teachers whose words we used to drink in and who turned out to be wretched flirts as we grew up, so many fine sermons that none but the little folks ever believed in. Why, look here," continued Vincent, taking up a copy of the morning paper from the table, "columns on columns of crime, almost a page on heresy trials, a celebrated Sabbatarian in in New York accused of bribing city officials —can it be that everyone is bad and deceitful?"

Vincent's companion sat in silence for several seconds after his friend had spoken. His face was troubled, as if the words had struck a tender chord and jarred.

"Vin," said Ellery, while his friend was still glancing over the columns of the paper, "not every one is bad. Not even the old Santa Claus myth is wholly without its truth. Santa Claus may be a lie, but the gladness of giving good things to friends and loved ones is a brilliant fact that shines behind the haze of myth. I should be sorry to believe that there was not more good than had in everything and everyone, even in those criminals whose evil ways the paper recounts. I know it!"

Ellery Channing spoke with more than his usual vehemence and his friend glanced at him curiously.

"I didn't mean to say exactly what I seemed to say, Ellery," said Vincent. "It would be false to what I know of you to say that humanity had not its worth beyond price. While you live, Ellery, I am always reassured in my belief in men and things."

After that Ellery sat so long in silence and the expression on his face was such that Vincent thought he must have hurt his friend by what he had thoughtlessly said.

"Come, old man, a dollar for your thoughts," exclaimed Vincent, cheerily.

Ellery Channing turned in his chair and looked his friend full in the face.

"Do you really ask me what I was thinking, Vin?"

"Certainly, old man. You look as if a thunder cloud had dropped into the room. You didn't ——."

"Vin, I was wondering if I could trust you."

Vincent Cole was puzzled and pained.

"Trust me, Ellery?"

"Yes, trust you with a story I have been tempted a thousand times to tell you, my dear friend—trust you with a story that may make you wish not to know me. Yes, Vin, I will. I am going to tell you the story of my life. You have been the best friend but one I ever had. It is cowardly not to tell you. Have you never wondered who I was and where I came from, Vin?"

"Do I not know you, Ellery," said his friend reproachfully.

"May be you know me now, Vin, but let me tell you," continued Ellery not waiting for Vincent to reply, "I am the adopted son of a counterfeiter, and my adopted father was the dearest friend I ever had. Don't ever judge people by what they seem to be or by their alleged deeds, Vin. There is good—there are

the best things to be found even in the heart of a counterfeiter. Let me tell you. Daniel Stone, the counterfeiter, was the noblest man I ever knew, while the world holds his memory among the worst. That man out of the kindness of his heart took me a waif out of the street, clothed me, cared for me when there was no other—taught me to try to be good and to learn the best things—worked for me, even wrought crime to obtain the money which he devoted to me when I was a child—and most of all, loved me at a time when I was a friendless outcast. Daniel Stone died in prison and his last word was a prayer for me. His last effort was to secure secretly the passage of a letter out of the prison for me telling me where I might find the means deposited in a bank to help me on to manhood. Vin, do you despise me for presuming to be in this college when I am living on the earnings of crime? I would never have done it, but it was his last wish—that I should fit myself to undo the wrongs he had done and be of as much service to the world as he had been harm. Thousands of times I have been tempted to cry out to the world and tell who I am, but his face that was only kind and loveable to me comes before my eyes and his looks beseech me to retrieve his past by using the means he left to fit myself for the good of my fellows. He guarded the secret well. Not a living soul but you, Vin, knows of my connection with him.

"Dear old father Daniel! Do you wonder, Vin, that I know there was goodness in the so-called worst of man? Can I forget the love of a counterfeiter that lifted me out of the gutter and perhaps saved me from a career worse than his own? My only ambition—I swear it, Vin!—is to live to teach the world that God loves even a counterfeiter! I am preparing myself now, with God's help, to declare the riches of His touch and love to men."

Ellery Channing had hastened through the recital of his past scarcely pausing for breath. Vincent Cole had listened as if spell-bound.

For an instant after Ellery had finished he

looked into his friend's eye. There he read only kindliness and sympathy.

"To think, Ellery," said Vincent, "that all these months I have gained comfort from you in my grief when your own was almost greater than mine!"

The rats scampered merrily over the ceiling of the old college building at Baymouth and the winter winds rattled the shutters. Heaven looked down kindly upon that room in the old college hall as Vincent Cole made of his own accord a promise to his friend that the secret of Dauiel Stone's career would be sacredly kept. And the story told by Ellery Channing that Christmas Eve bound the two young men together as were bound David and Johnathañ of old.   WILLIAM E. DANFORTH.

A HISTORY OF JOURNALISM IN LAKE FOREST.

Through the kindness of Professor Halsey, who placed his cosey study and his files of Lake Forest periodicals, a rare collection, at the disposal of the writer, the readers of the STENTOR may get a hasty glimpse of what attempts have been made in the past to find the key note of journalism in "lovely Lake Forest," and travel again over the road that finally led to the founding of the STENTOR.

The first paper published in Lake Forest was the *Lake Forest Gem.* Volume I, Number I of this journal appeared June 1, 1867. It was edited and printed once a month, by Wells C. Lake and William J. Fabian, aged thirteen and sixteen years, who had their printing office on the land near where Mr. Hinckley's private bridge now stands. The *Gem* was a two column folio 4½ x 8 inches. In their editorial greeting they promised to try "to make it as useful and entertaining as possible," and they certainly did succeed in making it a bright little paper. Their subscription price was fifty cents per year and their adver-tisements, of which they had a few, were charged for at the rate of fifty cents per line of six words.

The first three issues contain a continued fairy story, "The Golden Belt," which shows considerable imagination and literary ability on the part of its youthful author.

Beginning with the September number is a continued article, "A Trip to Lake Superior." A short step was made at Oconto, Wis., then a new town. It may be of interest to some to read a few extracts from the description of their visit to this place:

"Oconto is one of the many places where mills are located for the sawing up of pine trees. The mill to which we paid special attention was that belonging to Holt & Balcom."

In one of a series of articles on the "History of the University" in the STENTOR of October 7, 1890, Prof. Halsey has told the story of the *Gem's* demise, it only living six months. Of its editors one, Mr. Fabian, now resides in Evanston; the other, Wells C. Lake, died October 3, 1876. Prof. Halsey has the only complete file of the paper in existence.

With the November, 1867, issue of the *Gem* ended all efforts in the journalistic line until five years latter, when in August, 1862, the ladies issued the first and only number of the *Lake Forest Reporter.* This magazine con-tained twenty pages, 6 x 9½ inches. It was intended to be both a news and literary peri-odical. Editorially it says:

"Our first number is issued for August and will be followed in subsequent monthly as cir-cumstances shall warrant. Of this number we print 5000 copies."

On the last page are the words and music of the "Parting Hymn" of the Ferry Hall class of '72. Following is the first stanza:

"Farewell, our Alma Mater dear
    We leave thy loving care;
Yet not with trembling, not with fear,
    Life's burdens will we bear,
But going forth with precious seed
    We'll sow in life's broad field;
The kindly word and loving deed
    Will rich harvests yield."

We are told that the commencement pro-gram "was excellent in the main." Miss Annie L. Baldwin delivered the English salu-tatory, "The Niche that Belongs to Us," and

Miss Mary F. Benedict the Latin valedictory, "The Supremacy of Thought."

Among other notices is the following:

MARRIED.—In Lake Forest, July 17th, at Lindwood, by Rev. James H. Taylor, Miss Kittie E. Lind, daughter of Hon. Sylvester Lind, and Mr. Samuel C. Orr, of Chicago.

Newspaper enterprise in Lake Forest lay dormant from this time until 1880, a period of eight years. An awakening came in January of this year, when the *Lake Forest Review*, a distinctively literary magazine, was launched upon a career of nearly four years. It was a monthly issued from a printing office, started to give needy students employment, in the basement of the college building, under the management of Frank O. Harding. It contained at first twelve pages, 6¾ x 10 inches, later, in September, 1882, the size of the page was reduced to 6⅓ x 4¾ inches, and it was published only once in two months. In 1881 the printing office passed into the hands of the "University Printing Company," Mr. Harding going to California. The last number was the May-June number in 1883. Announcements of articles were made in that issue which were to have appeared in the September-October number of that year.

Miss Anna Farewell, '80 was editress-in-chief with Misses Josephine L. White, '80, and Lottie E. Skinner, '81, and Paul Bergen, '80, and Enos P. Baker, '82, as associates.

From the editorial column we take the following, thinking it may be appreciated:

"It has recently rained in Lake Forest somewhat. The famous weather 'down in Lincolnshire' which was so forcibly delineated by Mr. Dickens as to make the reader feel damp, was but a feeble effort by the side of the late vagaries of the Lake Forest weather clerk."

In December, 1880, the *Review* announced that its circulation was 1200. In this issue we find a notice of the first joint meeting of the Zeta Epsilou and Athenæan societies, which was held in the college chapel. From the local column of this issue we take the following excellent advice:

"Beware of cards. Many a young man has fallen into the hands of a knave and come within an ace of going to the deuce."

The issue of June, 1881, contains an account of the commencement of that year. Miss Charlotte E. Skinner was the salutatorian and Miss Anna D. Rhea the valedictorian.

The *Review* chronicles the fact that the first exhibition of the literary worth of the Aletheian society was held January 27, 1882.

During its last year, 1882-3, Prof. F. W. Kelsey was at the editorial helm.

The *Review* was the outcome of an attempt to establish in the west a university literary magazine. Throughout its tone was of a high character, and it was always ably edited.

The next attempt to enter the journalistic field was made by Dr. Gregory, Dr. Roberts' predecessor, in April 1886. One issue of the *Lake Forest* appeared in April of that year. It was an eight page paper, about the size of the STENTOR. It was to be managed by the Faculty and devoted to the "Interests of the Lake Forest University." Its career was brief if not brilliant.

It was not until June, 1887, that a paper could be established upon a permanent basis. In that month the STENTOR began its work "for the benefit of our undergraduates and Alumni," which it has so successfully carried on to the present. Under the able management of J. J. Boggs, '88, as editor-in-chief the STENTOR first saw the light. In February, 1888, H. H. Fish established a printing office in the Academy and for a time printed the STENTOR. In 1888-9, A. G. Welch, '89, was editor-in-chief, followed in 1889-90 by J. E. Smith, '90, who resigned in the Spring term remaining at home. In 1890-1, W. E. Danforth, '91, was responsible for the editorials. F. C. Sharon, '93, was elected editor in 1891-2 and is the first upon whom the honor of a re-election has been conferred.

The latest Lake Forest periodical, the *Red and Black*, the offspring of the STENTOR, was started during the fall of the present year and has so far been successful. H. L. Bird, '94, and E. C. Cleveland, '94, are the editors-in-chief.

At some future time we hope to review the work of the STENTOR, dishing up some of its old sauce, which has always been spicy, and telling something of, its organization and management.

N. H. BURDICK.

THE FOOTBALL TEAM AND SEASON REVIEWED.

As we look back on the season just closed we are apt to think it was not a gigantic success. Yet when all things are taken into consideration, we have no cause to complain. We were greatly handicapped by the injuries sustained and the fact that the captain was unable to be on the field every day to coach his men. In the future it would be well to select a captain from among the undergraduates, but Capt. Gallwey did the best he could and there is no question but that he rendered valuable aid. We present a picture of the team in this issue and the following is a list of the men with their positions:

W. B. Hunt, '94, center.
C. Durand, '97, quarter back.
F. A. Hayner, '95, right end.
M. Woolsey, '96, left tackle.
B. R. MacHatton, '95, right half back.
W. D. McNary, '93, left end.
D. H. Jackson, '96, left half back.
D. Williams, P. G., full back.
N.B.W. Gallwey, (capt.) P. G., right tackle.
N. Flint, '97, right guard.
J. A. McGaughey, '96, left guard.
C. Thom, '95; Rogers, '97; C. Everett, '97, and Dickinson, '97, substitutes.

W. B. Hunt, '94, is 6 ft. 2 in. tall, and weighs 190 lbs. This is his second year on the the team, having played substitute last year. He played his position well, and although weak at times was outclassed by no other center in the league.

Charles Durand is 5 ft. 10 in. tall, and weighs 150 lbs. This was his first year on the regu-

lar 'Varsity team, but he played on the second eleven last year. As a quarter-back he has no superiors and to his superb interference is due a large amount of ground gained.

F. A. Hayner is 6 ft. 2 in. tall, and weighs 158 lbs. He played on the team two years and was formerly captain of the West Division High School team. Although not in good physical condition his playing showed dash and a thorough acquaintance with the game.

Marion Woolsey is 6 ft. 2 in. tall, and weighs 192 lbs. This is his second year on the team and he has earned a reputation as a line breaker. His playing is steady and he seldom fails to get his man.

B. R. MacHatton is 5 ft. 9 in. tall, and weighs 164 lbs. This was his first year at the game and he clearly proved that he was made of "foot ball stuff." We have every reason to expect great things of him next year. He is quick and plucky and a good tackler.

W. D. McNary is 5 ft. 10 in. tall, and weighs 171 lbs. This is his third year on the team and up to the time his ankle was hurt he played the most brilliant game of the year. As an end rush he has few superiors, and is also a steady ground gainer.

D. H. Jackson is 5 ft. 7½ in. tall, and weighs 140 lbs. He played substitute on last year's team. His chief strength is in his dodging.

N. B. W. Gallwey is 6 ft. tall, and weighs 175 lbs. This is his second year as captain and he is a good coach. He formerly played on the Princeton team. As a line breaker and tackler he did fair work but was handicapped by lack of practice.

D. Williams is 5 ft. 7 in tall, and weighs 153 lbs. He played half back on the Williams team last year. His work was not up to his average, owing to injuries received the first part of the season. His chief strength lay in his bucking.

Nott Flint is 6 ft. 2 in. tall, and weighs 198 lbs. He played center rush in the only game he played in last year. He is a good guard and distinguished himself especially in the Beloit game.

J. A. McGaughey is 5 ft. 7½ in. tall, and weighs 170 lbs. This was his third year on the team as guard, and he held up his end nobly.

Of the substitutes Thom is 5 ft. 7 in. tall, and weighs 185 lbs. Rogers is 5 ft. 9½ in. tall and weighs 150 lbs. C. Everett is 5 ft. 9 in. tall and weighs 161 lbs. Dickinson is 5 ft. 10 in. tall and weighs 155 lbs. All played in some regular game.

The average height of the team is 5 ft. 10 1-5 in.; the total weight of the team is 2,359 lbs.; the average weight 168½ lbs.

We played five games, won two, lost two and tied one. We shut out our opponents once and were shut out once. We scored 72 points as against our opponents' 52.

As to the financial outcome of the season it can be said that we came out about even. The treasurer was lax in regard to collections otherwise there might be a balance in the treasury. Manager Crozier labored hard and conscientiously for the team's best interest and a great deal of credit is due him for his untiring energies. The task of management is a thankless one and no one can judge fairly of its difficulties until he has been in the position. Although we did not win every game and there was much dissatisfaction at times, yet the team under the circumstances did creditable work.

COLLEGE.

AMUSEMENTS FOR THE WEEK.

AUDITORIUM—Theodore Thomas,—Saturday night.
COLUMBIA—"Jane."
GRAND—"A Trip to Chinatown."
CHICAGO—Hermann.
HOOLEY'S—Digby Bell.
McVICKER'S—Pauline Hall.

" But, *Oh*, what a difference in the morning!"

Merry Christmas.

Have you a slab from the old reading room table to remember it by?

A few days of skating have been put to the best advantage by lovers of that sport.

Prof. Hale, of Chicago University, was out Friday of last week looking over the ground for the telescope.

The air has recently been thick with class "scraps," but at present something seems to have cleared it.

For a first-class shampoo, apply to the Freshmen, but if you want your hair cut, the Sophomores are the people.

The Sophomores and Freshmen have decided to hang up the scissors and the paint-brush and take down the pipe of peace and smoke it.

Last week's indoor ball game resulted 19 to 11 in favor of the town. A second game of five innings resulted 19 to 12 for the town.

It may be interesting to some to know that the wife of M. Ribaut, one of the present French cabinet ministers, was a Ferry Hall girl.

John David Russell, who graduated with the Academy class of '89, and was for a time with '93, has returned home, having spent the summer at Evansville, Ind.

The *Red Cross* and the *National Portrait Gallery*, the latter containing an illustrated account of Cleveland's administration, appeared in the reading room just before the wreck.

The Zeta Epsilon officers for next term are as follows: President, A. W. Doran; vice-president, H. Marcotte; secretary, L. A. Grove; treasurer, Dean Lewis; critic, H. W. Harris; sergeant-at-arms, Coolidge.

Once upon a time, long, long ago, in 1888, there was a scheme started to provide Ferry Chapel with a pipe organ, and a series of entertainments were planned, one of which was given, with this object in view. Where is the organ, and where is the money?

LAKE FOREST UNIVERSITY FOOT BALL TEAM.

Supplement to The Sexton, Dec. 20, 1902

THE STUDENT'S CHRISTMAS DREAM.

The Freshmen have elected officers for next term. Here is the list: President, D. Fales; Vice President, Miss Hopkins; Secretary and Treasurer, F. Grant; Poet, C. Thomas; Historian, A. O. Jackson; Sergeant-at-Arms, D. H. Jackson.

The following magazines and weeklies will be placed in the Athenæan hall for the use of the members of the society, while the University reading room is closed: *Cosmopolitan, Outing, University Magazine, Current Literature, Black and White, London Graphic, Chicago Graphic, Puck, Judge, Life, The Nation,* and *Magazine of Art.*

Thomas Kelley, the fireman of the freight engine which was wrecked here Thursday, Dec. 1st, and who jumped, died at his home in Joliet from the injuries received shortly after being removed from the hospital in Chicago.

Prof. Halsey offers as an elective for next term, open to both Juniors and Seniors, "Constitutional History." He continues "International Law" and that most popular elective, "Current Politics." Prof. Thomas offers a course in "Theism;" Prof. Walter Smith, Kant, "Critique of Pure Reason," and Prof. Stuart "Latin sight Reading," continuing his "Teacher's Course."

The Athenæan Society has chosen the following officers for next term: President, N. H. Burdick; vice-president, L. N. Rossiter; secretary, F. Grant; treasurer, C. G. Smith; critic, R. H. Crozier; sergeant-at-arms, C. W. Sherman.

A students' committee is to be formed to take charge of various matters of interest to the student body, to see about having a University button, a new reading room, order in the building, and other things of which we stand in need, and to act as a go-between between faculty and students. F. C. Sharon will represent the Athenæan on this committee, and E. L. Jones, the Zeta Epsilon.

The following new books have been placed in the library recently: " Tess of the D'Urbervilles," by Thomas Hardy; "The Death of Oenone, Akbar's Dream, and Other Poems," by Alfred Tennyson "; "Records of Tennyson, Ruskin, Browning," by Anne Thackeray Ritchie; " Decimal Classification and Relative Index," by Melvil Dewey, and the Twelve numbers of Annalen der Physik und Chemie for 1892.

The periodicals sold at auction to members of the Athenæan Society will be kept on file in its hall until the University reading room is refurnished. The Athenæans will in this way still have access to nearly all the reading room papers, and will suffer no inconvenience from the vandalism of some of the students. It is also thought that the Athenæan reading room will be kept open even after the University room is opened again.

It seems to have been forgotten or else never generally known, that the editor of the Chicago *Herald* established in Lake Forest the " Chicago *Herald* Scholarships." The conditions were that each competitor was to write during the year one newspaper editorial of 400 words, one contribution to some literary magazine or paper and one lot of reported items of from 600 to 800 words. We do not know, but presume the scholarship is still offered,

The second meeting of the Chicago Alumni was held in room 39, Athenæum Building Wednesday evening, December 14. The committee on constitution made its report which was accepted, and the constitution they presented adopted. The name is to be the Lake Forest College Club of Chicago. One full years' work in the college entitles to membership. The regular meeting of the club is to be on the first Wednesday evening of each month. The following officers were elected: President, A. C. Wenban; vice-president, J. H. McVay; secretary, F. M. Skinner; treasurer, G. W. Wright. The official organs of communication are to be the STENTOR and *Red and Black*.

The members of the Chess Club ranked as follows after Saturday's games in the tournament:

		PLAYED.	WON.	LOST.	PER CT.
1.	J. A. Linn	27	26½	½	.981
2.	A. B. Burdick	18	14	4	.777
3.	G. S. Wilson	15	11	4	.733
4.	N. H. Burdick	22	14	8	.636
5.	E. H. McNeal	24	14	10	.583
6.	C. G. Smith	20	11	9	.550
7.	S. B. Hopkins	21	10	11	.476
8.	W. D. McNary	15	7	8	.466
9.	Dr. Seeley	14	6½	7½	.464
10.	Prof. Dudley	13	5½	7½	.423
11.	L. N. Rossiter	18	5½	12½	.302
12.	W. E. Ruston	17	5	12	.294
13.	F. C. Rogers	21	3	18	.143
14.	C. W. Sherman	24	3	21	.125

The tournament will extend about four weeks into next term.

Early last week the dilapidated old table in the reading room was completely demolished. The result was accomplished gradually, all classes participating in the work, which required several days for its completion. The discipline committee of the faculty, sometime after the remains had been janitorially removed, decided that those who had done the deed were vandals, and voted to close the reading room to everybody until the students agree to refurnish it at their own expense, only those periodicals being accessible now which were sold at auction by the librarian early in the term. It is to be hoped that the vandals will do the right thing and not let the students suffer long for lack of light reading matter.

There will probably be no more "class scraps" in Lake Forest this year. The climax was reached last Monday night, when the Freshmen assembled en masse in College Hall to retaliate on the Sophomores for the other time. They found only seven victims, presenting each one with a vigorous shampoo and using a lavish amount of paint for decorative purposes. In the meantime, the Sophs. rooming out had been assembled, but judiciously refraining from attacking the assembled Freshmen, they waited until the leader and two other town Freshmen were on their way home, waylaid them, and deprived the leader J. A. McGaughey, of his long, highly-prized, bushy, black moustache. Prof. Halsey says this is the worst piece of hazing Lake Forest has seen for over fifteen years.

Exchange items often become so mixed up in their tour about the country as to be unre-cognizable. We give a good example below, taken from the Columbia *Spectator:*

My second famous note was published in the *Spectator* in its original form as follows:

"There are 2,000 matriculated students at Columbia, thirty of whom are Yale graduates. Foot ball is very popular this year, and very curiously six members of the eleven come from Indiana."

It is hardly necessary for me to do more thon submit for inspection some of the remarkable statements which were the offspring of this innocent remark. For six months I read and read them over and over again in the improved and revised additions until my head grew dizzy. Here are some of the extracts from the exchanges of that time:

"There are 20,000 students at Columbia, thirty of whom have played on the Yale foot ball team. The eleven will only play in Indiana this year."—*Daily Husler*, October 15.

"Columbia will play Yale this year with over 200,000 men on her foot ball team; many of whom are matriculated Indians."—*Harvard Bamboo*, October 17.

The climax was reached in the following note in the *Yale Current*, October 20:

"Over 2,000,000 Indians came to Columbia this year to play fool ball; they are very popular and it is hoped will soon matriculate at Yale."

TOWN TOPICS.

THEY ALL FAVOR A CLUB-HOUSE.

Every town of any importance now possesses its club-house, in which dances, receptions, dinners, lectures and social gatherings generally are held. Highland Park, our neighbor, has recently dedicated a new five thousand dollar club-house fitted up in the most modern style with parlors, reception room, dining room, dancing hall or lecture hall. etc. People down there are going to enjoy themselves. No place needs a club-house more than Lake Forest. The Art building does not fill the bill. If a club could be formed, a suitable fee charged for membership with annual dues, it would be a pleasant place for the younger members to pass their leisure time, while the older ones would enjoy the numerous receptions, dinners, etc. Apropos of this the STENTOR obtained opinions from several representative men.

Mr. Calvin Durand: I don't think you will get the people out. It is bad enough now for any gentleman after returning from business, to leave his family to go and see even a neighbor. I would like to see a club-house, however, and I believe the time is coming for one. I think a public hall, which would be wholly under the control of the townspeople, where entertainments and the like could be given, is needed.

Mr. Tuttle: I am in favor of a certain kind of a club. Of course, every one has a different idea on such a subject. I should like to see a Country Inn, a house where rooms and simple meals could be furnished to gentlemen friends of the citizens who come up to spend Sunday, and a place wholly under the control of the citizens. I think such an inn is needed, and would be a success financially. I don't think tennis courts and athletic grounds are needed. Large grounds would be too much work and expense to be worth while.

Mr. Sydney Taber: Of such a club as the Country Club at Evanston I should favor. I am personally very much in favor of anything that affords opportunities for tennis. Such a club would need to be very carefully managed; it could not be set on its feet at once. It is a sign of evolution in any town, and in a town like Lake Forest is sure to come sooner or later.

Prof. McNeill: Personally I should like to see a club. It would be a very good thing, although, of course, any wild management would spoil it. I think there are enough permanent citizens, aided by the summer residents to make it a success, though, perhaps, the item of expense would keep some away.

Mr. Aldrich: I would like to see one, but I have a little doubt as to whether there would be enough members to support it. There so few each member would have a great load of expense and debt. I would like very much to see a club with good athletic grounds.

Mr. M. T. Scudder, Jr.: I should favor such a scheme. Of course no liquors would

be sold there. The idea of having rooms for people to stay over night is a good one.

Mr. E. J. Warner: I have never thought much about such a thing. I would not, of course oppose any project of that kind. There was some talk of having a club building where the old hotel now stands, which would be a good thing for the looks of the town.

FERRY HALL.

Four new Sems. next term.

Misses Ada Barker, Dora Franklin, and Jorgensen will not return next term.

We had the pleasure Wednesday evening of listening to a very interesting paper on "Ideals" bp Mrs. Ralston.

Some of the Seniors had a delightful evening Tuesday, taking tea at Mrs. Holt's, and attending the Art Institute.

Wanted—to know if it is on account of the 'Cad's meekness' that they were not represented in last week's edition.

Miss Jeanie Smith, '92, on her return from Girard, Kas., where she has been visiting her sister, Mrs. Selby Vance, '85, spent Sunday with us.

The art exhibit given by Mrs. Seeley and Mrs. Mallory last Friday afternoon was a privilege for all lovers of art. The parlors were filled with the most beautiful specimens of embroidery and decorated china, and townspeople and students were delighted with what they saw. Mrs. Seeley's work especially deserves special mention. A pillow of roses and a table cover of sweet peas were exquisite. They will be on exhibition at the World's Fair. A tapestry representing Autumn, painted by Mrs. Mallory, was very fine. It sold recently for fifty dollars. Miss Robinson poured tea, and Mrs. Seeley, chocolate. Everyone voted a most enjoyable afternoon.

Thursday evening the University Club met with Dr. and Mrs. Seeley. Among the guests of the evening were Mr. and Mrs. Fales, Mr.

Harry Durand, Miss Harriette Durand and the Senior class. After carrying out the following program in the chapel the club adjourned to Dr. and Mrs. Teeley's parlors, where the rest of the evening was spent socially. As souvenirs of the evening we have very unique pen and ink programs prepared by Professor Stevens.

PROGRAM.

Duet—Symphonie No. 1,	- -	Haydn
Misses Ripley and Searles.		
Romanze—Op. 156, (Left hand alone),	-	Spindler
Miss Sizer.		
Saynoi,	- - - -	Selina
Mrs. Hester.		
La Tilense,	- - -	Roff
Miss Ripley.		
Duet—Serenade,	- - -	Krause
Prof. Eager and Miss Sizer.		
Solo,	- - -	Selected
Mrs. Hester.		
Valua,	- - -	Moskawshi
Prof. Eager.		
Duet—"Silhouetten aus Ungarn,"	-	Hofmann
Prof. Eager and Miss Sizer.		

The following program was very pleasantly carried out at the Pupil's Recital Tuesday evening:

Duet—" Silhouetten aus Ungarn,"	-	Heinrick Hofmann
Prof. Eager and Miss Sizer.		
Zigeunertanz,	- - -	Franz Behr
Katy Hagamann.		
Classical Music,	- - -	George Kyle
Mabel Messenger.		
'Tell, Oh! Tell Me,"	- -	Francis Thome
Bird Huddart.		
a. "Yawcob's Dribulations,"	-	Charles Follen Adams
b. Bugle Song,	- -	Tennyson
Mildred Lyon.		
Sonata—Op. 26, No. 3,	- -	Clementi
Lucia Clark.		
Ball Room Whispers,	- -	Meyer-Helmund
Ada Barker.		
Selection from " Widow Bedott,"		
(The widow retires to a grove in the rear of Elder Sniffle's house.)		
Nellie Dillin.		
Schmetterling,	- - -	Merkel
Martha Hartman.		
Goat Bells,	- - -	G. B. Allen
June Brett.		
Sonata—No. 1, C. Major,	- -	Mozart
Florence Tidball.		

' Mary Alice Smith,"	-	James Whitcomb Riley
Sadie Davis.		
Romanze—Op. 156, No. 1 (Left hand alone),	-	Spindler
Miss Sizer.		
Duet—"Silent Night,"	- - -	Nevin
June Brett and Bird Huddart.		

WHERE OUR ALUMNI ARE.

1879.

B. Fay Mills, evangelistic work, San Francisco, Cal., and Omaha.

1880.

Rev. Paul D. Bergen, mission work, China.

Mrs. Anna Farwell-De Koven, New York.

Rev. F. S. Forbes, pastor, Midland, Mich.

Rev. W. O. Forbes, pastor, Albina, Ore.

Mrs. Josephine White-Bates, Monterwy, Cal.

J. Kahout, lawyer, Chicago.

Geo. M. Entriken, with the Wabash R. R. Co. at Omaha, Neb.

Elmer Stearns, Kern Co. Land Co., Cal.

E. D. Stiles, World's Fair Transportation Co., Chicago, Ill.

John D. Pope, state senator, Friend, Neb.

1881.

Frank Jewett, studying medicine, Philadelphia, Pa.

H. M. Stanley, librarian, Lake Forest University.

Mrs. Charlotte Skinner–Thurston, La Grange, Ill.

Mrs. Anna Rhea-Wilson, mission work, Tabreez, Persia.

1882.

Rev. Enos P. Baker, pastor, Golden, Col.

Mrs. Carrie Ordway-Baker, Golden, Col.

Mrs. Etta Vaughn-Groeneveld, Butte City, Mont.

Arthur D. Wheeler, with Williams, Holt & Wheeler, attorneys, Chicago, Ill.

1883.

Mrs. E. Gardner-Halsey, Lake Forest, Ill.

Kenneth J. S. Ross, Spokane Falls, Wash.

Rev. J. W. Millar, member of faculty of Montana University, Deer Lodge, Mont.

Will Frey, lumber merchant, Freeport, Ill.

R. S. Davis, cashier Cox's bindery, Chicago.

1884.

Rev. N. D. Hillis, pastor, Evanston, Ill.

Mrs. I. Badger-Kelsey, Ann Arbor, Mich.

Mrs. Reid-Holt, Lake Forest, Ill.

H. H. Clark, partner in the Fredonia Linseed Oil and Paint Co., Fredonia, Kan.

Mr. Hotchkiss, superintendent Associated Press, Kansas City.

A. E. Jack, chair of English, Lake Forest Academy.

Mr. St. Pierre, mission work, Oroomiah, Persia.

W. W. Wirt, principal High School, Sandwich, Ill.

E. P. Hill, pastor Westminster church, Minneapolis, Minn.

1885.

Miss Anne E. Anderson, Lake Forest, Ill.

Rev. Thos. E. Barr, pastor, Kalamazoo, Mich.

Mrs. Bertha Balch-Barr, Kalamazoo, Mich.

Miss E. E. Lamson, teaching in High School, Atlantic, Iowa.

A. C. Neill, lawyer, Chicago.

· Rev. W. S. Shields, pastor Presbyterian church, West Point, Iowa.

H. W. Sutton, public school, Bonfield, Ill.

Rev. S. F. Vance, pastor Presbyterian church, Girard, Kan.

A. C. Wenban, member of the Chicago bar.

R. Porterfield, real estate business, Seattle, Wash.

1886.

Rev. W. E. Bates, pastor, Winnebago, Wis.

Rev. B. D. Holter, pastor, Prospect Park, Pennsylvania.

Miss S. Louise Mitchell, teaching at Duluth, Minn.

Miss M. E. Taylor, chair of Latin, Ferry Hall faculty, Lake Forest, Ill.

Rev. Geo. E. Thompson, pastor, Wilmington, Del.

1887.

Rev. John Hammond, pastor, Bangor, Pa.

Rev. G. D. Heuver, pastor, Milwaukee, Wis.

Mrs. Mary King-Armstrong, Winnebago, Illinois.

G. C. Findley, editor *Labor Herald*, Washington, Ind.

J. W. Dowdy, mission work, Yamaguchi, Japan.

C. E. McGinnis, pastor Presbyterian church, Lansingburg, N. Y.

1888.

Miss Mary Anderson, cashier in Anderson's dry goods store, Lake Forest, Ill.

Sidney A. Benedict, chemist in paper mill at Kimberly, Wis.

John J. Boggs, student McCormick Seminary, Chicago.

Rev. L. J. Davies, mission work, China.

Rev. C. H. French, pastor, Scotland, S. D.

Rev. W. N. Johnston, pastor Presbyterian church, Geneseo, Ill.

Rev. E. E. Nourse, studying abroad.

E. S. Wells, Jr., with the Chicago *Daily News.*

W. G. Wise, with the Chicago *Daily News.*

Miss Jane S. Wilson, chair of Greek and Latin at the Ossining Institute, Sing Sing, N. Y.

1889.

Keyes Becker, editorial writer on leading publicalion in Ogden, Utah.

Miss Anna Davies, post graduate course in the Chicago University.

Miss Carrie Griffin, teaching at Springfield, Ohio.

T. S. Jackson, in the law business, Chicago,

Miss May Horton, teacher, in Alcott School, Lake Forest, Ill.

Walter N. Halsey, teaching at Plattsmouth, Nebraska.

B. M. Linnell, attending Rush Medical College, Chicago.

Miss Mary L. Phelps, instructor at Ferry Hall, Lake Forest.

Grant Strob, pastor, Del Norte, Col.

Miss Harriet S. Vance, Eau Claire, Wis.

Edgar Wilson, on account of ill health, is at his father's home in Hopkinton, Iowa.

Rev. G. A. Wilson, pastor, Holyoke, Mass.

A. G. Welch, principal Elgin Academy, Elgin, Ill.

1890.

J. Anderson, surveyor, Lake Forest, Ill.

Miss Abbie E. Goodale, Wheelock Industrial School for Orphan Indian Girls, Indian Territory.

Rev. W. F. Lewis, pastor, Wilmington, Del.

Miss Mary MacNair, teacher, Crystal Lake, Illinois.

Miss Gracia G. Sickles, instructor of Latin in the Geneseo Collegiate Institute, Ill.

Miss Grace A. Stanley, teaching in the Alcott School, Lake Forest, Ill.

Mrs. Hobart Chatfield-Taylor, Chicago, Ill.

S. S. Durand is in business with his father in Chicago. He makes his home in Lake Forest.

H. C. Durand, with H. C. & C. Durand, of Chicago. He also lives in Lake Forest.

1891.

Miss Mary A. Davies, teaching in the Nashville College for Young Ladies, Nashville, Tenn.

Miss Florence S. Raymond, teaching in Dixon, Ill.

Miss Florence S. Phelps, teaching in Elida, Illinois.

W. H. Humiston, studying music in Chicago. Is organist of the First Congregational church.

Mrs. Juliet Rumsey-Stroh, Del Norte, Col.

W. E. Danforth, reporter on Chicago Tribune.

E. F. Dodge, reading law, Chicago, Ill.

J. H. McVay, studying medicine at the Homœopathic College of Chicago.

H. H. Davis, McCormick Seminary, Chicago.

J. S. Sutton, McCormick Seminary, Chicago.

N. B. W. Gallwey, McCormick Seminary, and residing at Lake Forest.

P. W. Linebarger, Spanish secretary to Hobart Chatfield-Taylor.

Sartell Prentice, Jr., studying theology at Princeton, N. J.

G. H. Steele, civil engineer with C. & N. W. R. R., with headquarters in Milwaukee.

J. E. Smith, La Crosse, Wis.

1892.

F. M. Skinner, with Chicago *Daily News*.

W. E. Pratt, with the Cleveland Rolling Mill Co., at Chicago.

L. E. Zimmermann, with Edmund B. McClanahan, real estate dealers, Waukegan, Ill.

W. B. Brewster, attending McCormick Seminary, Chicago.

M. McLeod, attending McCormick Seminary, Chicago.

W. R. Dysart, St. Paul, Minn.

Miss Agnes Brown, teaching at Racine, Wisconsin.

W. H. Matthews, attending McCormick Seminary.

E. S. Chaffee, same.

C. W. Irwin, same.

G. W. Wright, same.

W. F. Love, engaged to be married, attending McCormick Seminary.

A. S. Wilson, studying medicine in the hospital at Dunning, Ill.

W. D. McMillan, grain business, Fort Worth, Texas.

D. H. Williams, chair of mathematics, Lake Forest Academy.

A. M. Candee, superintendent of a department in the Radford Iron and Pipe Works at Anniston, Ala.

G. W. King, pickle business, Joliet, Ill.

E. G. Wood, teaching in the Woodstock Academy, Ill.

S. W. Goodale, at Amherst College.

Miss Charlotte Underwood, teaching at Racine, Wis.

J. F. Farris, reporter on the *Occident*, San Francisco, Cal.

W. Farris, attending college at the Leland Stanford, Jr., University, Cal.

H. D. Stearns, post graduate course, Leland Stanford, Jr., University, Cal.

W. R. Everett, lawyer, Chicago, Ill.

———

OGDEN, UTAH, Dec., 1892.

To those readers of the STENTOR who have always lived within shouting distance of civilization, the word "Utah" has a barbaric, polygamous sound that is the result of early training and schoolroom bias. There was a time when life among the Mormons was a dangerous venture for a Gentile, and few there were who tried it. But "tempora mutantur," as a Sophomore would say. The Gentile is now as safe in Utah as he is in Illinois. He has brought with him the essentials of civilization, and public schools, churches, libraries, newspapers, and free speech are matters of course here now, although they had to fight for a foothold.

All these things are having a salutary effect upon the Mormon, whose dense ignorance (which has been his chiefest sin) is becoming less and less apparent.

This Salt Lake Valley is a beautiful region. Ogden is about ten miles east of the Great Salt Lake, and thirty-seven miles north of Salt Lake City. Many of you doubtless think that Salt Lake City is on the shore of that great inland sodium chloride solution from which the modern Zion derives its name. Nay, not so. It is eighteen miles from the lake.

Never take a summer trip through Utah without stopping to bathe in Salt Lake. It is almost impossible to sink in the water, which is heavy with salt. But you must take care to keep the water out of your eyes and mouth, or perhaps I should say, keep your eyes and mouth out of the water, for it is accompanied by bitter tears and strangulation if it once gets in them. Otherwise the pastime is a most salubrious one.

The population of a western city is a human hash—a little of everything served hot. On Ogden streets one may see the Celestial direct from China, representatives of every European nation from Scandinavian to Italian, the American Indian wrapped in thought and a government blanket, the negro, the cowboy and the Mexican. In fact, there is almost everything excepting the dude. He does not thrive here.

This is a nervous country and the loafers are few, but gambling and drinking are common pursuits, and are looked upon much as matters of course by the community. Public sentiment is very loose regarding public morals. The first saloon I ever saw with a "ladies' entrance" is located in this town.

There are drawbacks to every location, however. The climate here is wonderful, the mountains are a constant source of pleasure, and the country round is fair and fertile. I shall hope to tell you more about Utah and her advantages, at another time.

With undiminished interest in L. F. U. and the STENTOR, I am   yours truly,
                              KEYES BECKER.

———

LATE NEWS.

The Senior class of the Academy has been suspended for three weeks after the holidays on account of refusing to learn a certain lesson.

The Freshmen and Sophomores will this evening indulge in a love feast and "bygones will be bygones." A banquet and reception will be given in the two society halls and the connecting corridor. The two class presidents will preside at the banquet, and among the toasts will be one by Forest Grant on "Reconciliation," and one by J. H. Rice on "Scraps." More in the next issue.

Mr. Ezra J. Warner offers the following prizes for Seniors in Political and Social Science: For the best essay on a given Economic subject a prize of $60; for the second best, $40. The essay shall not contain less than 2500 nor more than 3000 words and the awards will be made by the professors in Political and Social Science. Subject this year: "Shall the high tariff protection policy of the United States be abandoned?"

THE STENTOR.

VOLUME VI.   JANUARY 10, 1893.   NUMBER 12.

PUBLISHED EVERY WEEK
BY THE
Lake Forest University Stentor Publishing Co.

BOARD OF EDITORS.

F. C. Sharon, '93................Managing Editor
R. H. Crozier, '93..............Business Manager
N. H. Burdick, '93 }
S. B. Hopkins, '93 } ....Locals
L. N. Rossiter, '93...........Alumni and Personal
B. R. MacHatton, '95.................Advertising

ASSOCIATE EDITORS.

Harry Goodman, '94...............Athletic Editor
Forest Grant, '96....................Staff Artist
David Fales, '96·.........................Town

Terms—$1.50 per year. Single Copies—10c

——ADDRESS——
STENTOR PUBLISHING COMPANY,

LAKE FOREST, : : ILLINOIS.

Entered at the P. O. at Lake Forest, Ill., as second-class matter.

WE present this issue a. cut of the Chicago University foot-ball team as it appeared in the *Chicago Weekly* a short time since. *The Chicago University Weekly* will this week contain the cut of our team as it appeared in the STENTOR last issue. This is the first time to our knowledge that such exchanges have taken place between Western College journals, and we hope it will not be the last. The most friendly relations have been established between the STENTOR and the *University Weekly*, and we sincerely hope it is but a step toward a higher college journalism.

JANUARY 16 is the date set for the beginning of the base ball training. It is of the utmost importance that candidates should train well this year, neither overdoing it or shirking. Although we have lost some good men, yet it looks as if a successful season was approaching. We will have some strong teams to play against this coming season, and it behooves every man to hustle. We have a thoroughly proven manager and a conscientious and competent captain. Therefore if the candidates will apply themselves early and faithfully, we will have a team that can compete with the best of them.

A GYMNASIUM INSTRUCTOR.

We are at present without an instructor in the Gymnasium. What is to be done about selecting a new one? It is very important that there should be one appointed immediately, as the present term is the one in which Gym. work takes the place of all athletics. Under Mr. Everett's instruction the classes were doing nicely and the systematic training was doing a world of good. Now things are at a stand-still and everyone is awaiting the new instructor. This instructor should be a man who is well versed in anatomy, hygiene and physiology, a good athlete, and old enough to control the boys. Mr. Everett possessed these attributes to a remarkable degree, and we sincerely hope his successor will be as successful. And whoever he is, let us have him quickly.

IN REGARD TO ELECTIVES.

By the present system electives run one term only, and in this way a student gets barely a smattering of the subject. In the East electives run the whole year. A man electing a subject at the beginning of the fall term expects to continue it throughout the whole year. Accordingly students get some good, in fact a great deal of good out of such a system. We do not deny that some good is obtained in a one term elective, but it is easily forgotten, and the student in a year or so only has a vague confused idea of the subject, whereas if he had studied it hard for a year it would be indelibly impressed on his mind. It is perhaps rather late in the season to advocate this, and we do not like to appear as Faculty advisers, nevertheless we desire to see the change, and wish to put forth every effort to obtain it.

TRACK ATHLETICS.

In this issue we present a very able article on training for the track, by Mr. E. R. Baker, one of the best known of Chicago athletes, and also well known here. Track athletics are to a great extent neglected in the West. A few schools, notably University of Illinois, have taken a genuine interest in general athletics, and have turned out some very good track athletes. But in the East, on the other hand, general athletics have a great place, and track athletics stand at the head of them. Each College has its athletic team, as it has foot ball and baseball teams. There is no reason why Western Colleges should not become stronger advo-cates of the cinder track, and there are numerous reasons why this College should not only advocate, but support track athletics. A cinder track around the ball ground would improve the looks of the field and supply a long-felt want. We have good runners here. This has been proven beyond a doubt by the way in which prizes in the city and elsewhere have been carried off by our men. Let the athletic association look into this matter and see what can be done.

FIX UP THE BALL GROUNDS.

The approach of the ball season renders it extremely important that our ball grounds should be put in first-class order. It is not too early to speak of this, as the earlier we are ready the better. The only way to have the grounds fixed, is for the students *to fix them themselves* or to raise a fund and superintend the work. There is no use talking, the grounds must be fixed. Champaign last spring spoke of the grounds as "a mud-hole on the side of a hill." Of course Champaign was at the time laboring under a load of prejudice and defeat, but nevertheless the fact is patent to all that a field in the shape it was last year is not a fit place to play base ball on. Champaign *students* with spades and shovels made their grounds; Evanston *students* raised the money for their stand and grounds. Lake Forest students ought to do the same. It should be left to the athletic association to decide which plan is to be adopted, and every student should lend a hand with a will. The towns-people, the faculty, the trustees, will all be glad to see the students helping themselves, and will be all the more ready with their support when it is asked.

THE PROPOSED UNION WITH CHICAGO UNIVERSITY.

Chicago University wants Lake Forest to join it! This statement has caused many tongues to wag recently, both for and against, and they are still wagging. Briefly stated, the points are as follows: Chicago University is very desirous of forming a large University on the Oxford or Heidelberg plan. She wants Lake Forest to become a part of this system. President Harper therefore submitted to the Lake Forest Faculty seventeen propositions regarding the union. These were then laid before the Lake Forest Trustees, who appointed a committee to meet a similar committee from the Chicago University Trustees. This large committee then appointed a sub-committee, consisting of President Harper and Mr. Ryerson from Chicago, and Dr. McPherson and Dr. McClure from Lake Forest.

Although the scheme is regarded by some as very plausible and likely to be put through, it is now regarded by those who best know, entirely impossible. The first proposition by which all land and buildings belonging to Lake Forest will be turned over, at least nominally, to Chicago, is utterly incompatible with our charter, as is also the last proposition in regard to the course of instruction. Chicago at first proposed turning all her under-graduate work over to Lake Forest, said that the government, faculty, etc., of Lake Forest would be left as it is, and offered

to place the Yerkes telescope here if such an alliance was formed. Since then, however, President Harper has decided to have a college in Chicago also, so we might not get all the under-graduate work. There is strong talk also of Rush Medical withdrawing and forming with the other Chicago medical schools a great medical university. Taking it all in all, things are in a very chaotic state. One thing is certain: There will be no combination on the propositions originally offered. One of the Chicago trustees himself said that he did not see how Lake Forest could think of accepting for a moment. Whatever is done, will be done for the best interests of Lake Forest. Evanston has not yet been approached on the subject. If she is, it is very certain she will not accept.

TRAINING FOR THE TRACK.

POINTS THAT SHOULD BE OBSERVED.

Before attempting to discuss the question of track-training, is might be well to ask what is the object of such training.

To develop the body and train the mind to the fullest extent in order that the athlete may be able to win races, is undoubtedly the object to be attained.

I will not endeavor in this short paper to point out the benefit to be derived from a systematic course of training, but will take it for granted that it is admitted to be sufficient to repay the ambitious aspirant even if he fails to acquire distinction as a runner.

Before beginning to train the novice should consult a physician and satisfy himself that his heart and lungs are sound. A man who has once been thoroughly developed will get himself into condition much sooner than one who has never trained before. For such a person as the latter to begin training three weeks before his event, is generally a detriment instead of a help. He should begin at least three months before and take his routine of work regularly every day, never missing a day except for some sufficient reason.

As to the best course to pursue when preparing for a race, I may be excused for quoting the old adage, "what's one man's meat is another's poison," for the truth it contains when applied to athletic work. The preparation which a distance runner will find best suited to his purpose, will utterly unfit the sprinter for the work ahead of him.

While I believe the old time style of dieting and physicing frequently did a man more harm than good, still a certain amount of the same is permissable. A man may eat what he relishes and can easily digest. If he is inclined to be fleshy, he should avoid fat-producing foods, as it will require that much more work to get him into condition; but if he is of slim build, those foods will assist him to maintain his strength.

Gymnasium apparatus may be used to advantage as an aid, but no amount of such work will take the place of the daily spin upon the track.

Let us suppose that the sprinter has observed the foregoing directions for a month or so, and by means of moderate work has his lungs, heart and muscles in condition to stand a lively spurt without danger of straining. Let him obtain the services of a friend to accompany him to the training ground and assist him. Do not rub down before taking a practice run, although this is a benefit before a race.

Let the friend act as starter and give half a dozen starts with a short run of about 10 yards at full speed with each. Then follow this up with a run of 50 yards, another of 75 and another of 100 yards. Adjourn immediately to a warm dressing-room; strip off and be well rubbed down, using a little Witch Hazel, which is acknowledged to be a standard liniment.

Too many baths have a debilitating effect and as a general rule water with the chill off it is better than the cold *douche*.

A sprinter should never run at a slower gait than his full speed while training. He should begin at one-third to one-half his distance and gradually increase until he is able to sustain his speed for the full distance. It is a much better plan to run 50 yards three times a day than to run 150 yards once a day, and the same idea will hold good in training for any event.

The sprinter does not require a knowledge of pace, except perhaps in a quarter-mile run, when he should not start at the limit of his speed, but reserve his strength for a strong finish.

On the other hand he must be careful not to go to sleep and find himself beaten while still possessing plenty of strength.

A good start is all-important in a sprint, as the race is of such short duration and encourages the runner to put forth his best efforts, while exerting an equally depressing effect on his opponent.

Probably the best way to start is to stand with the left foot at the mark with the other foot 15 or 18 inches behind and slightly to the right with the toe pointing at an angle of 45 degrees. Bend both knees and extend the left arm in front and the right arm behind. At the crack of the pistol bring down both arms with a jerk without bending the elbows, and step forward with the left foot about twelve inches. This will at once put the runner in motion and give him his full stride quicker than if he stepped off with his right foot.

While resting between heats never stand still for a mement, and always have an overcoat or some wrap to put on, as contact with the air, even on a warm day, will stiffen the muscles and render one liable to take cold.

About as good a plan as any for the distance runner to follow is to have a watch held on him each time he runs. I would advise him always to run his full distance, but to begin his training by merely jogging along at a dog-trot. As he begins to get into shape, he can put on more steam until about two weeks before his event he is going the distance at the limit of his ability.

But little work should be done on the last week and only of such a nature as to keep himself in shape. Under no circumstances should he run on the day before the race.

The distance runner has the utmost need of a knowledge of pace and should study as far as possible the peculiarities of the men he is to run against.

If he is something of a sprinter it is well to trail the other and depend on a strong spurt to win at the finish, but, on the other hand, if of a plodding, persevering disposition, let him set as hard a pace as he can himself stand and endeavor to discourage or kill off his opponent. Do not stay out of races because you are afraid you are not likely to win, for you will gain a knowledge of details in that way, that no amount of theory will supply.

In this sport as in everything else, authorities disagree, but the foregoing are some of the conclusions arrived at as a result of a somewhat extended experience on the track, and if they should prove of service to any having the interests of the pastime at heart, I will feel that my effort to help along the cause has not been in vain.   ED. R. BAKER.

WHAT THE STUDENTS THINK OF ANNEXATION.

The question of whether Lake Forest University is to become the undergraduate department of Chicago University is the one which greets the students and friends of both universities upon their return from the holidays. The STENTOR prints below the opinions of some of the students gleaned from personal interviews. The summary is as follows: Out of sixteen students interviewed, twelve are decidedly opposed to the plan and four favor it.

N. H. Burdick, '93: Not in favor of it. Would like to see Dr. Grey's monument to Prof. Harper at the World's Fair.

W. D. McNary, '93: Not in favor of annexation. Thinks that Lake Forest would be giving more than it would be receiving.

J. A. Linn, '93: In favor of annexation.

It would be a step toward a real university in America.

L. N. Rossiter, '93: Not in favor of annexation. Thinks that Lake Forest would become a Baptist university.

E. L. Jones, '93: Not in favor of annexation. Came to Lake Forest because he wanted a diploma from a Presbyterian and not from a Baptist university.

R. H. Crozier, '93: In favor of annexation. Wishes Lake Forest to be one with educational progress and truth.

C. S. Davies, '93: Not in favor of annexation. Is thankful that its failure to pass is assured.

F. C. Sharon, '93: In favor of it. Thinks it would raise Lake Forest to a position of greater usefulness in the educational world.

H. Marcotte, '93: Opposed to annexation. Does not think the advantages are what they are claimed to be.

H. Goodman, '94: In favor of annexation on certain grounds, but opposed to the 999-year lease of Lake Forest property. Thinks that athletics would be helped.

E. A. Drake, '94: Not in favor of it. Thinks it would be drowning Calvanism in cold water.

G. T. B. Davis, '94: Not in favor of annexation. If he is to attend any sectarian college, he wishes it to be Presbyterian, not Baptist, else he would not have matriculated here.

H. L. Bird, '94: Not in favor of it. Thinks it would be a Baptist educational monopoly with no equal compensation to Lake Forest.

W. E. Ruston, '94: In favor of annexation. Thinks it would be a financial help to Lake Forest.

E. C. Cleveland, '94: Not in favor of it. In spite of all possible advantages, we would be Chicago University and not Lake Forest University.

R. B. Spellman, '95: Not in favor of it. Does not want to see a Presbyterian college swallowed by a Baptist.

W. B. Hunt, '95: Not in favor it. Thinks it a scheme to get good Presbyterian money not otherwise available for the purpose to back a Baptist university.

C. W. Sherman, '96: Not in favor of annexation. Believes that Lake Forest would lose her individuality without any adequate return.

F. C. Rogers, '96: Not in favor of it. Lake Forest would merge her personality in the great Chicago University.

Chauncey Thomas, '96: In favor of annexation under some circumstances; others not. Favors whatever would benefit Lake Forest and the cause of higher education.

COLLEGE.

AMUSEMENTS FOR THE WEEK.

AUDITORIUM—Theodore Thomas,—Saturday night.
COLUMBIA—"A Parlor Match."
GRAND—Sol Smith Russell.
CHICAGO—Stuart Robson.
HOOLEY'S—E. S. Willard.
McVICKER'S—Pauline Hall.
SCHILLER—"My Official Wife."

Happy New Year.

To annex or not to annex; that is the question.

Ice was cut from the college pond this year for the first time.

Clayton Sherman and mother spent the holidays at their old home in Beloit.

J. A. Linn contemplates a " p. g." course in Latin at the Chicago University next year.

Reports are now sent out in large square envelopes. Beware of that kind next vacation.

Of the college faculty Prof. Morris was the only one not seen here most of the time during the holidays.

Charles S. Hucker of the Freshman class will not return to school this term. He has gone into business in Waukegan.

Prof. Harper has substituted botany for anatomy in the Sophomore year.

Prof. Harper has transferred the Senior chemistry class to Prof. Stevens.

A rumor is current that in case Lake Forest is annexed to Chicago University the class of '94 will graduate elsewhere.

Quite a large number of our students were present at the three college glee club concerts in Chicago during the vacation.

An article entitled "Training for the Track" appears in another column of this issue. It is an article that should be read by every man in school.

As soon as the trustees are prepared to announce final action with regard to the presidential chair, the annual catalogue will be issued.

It is rumored that R. B. Spellman will soon have a line of "slightly soiled and ruined by water" goods for sale at a reduction at his store in the college.

Prof. Alfred Emerson, of Cornell, formerly incumbent of the Greek chair here, delivered an illustrated lecture at the All Soul's Church, Chicago, on "Pompeii; Its Architecture and Pictures," Tuesday evening, January 3.

Fewer students than ever before remained here during the holidays. The unlucky ones were Messrs. Chauncy Thomas, McDonald, Smith, Rossiter, Tom Hopkins, Gibson, Haberli, McKee, Wilson, Jones, Davies, and the Moore brothers.

The Freshmen and Sophomores as a penalty for not returning on time from their love feast, will not call at the Sem. this month. Consequently wailing, gnashing of teeth and imprecations on the powers that be, by the lower classmen.

The college bell, as usual, was rung New Year's eve. This time the ringing was slightly overdone as it commenced at 11.00 p. m. and continued till after 12. At 11.45 the church bell commenced ringing and continued till 12.05. This latter was more as it should be and did not become monotonous.

Of the students who remained here during the vacation those rooming in the college building were, by order of Frye, forced to move over into Academia, much to their inconvenience and that of the regular roomers at the latter building.

N. H. Burdick and "Sport" really got back on time, and "Buck" was only half a day late. S. B. Hopkins has not yet appeared, but we hear that he is running Fort Wayne and cannot readily find anyone to whom he is willing to trust the care of his native city.

The one topic of discussion is annexation. If no further good comes from this agitation Lake Forest will reap one benefit, it will be thoroughly advertised. Many blue Presbyterians are awaking to the fact that there has got to be some "hustling" done if they are not to be outdone by their Baptist brethren.

We are indeed sorry to chronicle the fact that Dr. Hursh, for some years in our midst, has decided to make Chicago his home hereafter. Dr. Hursh has gained many friends while here, in the college as well as in the town, and the students regret his departure exceedingly. We wish him success in his new position, that of resident physician in the National Bi-Chloride of Gold Institute.

The Zeta Epsilon Literary Society have secured Eli Perkins for one of his inimitably humorous and funny entertainments to be given at the Durand Art Institute building Friday evening the 13th inst.; admission fifty and seventy-five cents. This is one of the treats which the literary societies delight in giving and which no one should miss. As a humorist Mr. Perkins is of world-wide reputation.

On account of Frye turning off the steam at the close of school last term the steam pipes in *only* sixteen rooms in the college building were frozen and consequently broken. The water meter in the gymnasium burst, and a water pipe in the Art Hall burst, flooding part of the basement ankle deep. The frozen and broken pipes in the college building caused quite a loss to several of the boys who had left their things in their rooms. R. B. Spellman suffered most, while many others barely escaped serious damage. It took Frye and four men all the week after Christmas Day, when the accident happened, to repair the damage in the college building alone, and it cost the University more than it would to maintain steam through several winter vacations. Perhaps some day our engineer or "the committee" on whom the engineer tries to throw the blame, will learn that water left exposed in a temperature below 32 degrees will freeze and burst its bounds.

TOWN TOPICS.

Mr. Wells is building an addition to his house.

Mr. Wm. Henry Smith is now living in Mrs. Warren's house.

Mrs. Reid and family have returned from the south, where they spent the holidays.

Mr. C. E. Latimer has moved into his new house, which was building last term, to the north of Mr. Wells.

Quite a party of Lake Foresters went to the "North Shore Limited" Wednesday to see Miss Mabel Durand and Henry Rumsey off to the east.

Miss Catherine Fales and Miss Mabel Giles returned Thursday, January 5th, to Ogontz Seminary, together with quite a company of Ogontz girls.

A few young people informally met the last evening of the old year at the house of Mrs. Calvin Durand for a little merriment, and till nearly '93 the time was passed in dancing and music.

Mr. Blackler is doing a good business in ice this year. Both Farwell's and the college pond have yielded an unusually thick, clear crop, and probably will freeze over in time for another harvest.

Mr. Schreiber, of Chicago, is giving a series of lectures at Mrs. Ralston's on "The Sculpture of the Columbian Exposition." It would be of great benefit to the students if these lectures could be obtained for them.

The assessments for paving will be approved at the January term of the County Court. Beside the block paving, there is to be macadam on Westminister avenue—the road running east from the north end of the depot—to Mr. Scudder's corner.

Charles W. Deering and Cyrus H. McCormick have bought the tract of land adjoining the south line of Lake Forest for $54,900. This property has a frontage of 1,400 feet on the lake and 1,400 feet on the Sheridan Drive, and is directly opposite the twenty-eight-acre piece sold last November to Cyrus Bently for $41,500.

Mrs. Jesse L. Moss entertained a number of young people Monday evening, January 2d, from 7.30 till 11. Before dinner old fashioned games were the order of the evening.

The same evening Mrs. J. B. Durand gave a dinner for her daughters, Misses Helen and Florence Durand, to a select party of Lake Foresters.

Christmas was observed in the usual manner this year at the church Sunday evening. The singing of the children was especially beautiful, and Mr. Gallwey is to be congratulated on his success in training them. Instead of the customary half-box of candy and an orange, an ornamented calendar was given each Sunday School scholar. The exercises were prettily concluded with a Christmas tree.

Perhaps the only general gaiety of vacation was a five o'clock tea given by Mrs. Shirley V. Martin and Miss Bertha Hands, Monday, January 2d. Miss Hands poured chocolate, and Miss Bergen, of Highland Park, officiated at the tea table. Music was furnished by the orchestrian, which rendered selections with the power of a full orchestra, and of greater variety. Everyone enjoyed that way of passing an afternoon.

ATHLETICS.

NOTICE—All those desiring to enter into competition for positions on the base ball team will please hand in their names as soon as possible to Capt. McNary, or the manager.

HARRY GOODMAN,
Mgr. B. B. C.

Active training for the base ball season will begin in the gymnasium January 16.

The athletic committee of the Faculty are negotiating for an athletic instructor in the gymnasium. The plan is to have Mr. Everett come out two afternoons a week to take charge of affairs for the rest of the year. The students, appreciating the worth of Mr. Everett, sincerely trust that the plan may meet with success.

"Northwestern has undoubtedly won the league championship in foot-ball, but her success is largely due to forfeited games, which for various reasons were quite numerous. Until within two weeks of Thanksgiving it was understood that Lake Forest would play here on that date, but we were at last informed that we must play the game at Lake Forest or lose it by forfeit. Knowing that the game between the elevens of the Chicago and Boston Athletic clubs on that day would draw the crowd away from the game at Lake Forest, Manager Ames decided to let that game go, and made arrangements for the Chicago University game here. Why the schedule as originally made out was not conformed to can only be explained by the president and secretary of the league, who evidently thought they had waited until it was too late for us to get any other game for that day, and so we would be forced to play at Lake Forest or not at all."—*Illini*, Dec. 13.

It is quite evident that the writer of the above article is totally unacquainted with facts. In the first place, Northwestern did not win a single game by forfeit, but that is of little consequence. In view of the fact that we played the University of Wisconsin the year before at Madison, she was to play a return game in Lake Forest last Thanksgiving day. Champaign taking Madison's place in the league, the duty of filling the engagement devolved upon her. Manager Ames, it is true, wrote to Manager Crozier, offering (without anthority) an equal division of the gate receipts if he would play the game at Champaign. Manager Crozier replied, enclosing a written agreement for Manager Ames to sign, to which he received no reply, and Champaign was notified by the proper officials that she must play the game at Lake Forest. Such conduct on the part of Champaign should be most heartily condemned. They have come into the league evidently with the idea that they are to run affairs, and that they will conform to the official schedules only as it suits their convenience. At the next league meeting they should be severely reprimanded, and a repetition of such conduct ought to be met with expulsion.

FERRY HALL.

How we envy the Seniors their class pins!

Who thinks reduced fares with a stop over in Chicago a fine scheme?

Miss Searles spent the holidays with Miss Ripley and Miss Goodwin.

Miss E. J. Smith spent several days with Miss Sara Buell, of Sterling.

Miss May Bailey visited Miss Margaret Conger at her home in Clinton.

Remarks overheard in Miss Hopkins room: "O girls I can wear double A shoes."

Topics lately discussed: A horse's fur. A baby's paws. Moses' coat of many colors.

Inquiring Sem.—"Do you think there will be any *ranks* in heaven?" (We trust not.)

Mrs. E. J. Bones, *nee* Ketcham, has gone to Pass Christian where Mr. Bones is sick with sciatica.

We are glad to welcome Miss Norton, of Chicago, who will have charge of the French classes.

Miss Bessie McWilliams spent part of the holidays with Miss Theo Kane, at the latter's home in Chicago.

Misses Creswell, Marshall and Williams spent the holidays with Miss Beatrice Taylor at her home in Princeville, Ill.

The halls are well filled with trunks, and expressions such as this are frequently heard: "O, consarn it all, I've torn my dress."

We regret that Misses Theo Kane and India Wilson are not to return this term, but hope they will be with us in the spring.

Miss Ada Mathes, a former student, has returned and intends completing the course next year. The Misses Stoddard are also with us again.

Are the Sems. indifferent as to whether L. F. U. becomes an undergraduate department of the Chicago University? We have heard no opinions expressed.

The statement in the last STENTOR that Miss Florence Phelps is teaching at Elida was incorrect. Miss Phelps is teaching now in the schools of Independence, Iowa.

The officers of the Aletheian society for the winter term are: President, Miss Marshall; Vice-President, Miss Creswell; Secretary, Miss Gilleland; Treasurer, Miss McKee; Critic, Miss Oberne; Sergeant-at-arms, Miss Heron; Program Committee, Misses Hopkins and Hickok.

ACADEMY.

The statement made recently in the *Tribune* that I received only restrictions when the Senior class was suspended is entirely false. I received no favors whatsoever, nor did I want them. E. C. YAGGY.

Prof. E. J. Swift, who was a Cad Prof. five years ago, is in Lake Forest at present.

Paul Owslye was seen around town recently. He was once a Cad, as Prof. Mendel will testify.

Smith, Laflin, and Brown are new Cads. They deserve praise for selecting so desirable a school.

It has been announced that the Everett brothers will return within a week. We rejoice and welcome them back.

The society elections have not yet come off. It is getting late, and we must shove them through. Let's get a move on.

Joe Rogers will not return to the Cad this term. Joe was a foot ball man, a Tri Kappa, and a good fellow. We regret his departure.

It is unnecessary to say that the Cads had a glorious vacation. The art of doing a vacation seems to fall into the domain of the Cads. We recognize only one other adept out, namely, the Sem.

AMONG THE ALUMNI.

J. F. Faris, '92, is now in Chicago.

The Rev. E. P. Hill, '84, is pastor in Freeport, Ill.

A. C. Wenban, '85, was a visitor here on Christmas day.

E. G. Wood, '92, spent the holidays with his parents in Lake Forest.

Mrs. M. McKinney-Bergen, '83, is with her husband in Baltimore, Md.

L. E. Zimmerman, '92, of Waukegan, spent the holidays in Fulton, Iowa.

H. R. Marsh, ex-'95, now at Champaign, spent a few hours here Dec. 23.

The Rev. Paul D. Bergen '80, is this year attending the John Hopkins University.

Sartell Prentice, Jr., '91, will attend McCormick Seminary during the coming term.

Miss Gracia G. Sickles, '90, is now Mrs. A. G. Welch, and makes her home in Elgin, Ill.

J. Z. Johnston, ex-'93, now of McCormick Seminary, spent the first week of the vacation here.

E. S. Cass, ex-'93, now at Amherst, visited his old schoolmates here the last two days of last term.

Miss Loveridge, ex-'93, who has been spending the fall in the Wisconsin pineries, has returned to her home in Waukegan.

J. A. Bloomingston, ex-'95, visited his old friends here last Thursday. Bloomingston is now attending the Pennsylvania Military College.

H. A. Rumsey, ex-'94, now attending Williams, returned to his home here for the Christmas vacation Thursday after school closed, and remained till last Wednesday.

LATE NEWS.

Quite a number of our college men attended Willard's Saturday matinee.

From some of the reports it looks as if A's, B's, and C's were dished out indiscriminately for last term's work.

Fraternities are to be represented at the World's Fair. Not more than $3,000 will be expended on their exhibit.

A gay party consisting of sixteen boys and girls and a dozen tin horns enjoyed a merry sleigh-ride Saturday evening.

Frank W. Pine, a well-known Academy student here in past years, visited here last Saturday and Sunday. He is now at Ann Arbor and a classmate of Clarence Church, also well known here.

THE STENTOR.

VOLUME VI.   JANUARY 17, 1893.   NUMBER 13.

PUBLISHED EVERY WEEK

BY THE

Lake Forest University Stentor Publishing Co.

BOARD OF EDITORS.

F. C. SHARON, '93................Managing Editor
R. H. CROZIER, '93...............Business Manager
N. H. BURDICK, '93 }
S. B. HOPKINS, '93 } ....Locals
L. N. ROSSITER, '93...........Alumni and Personal
B. R. MACHATTON, '95..................Advertising

ASSOCIATE EDITORS.

HARRY GOODMAN, '94...............Athletic Editor
FOREST GRANT, '96.....................Staff Artist
DAVID FALES, '96...........................Town

Terms—$1.50 per year. Single Copies — 10c

———ADDRESS———

STENTOR PUBLISHING COMPANY,

LAKE FOREST, : : ILLINOIS.

Entered at the P. O. at Lake Forest, Ill., as second-class matter.

DISCUSSIONS on the annexation laggeth. We no longer hear the strict Presbyterian stating that he is afraid of mingling his outer garments with those of Baptist brethren. What is the matter? Has everyone dropped back into the same old rut and become entirely oblivious as to whether his Calvinism is to suffer or not in this combination?

THE Senior class is certainly to be upheld in raising a vigorous protest against depositing ten dollars for being allowed to work in the laboratory. The amount required is exorbitant considering what it is deposited for. Not every student can find ten dollars to hand over immediately, nor is there any use of having the deposit so high. A student with any degree of carefulness will not break ten dollars' worth of test tubes and bottles in four years. Five dollars is an ample deposit. The Seniors should try their utmost to bring it down to this.

NEVER in the history of the institution has the game of chess been so enthusiastically played and supported as this year. It is a game which requires both skill and thought, and it is certainly a credit to the school that so many have taken hold of it and such interest is displayed. The article in this issue on the game is written by one who is thoroughly versed in its mysteries and who knows whereof he speaks. The STENTOR would especially urge upon the attention of Northwestern University and Chicago University the writer's scheme of organizing an intercollegiate league. We would suggest that each of the colleges delegate this matter to a committee and that immediate steps be taken toward the organization of such a league.

OUR BOOK REVIEW DEPARTMENT.

With this issue we add a new feature to the STENTOR—a book-reviewing department. We have at the head of this one of the best students and

critics of literature in the University
and his criticisms are bound to be fair
and to the point.   The best and latest
books of A. C. McClurg & Co., Ginn
& Co., and D. C. Heath & Co. are
given us to be reviewed, and we hope
this new department will be hailed
with pleasure by the STENTOR's readers.
We will endeavor to give them reviews
of the very latest books.

THE STUDENTS' COMMITTEE.

The Students' Committee, recently .
appointed to act as a medium between
students and Faculty, is for the pur-
of acquainting the Faculty with the
grievance of the students and devising
or seeking a remedy if possible.. This
committee means to act in all serious-
ness for the best interests of the students and it asks their hearty coöperation and support in all contemplated
reforms.   This committee is not to be
a general waste-basket for everyone's
private petition, or every little petty
grievance, but is for the consideration
of matters of general interest and
moment. Now that the students have
empowered such a committee to act for
them they should show proper consideration and respect for its actions.
If its work is not respected it will
become a mere figure-head.   Let the
students see that it does not.

A SUGGESTION TO OUR ALUMNI.

The number of our alumni is not as
the sands of the sea, and yet they form
a goodly body and taken all together
represent not a little of this world's
wealth. Now we have a suggestion to
offer them which we hope will meet
with their hearty approval.   It is the
custom of alumni in other schools to
give something to their Alma Mater,
to endow some chair or support its
athletics in some. way.   This is the
way Eastern institutions have grown.
The Nebraskan says that all their
alumni do is to get together every year
and "feed."   We hope our alumni will
not stop at the same thing. At present
nothing is needed here in athletics so
much as a trainer.   The only way we
can have a trainer is to pay for one.
We realize our alumni are not strong
enough to give toward any building or
chair, but they could, we should think,
raise a fund for athletics to go towards
securing a trainer.   Evanston alumni
have raised a fund of $2,500 for this
very purpose. Of course we could not
ask a like amount, but a smaller fund
perhaps might be raised.   The Alumni
Association of Chicago soon meet.
Why could they not start the movement
and communicate with other alumni
througout the country?

This is not merely idle talk for we of
the class of '93 will soon be members
of this association and will do our part
in this matter. It will be a fruitful subject for discussion at the next meeting.

OUR BOOK REVIEWS.

"Some Rhymes of Ironquill of Kansas" is the title of a handsome volume
in blue and gold recently published by
A. C. McClurg & Co.   There is poetry
here of all descriptions, and "Ironquill"
seems equally felicitous in the various
fields.   "The Prairie Storm" is a
charming little poem of three stanzas,
showing perfect sympathy with the

workings of nature and an ability to express them in beautiful verse with an accompaniment of exquisite imagery. As a philosopher, he takes us themes as varied as the death of Tarpeia, a game of whist, the reliques of the glacial period, and the falling of the leaves, and from each draws a moral, a principle of life. He is less happy in his fables, where he creates that from which he draws his moral: all but the first two are very far-fetched, slangy and low in tone. As a satirist, he goes for politics, doctors, the law, and particularly the Kansas bar, with great vehemence and says some very funny things about them. The poetry is marred in many places by the introduction of that old-as-the-hills idea of living on the stars (!) before or after death, a theme so hackneyed as to appear almost ludicrous in modern verse. We hope Ironquill will write more poetry as beautiful as "The Prairie Storm," as grand as "The Sunset Marmaton," as pathetic as "Whist" and "The Old Pioneer," as full of rich satire as "An Agreed Statement," and "The Medicine Man." If he does, without further reference to the sergeant from "the Violet Star" and the princess "now living in Altair," he will easily take high rank among American poets. The typography of the volume is perfect, and the binding would ornament any bookshelf.

*
*

"Our Cycling Tour in England," by Reuben Gold Thwaites, of Madison, Wis., is a bright, very readable account of a trip by wheel through seven hundred miles of historic country. The descriptions are accurate and detailed,

yet never the least bit uninteresting. All the important history of each point reached is given in an entertaining and instructive manner. The method of touring by wheel allows the author much "communion with rustic folk," and he introduces into the book many delightful conversations in "native English," full of quaint and original humor. Arundel park arouses him into an energetic defense of the baronial parks—"beauty-spots, heavenly places, rescued from the humdrum world. Here the English sense of the beautiful is developed, the heart cultivated, the soul trained." The charm of the book is due to the faithfulness with which it tells "what the hedge-rows say, and how John and Mary live in their wayside cottage." It is by all means the best substitute for a trip through the parts so pleasantly described that we have yet seen. The numerous illustrations in the volume are superb. Few books of travel, few books of any kind except art books, contain more beautiful pictures than those of Bath and Shanklin Village in "Our Cycling Tour in England." (A. C. McClurg & Co).

*
*

"How Do You Spell It?" by W. T. C. Hyde, is a reference book of the "visual method of teaching spelling." We give in Mr. Hyde's own words some of the special features of the book:

1. The orthography is that recognized in the body of Webster's dictionary and preferred in his lists of words spelled in two or more ways.

2. It teaches spelling without rules.

3. It is adapted to persons of any age who can read.

4. It contains, in alphabetical order, practically all the words including derivatives, in general use, which are at all liable to be misspelled, and also the primitives, the derivatives of which are of perplexing orthography.

5. In every word liable to be misspelled the letters which are ordinarily transposed, misplaced, omitted, or otherwise misused, are printed in bold-faced type, thus emphazing to the eye the picture of the word as correctly spelled.

6. It contains the largest compilation of homophonous words (those alike in sound but different in spelling and meaning) ever published.

The theory is that when we look up a word in this list, its grotesque appearance will fix an indelible image of its peculiarities on the " mind's eye," we will never have to look up the word again. This may or may not be true; at any rate, the book is a more handy reference book than a large dictionary, and will be a profitable investment even if we have to look up the same words several times. (A. C. McClurg & Co).

CHESS; AN HISTORICAL SKETCH.

To write an exhaustive or complete article on chess, or even on any division of the subject within the space allotted to me, would be so manifestly impossible that it would be folly to attempt to do more than to string together a few facts and theories which possibly may be of interest to some readers of the STENTOR.

No other game approaches chess in the scope afforded by the number of the pieces and the variety of their powers, for skill and foresight involving as it does the faculties of memory and conception.

The game is of great antiquity. Some slight modifications have been made in it in modern times, but the game appears to have been in its most essential characters the same for two or three thousand years. The legends and traditions assigning the place of its nativity have been as varied and as numerous as the theories concerning the home of the first man.

Zenobia and Semiranis, Cæsar and Alexander, Xerxes and Herodotus, indeed almost every one of the ancients whose names we know, with countless others of whom most of the world has never heard, have in time been pointed out as the inventors of the game.

Van der Linde says that chess certainly existed in Hindustan in the eighth century and that probably it originated there. He thinks that the game was invented by the Buddhists, "according to their ideas, war and the slaying of one's fellowmen, for any purpose whatever, is criminal, and the punishment of the warrior in the next world will be much worse than that of the simple murderer. But they ministered to the combative propensities of human nature by inventing the bloodless warfare of chess as a harmless imitation of and a substitution for the carnage of the battle field."

The game was introduced into Europe about the ninth or tenth century but was known as *shatranj* until the fifteenth. Then the name chess was first used in speaking of the game. At that time, chess was the same game, almost exactly, that we play.

Many of the terms used in chess betray its oriental origin. The word "check" is a corruption of the Persian word "shah." Checkmate is *shah mat* which being interpreted is king overcome. Rook is the Sanscrit rukh, which seems to have designated some animal used in warfare, perhaps the elephant.

The rapid development of chess and the increased interest in the game date from the first International Tournament at London, in 1851. Numerous such meetings have occured since then and have kept the game before the world more prominently than ever before.

A chess league of the colleges has often been

suggested but every one seems to have shrunk from taking the initiative in the matter.

We have here a flourishing chess club, which has almost completed its schedule of games, although there has been no incentive to good work except, perhaps, the doubtful one of rank in the club.

But if the club should invite Northwestern and Chicago to enter into a small intercollegiate contest, it would give each member of the club an incentive to work hard for the honor of representing Lake Forest in such a meeting.

If the league proved successful, Wisconsin, Michigan and others of the Western universities could be admitted. Then we would have annually a chess congress which would truly represent the West.

Ibnul Mutâzz, in praise of chess, has well said:

> "Oh thou whose cynic sneers express
> The censure of our favorite chess,
> Know that its skill is science's self,
> Its play distraction from distress,
> It soothes the anxious lover's care,
> It means the drunkard from excess,
> It counsels warriors in their art
> When dangers threat and perils press,
> And yields us, when we need them most,
> Companions in our loneliness."
>
> JOHN A. LINN, '93.

SPECIAL ANNOUNCEMENT.

There will be a meeting of the Lake Forest Club of Chicago, at Athenæum Hall, Room 39, Wednesday evening, at eight o'clock. All Alumni are earnestly requested to be present.

F. M. SKINNER, Secy.

A new system will be introduced at Columbia in the near future. Instead of the present system of numerical grades, students will be classified into five groups, according as their work has been excellent, good, fair, poor, or a failure.—*Daily Princetonian.*

The Lawrence (Kas.) University Glee and Banjo clubs have recently returned from a four weeks' trip through Kansas, Colorado and Missouri, having appeared before 10,000 people.

COLLEGE.

AMUSEMENTS FOR THE WEEK.

COLUMBIA—Hallen and Hart in "The Idea."
HOOLEY'S—E. S. Willard—Repertoire.
GRAND—Sol Smith Russell in "Peaceful Valley."
CHICAGO—Helen Barry in "The Duchess."
McVICKER's—Marie Wainwright in "The School for Scandal."
SCHILLER—Minnie Seligman (Cutting) in "A Modern Match."

Good sleighing.

R. J. Dysart was visited by his father during the week.

The societies adjourned Friday evening for the lecture.

Go to French the druggist for anything in the line of toothbrushes.

The new Science Hall at Beloit, the gift of Dr. D. K. Pearsons, was dedicated with appropriate ceremonies Friday.

We have no remarks to make upon the recent weather save that the mercury hovers about the —10 mark. Facts talk.

Ruston has a fine lot of gymnasium suits on hand. Call and examine them. All sizes.

While the Sophomore class continues its last term's work in chemistry the Seniors have made a change, taking Inalitative Analysis.

The readers of the STENTOR should not miss the article on chess nor the new department, "Book Reviews," appearing in this issue.

Buck, the Waukegan jeweler, has a fine line of jewelry and repairs watches in first-class shape.

During vacation some one who ought to have known better, if he knew anything at all, threw the boxing gloves at the gymnasium into kerosene oil.

Forest Grant, staff artist of the STENTOR, in addition to his college course, is taking a course of instruction at the Chicago Art Institute.

The young ladies of the college elected Miss Lizzie Williams to represent them on the Students' Committee. The other members of the committee are F. C. Sharon and E. L. Jones.

A social organization, to be known as the Pleasure Club, with a charter membership of fifteen, has been formed by the young people of the town and University. The object sought is to promote the social interests of its members.

The Sophomore class have elected the following officers for the winter term: President, B. R. MacHatton; vice-president, Miss June Brett; Secretary, Miss Lottie Leise; class poet, Miss Mamie Pratt; sergeant-at-arms, E. U. Graff.

The ancient, weird, mysterious and unknown M. O. T. A. has been revived. Were it not that the penalty is so awful and the results so dire, we would endeavor to give our readers some of its dark doings. But the seal of silence is upon our pencil point.

Among the various things which the recent cold snap has inspired is the reorganization of last year's German club. This was of much profit as well as pleasure to its members last year and we trust that its revival will be welcomed by many new as well as old students.

The first effort of the Students' Committee did not result as felicitously as might have been desired. They attempted to bring before the Faculty a request to reconsider the deposit of $10 required from those entering the chemistry classes, but encountered an obstacle wondrously like to the laws of the Medes and Persians. They were informed that no satisfaction could be obtained by any such procedure because the Faculty had decided upon it once for all.

Mr. Melville W. Landon, more popularly known as Eli Perkins, delivered his lecture "The Philosophy of Wit" to a fairly good audience Friday evening. While as a scientific study of his subject Mr. Landon's lecture may have left something to be desired, yet as a humorist, wit and good story-teller, and we might add as a moralist, he was fully satisfactory. We should like to hear him again when the weather is not so cold as to prevent a full audience. The Zeta Epsilon Glee Club so pleased the audience that they received a hearty encore.

TOWN TOPICS.

Mrs. E. J. Warner gave a sleighing party to a company of young people last Saturday afternoon.

Friday afternoon the whole Alcott school enjoyed a lively sleigh-ride, and afterwards stopped at Mrs. Warner's for refreshments.

The Art Institute met last Tuesday night at Mrs. Warner's. Mr. M. L. Scudder, Jr., delivered an illustrated lecture on "The Cliff Dwellers," to an unusually large number. After the lecture the usual informal reception took place.

We mourn to announce the funeral of Mr. Taylor's baby, which took place Thursday morning at the church. Dr. McClure conducted the services. The little child, which was 14 months old, died Tuesday, January the 10th, of croup, and was buried in the Lake Forest cemetery.

The late fall of snow and the prolonged cold weather are the most severe Lake Forest has seen for five years. Five years ago the thermometer reached 20 degrees below zero at one time, but the cold did not continue for so long a period. Very seldom, also, has the sleighing been so good as it now is.

The pleasant meeting of the Ladies' Missionary Society last Thursday afternoon was largely attended by townspeople and students. Mrs. Haworth's talk was very interesting, and her reception, aided by a number of young ladies in Japanese costume and according to Japanese etiquette, was charming. Light Japanese refreshments were served in the form of wafers and tea in dainty little cups which were for sale. Everything flavored of Japan, and on leaving, one really seemed to have been at a Japanese social. Following is the list of young ladies who assisted Mrs. Haworth: Misses Holt, Jean Steel, Mamie Pratt, Minnie Rumsey, Harriet Durand, Florence Durand, Helen Durand, Lucy Rumsey, Bessie Mc-Williams.

ATHLETICS.

Training for the base ball season began in the gymnasium yesterday.

The probabilities are that there will be twenty-five candidates for the base ball team this year, the largest number yet recorded. About twenty have already handed in their names.

Champaign seems to be determined to enter some larger league. Undaunted by their rejection by the Northwestern Inter-collegiate Athletic Association they applied for admission to the Western Collegiate Foot Ball Association, including the State Universities of Kansas, Nebraska, Missouri and Iowa, but were refused.

The following are some of the rules adopted by the management of the base ball team:

The candidates must be at the Gymnasium promptly at 4:20 P. M. each day.

For the first week or two running will occupy most of the time. Ten laps the first day increasing two each day until 58 laps (2 miles) is reached as the limit.

Smoking and all use of tobacco is strictly prohibited.

It is the intention of the management to procure new suits if possible. Until they are procured the men must appear for practice in some sort of uniform. Uniforms are not to be worn at any time except during training or practice. A system of marking will be kept up and two per cent. substracted from a man's standing for offenses at the discretion of the captain, a man falling below a certain grade irrespective of his playing abilities relinquishes his chances for a position on the team.

The men will be required to take a shower bath three times each week and will not be allowed to stay in the tank more than fifteen minutes at a time.

A strict observance of the above rules is absolutely necessary.

It has been suggested that Athletic relics and pictures of Athletic teams be placed in the gymnasium, but as yet nothing has been accomplished in that direction. Athletics here are fast approaching that degree of excellence which is really remarkable when all things are considered. Last year we turned out a champion base ball team and our foot ball eleven was one of which we might feel justly proud. It would then seem to be the duty of the students to leave behind them an indication of their appreciation of the merits of these teams and the precedent once established could easily be carried out. It does no good to simply talk of it. Let some action be taken at once.

FERRY HALL.

New definition of conceit: " Maintaining my social position."

Miss Bessie McWillams spent Sunday, the 15th, with Miss Theo Kane.

The Misses Comstock of the same place visited Miss Lucia Clark.

Miss Evelyn Dunne of Hyde Park spent Sunday with Miss Mildred Lyon.

The Seniors have presented each member of the Faculty, with one of their class pictures.

The naming of salt-cellars has afforded much amusement, but the owners do not wish the names printed. Why not?

Wednesday afternoon the Psychology class realized the effect of the physical upon the mental.

Miss Searles and Miss Goodwin entertained the Seniors very pleasantly at a five o'clock tea, Wednesday afternoon.

The girls who failed to be present at the opening January 4th, feel that for them '93 bids fair to be a year of lost opportunities, should they continue to make such mistakes as that was, or rather should Dr. Seeley surprise them with many more announcements such as this,—"all who were present at the opening chapel exercises whose daily record reaches ninety per cent. will be excused from examinations.

First Sem. "Are you going to the Missionary meeting Thursday?"
Second Sem. (With indifference approaching disgust.) "What, at the church? No. Are you?"
First Sem. "I guess not."
Second Sem. "We don't wan't to go to that."
First Sem. "No. I thought maybe you would, as the boys are invited."
Second Sem., (with sudden enthusiasm.) "O, are they! Let's go."
(And they went.)

ACADEMY.

GAMMA SIGMA.

Kennedy has moved to Mitchell Hall since his return to school.

Parker has quit school to go to work and will probably not return this year.

Cross rooms in the dormitory this term instead of staying at Mitchell Hall as he formerly did.

Hannant, who formerly roomed and boarded outside, has moved into the dormitory for the coming term.

Hannant has been indisposed for the last day or two, but is better at present, and is able to attend his classes.

Allan has been on the sick list for the last two or three days, but is rapidly convalescing and will soon be out again.

Roberts has returned to work again, after a most delightful visit of over two weeks, spent for the most part in Chicago.

Rheingaus, MacDonald, Condon, and Smith were the only unfortunates who remained in town during the holiday season.

Rev. A. R. Mathes, of Canton, Ill., visited his son Archie, who is attending the Academy, last Wednesday and Thursday.

S. C. Richards was damaged "several dollars worth," so he says, by the bursting of steam pipes in his room during vacation.

Arthur Reed has returned from his southern trip and resumed his school work last Monday. He went as far south as Augusta, Georgia.

There is evidently a ghost in the dormitory, as Rohn's room has been entered two nights in succession, when everyone is supposed to be wrapt in slumber.

Gruenstein, feeling uncertain about his future relations to the Seminary, visited a phrenologist on Madison Street last week and returned happy and satisfied.

The society owe a vote of thanks to ex-Pres. Cherver for the able and efficient manner in which he has presided over, and the interest he has taken in the welfare of the society.

The new officers for the Gamma Sigma society are: Harvey, president; Graham, vice-president; Vincent, secretary; Roberts, treasurer; McKinnie, STENTOR correspondent.

An invitation was given the Academy Faculty and students by the Ladies' Home Missionary Society to attend their entertainment and reception, given in the church last Thursday, from 3 to 5 p. m.

A new student by the name of Taylor, hailing from Galesburg, took rooms in the dormitory, but being smitten with that ancient malady known as homesickness, held an auction in his room last Sunday evening, and took an early train for home the following morning. He returned, however, as suddenly as he departed, meeting, in all probability, with a very practical parent at the other end of the line.

Prof. Palmer has assigned the following essay subjects to the various members of the Cæsar class:

1. Cæsar's First Campaign; S. R. Brearly, January 17.
2. Cæsar's Second Campaign; A. A. Cobb, January 17.
3. Cæsar's Third Campaign; U. B. Hewitt, January 24.
4. Cæsar's Fourth Campaign; L. H. Gilleland, January 24.
5. Gaul and its People; A. Cooke, January 31.
6. Ancient Germany and its People; G. H. Heineman, January 31.
7. The Organization of a Roman Army; J. H. Rheingaus, February 7.
8. The Compositions of the Roman Legion and its Tactics; E. M. Breckenridge, February 14.
9. Roman Arms. Offensive and Defensive; W. Jager, February 14.
10. The Roman Camp; W. W. Keyes, February 21.
11. Operations against Fortified Places; D. Kennedy, February 21.
12. Roman War Ships; J. P. Cobb, February 28.
13. Provisioning and Pay of the Soldiers; G. Keith, February 28.
14. The Roman Cavalry; A. G. Randolph, March 7.
15. Cæsar as a Writer; W. Jackson, March 7.
16. Cæsar as a General; C. J. Hannant, March 14.
17. Cæsar as a Statesman; E. J. Warner, March 14.

LATE NEWS.

S. A. Benedict, class of '88, spent Sunday at home.

W. E. Danforth spent Sunday with his Lake Forest friends.

The Art Institute hope to hear Eugene Hall at their meeting next week.

Miss Marie Thompson, of Chicago, assisted the choir both morning and evening last Sunday.

A game of indoor ball between two scrub teams from the College and town resulted in a score of 20 to 36 Saturday evening.

There was a sleigh-ride Saturday. The Faculty were participants. The sleigh capsized. So did the Faculty. Some damage was done. Prof. —— tore his clothes. It was his trousers he tore. He rode home under the robes in the broken sleigh.

The following is a correct record of the games played at the Chess Club tournament and the standing of the members:

		PLAYED.	WON.	LOST.	PER CT.
1.	J. A. Linn	33	32½	½	.984
2.	A. B. Burdick	24	16	8	.666
3.	G. S. Wilson	29	18	11	.620
4.	C. G. Smith	23	14	9	.609
5.	Prof. Dudley	19	11½	7½	.605
6.	E. H. McNeal	24	14	10	.583
7.	N. H. Burdick	28	15	13	.535
8.	Dr. Seeley	17	8½	8½	.500
9.	S. B. Hopkins	21	10	11	.476
10.	W. D. McNary	18	8	10	.444
11.	L. N. Rossiter	25	7½	17½	.300
12.	W. E. Ruston	26	7	19	.269
13.	F. C. Rogers	27	6	21	.222
14.	C. W. Sherman	30	4	26	.133

THE STENTOR.

VOLUME VI.   JANUARY 24, 1893.   NUMBER 14.

PUBLISHED EVERY WEEK
BY THE
Lake Forest University Stentor Publishing Co.

BOARD OF EDITORS.

F. C. SHARON, '93 ....Managing Editor
R. H. CROZIER, '93 ....Business Manager
N. H. BURDICK, '93 }
S. B. HOPKINS, '93 } ....Locals
L. N. ROSSITER, '93 ....Alumni and Personal
B. R. MACHATTON, '95 ....Advertising

ASSOCIATE EDITORS.

HARRY GOODMAN, '94 ....Athletic Editor
FOREST GRANT, '96 ....Staff Artist
DAVID FALES, '96 ....Town

Terms—$1.50 per year. Single Copies—10c

————ADDRESS————

STENTOR PUBLISHING COMPANY,

LAKE FOREST,   :   :   ILLINOIS.

Entered at the P. O. at Lake Forest, Ill., as second-class matter.

IN REGARD TO THE READING ROOM.

The question of the reading room should be seriously considered. It is not that we want a *reading room* so much as that we want a *new* reading room. The students are not desirous of going back into the old place dignified by the name of reading room. We might just as well not have a room. No one acquainted with the place goes there to read It is a cold, disagreeable dirty room situated so that every class pours into it and makes it a general loafing place. The bareness of the place tempts mischief. If we want a reading room *now* is the time to change.

The Academy will soon be vacated, there will then be room for all classes, and the President's room adjoining the library would make a splendid reading room. The students would help fix such a room up and take a pride in it. The old room however will *never* be kept decently, no matter what the promises are. We do not wish to uphold vandalism, but it seems that in the reading room case it was as near justifiable as it ever is.

WANTED: A WAITING ROOM.

One of the crying needs of the college is a gentleman's waiting room. The ladies have their waiting room and it is very nicely furnished. But the boys, especially those rooming outside, have no place whatever in which to study or wait between classes. It is too far to go to one's room between classes, but where can these students study or pass their time. There is no way except to "sponge" off classmates in the building and make their rooms general hotels or loafing places. This is manifestly abusing the hospitality of the boys and the thing is becoming a nuisance. But where can these outside students go? Must they hang round the halls? There is, absolutely no alternative. There should be a room for general assembly. This is no vague and idle scheme. Such a scheme can easily be put into practice. The old reading room should be thrown open, not as a reading room, but as a general assembly and waiting room. There will be no expense entailed. The simple unlocking of the door will provide it. At least the Faculty should look into the feasibility of the plan. It's a good subject for the Students' Committee.

PROMPTNESS IN COMMITTEE WORK.

There is one thing that students of this University lack in common with other students, and that is promptness in committee work and college matters generally. It is extremely hard to get the students roused enough on any subject to hold a mass-meeting, but even when such a meeting is held after prodigious efforts, it usually amounts to nothing. After discussing the subject a committee is appointed. There it stops. The secretary forgets to notify the committee; the committee forgets what if is to do, and, finally, the members forget they are on such a committee. No one ever thinks of having a meeting to hear the report of the committee. In fact most of the students have forgotten all about such a thing and the matter drops. Appointing a committee here is equivalent to laying the subject on the table. Naturally, however, there is little effort in the committee because of the apathy of the general mass. The prime object of every meeting of classes or general body seems to be to appoint a committee and then adjourn. As "adjourners" the students here beat anything on the boards. Half of them do not know what the committee is appointed for. The committee merely partake of the

general apathy. The only way to reform this or wake the men up is for every student to take a more active interest in college affairs and not leave the bulk of the work to the few.

THOSE COMMENCEMENT ORATIONS.

There is a great deal of talk here about doing away with commencement orations and the present Senior class has expressed itself as decidedly in favor of abolishing the system. The following clipped from the *Ariel*, is to the point and leaves nothing unsaid:

" A petition will shortly be presented to the faculty by the Senior class asking for a change in the nature of the commencement exercises. That the present system is not suitable for the graduation exercises of a modern university is evident. The time has gone by when fancy exhibitions of knowledge and Latin orations furnish a suitable end to a university career. A commencement oration is no test of the orator's ability; gives little chance for original thought; is extremely fatiguing to the audience, and it serves no useful purpose visible to the naked eye. Other colleges now have exercises more fitted to the occasion which makes it one of profit and enjoyment instead of a tiresome "out-pouring" of learned nothings. The present petition asks, we believe, that some orator of national fame as Phillip Brooks, Gunsaulus or Bishop Huntington be invited to deliver an address to the class and public, and that the valedictory and salutatory addresses be the only part taken by the members of the class. In this way it is believed that the highest honor will be rewarded and that those who attend graduation exercises will hear a speech "that is a speech" instead of—but we have already given our opinion of the average commencement oration and will say no more. There is no better time to begin such a reform than the present year, especially as the Senior class almost unanimously desire it, and if the class is satisfied, we do not see why the faculty should not be so."

BOOK REVIEWS.

"Marianela: A Story of Spanish Love," translated from the Spanish of B. Perez Galdos by Helen W. Lester, is the fifth in a series of "Tales from Foreign Lands," published by A. C. McClurg & Co. The events of the story take place in and around the zinc mines of Socartes. All of the principal characters have begun life in extreme poverty, some of them as street beggars. The Golfin brothers, Carlos and Teodora, have risen by persistent effort to be the possessors of enormous wealth, Carlos being chief engineer of the mines and Teodoro a widely travelled doctor with much skill in treating diseases of the eyes. The Centeno family are just able to earn a scanty living by the combined efforts of the father and four children, one of whom runs away during the course of the story to become, as he boastingly asserts, a second Dr. Golfin. Senor de Penàguilas, patriarch of Aldeacorba, and his brother of Santa Irene de Camfò, have both received large fortunes by inheritance and the effects of this suddenly acquired wealth on the two men are admirably set forth. Marianela, daughter of a lamp-lighter, deformed in infancy by a terrible fall, alone remains dependent. Her moral character is wonderful, considering her wretched life with the Centenos. She gives every bit of money she receives to the youngest Centeno to enable him to run away and make something of himself. She possesses all the Christian virtues in a remarkable degree, though she knows almost nothing about religion. Yet, in spite of her beauty of character, she is made to endure the worst of torments and a most pitiful death; the reader cannot help rebelling against her undeserved misfortunes. We will not tell the story of her life, nor speak at any length of the blind Pablo, whose eyes she was until the rich doctor restored him his sight. The author shows great skill in mind analysis and is severely critical of "the singularity of the customs of a society that does not know how to be charitable without charity balls, bull-fights,

and raffles." These are two good points of the book, the two principal faults being the wretched fate of the heroine and a noticeable lack of smoothness in style, due probably to the translator.

TESS OF THE D'URBERVILLE'S.

A CRITICISM.

There can be no doubt that Thomas Hardy's novel, "Tess of the D'Urbervilles," has attracted more attention at the hands of the critics and the reading public than any other novel since "Robert Elsmere." Though the story appeared as a serial in 1891 and in book form early in 1892, it may not be amiss, even at this late date, to consider some of its most striking characteristics.

That it is to be absolutely different from the ordinary modern English novel is evident from the beginning. It has to do with English country life, but not with that of the proprietors of the estates: the characters are the peasants themselves, the tenant-farmers and their associates. Many of these people are densely ignorant, indolent, and emotionless; but there are also many of a somewhat finer mould, capable of the intensest feeling, but unable to control and direct it on account of lack of training, who are perfectly helpless in the hands of a person with a little experience of the world, whether his intentions be good or evil. Such an one is Tess Durbeyfield, supposed to be descended from the ancient Norman D'Urbervilles. This supposition and her poverty, due to the indolent habits of her father and mother and increased by an unfortunate accident, lead her to Alec D'Urberville, who is not a D'Urberville at all, but a Smith, who has assumed the defunct name as better in keeping with his wealth than his own plebian one. She is helpless before his experience of the world, and thus her misfortunes begin, to end only at her death.

We have found one point in favor of the story: it deals with a phase of life to which we are not accustomed to pay much attention.

Who else has written the life of a dairy-maid? All the surroundings are new to us; we read the novel and find out much that we never knew before.

Another point strongly in favor of the book is the style in which the story is presented to us. Never were emotions so varied and so intense—passionate love, consuming remorse, implacable anger, contempt—presented in a more potent guise. There is a kind of subtle change in the style which enables us to tell when something of importance is being led up to, there is an indescribably touching way of presenting the nobler emotions. The very simplicity and unworldliness of it all contribute to the same end.

Can any fault be found with "Tess of the D'Urbervilles," then? We answer that it is open to adverse criticism in several regards. The principal male characters are abominable. Such characters should not be necessary in any story. Alec D'Urberville is a very slave to the animal nature; he is vindictive, unprincipled, worthy only of contempt. Angel Clare, while admirable in many respects, behaves the very fool in the crisis of his life, and is the cause of untold misery. Moreover, his character is not consistent. Though he abandons Tess most foolishly and cruelly just after their marriage on receiving from her own lips the story of her shame, for which no reasonable human being would hold her accountable, he resumes the interrupted relations with her after his return from Brazil, though he knows that she is now guilty of murder in the first degree; he will have nothing to do with the victim of another's wiles, but is not averse to a red-handed murderess soon to suffer death on the gallows for her crime. The fact of his repentance for the former deed can scarcely excuse the latter.

Then again the ending of the novel is very unsatisfactory. Is it impossible nowadays to write a strong novel with a satisfactory ending? Almost every criticism of a modern novel contains something about an unsatisfactory ending. For the heroine to be hung for murder, while

he who was long her husband in name, but really so for a very short time, walks slowly out of town leading her younger sister by the hand, none being allowed to see the execution, is surely about as unsatisfactory as an ending could well be.

In conclusion, the power of the story may be said to depend on the success with which character is developed, the only defect being that mentioned in the case of Angel Clare. It is no exaggeration to say that Tess Durbeyfield is the most interesting character study in modern fiction. Two further sources of power are the vividness with which emotions are presented and a peculiarly forcible narrative style. And, finally, the fact that fiction has never heretofore found its characters in these walks of life causes much unwonted interest to attach to the story.

On the other hand, the prominent male characters, though well presented, are repulsively immoral or priggish. Tess is the victim of both faults. But the imperfection is entirely in the conception, not in the presentation. The latter could scarcely be improved. The style is fully equal to that of any of the so-called "standard" novelists. The description of the threshing machine, engine, and engineer, and the narrative of the events of threshing day at Farmer Groby's, have never been eclipsed, in vividness of imagery, originality of conception, and power of presentation by any writer of English fiction, I care not what his reputation.

But in the lack of a firm and abiding sense of moral responsibility, in the loose religious tone of the book we find the great objection to it. Angel Clare, the son of a minister, with two brothers in the ministry, intended for the ministry himself, takes up farming instead, on account of some very free ideas. These are readily taken up by Tess, who was never taught any religion at all. She imparts them in turn to Alec D'Urberville, thereby causing him to backslide after being converted soon after her marriage to Clare. Temptation is placed in the way of Izz Huett, one of Tess's companion's at Crick's and Groby's, and she is anything but firm. We have mentioned Tess's murder of Alec, and the latter's total depravity except during the period of his conversion. These things, together with the slurs thrown at Clare's brothers and even Providence itself, will doubtless prevent "Tess of the D'Urbervilles" from attaining that lasting fame which would undoubtedly be its due without them.

AMHERST GLEE CLUB CONCERT.

The Amherst College Glee and Banjo Clubs will give a concert here in the Art Institute on Thursday evening, April 6th. The clubs comprise twentysix men and have the reputation of being one of the very best organizations of the kind in the east. The clubs sing in Chicago on the 5th, where it will be made quite a society event. It is proposed to make it a society event here also. The ladies of the town will be asked to act as patronesses and a reception will probably be given in the afternoon. This is a town entertainment, and as the town has always heartily supported college entertainments, this is a chance for the latter to return past favors, and it should do so heartily. Those having this in charge are at considerable expense and the students should see that they are nothing out and should give the club a rousing reception. Prices will be moderate. It is a great chance to hear a fine club. Our own E. Smith Cass will probably be requested to sing his inimitable solo, "Chick-a-dee-dee."

Francis W. Kelsey, the well-known author of text-books, will spend the coming year traveling and studying in Rome, France, Spain, North Africa and Sicily.—*Wooster Voice.*

The debate held Wednesday the 18th, between Harvard and Yale was won by the former by 100 points. Harvard had the negative.

COLLEGE.

AMUSEMENTS FOR THE WEEK.

COLUMBIA—Louise Leslie Carter and Lottie Collins in "Miss Helyett."
HOOLEY'S—Nat C. Goodwin in "A Gilded Fool."
GRAND—Alexander Salvini—Repertoire.
CHICAGO—"The Crust of Society."
McVICKER'S—Marie Wainwright in "The Social Swim."

The second crop of ice is being harvested from the gymnasium pond.

Go to French the druggist for anything in the line of toothbrushes.

J. A. Linn has been confined to his room by a severe cold during the past few days.

Ruston has a fine lot of gymnasium suits on hand. Call and examine them. All sizes.

W. E. Ruston favored a social gathering in Evanston, Thursday, with his gracious presence.

Buck, the Waukegan jeweler, has a fine line of jewelry, and repairs watches in first class shape.

The Freshman exuberance vented itself in a sleigh-ride Monday evening. About thirty of the young folks participated.

The Senior class in Ethics are to prepare a "very short essay, not to exceed 1,000 words," on the "Freedom of the Will."

Next Thursday, January 26, is the annual Day of Prayer of Schools and Colleges. As usual it will be duly observed in Lake Forest.

For the first time during the year the Seniors have been recognized as a class. Mrs. Seeley very kindly gave them a tea yesterday (Monday) afternoon. The entertainment was such as only one like Mrs. Seeley knows how to give, and all enjoyed themselves as enjoyment can be found only at Ferry Hall.

The Athenæan Society had the privilege of listening to a talk on Socialism by one of its disciples, in the person of E. J. Swift, last Friday evening.

We wish to state that the gymnasium was not damaged by the impact of the boxing gloves, but that the gloves were ruined by their bath in the kerosene tank. For explanation see last week's STENTOR.

You may notice a kind and benignant smile upon the countenances of the Sophomores and Freshmen, and you may wonder thereat. But it is only because good Dr. Seeley has removed the restrictions from the "Sem" imposed by him on the occasion of last term's love feast.

R. B. Spellman has discontinued his studies and gone to other fields. What his future intentions are could not be learned. He left his "cash basis" in the care of the Vance brothers, who may hereafter be found at his old stand. "No trust, no bust," is their motto. The STENTOR sincerely regrets Mr. Spellman's departure, and wishes him success in his new field.

During the week the students of the college held a mass meeting to take some action looking to the establishment of a reading room. If by contribution the students will raise a certain specified fraction of the cost, it was stated, the Faculty will make up the deficiency and place a plain deal table in the old reading room and restore the papers and magazines to their places.

The Sigma Phi fraternity, of Williams, lost their chapter house by fire Saturday morning, January 7. This was one of the finest chapter houses in the country, and the loss, fully covered by insurance, was in the neighborhood of $35,000. The fraternity will rebuild. It seems that Williams is at the same disadvantage that Lake Forest is in, that it has inadequate fire protection. When, after much delay, sufficient hose had been found to reach from the water supply to the fire it was found that the hydrant was frozen. By the time that the water was gotten to flow the fire had passed beyond control. The *Williams Weekly* takes occasion to emphasize the need of at least supplying a sufficient amount of hose for such emergencies and characterizes lack of such precautions as little less than criminal. It says, which is applicable as well to Lake Forest as to them, that fire escapes and hand grenades should be provided for the dormitories, which in case of fire would become veritable death traps.

TOWN TOPICS.

Mrs. Dwight gave a luncheon to about fourteen Chicago and Lake Forest ladies Friday last.

Saturday afternoon Miss Elsie Larned gave a sleigh-ride to about twenty friends, afterwards entertaining them with an informal dinner.

At a meeting of the shareholders of the Alcott school it was decided that every patron of the school should purchase shares of school stock. This method has been taken of decreasing the debt of $650 on the school.

The Dancing Class met Thursday evening at the home of Mrs. Joseph Durand. The class will meet every alternate Thursday throughout the winter. The members are: Misses Florence Durand, Helen Durand, Jean Steel, Mamie Pratt, Harriet Durand. Messrs. F. C. Sharon, W. R. Nash, E. C. Yaggy, Harry Durand, J. H. Jones, B. R. MacHatton.

ATHLETICS.

Training continues in the gymnasium under the direction of Capt. McNary. There are quite a number of candidates for each position which makes the rivalry sharp. A great deal of interest is manifested in the work, which augurs well for the future welfare of the team. In time the training will be put on a more systematic basis. As it is now individuals get but little practice. Capt. McNary seems to be thoroughly capable of bringing to a successful issue the task he has undertaken.

At this early date it is rather difficult to pass criticism on the merits of the team. However, Kimball and Curry plainly show that they are made of baseball stuff, while Rogers, Sherman and Gilleland are hard and conscientious workers.

Almost all colleges of note have put their ball teams in training. Amherst has adopted an excellent plan for developing the powers of candidates for battery positions. The men indulge in hand-ball play one hour each day in addition to other work.

There seems to be a disposition on the part of a few candidates to shirk daily practice. This is especially noticeable among last year's players. It should be understood from the outset that in justice to new men, the old players go through the same course of training.

It may be of interest to students and athletes to know how Yale and Chicago Universities will train their men for the ball team. We copy the following from the *University News:*

"Laurie T. Bliss, captain of the Yale base ball nine, has outlined the work for the coming season, and will put the candidates into active training about the first of February. The practice will consist of gymnasium exercise for some time. About the first of March cage-work in batting grounders and base-sliding will be attempted.

"John G. Clarkson, of Cambridge, the former pitcher of the Bostons and Clevelands, will coach candidates for pitcher's position, commencing early in March. This engagement is very satisfactory to Yale students, as Mr. Clarkson is considered an excellent coacher.

"Every member of last year's nine is now in college, and will occupy very nearly the same positions as last year. Jackson will probably be substitute catcher this year; Bowers will do the greater part of the pitching. "Yale's nine will take a southern trip, starting March 29. The universities of Pennsylvania, Virginia, John Hopkins will be played. There are two open dates.

"Mr. Stagg has commenced to polish his baseball material. Twenty seven men have been found who want to play on the University team in the spring. They are nearly all from high school, academy and small college teams There no stars that come with laurels from the larger colleges. They know the rudiments of baseball, and there is plainly the making of a team among them, but they are not fup on the hundred and one fine points of the game, and the many tricks of the trade. So Mr. Stagg has commenced putting on the finishing touches in ball stopping, base

sliding, catching and pitching. Work will be done daily in the gymnasium by the candidates. Training facilities in the gymnasium are ample. Up at the end of the long interior a space for ground bounds, 40 by 50 feet, has been left unfloored. And along this end wall, at a certain hour every day, may be seen crouching a line of candidates, awaiting in turn the ground ball which Stagg, with a deft turn of the bat, sends down. It is not much of a trick to stop a ball on a smooth wooden floor, but on the ground, as on the field, the angle of deflection is more uncertain. The players are taught the utmost quickness, both in stopping the ball and in recovery; to close their feet when it comes spinning down the ground; to return it underhanded as well as overhanded; to slide bases easily and naturally, head foremost and feet foremost; to slide around and in front. Batting is the hardest of the accomplishments to be cultivated. A cage consisting of cord netting suspended from the ceiling and enclosing a space 70 by 30 feet, will be placed in position in a week or two for batting and battery work.

"In addition to the actual practice in the game, Mr. Stagg has prescribed a set of exercises intended to make a suple body. These will be taken every day. The veteran of famous battles on the college field will play on the first baseball team of the University. He will not try to gain new honors in the box, but will probably take the place behind the bat, for no one else has been found yet who has the making of a catcher."

FERRY HALL.

Miss Rogers is attending Madison University.

Miss Cabot will not return to Lake Forest College.

Miss Grace Linnell has been suffering with the quinsey.

Miss Oberne attended the recent charity ball in Chicago.

Miss Edith J. Smith spent Saturday with Miss Glenrose Bell.

Mrs. Seeley enjoyed a visit from her brother, Mr. Franz Hesse, Sunday.

Mrs. Lyon, of Chicago, spent Wednesday with her daughter, Miss Mildred.

Miss Maude Bohn, of Chicago, spent Sunday, the 15th, with Miss Goodwin.

Dr. Seeley was confined to his room several days last week with tonsorial throat.

Miss Liese was one of the guests at the reception at which Miss Dixon of Chicago made her debut.

8 THE STENTOR.

Miss Mildred Lyon has been confined to her room the past week with a heavy cold.

The Seniors have no faith in superstitious sayings. They now sit thirteen at table.

Miss Robinson entertained the young ladies of her table at an afternoon tea, Tuesday.

Miss Bessie Galt, of Sterling, has gone to Pasadena, Cal., to visit Miss Lida Fife, '90·

What interested the brakeman for fifteen minutes on the 5:40 train Saturday evening?

Miss Martha Matzinger will spend the remaining part of the school year studying music in the city.

Several members of the Faculty indulged in a sleigh-ride Wednesday afternoon, in honor of Miss Goodwin's birthday.

Misses Searles and Goodwin gave a pleasant little tea to the ladies of the Senior classes of the College and Ferry Hall last Wednesday.

Friday evening the following program was carried out by the Nu Beta Kappa Society:
Essay, - - - - - Miss Black.
Recitation, - - - - - Miss Craven.
Life of Ole Bull, the Norwegian violinist,
Miss McIntosh.
Reading—Extract from Ole Bull's Christmas Story,
Miss Green.
News of the Week, - - Miss Louise Conger.
The society has now forty members enrolled. At present many of these never appear on the program. With such a large number, meeting but once in two or three weeks, anything else is impossible. So much of the work too has been purely musical that necessarily it must fall to a certain few. Isn't a better literary society necessary to the good of Ferry Hall, and to a higher student life? Why not make a division, organize a rival society, and so arouse the students to better work? Time? Haven't we as much time as other colleges and seminaries? Are the rules of the constitution carefully carried out, members fined when they are absent without excuse, or fail to perform their part, or provide a substitute to take *that* part? Are "Roberts' Rules of Order" studied? Does the aspect of the room upon entrance inspire one to real literary effort? The curtains have not been seen this year, except as used in decorations in the chapel, and one of them has been folded and hanging over the back of one of the seats there since November or the first of December. The society *ought* to have a room which they could keep locked. Standing open continually, being used as a practice room, recitation room, general gathering place on all extra occasions, it is almost impossible to keep it in the order in which it should be. Many realized the condition of the society. Is not some one ready to act? Instead of saying, "yes it's awful; something ought to be done," get together and do it.

ACADEMY.

GAMMA SIGMA.

Hannant visited Evanston friends last week.

Fred. C. Smith was visited by his father last Wednesday.

Mr. Fontleroy visited the Academy classes one day last week.

Geo. Rice read an essay before the Cicero class last Friday, entitled Priestly Colleges.

Anderson and Dewey spent Wednesday evening in Waukegan with a sleighing party.

Rogers and Gilleland are training with the base ball team, hoping for positions on the nine.

Quite a number of college students were examined in English history by Prof. Burnap last week.

McDonald, who has been confined to his room with neuralgia of the face, is again able to be out.

A class in mechanical drawing has been organized with a membership of eight. Any who feel able to pay the price are invited to join. A competent instructor from the city has been secured.

The Gamma Sigma society will hold its preliminary contest in declamation on Wednesday, January 25th.

The Academy boys hope the services of E. W. Everett may be secured as gymnasium instructor for this term.

It required the combined efforts of four of the Academy boys to get a certain young lady from Ferry Hall started home from church recently.

Prof. McNeill, Prof. Morris and A. A. Hopkins acted as judges in the preliminary declamation contest of the Tri Kappa society last Wednesday.

Prof. Williams will hereafter have a special algebra class one afternoon of each week at 4 o'clock, for the benefit of those who miss regular recitations.

The new dormitory is finished and kept heated to prevent the plastering from cracking. The cottage is nearing completion, and the chapel is being plastered.

The Academy boys who use the gymnasium for physical development wonder if it is to be monopolized by a few indoor baseball players for the remainder of the winter.

Dewey and Severing gave an exhibition of some very unscientific slugging to a small and select audience, as a result of Severing's attempt to play a practical joke upon Dewey. No one was hurt.

Mr. Burke, state secretary of the Y. M. C. A., led the prayer meeting in the Academy chapel last Tuesday night and organized a Y. M. C. A. of Academy students. He was assisted by E. L. Jones of the college.

Thanks to Prof. Jack's selections, the Academy is now provided with a strictly first-class library, which, though small, is worthy the attention of every student who is at a loss to know what to read. Additions to it will be made from time to time.

TRI KAPPA.

Frank Spring is able to attend classes again after being on the sick list for a week.

Mr. H—t has been duly initiated into the every-day manner of living in the Academy Hall, by the usual method of baptism.

Nott Flint was absent from recitations on Monday on account of illness (?), but we were glad to note that his ailment lasted only one day.

Those awful burglars that came so near gaining entrance into the apartment of Rohn last week are still at large. It is, indeed, thrilling to hear Mr. R. relate his experience with them.

Complaints are continually being made by Academy students and others that money is taken from clothes left in the gymnasium. This annoyance keeps reminding us of the need of lockers in such a place.

A movement is on foot now among Academy students to organize the Academy department of the Y. M. C. A. into an independent association. This is a movement in the right direction, and will undoubtedly be a means of doing better work in the Academy.

Last Wednesday the preliminary contest in declamation took place, and was, in every way, an honor to the society. There were five contestants, and all spoke in a manner deserving of praise. B. S. Cutler was accorded first place and Cobb second. These gentlemen will represent the society on the annual contest with the Gamma Sigma society.

AMONG THE ALUMNI.

H. A. Rumsey plays first banjo on the Williams Banjo Club.

W. E. Danforth, '91, is this term attending McCormick Seminary.

H. E. Royce, '91, is now engaged in the real estate business in Chicago.

It is announced that L. E. Zimmerman, '92, will soon change his place of business from Waukegan to Chicago.

The Lake Forest University Alumni Association of Chicago held a special meeting Wednesday evening, January 18, at Room 39, Athenæum building, Chicago.

Miss Dora Franklin, Ferry Hall, '95, is this term attending the Loring School, 2539 Prairie Avenue, Chicago.

The Lake Forest College Club, of Chicago, met Wednesday evening, January 18, at Room 39, Athenæum building. Quite a large number attended, considering the cold weather on that particular night. In the necessary absence of the president, Mr. Wenban, Mr. McVay took the chair. After preliminary discussion of business, which consisted mainly in accepting an invitation from Mr. Wenban to meet at the Hamilton Club February 2nd, the Club listened to a carefully prepared program. College songs were sung; Wright and Matthews gave readings, and there was a debate on the question should Lake Forest College be annexed to Chicago. Humiston read a Latin poem and the Association adjourned to an adjacent restaurant.

COLLEGE WORLD.

It is stated that some one hundred college men are connected with the New York *Tribune, Sun* and *Times.*

The Freshman class of Yale, by a recent action of the faculty, is declared from entering any intercollegiate contest in baseball during the year.

Beloit claims to have the best college paper in the West. The *Round Table* is a good journal, but it is semi-monthly and can not be compared therefore with a daily or a weekly.

The manager of the athletics at the World's Fair is endeavoring to arrange a boat race between Cambridge, Oxford, Yale and Harvard for the college championship of the world.

The statement going the rounds of the college press that the football game between Stanford University and the University of California, which resulted in a tie, will be played off in a few weeks is totally incorrect. It will not be played off until next Thanksgiving.

Certain changes in the method of scoring in foot-ball are being discussed. It is proposed to abolish the place kick altogether. The Philadelphia *Press* suggests the following: Safety, 1 point; goal from field 3 points; touch-down, 5 points; and goal from touch-down (if not abolished), half a point.

One of the corridors in Mammoth cave is known as Fraternity Hall. It contains pyramids of stones representing fourteen different fraternities. Each visitor adds one stone to the pile representing his fraternity. It is a wonder that some enthusiastic bard doesn't throw rocks at the whole group.

Of the former members of the Hasty Pudding Club four have risen to be presidents of Harvard College, eleven to be deans of the various departments, eighty-two to be instructors or professors, ten presidents of other colleges, seven United States cabinet officers, eight United States senators, forty-one members of congress and five governors of states.

> A maiden in the parquet sat,
> On her head a mammoth hat;
> Just behind, a man with rage
> Swore he couldn't see the stage.
> Hardly had the words been said
> When the maiden bared her head.
> Man now smiles—feels hunkidori.
> Reader, this is a fairy story.

THE STENTOR.

VOLUME VI. JANUARY 31, 1893. NUMBER 15.

PUBLISHED EVERY WEEK
BY THE
Lake Forest University Stentor Publishing Co.

BOARD OF EDITORS.

F. C. SHARON, '93.............Managing Editor
R. H. CROZIER, '93.............Business Manager
N. H. BURDICK, '93 }
S. B. HOPKINS, '93 } ....Locals
L. N. ROSSITER, '93...........Alumni and Personal
B. R. MACHATTON, '95.............Advertising

ASSOCIATE EDITORS.

HARRY GOODMAN, '94.............Athletic Editor
FOREST GRANT, '96.............Staff Artist
DAVID FALES, '96.............Town

Terms—$1.50 per year. Single Copies—10c

————ADDRESS————
STENTOR PUBLISHING COMPANY,
LAKE FOREST, : : ILLINOIS.

Entered at the P. O. at Lake Forest, Ill., as second-class matter.

THE LENIENCY OF OUR FACULTY.

Here, as in all other institutions, a vast amount of unnecessary grumbling is done, and a great deal of fault found with the Faculty. We acknowledge that we have not been the least in this, and yet it has been forcibly brought to our mind recently that we should be deeply thankful for the leniency and good will it has always shown us as students. When we compare our restrictions, and they are few, with those put on the Yale, Harvard, Princeton and other college students by their Faculties, we cannot but thank our Faculty with grateful hearts that "we are as we are." Recently, the Faculties of Yale and Harvard have put very severe restrictions on their students, and now no Yale freshman can compete in any athletics; the Harvard freshmen glee club cannot leave town, and no Harvard athletes can go outside of New England. Other colleges are just as severe. Here, on the contrary, we are given every privilege and allowed every freedom that can be consistently allowed. The members of the Faculty are easily accessible and take an interest, in fact, a great interest in all student affairs; and yet, when something goes wrong, we make the Faculty bear the brunt. The Faculty treat us as men and gentlemen. Do we entirely deserve the trust reposed in us?

LET US DEBATE.

The colleges of the land are not given over entirely to athletics. This is the season of rest from sport, and greater attention is being paid to literary work. Great interest was manifested in the recent Harvard-Yale debate, in which Harvard won after a close fight. Dartmouth has recently challenged Amherst, and Ann Arbor has thrown down the gauntlet to Wisconsin for a similar contest. This is as it should be. We will venture to say that, outside of the curriculum, there is nothing that benefits a student so much as the debating society. It quickens his thinking and makes him logical. It helps his speaking and improves him generally more that any other literary exercise. We see no reason why we shouldn't have a debating society here, or have a prize contest between the societies or classes as desired. Then the winners of this debate should contest with representatives of Evanston or Beloit. It seems to us that debating is not fostered here enough. Prizes are given for declamations, essays and orations, but debates are not recognized in any way except by the societies. Now, if anyone contemplates giving a prize, let it be for a prize debate, and let this debate occur sometime in March or April, or earlier, and *not* in commencement week. Too much is jammed into commencement week now. After such a debate we would be prepared to meet Evanston, Beloit or any other Western school, and give them a hard rub. We have excellent debaters here if we will only develop them. Besides, we do not have enough to do with outside schools, in a literary way. It is entirely confined to athletics, and this is manifestly unfair to our literary department. Think this over, students, and let us see some action taken.

THE BASE BALL SITUATION.

The situation in the Western College League is rather queer at present. The Beloit Faculty have practically shut down on athletics there, and Evanston is undecided whether to remain in the league or not. If these two do remain, they are anxious to have Champaign dropped. So what is to be done? As yet there is no base ball news from any of these colleges, so that we cannot say what the prospects are for a good season. As for us, we hope that winning the championship last year will act as a great incentive this year, and arouse some enthusiasm. Evanston should remain, if for nothing more than to better her record of last year. It would ill befit her to desert with such a record behind her. Champaign should continue a member because she is a good base ball school, and has a great deal of enthusiasm and push. Beloit has always made a good record in base ball and should strive to awaken her Faculty to the fact that athletics have some place in college. The Western League should continue by all means, and, in in order to do it, the members should bury their little differences very deep, and begin the new season with the most cordial feelings.

THE NEW FOOT BALL CAPTAIN.

Fred. A. Hayner, of the class of '95' has been elected captain of the foot ball team for next year. Hayner has played end rush on the team for two years and made a good record, in fact, an excellent record both years. He has shown good head work in most of the games and a capability of taking charge of a team. While he has had no chance as yet to prove his generalship, the STENTOR feels sure he will do well, and wishes him and the team all success possible.

The chess club has been a success. Now, why not combine either a whist club with the chess club or organize a whist club separately? There are many good whist players, and the game is no less scientific than chess, though in a different way. Let the whist players talk this matter up.

THE ETHICS OF SOCIALISM.

Not many months ago, a man, presumably a believer in the good old adage, "might makes right," certainly not an adherent of what he contemptuously calls the new "schemes for regenerating the world," derides socialism thus: "One main objection of mine to these schemes is that they are mere mechanism. They are unethical. They appeal not to the moral nature of man but to the stomach. They are a chapter, and a very ignoble chapter, in pig philosophy. Not more light, but more swill, is the cry which ascends from socialists and anarchists alike. I grant that there is some reason in the cry, and I would say, 'Well, by all means, have a little more swill then; but do not expect to wallow in swill. I will not suffer you, in order to that consummation, to upset the fair civilization and reduce all things to one dead dull level, flatly contradicting every worthy idea of the social organization. I have the hangman to break your necks, and the cannon to blow off your heads, if you attempt forcibly to realize your abominable Utopia.' That such will be the language of Germany, with whose strength the existence of civilization is bound up, I have no doubt. As to England, she is so far gone in maudlin sentimentality, so advanced on the road to 'self-government by the basest' that I greatly fear for her future."

But, you may say, it is no concern of ours to defend socialism. Yet, do these words seem either true or just? Assuredly they misconstrue the nature as they distort the motive of those economic changes which are certain to come about, and which will have something, be it more or less, of an affinity with these "schemes for regenerating the world." This stern tirade is worthy of thought. That man meant what he said. His accent was that of contempt, anger, of instinctive alarm, such as always betrays the intrusion into one's comfortable existence of an unknown and not easily measured force. There spoke the voice of threatened interests, of limited liability, and

the funded debts of all nations. He but gave utterance to what many are saying in their hearts, and would be delighted to proclaim aloud had they the courage. In every land there is a minority, few of us compare them with the millions, yet powerful by reason of their wealth and social influence, and whose share of what our friend has kindly termed "swill" has always been secure, thanks to sheep skin and sealing wax. To such, the "little more swill," which our sarcastic friend is willing to distribute among the starving, cannot greatly matter. "Why," he asks, "do the people cry for bread?" Why, indeed? Is it not their ignoble motive to fill their stomachs, the said stomachs being empty and clamorous for food? "Well," said he, with an emphasis worthy of the great Duke of Wellington, "let them fill them and be damned."

I need not apologize, even to the most fastidious, for quoting this vehement language. It is not only genuine but instructive. It sums up the position of the ordinary monopolist who is convinced that on the side of the *habentes* among whom he has gained a footing, there stands not only legal justice, represented by parchment and red tape, but also the nature of things; yes, reason and the will of God. The highest powers, he thinks, are with him. The inheritance of man from past ages, the arts, literatures, sciences, distinction of manners, individual freedom—all, he cries, repose upon the unlimited right of private property as their sure foundation. Ethics is the science of moral obligation. In what direction then does it bid us advance—on the path of free competition where the capitalist drives his herd of slaves like struggling swine; demon possessed over the precipice; or up the difficult, yet surely ascending way of perfection, leading to the true human sphere in which, not brute force, but the law of duty holds sway, and the love of one another.

But what do we understand by economic revolution? Are we denying a man's right to do what he will with his own? Must private property be abolished? If private property has assumed forms beyond reckoning, and most unlike, to decide against the right of private property in certain modern shapes is by no means to overthrow the principle itself. We must look capitalism in the face as an existing system, and ask ourselves whether it ought, on moral grounds, to endure. If it ought not, if, in spite of our critic's contention, it has no ethical basis, then go it must and will.

Ireland has suffered many conquests, uncounted confiscations, yet the Irish nation will never be subdued, and the quarrel of centuries, unappeased by parliament law, is alive at this day. Poland, smitten to pieces by public treaties, is yet one nation. Italy, after three centuries of shameful degradation, has been raised from the grave to take her place among the powers of Europe. Can we imagine that the greatest and most deeply enslaved of all nations, the nation of the poor, will never have its turn; that the bad old custom of living on what others have toiled for will stand good everlastingly in the chancery of heaven.

We have before us an amazing spectacle. We see a great multitude plowing the fields, raising the harvests, digging mines, weaving, and fashioning all manner of beautiful and useful things by means of the machinery which they themselves have made, carrying the produce of their toil to the world's end and carrying thence in exchange what like multitudes have in like manner created! And then the transformation! The banquet of civilization is spread and the company sit down. Are they the toilers of land and sea whom we beheld so busy? Do these eat the fruit of their hands? By no means! They have withdrawn out of sight to their dog-kennels, otherwise called hired tenements, and to their festering scraps, too often raked out of the refuse, in the strength of which they are allowed to live, to profligate and to create fresh capital. This is our law of supply and demand. Supply, the number of those who must work for wages or starve; and demand, the least amount on which, whilst working and breeding workers, they can contrive, *not* to starve until their average tale of

life has been told. Here is an ethical system, indeed, that confiscates for the benefit of a few the land of whole continents; that monopolizes the cotton industry, the coal industry, the iron industry; that snatches the corn from the Russian peasant on the Volga in order to drive down prices for aristocratic England; that depopulates Italy and fills its hospitals with starving women; that in the rich, democratic and educated states of America is repeating these marvels of the old world, laying its dead hand upon millions of acres, and raising up a proletariat not only on the shores of the Atlantic, but in Chicago, and at the Golden Gate. The *reductio ad absurdum* of industrialism can be but one step further—commercial ruin, and thither the system of the monopolist would hasten us.

Now which, if we have faith in God, is right—the pessimist, to whom the bulk of mankind are slaves at the mercy of a few; or the scientific student who, analyzing experience and finding progress, declares injustice to be no rock of ages but a thing to be grappled with and overcome. Yet with what front are we told that there is now a confederacy of God and mammon, or, in smoother phrase, that capitalism is rooted and founded on the moral law, is identical with justice and civilization? Is it just, or Christian or civilized that men should be slaves? Is there any shame in beginning where our Master did, with the wants and diseases of mankind; in feeding the thousands scattered through the wilderness ere we break to them the bread of a higher life? "Then are there not things which a man may call his own?" Let us say yes, cheerfully. "And a man may do as he likes with his own?" The answer is no. He must act as becomes a member of the great human family, as one who returns to his brethren, for the good they render to him, an equivalent— not a competition wage. Instead of prescription and competition, we want an acknowledgment that society is a rational organism, in which every human being has his appointed place,

There are many doors of escape from slavery, but the widest of all is the preaching and teaching of justice as due to men because of their humanity. To civilize is to make men feel that they are brothers, and from that brotherhood the Father will not be absent. Socialism and kindred doctrines may distort or misapprehend the Christian message, but capitalism has never heard of Christianity, of ethics, or of humanity.

LÆRTES '99.

THE LORELEI.

I know not whence it rises,
This thought so full of woe;
But a tale of times departed
Haunts me and will not go.

The air is cool and it darkens
And calmly flows the Rhine.
The mountain peaks are sparkling
In the sunny evening shine.

And yonder sits a maiden,
The fairest of the fair,
With gold is her garment glittering,
And she combs her golden hair.

With a golden comb she combs it
And a wild song singeth she,
That melts the heart with a wondrous
And powerful melody.

The boatman feels his bosom
With a nameless longing move.
He sees not the gulf before him,
His gaze is fixed above.

I believe o.er boat and boatman,
In the end the billows run,
And 'tis this that with her singing
by the Lorelei was done.

EMIL MENDEL.

Lake Forest, Ill.

COLLEGE.

AMUSEMENTS FOR THE WEEK.
COLUMBIA—J. K. Emmet in "Fritz in Ireland."
HOOLEY'S—Nat C. Goodwin in "A Gilded Fool."
GRAND—Alexander Salvini in "L'Ami Fritz" and "Cavalleria Rusticana."
CHICAGO—"The Crust of Society."
McVICKER'S—Mr. McKee Rankin in "A Kentucky Colonel."

COLLEGE NOTES.

The "World's Fair" class, '93, of the college mourns the departure of the sem seniors from the class in American Politics.

The tintinnabulation of the tinkling sleigh-bell merrily rings out upon the icy air of night every evening. Sleigh rides galore have been in order. To even name the different parties during the last ten days would take too much room. Parties of twenty, parties of ten, parties of four, parties of two, and, sad to tell, even parties of one have taken advantage of the splendid sleighing and the beautiful nights. It has been several years since it has been possible to enjoy this kind of pleasure, and it seems as if everyone was making up for lost time.

Have you ever been in Redda's room? A cad got in there the other day and wrought such a marvelous transformation that the owner has not even yet become accustomed to his new environment. The cad reduced chaos to order upon the table, he picked half a dozen collars out of a pile of shoes, hung up several suits of clothes, etc. This was the only way Jim could "do up" the room.

The tea given by Mrs. Seely to the senior classes of the College, Ferry Hall and Academy last week, Monday afternoon, was a very pretty and enjoyable affair. Mesdames Yaggy and McClure occupied the places of honor at the refreshment table, dispensing delicious tea and chocolate. The classes appreciate the honor done them.

The late Gov. Bross established in his will a lecture fund of $40,000, the interest of which was to be expended once in ten years upon a lecture course for the benefit of the students. It was suggested if the heirs of the Bross estate would not object that this income might be more profitably spent by using it for the purpose designated year by year. The matter is now in the hands of the students' committee, and they will circulate a petition which you will be asked to sign. This petition will then be turned over to the proper persons, who will try and accomplish the end sought. This is a very commendable move, and the STENTOR hopes to see it succeed.

Thursday, the 26th, was observed as the day of prayer for Schools and Colleges. In the morning the Rev. Mr. Hall, of Chicago, whose face is not unfamiliar to us, spoke at the church lecture room from the text "Multitudes, Multitudes in the Valley of Decision," laying special stress that between the ages of sixteen and twenty-one bears the whole future life is mapped out by the decision then made. In the afternoon, at Ferry Chapel, the Rev. Alexander Patterson spoke from the text "Speak, Lord, for Thy Servant Heareth," with special reference to the call to the gospel ministry. Both addresses were earnest and convincing.

J. Arthur Mitchell visited his old friends Friday. "Mitch" is the same genial, openhearted fellow that he was when he was one of us.

"Dick" McCleod, '92, was the guest of R. J. Oysart Thursday.

The students all feel that with the death of Mr. Wood there has passed away one who was always a friend to the young, and whose life was to them a shining example of truest Christian character. Although called almost

without warning, yet he met death most beautifully.

"As one who wraps the drapery of his couch about him,
And lies down to pleasant dreams."

The influence of Mr. Wood's life will long live in the hearts of those with whom he came in contact, and the force of the example of his life will always be felt for good by those who knew him.

The latest fad in the College is the eating of those repulsive licorice tablets. Ough! We have one in our mouth now.

TOWN TOPICS.

The Rev. Glen Wood died at his home, Wednesday afternoon, of neuralgia of the heart. He was ill only a few days and the end came unexpectedly. The funeral took place at his home Friday afternoon. The Reb. J. G. K. McClure, pastor of the Lake Forest Presbyterian Church, conducted the ceremony at the house, while the Rev. J. M. Strong, of Evanston, conducted that at the grave in Rose Hill. Several of Mr. Wood's favorite songs were sung by a quartet of students. The active pallbearers were six colored men, and the honorary pallbearers were H. Horton, E. S. Wells, G. Rossiter, D. Fales and E. S. Skinner, of Lake Forest, A. H. Castle and John W. Tindall, of Chicago, and H. B. Hurd, of Evanston. For years Mr. Wood was General Western Secretary of the American Tract Society, and travelled extensively, doing the work in which his life was bound up, faithfully and earnestly. Mr. Wood was born in Greenbush, N. Y., in 1818. He graduated from Yale with the class of '42. After graduating from Burr Seminary he founded the Presbyterian Church of Keokuk, Ia., which was the only pastorate he ever held. In 1878 he came to Lake Forest, where he has since resided, giving his time to various charitable works. The bereaved family have the sympathy of the entire community, each member of which, in Mr. Wood's death, feels a personal loss.

Fred. Wenban left this week for an extended trip through Wisconsin and Iowa.

Wednesday, a car containing a stallion and a bull was derailed in a flying switch; the shock drove the bovine's horns through the side of the car, and threw the horse upon an attendant, inflicting slight injuries.

A man by the name of Higgins was slightly injured by falling from the depot platform under a passenger train one day last week.

ATHLETICS.

The new riding of the athletic committee of the faculty is going to work irremediable harm as far as the interests of baseball are concerned. If we are to have a baseball team to represent us in the spring it is certain that the men must be trained beforehand. The management, after careful consideration, adopted a method which seemed most advisable, and it necessitated the use of the gymnasium floor at least three afternoons a week, between the hours of 4.20 and 5 o'clock. It is impossible to use the ball-cage provided, for reasons so obvious that it is unnecessary to state them. But few ever use the gymnasium between these hours, and these men can see no possible objection, as the apparatus used by them is not interfered with. Some entertain the mistaken idea that an athletic team is for the glorification of a few individuals, but an examination of the facts would clearly prove that teams are organized for the benefit of the University as a whole. Either the decision of the Faculty must be revoked or amended, or else we will have no ball team. It is not sufficient to simply develop the physical prowess of the men as in football, but practice must be had in handling grounders, pitching, catching, etc. Enthusiasm must be kept up, and if the men will not develop themselves physically of their own volition it is evident that some incentive must be offered. It is a question of vital importance to everyone, and some means must be secured by which the ball

team does not suffer in consequence of being deprived of the gymnasium as a place for practice.

At the Board of Directors meeting, held last Wednesday, Messrs. McKay, Crozier and Goodman were elected to represent the college at the regular February meeting of the Western College League. It was also decided that these committees be appointed by the President, one for Field Day and two in athletic entertainments. These meetings come but once a month, and it does seem as though all members could be present. As it is now there is great difficulty in securing a quorum.

The Athletic Association held a meeting in the College Chapel, Friday, Jan. 27, and elected Charlie Durand as director from the Academy, to succeed Warren Everett. It was reported that the Athletic Committee of the Faculty were endeavoring to secure a new athletic instructor for the gymnasium. These mass meetings should be held oftener, as during the winter term athletic interests are liable to lag, and the enthusiasm needs to be kept up.

Fred Hayner, '93, was elected captain of the football team for the year 1893-'94.

Last Monday the new Yale Gymnasium was formally presented. It is one of the finest gymnasiums in the world, as regards appointments, and was constructed at a cost of $200,000.

Forty-two men have applied for positions on the Cornell baseball team, and yet among this number not one is capable of filling the pitcher's box. All their efforts are being concentrated in this direction.

The outlook at Evanston is rather discouraging to baseball enthusiasts at that institution. But two men of last year's team, Bass and Griffith, have returned to college, and it is reported that the latter is going to Ann Arbor. It seems impossible to get new men out, and it looks now as though North-Western would make a poorer showing than last year, which is saying not a little.

Notice.—The next regular meeting of the Board of Directors of the Athletic Association will take place Monday evening, Feb. 6, at 7:45 p. m., in the President's room.

By order of the President,

B. R. MacHatton, *Secy.*

FERRY HALL.

Sleigh-rides have been the order of the week, parties having been out every evening.

Dr. and Mrs. Seeley spent Sunday, the fifteenth, in Chicago, at the home of Mr. and Mrs. Greenlee.

Thursday, Ferry Hall was well represented at the meetings. Consecration meetings also were held for a few moments in the morning on the different floors.

Miss Theo. Kane spent Sunday, the twenty-ninth, with Miss Bessie McWilliams.

Miss Ida Kehl has gone to California to spend the winter.

Girls, what are we going to do Washington's Birthday? Let's not leave the planning till the last minute.

Miss Gertrude Greenlee, '90, spent Thursday with Miss Alice Conger.

Miss Ada Barber, now in California, expects to go to Mexico by water, then return to Los Angeles, where she will remain till spring.

Four of the Senior entertained four young gentlemen at supper last Monday, after being sufficiently urged by said gentlemen.

Mr. Hays was summoned by telegram to Lake Forest to see his daughter, Miss Edna, who has been quite ill. Miss Hays has been taken to her home at Albion, Ind.

Misses Alta Barnum, Jeannette Kennedy and Beatrice Taylor were guests on the Freshman sleigh-ride.

The all-engrossing subject now is sleigh-rides. The Athenaens had one Tuesday evening, Jan. 24, and the the Zetas, Jan. 26. Everyone reports a pleasant time.

ACADEMY.

GAMMA SIGMA.

The senior class were entertained by Mrs. Seeley last Saturday afternoon from four to six o'clock.

Small amounts of money are reported missing from clothing left in gymnasium, and also from private rooms. It is hoped the matter will be looked into with the intention of catching the thief.

One of the Academy boys has shortened the usual form of salutation upon meeting an Academy master to "Hello Prof."

A number of the students attended the sleighing party and dinner given by Miss Larned last Saturday, and enjoyed a very pleasant time.

The gymnasium is now very generally patronized by the students, and they may be seen upon the running track nearly every evening.

The Gamma Sigma Society held its preliminary in declamation last Wednesday. The contestants were Heineman, Bournique, Graham, Cross, Scudder, the first two being successful. Prof. McNeil, A. A. Hopkins and McGauhey acted as judges.

There were no recitations last Thursday, it being the day of prayer for colleges. Instead of Chapel exercises the students were invited to attend the services at the church.

A large number of the students procured a sleigh and took a trip to Waukegan last Sunday, but since a recent meeting of the faculty they are made to recognize the error of their way.

Creswell was showing a friend from home the University last week.

The Tri Kappa Society adjourned last Wednesday to accept the invitation of Pres. Harvey to attend the Gamma Sigma contest.

McGauhey and Jackson Bros., former members of the society, witnessed the contest in declamation last week.

The Academy students who subscribed to the reading-room fund find it rather hard to get the worth of their money this term owing to the fact that the room remains closed.

S. C. Richards was visited by Rev. Thos. Marshall of Chicago last Wednesday.

Roberts was in the city Wednesday afternoon preparing for the preliminary contest in debate.

Hubachek has left Mitchell Hall, and will room outside for the remainder of the year.

It would certainly do no harm for those who sit in the church gallery on Sunday mornings to at least make a pretense of paying better attention to the sermon.

Lost.—In the Academy dormitory, last Wednesday evening, between the hours of 9:30 and 10 p. m., one temper, the property of Prof. Dudley. A suitable reward will be given by the students for the return of the same as soon as found.

The College people sleigh-ride; the Ferry Hall folks give spreads, but the Academy boys sit for three hours every holiday on the rough side of a pine seat in the chapel enthusiastically storing up knowledge for use in the dim and distant hereafter.

AS AN ALUMNUS LOOKS AT IT.

St. Paul, Minn., Jan. 23, 1893.

DEAR STENTOR:—

I believe there is a time for speech and a time for silence. At the present time I believe speech is not out of order, and as an Alumnus of L. F. U., I hasten to put my opinion on record *in re* the proposed union of Lake Forest College with the Chicago University, which union has a tremendous bearing on the future of L. F. U. By way of preface, before adding my *mite* to the concensus of opinion regarding the scheme, I wish to say I am a non-unionist. Following causes to their effects, it would seem that such a course would mean defeat and ultimate suicide.

It would mean the relinquishing of the institution's independence, and of its well-founded expectation of future greatness. Its identity would be submerged and its hope overthrown. To tack it on as a tail to the U. of C. kite would be to diminish materially much of its present well-merited distinction as an educational institution of great promise. It would become merely a "feeder" to the mill, and could rise no higher by reason of its subordinate position. Well might a person as well try to lift himself by his boot straps.

As it is at present, it stands on its own pedestal, fights its own battles, wins its own laurels and asks no quarters from any institution, feeling, as it does, amply able to honorably and successfully cope with any of them. With such a record why retrace its steps?

With such a start as it now enjoys, it seems almost absurd to contemplate for an instant being swallowed by a would-be gormandizer. Then again, would not such a course re-act unpleasantly on the professional departments, and would there not be a general abatement of individual interest in the institution and the city departments follow in the wake of the college and become a part of the expanding anatomy of the ambitious, precocious and omnivorous young monster institution of Chicago?

Would in not be more creditable, more honorable, even though its growth be somewhat slightly retarded by its proximity to such an amazingly covetous institution as adorns the brow of Chicago's pride, to preserve its identity and thus its power, and thus insure its future renown, for, with a distinct individuality, would not its scope for enlargement be widened, its influence extended and its usefulness increased?

Would not the sympathies of more well-filled purses be touched, and a consequent increased influx of funds follow?

Again, would it not be an exhibition of cowardice caused by the aggressiveness of this educational minerva, sprung full-fledged from the replete pocketbooks of a few philanthropists of large liberality, and of a baseless dread of extinction, to attach itself to the hem of another's garment?

If we but persevere, a broad and disinterested philanthropy will smile upon us, and bring into full bloom the latent possibilities · inherent in our institution.

No, a thousand times no, to the question of union! ·Let us abandon forthwith such a disastrous course, and fight it out on the old line if it take additional years.

"There can be no backword movement," as our retiring President eloquently said. We must rise to our destined eminence and become a still larger factor in the educational realm. But we can, I hope, never submit to become a cypher, to be placed at the will of another. Therefore, let us, with one accord, raise our voice against any such scheme, and with such an unmistakable refusal to any proposition to take shelter under the wing of our sister institution that her impertinence will be rebuked; that our future greatness may be assured, and that we may proclaim to the world that L. F. U. can paddle her own canoe.

No, we will be a sister to you. but no more. We can never consent to marriage, for we mistrust you, and feel that you would rule or ruin.

Fraternally,
W. B. BREWSTER.

Cotangent, cosecant, cosine,—
All co.'s that can be said,
Are not to be compared with thee,
Thou best of co.'s—co.ed.
— *University Herald.*

THE TWO MAIDS.

Two maids as fair as fair can be;
Fair twins, both blondes are they,
But both coquettes and shallow-souled,
Dressed up in style to-day.

They paint sometimes when color fails;
Delight in laces fine;
Two maids, two ready-mades are they,
These russet shoes of mine.
— *Williams Weekly.*

REVISED VERSION.

Beneath the tum-tum tree they sat,
He squeezed her hand; she smashed his ha —
They scrapped—
I saw them do it.

(One stanza more completes the rhyme.)
I snapped the Kodak just in time.
I clapped—
They heard me do it.
— *Williams Weekly.*

A PHYSICAL WRECK.

He cannot draw for want of "eye,"
He cannot sing for want of "ear,"
He cannot play ball for want of "head,"
Nor bluff for want of "cheek"—how queer!
— *Williams Weekly.*

"A fellow feeling makes us wondrous kind."
Perhaps the poet might have changed his mind
If, in a crowd one day he chanced to find
"A fellow feeling in his coat behind."
— *Exchange.*

The harp that once through Ta-Ra-Ra Boom
De-Ay's Halls
The soul of music shed, ·
Must soon hang silent on the walls,
Or we shall all be dead.
— *Wesleyan Echo.*

THE STENTOR.

Volume VI.   FEBRUARY 7, 1893.   Number 16.

PUBLISHED EVERY WEEK
BY THE
Lake Forest University Stentor Publishing Co.

BOARD OF EDITORS.

F. C. SHARON, '93................Managing Editor
R. H. CROZIER, '93...............Business Manager
N. H. BURDICK, '93 }
S. B. HOPKINS, '93 } ....Locals
L. N. ROSSITER, '93..........Alumni and Personal
B. R. MACHATTON, '95.................Advertising

ASSOCIATE EDITORS.

HARRY GOODMAN, '94..............Athletic Editor
FOREST GRANT, '96....................Staff Artist
DAVID FALES, '96........................Town

Terms—$1.50 per year. Single Copies—10c

——ADDRESS——

STENTOR PUBLISHING COMPANY,

LAKE FOREST, : : ILLINOIS.

Entered at the P. O. at Lake Forest, Ill., as second-class matter.

THE CHESS LEAGUE.

The *Northwestern* editorially seconds the STENTOR's suggestion that Northwestern, Chicago and Lake Forest Universities organize an inter-collegiate chess league, and quotes the STENTOR's editorial. As Lake Forest took the initiative in making the proposition it seemed best for her to follow it up by appointing a committee with power to act upon the question. J. A. Linn is the chairman of this committee. The present inter-collegiate contests all belong to the department of athletics. If a man has the right physique he has a chance of a place on these contests; otherwise he can be no more than a spectator, more or less interested, and give money to their support. A chess league would furnish intellectual contests, and if a man has brains and application he may win for himself laurels here when he would fail as an athlete. The chess league would not be a competitor with athletics, but would supplement them. We hope to see the universities mentioned take an active interest in this new movement, and appoint corresponding committees.

A DEARTH OF VERSE.

As we glance over exchanges we cannot but think how very lacking we are in versifiers. Scarcely an exchange comes to our table, that is from the more reputable schools, that does not contain specimens of verse, some of them very bright, some comic, and some containing real beauty. College verse is gaining a great place in college literature. Several colleges are issuing bound volumes of original poems, and they are selling at a wonderful rate. It is seldom in the best college journals that we see poor articles of verse, and one of the very choicest souvenirs, we should think, would be a volume of these poems, written at one's own college. There is a great dearth of poetry here. All that has been attempted has either been so deep as to have sunk the author before he is half through, or else mere doggeral. Can't something be done to start a train of thought that will bring out verses? Why should we be behind every other college in the land in this respect? We believe good specimens of poetry could be produced here if the fellows would but wake up and become interested in something beside themselves. The fact is, the students here are either too lazy to think or else—they can accomplish nothing when they do think. We would rather believe it is the former.

A SUGGESTION FOR THE SENIOR CLASS.

The present Senior class has been a class that has never done things by halves, and it will leave a name and reputation behind it that will be very enviable; and yet, it should leave some lasting memorial; should establish something that would keep its name and memory green for many years to come. This institution is growing every year. A new president soon will send things forward with a great boom. The literary work done here has always been a boast of both Faculty and students. It will soon be greater. Then why should we not have a literary magazine? We have two papers which fill the bill very acceptably from a news standpoint. Why shouldn't the present Senior class make its name immortal by starting a literary magazine, to be published once a month? There is plenty of ability in this year's class, and we are capable of publishing a magazine that will be a credit to the school. It has been claimed that such a magazine could not be published successfully here. We believe

it could. It was also said that this school could not support a weekly. Lo, and behold, it supports two! Such a magazine could be started soon, a few numbers issued, and everything established on a firm footing for next year's class. It would be a scheme worthy of '93' and we are anxious to see it put through.

AN INCENTIVE FOR CLASSES.

We see that recently Yale has offered prizes to the class teams that win in the inter-class athletic sports, and that Williams graduates have offered a silver cup for the winner of the inter-class ball games. The *Williams Weekly* has the following to say on the matter:

"The purpose is to arrange a series of inter-class games, including all four classes, to be played during the spring term. The victorious team will gain the honor of holding the class championship cup during one year, and of having the name of the class engraved upon it. The cup itself will pass from one victorious class to another, and gain from year to year in prestige and importance.

"The advantages arising from this plan are so obvious that they need scarcely be mentioned. First and before all here is something to meet and oppose, the deplorable decline of 'class spirit.' With the abolishing of hazing, rushes and class sings, inter-class feeling has become, like the excuse committee, a parody on itself. Class feeling is in the nature of things necessary and must have its expression, while the decline of such expression is a sure indication of an unhealthy state of affairs. A contest of some sort is implied in any idea of rivalry, and such contest as that proposed is beyond the reach of objection from well meaning though misguided trustees. Let us centralize our enthusiasm upon carrying out this scheme. We have enthusiasm for our college games and to spare. Enthusiasm too, is a commodity that increases

THE STENTOR.

in expenditure. There are many Wednesday and Saturday afternoons during the spring term, when the college team is playing out of town, or for which no game is arranged, when we would be glad of an exciting class contest. Then the practice games will afford the needed training for the 'Varsity team much better than any disinterested second nine can. Still further, a good system of class nines will bring out athletic talent which otherwise would remain latent. There are always many fellows in college who would like to play, but are discouraged from trying because they are sure they would be defeated. It is a trite saying that one does not know what he can do until he tries, but it will bear repetition."

Undoubtedly this is a good thing. The class spirit is dying out here in the same manner. Only occasionally does it flare up for a brief time in some class fight. Last year the class games were quite successful, but the schedule was too long, and consequently the championship was not decided, although '94 was slightly ahead at the time. This year, with a shorter schedule and such a prize as a cup, the season would be eminently successful. There is no doubt but that the class league last year developed many players who otherwise would not have come forward. Let the league again organize and consider the matter seriously.

THAT MOUNT ORNO BUCK.

'Twas Christmas Eve again. Once more the whole family of six were gathered around the fire. Each year saw them scattered to the four points of the compass. Each Christmas saw them together again. No one else was welcome there that night. So had it been for twenty years. The father, an old-timer, had told stories of early days in Colorado; of buffalo, Indians and stage-coaching; of the Leadville stampede, and the Cherry Creek flood. Then Will, one of the brothers, told how was killed the wild goose we had had for

dinner—a belated straggler along the Platte. Then silence followed. Suddenly the youngest broke out with: "Say, Chance! Tell 'bout the big buck!" She had heard the story before; but a murmur of assent following, "Chance" put a fresh stick on the coals and began:

"We were camping with John Glascow at the foot of Mount Orno, in Egeria Park, Colorado, that summer. A mile away down the valley from his little log cabin was the mail. Whoever went to the post-office, about twelve miles away, usually brought it up for the whole valley. Taking Rattler (my 45-90 Winchester) along for company, I went after a letter or two that I knew some of you had written me. Coming home again along the left of the ridge, I shot the head from a grouse. Still further on I saw three deer, but they were too far off to tell whether bucks or does. Not being on a regular hunt, the glasses had been left at the cabin. The deer were feeding in the head of a steep gulch, and in the shadow cast by the now setting sun. Mentally marking the place by a slight raise in the ridge, I stepped across to the other side and I was soon opposite them, I thought. The top was covered with coarse gravel there and sounded altogether too loudly under my feet to be pleasant at the time. At this point grew brush about eight feet high which hid me well. A few feet farther down on the other side it was about breast high. Which way the wind was, I do not remember; but, as it did not interfere with the shooting later, I think that it must have been blowing across the ridge. Stepping quickly, but noislessly as possible, across, I stood looking over the lower brush. Nothing was to be seen. Everything was perfectly still——when, about forty yards away, stood the largest buck I have ever seen. Broadside he stood, with head thrown back, cropping the leaves above him. How he got there I never knew. His tawny color contrasted sharply with the dark green background. So did the little ivory bead when I pulled the trigger! The buck gave a plunge and stood still. Another decided contrast! Then away he went along the ridge—almost straight away from me slightly towards its crest. Again the repeater spoke; but the white showed against the green that time. With set teeth two more shots were sent after him, in such fashion as to make Rattler worthy of his name. One of them caught the flying buck in the left hip and went through him lengthways. It tore its way through most of the important organs, including the heart (but not cutting a ventricle) and left a ragged hole in his breast. This made him stagger. The other bullet went in just back of the right fore-leg and out the same hole. The buck staggered over the top of a little ridge branching from the main one. Running along the latter, I came suddenly upon him—standing broadside again with his head lowered and turned toward me. His feet were firmly braced and blood was dropping from his nostrils. A perfect statue of blended defiance, wonder and helplessness he stood. Another quick shot at his neck, but my running made it harmless. [Never have I done better nor worse shooting than I did that day.] With a toss of his velvet antlers, he disappeared with stumbling gait down the smaller ridge. Knowing him to be fatally wounded, I rapidly followed for about one hundred yards. There he was, crouched down in the brush with his legs folded under and that powerful neck flattened almost to the ground. He made no effort to rise, but still had entirely too much life in him·to be approached without danger; so a bullet broke his neck.

"This was in plain sight of our cabin, not half a mile away, on the edge of the little hay-field below. Sticking him and pulling his head down hill, I left him to bleed; while I tried, by yelling and hat-waving, to get some one to bring a horse. But, as usual in such a case, no one saw me in the brush and deepening shadow, although they had all heard the rifle. After dressing the buck—being careful to save the tallow for candles (we used no oil) and to cut out the toothpicks from the legs for mementoes—I started home in the twilight, my arms covered with dry blood to the elbows —a nice feast for the mosquitoes. Next day, the wisest, meanest horse in Colorado, Old Moll, [You remember her, Will?] had the honor of packing that deer to camp." [The query brought a vigorous nod from Will. The remembrance of a certain fifteen-mile walk, partly along the old Ute trail, from Twenty Mile, when there after antelope, still lingered.] "And a load the buck made too," the speaker continued. "Milo, my companion, held his coat over Old Moll's white head with one hand and took up the three-inch slack of the rope with the other. We had to put the rope over a limb and around a tree in order to get such a load into the air. When nicely balanced across the saddle, the rope was untied—just in time to let the deer take his last plunge, with Old Moll's help, of course. With the grain of the

hair it went down hill about ten feet, much to her satisfaction, no doubt. No tree being convenient, we had to pull it up again. The next time my private deer hitch put a stop to such antics. Then, with one eye on the deer and the other everywhere, Old Moll brought the deer into camp. How much it weighed, I do not know. No one there had ever seen a larger one. I put several ordinary sized deer on a horse that summer when limber, but could barely lift this one when stiff. The skin was nailed up in John's winter cow-shed along with that of the bear. Two elk-hides soon followed. It may be there yet, as I gave it to John when I left." The speaker held his battered silver watch to the now dying fire. "Merry Christmas! Little one," he said, "I beat you that time. But come! To bed! Or Santa Claus will get tired of waiting and forget to leave you anything." Then the magic circle was broken, to be united again—*Quien sabe?*

—CHAUNCEY THOMAS, '96· *Sports Afield.*

COLLEGE.

AMUSEMENTS FOR THE WEEK.

COLUMBIA—Bostonians in "Robin Hood."
HOOLEY'S—Nat C. Goodwin in "A Gilded Fool."
GRAND—De Wolf Hopper in "Wang."
CHICAGO—August Junkermann in "Onkel Braesig."
McVICKER'S—Mdlle. Rhea in "Camile."

Prof. Halsey now occupies the recitation room in the south gable of the Art Building.

The inclemency of the weather has made sleighing parties less popular than last week.

It is reported that the Discipline Committee of the Faculty is to give another of its delightful entertainments soon.

A large number of students during the week applied at the World's Fair grounds for positions as guides during the Exposition.

During the week enough rain fell and froze to make the sidewalks impassible, forcing pedestrians into the road.

The University Club at its last meeting, held at Prof. Thomas' residence, listened to a paper by Prof. Jack, on the Philosophy of Tennyson.

Prof. Walter Smith will read a paper before the Art Institute, which meets at Mr. Yaggy's next Tuesday, on Schopenhauer's Theory of Art.

Prof. Thomas delivered an address on the Claims of Lake Forest on Chicago Presbyterians before the Minister's Meeting in Chicago, Monday.

Thursday the class in Current Politics resumed work, a recitation room being at last found, the want of which has until now stopped the work of the class since the opening of the term.

The class of '92 have established a laudable precedent in presenting the University with their individual photographs grouped around the likeness of Dr. McClure, all placed in a neat frame, and hung over the first landing of the main staircase in the Art Building.

Mr. E. M. Wilson, of Waukegan, who won the chess championship of Idaho in a 15-game tournament last winter, spent Friday afternoon and evening with Mr. Linn. They played four games, Mr. Linn securing 2½ to Mr. Wilson's 1½.

The college students who heard the Tri Kappa debate last Wednesday report themselves very much pleased with the debate of the winner, and also with that of Yaggy. The Gamma Sigma debater will have to get up a very strong debate in order to win from Cook.

February 3, the students attending North-Western from Menominee, Mich., gave a party in Evanston to the Menomineites who are attending school at Lake Forest, Kenilworth and Chicago, as well as others now in the vicinity of Chicago.

Our Chess Club, together with our proposition that an intercollegiate club be organized, has attracted the attention of Northwestern and Chicago, and the matter is being worked up in these universities. Mr. Linn is chairman of a committee to formally invite the players in these two neighboring institutions to play a tournament with ours.

The Chicago Chess Club have invited the Lake Forest Chess Club to visit them and play chess. The chess club voted to accept the invitation, and to send as representatives all those whose averages in the tournament now being played were above 500 per cent. The time of the tournament was extended two weeks, now closing February 18. A committee was appointed to try and organize a chess league, with Evanston and Chicago Universities.

Among the recent additions to the library are the following:—First Volume Hegel's History of Philosophy, translated by E. S. Haldane, the entire set, consisting of three volumes; Studies in Logic, by members of John Hopkins University; Essays on Literature and Philosophy, by Edward Caird, M. A., LL. D., two volumes; The Art of Poetry, translations from Horace, Vida and Boileau, edited by Albert S. Cook, of Yale; also the Defense of Poesy, by the same author; Essays in Literary Interpretation, by Hamilton Wright and Maline; Newman's Essays on Aristotle, edited by Albert S. Cook; Education of Man, by Friedrich Froibel and Poet Lore, volume four.

The day of the week was Thursday; the time was 10 a. m.; the place was the campus; the actors were Davies, Doran and Marcotte. Now it came to pass at this time that Davies, the strong, and Doran, the giant, met Marcotte, the innocent, and immediately began to sorely harass him. Be it known that Marcotte is of a brave spirit, and when his adversaries did beset him he was filled with a mighty indignation, and forthwith began to cast about him for means of retaliation. Seizing Davies, the strong, he did throw his adversary so that he fell with a dull thud—and great was the fall thereof. Then did the valiant Marcotte proceed to cast snow and ice in his enemy's face, even to the choking off of the wind. Having thus conquered the first, he turned the vials of his wrath loose upon the greater of his antagonists, and so defeated him that he did cry aloud in his defeat. Whereupon the magnanimous Marcotte did arise and run amid the cheers of his admiring classmates.

TOWN TOPICS.

Several of the town girls went to the German given at the Seminary last Friday night.

Mrs. Henry Ralston gave a dinner to Lake Forest friends Friday, Feb. 3rd.

Mr. E. F. Chapin was lately called east by the sickness of his father. His father died at Brookline, Mass.

Mrs. Jesse L. Moss gave a dinner party, Thursday, February 2, to a company of outside friends.

Mr. Alex is putting an addition on his house, which he has lately bought of Mr. Wm. Henry Smith.

On account of the lack of enthusiasm among the members, the Dancing Class will hereafter be discontinued. The last meeting of the class was held at Mrs. Calvin Durand's, Thursday, February 2.

Mr. Frank Rumsey's son, Joseph, who was taken with diphtheria just after Christmas, has just been released from forty day's quarantine of complete isolation from the rest of the family. Mr. Rumsey's other children escaped the disease.

It has been decided to renew the Dante Class, over which there was so much enthusiasm last winter. The class meets for the first time Tuesday morning, Feb. 7th, at the home of Mrs. Larned. Prof. Walter Smith will take charge of the class as before.

It has lately been heard from some of those who live in the town, that they have never yet heard a student's serenade. Although this is hardly the season for serenades, it is a good point to bear in mind that serenades are welcome at other places beside the Seminary, and would be as heartily appreciated as there.

ATHLETICS.

Warren Everett was in town last Tuesday to take charge of the classes in the gymnasium. From now on he will be out regularly twice a week. We are to be congratulated that the services of so efficient an instructor could be retained.

Henry, Marcotte and Harvey were appointed the committee on Field Day, and MacHatton, Fales and Flint the committee on entertainment, the first named being the chairman of the respective committees. The committee on athletic exhibition has not as yet been appointed.

The evil effects of the ruling of the Faculty restricting candidates for the ball team from the gymnasium floor are already plainly visible. The men do not show themselves at the gymnasium at all, and enthusiasm is a thing of the past. It will seem rather strange not to have a ball team this spring, as it will be the first time such a thing has happened since baseball first started here. The management regrets exceedingly that a ball team cannot be organized, especially as it was learned that through the instrumentality of a certain few the use of the gymnasium was forbidden.

Advices received from T. M. Blackman, the manager of the Beloit Ball Club, would seem to indicate that baseball interests at Beloit were in a flourishing condition. Although but five of last year's team have returned to college, they are confident of a stronger team than last year's. At present the candidates are doing light work in the gymnasium for a half-hour each day, working with light dumb-bells, Indian clubs, etc., together with various "setting up" exercises. This is followed by a half-hour's work at the bat, pitching, catching, picking up grounders and sliding bases. Then follows a sharp run, gradually lengthened from day to day, a bath and rub down, which ends the day's exercise. We wish the Beloit all possible success, and trust that the friendly relations which have heretofore existed between us may be kept up. We hope, in the near future, to be able to give the methods of training employed by other leading western colleges.

FERRY HALL.

Miss Jessie Lindsay, of Milwaukee, spent Sunday with the Misses Kennedy.

Miss Lucy Smith has gone to Chicago for a weeks rest on account of her health.

Rumors are afloat of an open meeting of the Tri Beta Kappa Society in the near future.

Lost:—(By the Sophomores, Nov. 8th.) Class Hats.

Lost:—(By the Freshmen, Nov. 10th.) All their clothes.

Freshman bill-of-fare, Nov. 10th.

Crackers : - - - - Cheese

Freshman motto.

"The wicked fleeth and no man pursueth."

The F. H. library has been removed from the first floor to rooms 107 and 109 second floor.

Senior, picking up a small "Madonna," and holding it at arm's length.—"Who took this tin-type?"

In the Logic class.—"It is hard for some people to distinguish whether a fish is vegetable or animal."

Brilliancy of the Seniors.—Who wrote "The Fair Barbarian?" "The Fair God," you mean, don't you? Ben Hur wrote that.

We regret to say that Miss Robinson was called to her home in New York, Tuesday, by the serious illness of her mother.

Ferry Hall gas is about as reliable as a board of trade speculation. The girls in the middle part of the building dwelt in darkness three nights out of the past week.

Miss Hall, of the Columbia School of Oratory, entertained the Aletheian Society November 4th with two selections from Dickens' Works, and a talk on Physical Culture.

Last term, at morning chapel, we were favored frequently with music from Prof. Eager or Mrs. Hester. This term, we have had such a treat but once, Friday morning, when Prof. Eager played for us.

Miss Vera Scott and Miss Edna Smith gave a little informal dance in the gymnasium Friday evening. Among the guests were Miss Irene Smith, of Hagerstown, Md., Miss Mary Travers, of Amboy, Ill., and Miss Mina Howard, of Glencoe.

The first edition of the "Aletheian Kicker" made its appearance in society last Friday evening. It discussed the impropriety of saying good-night under the flare of the gas light; the necessity of having a chaperon when going to lectures in carriages, and several sensible things.

Saturday evening, at eleven o'clock, the Misses Kennedy gave a very enjoyable spread in honor of their guest, Miss Lindsay. The young ladies were all in evening costume. Covers were laid for twenty. Miss Jeanette Kennedy in an exquisite costume of tan, girt about the waist with a golden-brown cord, presided at the head of the table, her guest at her right hand. Miss Lena Kennedy did the honors at the foot of the table. She wore a beautiful gown of mousseline de soie. The Misses McWilliams, McCord and Lyon looked charming in simple dresses of white embroidered mull. Neither space nor imagination will permit us to further describe this most pleasant of feasts.

The College girls petitioned the Faculty a long, long time ago for the use of the gymnasium one afternoon in each week. The request was granted on the conditions that curtains should be purchased for the windows, that a chaperon should be secured, and that there should be regular classes. Now, the trustees furnish an instructor for the boys, and the girls do not think it any more than just that the same should be done for them. They accordingly made their request to that effect, and even went so far as to agree to pay half of the teacher's salary, but——perhaps the present Freshmen will get a reply when they get to be Seniors. We wish the College boys to remember how long it took them to get the Gym., how long it took them to get possession of it after it was finished, and *please* have enough mercy on us *not* to ask us any more "Why don't you hustle?"

ACADEMY.

GAMMA SIGMA.

Heineman was visited by his father recently.

Reinhart has been ill for the last few days, but is again convalescent.

Kilgore and Condon are training their voices to shout for the baseball team.

Several of the day students were in Waukegan one evening 'last week with a sleighing party.

Taylor, who has been in the city this past week having his eyes treated, has returned to school again.

An athletic exhibition will be given by the students if sufficient interest in the matter can be aroused.

MacHatton, Fales, and J. H. Rice of the college attended the Tri Kappa debate last Wednesday.

The Glee Club will meet hereafter from 11 to 12 on Thursdays, instead of Tuesday and Friday evenings as formerly.

Prof. Smith will hereafter have charge of the Ancient History class, Prof. Burnap devoting more of his time to Greek.

Prof. Allen, whose death has before been mentioned in this paper, was director of the Academy Orchestra last year.

Most of the declamation contestants are hard at work drilling under Prof. Booth. The contest promises to be very exciting.

Prof. Smith addressed the students in Chapel last Wednesday concerning the life and character of Blaine. His talk was very enjoyable.

The rumored election of a president for the University was a subject of conversation one day last week with those who contemplate entering the college next year.

A great many of the boys took advantage of the pleasant weather and bright moonlight last Monday night to enjoy an evening of skating on Farwell's Pond. A pleasant time is reported.

Warren Everett has been secured as gymnasium instructor again, and will come from the city three times a week, Monday, Thursday and Friday. All are glad to welcome him back.

Everyone admires the ease and grace with which Marshal establishes himself in the esteem of the Academy students. By his joy and mirth he has been truly termed a cloud with a silver lining.

The Tri Kappa Society held their preliminary contest in debate last Wednesday morning. Rice, Yaggy and Cook were the contestants, the latter being successful. Sharon, S. B. Hopkins and Prof. Bridgman acted as judges. The Gamma Sigma accepted the invitation of Pres. Durand and attended in a body.

Judson Williams, "to get the worth of the money he paid for oil," left his lamp burning while he spent Sunday evening visiting a friend. Upon his return he found it would take about two hour's work to remove the soot from clothing and furniture, his lamp having smoked away during his absence like a first form cad.

Some of the boys who room in the president's house, took advantage of the recent thaw to storm the Mitchell Hall boys with snowballs. They at first held them in their own building, but the Mitchell Hall boys massed their forces, made a sudden rush and routed the attacking party. Heineman and Alexander were for a time held as prisoners.

The following were elected officers of the newly organized branch of the Y. M. C. A. in the Academy:

Pres., Geo. Rice.
Vice-Pres., R. L. Roberts.
Rec. Sec., M. K. Baker.
Cor. Sec., T. M. Hatch.
Treas., C. J. Hanant.

The association starts out with a body of earnest Christian young men at the head of it, and it is to be hoped much needful work will be accomplished. Heretofore the organization was in connection with the College Association, and many who would like to have joined were for this reason prevented from doing so.

THE STENTOR.

VOLUME VI. FEBRUARY 14, 1893. NUMBER 17.

PUBLISHED EVERY WEEK
BY THE

Lake Forest University Stentor Publishing Co.

BOARD OF EDITORS.

F. C. SHARON, '93 .... Managing Editor
R. H. CROZIER, '93 .... Business Manager
N. H. BURDICK, '93 ⎱
S. B. HOPKINS, '93 ⎰ .... Locals
L. N. ROSSITER, '93 .... Alumni and Personal
B. R. MacHATTON, '95 .... Advertising

ASSOCIATE EDITORS.

HARRY GOODMAN, '94 .... Athletic Editor
FOREST GRANT, '96 .... Staff Artist
DAVID FALES, '96 .... Town

Terms—$1.50 per year. Single Copies—10c

———ADDRESS———

STENTOR PUBLISHING COMPANY,

LAKE FOREST, : : ILLINOIS.

Entered at the P. O. at Lake Forest, Ill., as second-class matter.

SOMETHING FOR LATIN STUDENTS.

We notice by the *Illini*, the official organ of the University of Illinois, that it will publish in every issue from now on, English verse translations of Latin poems made by students in the University. This is an excellent plan and if a University can produce no original verse it should at least produce passable translations. Here is a chance for Latin students at Lake Forest. Turn out some metrical translations and we will give them space.

THE GIRL OUT OF SCHOOL.

There is no problem perhaps so hard for a girl to decide as what she shall do when her school days are over. She wants to have a good time and yet she wants to be literary, she wants rest and yet she wants to be on the go, she wants to read "something light" and yet she wants to study, in fact she is made up of impulses. Correct us if we are at fault for this a masculine view. A girl at best must lead a rather monotonous life and active men cannot but sympathize with her. However realizing our inability to cope with this problem we asked Mrs. Ferry to write on the subject and the admirable paper found in another column will explain itself.

ST. VALENTINE---YOUR PATRON SAINT.

What visions the mention of St. Valentine brings up before our minds, especially those among us who are imaginative. We seem to be carried back to the times when on the 14th of each and every February we looked forward to the coming of the postman with his bundle of filagreed, embossed, and *beautiful* valentines all directed in strange handwriting—the handwriting is always strange on this day, but the sender at the last minute thinks the writing is *too* strange so into the corner go his initials. We scarce thought such beautiful things could be made out of paper. And then the verses! Sit still, our heart! How they breathed out true love and beautiful cheeks and pearly teeth and breath of roses and other attributes. Oh those days have gone— unless some one kindly sends us some verses today. And in their place have come these days of cynicasm when the college man is abroad in the land and declares that "we do not exist" that "St. Valentine never existed" and that "Santa Claus is a Myth." O ye heretics, ye Sophists, take away ourselves, take away Santa Claus but leave us St. Valentine. P. S. As the last mail is in however and we are still empty handed, you can take away St. Val. to.

SOME MASCULINE ADVICE.

If we are too over-bearing, girls, don't hesitate to inform us and enclose a two cent stamp for reply. But we noticed in a recent STENTOR that the Ferry Hall correspondent complained that the girls took no interest in Society work whatever, that they preferred paying a fine to appearing on the program. On this statement we want to make a few remarks. In the college and academy, contests of various kinds are held, class contests, society contests, declamation, oratory, essay, and debate contests and prizes are given for these. And Ferry Hall, the largest department, has no contest of any kind, no prizes for anything, not even any society spirit! *Girls why don't you contest?* Organize another society, get up some pride as to which society shall lead and you will be surprised at the amount of interest you will take in your literary work. If you will but organize and show yourselves in earnest, people will be ready enough to offer prizes. And think of the fun and excitement! A real Ferry Hall contest instead of a Cad contest or a College contest. Ferry Hall could give splendid contests in music or elocution. What do you say, Ferry Hall? Will you accept our advice?

TO OUR GIRLS.

Dear Girls (can't we say dearest girls?) we realize what an important part you play in college life and with contrition we acknowledge that in the past we have not paid enough attention to you, that is—excuse us--we—we mean *editorially* of course. In our blind selfishness and egotism we, of the male persuasion, have gone forward day after day saying, "there are none like us," "we are the people," "Was ist los mit us" and other touching phrases. But when we reach this day dedicated to that noble saint, the guardian of lovers, we are arrested in our mad career as we realize that this day of all others is set apart for *you* and that it behooves us to prove that "we are the people" by composing some sweet verses, tacking them on some illuminated paper, and sending them to our lady-loves. But we have so many girls (pardon our modesty) and the old way would take so many new Columbian stamps that the best and most inexpensive way we could think of, was to send our love through the STENTOR, so here it is. We know it is not so tender as some we have seen as we have said nothing about "azure hair and golden eyes" but we have lost much of our tenderness in this cold world, and to speak confidentially a great deal has been wasted (?) no we mean *lost* on you already. With these thoughts dear girls we hope to keep you on our subscription lists another year.

ST. VALENTINE AND THE WAY THE SEMINARY REGARDS HIM.

Do girls like Valentines? Yes, they do in their tenderer years. But when they reach the advanced age of eighteen, they say they never think of them. No (?) Watch the maiden who would speak thusly. It is the fourteenth of February, a missive comes to her, with blushing cheeks and down-cast eyes she takes herself from our midst and in some secluded spot, learns who would have her for his valentine. We never think of things till they are brought to our minds, and now do you suppose that maiden will forget her valentine?

*_**

Who ever accepts this valentine
Will be forever a love of mine,
For I know nothing much to write
Trying hard with brains and might.
But of the kinds of valentines let us speak.
There's one for the lowly and one for the meek,
One for the bride and one for the groom,
And one for the person who wields a broom,
One for the fat and one for the slim,
One for Johnny and one for Jim,
Pretty ones, comic, little and big,
But for the whole pile I don't care a fig,
We'd rather have fruit and candy and cake,
And all the good things that cooks can make,
But above everything else that we can recall,
Is the life that we lead at Ferry Hall.

Nancy Hanks.

*_**

I used to think Valentine's Day was great fun, and used to expect a valentine, but since I've grown so old I don't know anything about it any more.

M. S. age 19.

*_**

Modern St. Valentine sits all the day
This big book before him lies open,
He checks off the slams that he has to repay,
And smiles at the numerous love-tokens.

Would-be-Poetess.

*_**

It seems to me the dear old custom of St.

Valentine's day is fast being elbowed to the rear among our social observances! This legendary saint once held the highest place in the hearts of the young people of a household. How the mails were watched, and with what eagerness its treasures were born away by some blushing maid, to be opened in the privacy of her own room. A still better period in the annals of this lore was the time when original stanzas were Cupid's messengers. The return of such a time would be warmly welcomed. A sheet of paper with some one's honest sentiments would be far more welcome today, to a sensible girl than a ream of "printed prettiness."

Cupid's Advocate.

*_**

St. Valentine's Day is the time when young love
Finds vent in the form of a token,
These valentines may, in some shape or way
Mean very much more than is spoken.
The saint, though old, shows his wits are still young,
By the way he composes his rhymes,
For the spoony expressions he puts in his gifts,
Shows he keeps up with the times.

Shy Maiden.

*_**

See yonder maiden tripping down the street, happy, joyous, gay. Sly Cupid hails her, and hands her missives many. Away she goes waving her missives high, and telling of conquests many,—who *is* her valentine?

Five—ten—fifteen years have passed. Sly Cupid, young as ever—for we are told with every generation he is re-born, comes gaily down the street. That maiden, a maid-en still, sits at the window. Will he stop? Does her heart still flutter? Yes—no! But Cupid with his pack goes by—and as we look we are forced to murmur those time-worn, tongue-worn words—

Of all sad words of tongue or pen
The saddest are these, "it might have been."

Coquette.

*_**

Valentine's Day! Cupid's Day! Yes, his majesty king Cupid holds forth to-day. Hearts is the game. Every youth and maiden must play their cards well. Each would capture the ace. King Cupid would assist, and slyly slips a second ace into the pack. The game is ended and each stands triumphant—the youth with the heart of the maiden—the maiden with the heart of the youth.

THE SCHOOL-DAYS OVER—WHAT SHALL SHE DO?

How to pursue one's education independently is a mixed question in this progressive age, and especially for women. The result of the combined wisdom of all the sages could not lay down laws that would cover the needs of any one woman. The most that an interested outsider can do is to point out some mistakes that can be avoided. The great danger of the present age is its complexity, which tends to dissipate and weaken the powers. There are many things to learn and many openings hitherto closed to women. It reduces everyone to the necessity of wise selection.

This is an age particularly stimulating to woman's ambition. Not only are women holding out the helping hand to each other, but the wisest and best men are still firing us on with words of praise and encouragement, while the voices of the weak and foolish brothers who have been tiring our ears with the old refrain of "woman's sphere" are growing weaker and dying gradually into irrecoverable silence.

Doubtless every girl feels, more or less, the inspiration of the hour, and a struggling ambition to be among the best.

To leave generalities for the familiar and special, let us note a single specimen of the great genera—"The Sweet Girl Graduate."

It is not necessary to dwell upon the girls who have a decided bent in any direction; who expect to teach, paint, study music, or enter upon the hundred and one occupations open to women. They need no help or advice that they cannot hunt up themselves.

But there is one poor creature, a sample of the large majority who are bright, conscientious,

and who do not have to do anything. She could paint, draw, teach, write and be an artist in any profession she chose to be proficient in.

We have all seen her. She has (been) graduated with honor and is filled with ideas of progress, and desires to keep up her studies, as the phrase goes. She hangs on to her education as a belle to her favorite terrier, jerking it along and holding on to it as if it was bound to get away from her. She joins all the classes she is asked to. German, French, Italian and Spanish are studied with devouring eagerness for fear she will forget how to say "Have you seen the red cow of my sister-in-law's grandmother?" correctly in all four languages.

This young woman has come out, of course, and has her train of admirers.

The multifarious calls that society continues to make upon its buds must be responded to. That time-honored institution, now as of old, looks to woman as its guiding star.

Is it reasonable to suppose that a young girl of ordinary endurance can pay attention to the social demands made upon her during the two or three years after the school-days are over, and also pursue, to any great extent, her studies?

A thousand times no! Many more break down from a sense of this double responsibility than from the assigned cause, social dissipation. The truly frivolous, those who care not for the deeper nature, never break down. It is generally the girl who, naturally enough, is fond of fun but also feels that education must be maintained as if it were a tangible something that, in order to be kept, must be fondled and cared for.

She even grudges the time for the girlish dreams (remember what grand endings are likely to result from them) which must be interrupted ever and anon by a page of mental philosophy or a conjugation of a waning verb.

This is not as it should be. Do not think of study for at least two years after graduation. I mean the memory drudgery of it. If your education is worth anything it will not run away from you. It cannot. You have not been putting on so many shells of education, onion like, but you have absorbed whatever will be of use to you.

Give yourself a chance to grow and develop and work out those principles and maxims that were instilled into you as the morning dew upon the tender herb.

Webster says: "Education is properly to draw forth, and implies not so much the communication of knowledge, as the discipline of the intellect, the establishment of the principles and the regulation of the heart."

There is a great deal said about the elevation of the stage, but society can have a vast amount of elevating and every woman should consider herself a lever for that purpose.

Society itself is inevitably the great school of tact in which the art of gentle breeding is taught by experience and observation.

When we smilingly observe "She treats everyone as though he was the favored one," we are noting the behaviour of one who has mastered the art of courtesy. It is frivolity and heartlessness that have brought down the anathemas of the severe upon the "great belle."

Now, time and space are used up and nothing is said about religious culture, but you can read Henry Drummond..

Nothing about reading? There are courses and courses marked out for you. All I wish to say is: Learn to skip voluminously; the best is always scanty; let us be thankful for that in one respect. Learn to select the best, and bravely ignore even much that is good.

To sum up, regulate your conduct and way of life so that when you are doing one thing you shall not worry because you are not doing a hundred other things. For this feeling is the great bug-bear of woman's existence.

ABBY FARWELL FERRY.

A GRIM (M) FAIRY-TALE.

BY AN ARABIAN KNIGHT.

Once upon a time long, long ago almost before "time was," there lived in a certain land a king by the name of Onwee. (Now if this king were French we would call him *Ennui* but being an ancestor of Pres. Clevenson we use the English.) King Onwee had everything his great heart could desire even from his ten meals a day to the crease in his trousers, for be it known that his mighty sovereign wore trousers and had a crease long before "hand-me-downs" came in style. Everywhere the people loved him, thousand of servants were at his beck and call, he had musicians, and clowns and sooth sayers galore. And yet was this monarch not satisfied. He continually longed for something new. He was intensely tired. Everything around him was tired. He ordered a bicycle one day but that was *tired* too. Even the names of his ministers suggested weariness. His prime minister was R. E. Pose, his secretary of amusements was U. Makemetired, his gauger of the public weariness was S. Leeper. The king became so weary that finally he assembled his ministers and held a consultation. They decided that King Onwee was dying of *ennui.* So the word went forth to the uttermost limits of the Kingdon that the king must be amused. That if he wasn't amused in twenty-four hours he would amuse himself by severing the jugulars of his ministers which the ministers avowed would not be amusing at all. Naturally the ministers arose and shook themselves and messengers were dispatched in every direction to hunt up something amusing.

Now it so happened (everything happens just right in a fairy tale you know) it so happened that a youth yclept Cupid had wandered into the kingdom that day and hearing and seeing this wonderful commotion desired to know "Was ist los." The anxious people told him their beloved king must be amused or he would die and then it would be amusing to see who would succeed him. Cupid thunk a great think and finally saying in stage tones "It must be done," journeyed onward toward the palace. Walking into the king's presence he took out his bow and arrows and, taking aim, deliberately shot the great king through his great unamused heart. The king gave a mighty leap but Cupid vanished in thin air and the monarch setting back in his throne again, found he was still alive and apparently unhurt. But he gradually became aroused and awakened and made things lively for the sleepy court and became so nervous and restless that R. E. Pose had to skip around lively to keep up with him. Still all this perplexed the king as much as his loving subjects and he would fain know the reason thereof. So he caused all his soothsayers and prophets to come before him and demanded that they should tell him whence this whichness. But they were even more at a loss for a reason than the king himself. Then was the king enraged and cast them from him and sent out into his kingdom saying that to any one who would interpret his changed feelings he would give honor and great wealth.

So it came to pass that one day a venerable man was brought before him who had been captured near the royal chicken coop. The people demanded his life, and the king himself was in a great rage, but finally said: "One chance I give thee for thy life. Tell me whence this change of nature that has come over me and I will not only give thee life, but great riches beside."

Then the old man prostrated himself before the king and said in a trembling voice: "O King Onwee, greatest of the kings, since thou wilt grant me my unworthy life for this knowledge, be it known unto thee that thou art *in love*, and that the arrow which entered thy heart was from cupid, the god of love."

"In love!" shouted the king, "and with what?"

"With a woman, your most sacred majesty."

"Go forth," said the king with eagerness to his ministers, "go forth and fetch in the fairest woman in my kingdom till I prove his words."

Then they went forth and brought in the fairest woman, and the king looked on her and *loved*.

Then was there great rejoicing in the king's heart. "Ho, ho, ho," laughed he in what we of the present would call a horse laugh [but horses were not invented then, neither was Latin]. "Ho, ho, ho, thou art a philosopher

truly. And what is thy name, O man of wisdom?"

"Valentine, an' it please your majesty," responded the old man."

"It pleases me mightily," quoth the king, "and we shall remember thee. S. Leeper, what day is this?"

"The 14th of February, your majesty."

"Ah, Valentine, since thou hast shown us love, henceforth thou shalt be called St. Valentine, and this day shall be set apart for thee as an everlasting memorial for thee."

Then was there feasting and much drinking of wine as St. Valentine took his place at the side of the king, which place he has held ever since. [This version has never before been in print because it has just been discovered in the cave of the Forty Thieves, and was read by the light of Aladdin's Lamp.]

S.

COLLEGE.

AMUSEMENTS FOR THE WEEK.
Columbia—Bostonians in "The Knickerbockers."
Hooley's—Rosina Vokes.
Grand—De Wolf Hopper in "Wang."
Chicago—August Junkermann in "Hanne Nuete."
McVicker's—Wilson Barrett.
Schiller—"Surrender."

Have you been vaccinated?

Have you made application to be a guide at the World's Fair?

More snow during the week. Sleighing parties are again popular.

W. H. Hummiston was the guest of the G. P. Club the first of last week.

G. W. King spent several days among his old friends last week.

A number of the boys attended the Saturday matinee of "Wang."

Who looked at the Sun clock at ten o'clock Friday night? Naughty boy.

.French, the druggist, has everything in the line of tooth-brushes and toilet articles.

Gymnasium suits, shoes and other athletic goods on hand. Low prices. Ruston, College Hall.

One more week and then the chess tournament will close. If you have any back games you'd better play them off.

Buck, the Waukegan jeweler has the finest gems in the west. Give him your order for anything in the line of jewelry.

Step up, gentlemen, and plunk down the goodly coin of the realm and never again be tempted to burn barrels without setting a guard to watch lor the enemy.

Reports have reached us that G. D. Schofield continues to regain his health, though but slowly. It is his intention to take a Southern trip as soon as consistent with safety.

The favored few who attended the Aletheian open meeting Friday evening were very enthusiastic Saturday morning in their praise of the ladies' efforts. Those who were "not sufficiently urged" feel that it is a serious misfortune not to "stand in."

The afternoon reception given Friday afternoon by Dr. and Mrs. McClure was attended by most of the students who, without exception, report a very pleasant affair. The Misses Rumsey, Stanley and Holt were at the chocolate and tea tables.

Many of the students went to Jackson Park Saturday to make application and take the examination to be guide at the World's Fair next summer. Evanston was well represented and the guying between the representatives in the rush was good natured and hearty.

The dates of the closing of the winter and spring terms have been fixed. The present term will close March 22nd and the next term June 14th. This has been a much vexed question and it is to be hoped that this announcement will be a relief to those interested.

Some town hoodlums threw a snowball through the Crozier & Ruston window one evening last week. They also annoyed two young ladies who were returning home from Ferry Hall unattended. Such things should not be and the fact that they are shows that something is wrong.

The reading room is again open! After two months the powers that be have decided to abandon the anachronism of a college in which a reading room has no place. The magazines and papers may once more be found in their old places. The proposition made that the students furnish a table, or bear part of the cost of one, was not accepted by them. A substantial table, however, has taken the place of the old ram shackle affair, but just who is to be thanked for it is not stated. Whoever it may be the students appreciate the kindness.

One of the most delightful affairs of the season was the party given by Mr. and Mrs. N. D. Pratt to the Athenaean Society last Saturday evening. About thirty couples were present and enjoyed a progressive spelling game most of the evening. Miss Grace McCord and F. C. Sharron won the head prizes. The rest of the evening was spent in singing and "Willie" Danforth, "Rad," "Robbie Frazier" and "Niddie" gave their inimitable solos. To sum it up it was a time such as can only be enjoyed at Mr. Pratt's.

The engagement is announced of Herbert Alward, of Chicago, and Miss Jessica Stevens, of Neenah. The prospective groom is well known in this city, having been a member of the Menasha base ball team of '88. The gentleman is well known to the old students of Lake Forest. For some time he was a prominent player on the defunct Racine College base ball team and played during the first years of its existence in the Northwestern College Base Ball League. His many friends wish him all possible happiness. He is quite prominent in Chicago and Milwaukee.

A certain firm in a certain state—we withhold names for ethical reasons—have sent out their annual circulars announcing that they are "supplying the busy students of the country with all kinds of literary productions." These "productions" are all written by "alumni of first class colleges" and are warranted to relieve "those who are obliged by a tyrannical college faculty to waste both mortal time and parental money" in useless work. High school orations are worth from "$3.00 to $8.00, according to style, length, subject, etc." Sermons $1.00 to $25.00, ditto. The circular is "yours confidentially." We are going to frame ours.

There is to be at the World's Fair a National Inter-collegiate Base Ball Tourney in which it is proposed the five best teams of the west will be pitted against the five best in the east. The five proposed for the east are Yale, Harvard, Princeton, Pennsylvania and Cornell. The west will be represented by Michigan, Madison, Univ., of Chicago, Minnesota and Northwestern. At least this is the way they are chosen by the president and secretary of the scheme, who are respectively from Northwestern and Chicago. Northwestern will have to pick up wonderfully. There are numerous teams in the west that can beat her. She won our game last year. We should judge from records made that the University of Iowa or Lake Forest would stand a much better chance than Northwestern. We understand Grinnell will have a strong team this year and then what is the matter with Leland Stanford? Who takes it upon himself to pick out the five best teams in the west?

TOWN TOPICS.

Miss Hattie Durand is visiting her aunt, Mrs. Downs, in Chicago.

Mrs. J. H. Dwight has been confined to the house by injuries received from a fall on the ice.

Mr. C. K. Giles spent Sunday, February 5, at Ogontz School, with his daughter, Miss Mabel Giles.

The Art Institute met last Tuesday at the home of Mr. Yaggy. Prof. Walter Smith delivered the lecture.

The Misses Florence and Kathryn Durand are visiting their aunt, Mrs. Dewey, in Milwaukee. Mrs. Joseph Durand spent Friday with Mrs. Dewey.

At the next meeting of the Young Ladies' Musical Class, the musical number will be a quartette of young ladies, composed of Misses Pratt, Grace Stanley and Minnie Rumsey, and Mrs. Shirley U. Martin. The object of the class is to promote a higher knowlege of music.

FERRY HALL.

The Misses Phelps visited Evanston last week.

Miss Chandler, of Chicago, spent Saturday with Miss McIntosh.

Miss Searles gave a tea to the young ladies of her table Thursday p. m.

Mrs. McWilliams, of Odell, spent Thursday and Friday with her daughters.

Mr. Lord, of Evanston, spent Tuesday afternoon with his daughter, Miss Annie.

Miss Cresswell has been confined to her room for two weeks past because of illness.

Several of the girls enjoyed a sleigh-ride given by the Academy boys Friday evening.

Girls, let us protest if there is to be no ball team this year. What will the spring term be with no base-ball games?

Some of the callers on the eve of February 4th seemed to be rather embarrassed. At any rate, the ladies had to do all the talking.

Miss Marie Halloway, '88, is spending the winter with her sister in Omaha. She expects to spend the months of March and April in California.

Young man, burn not the barrel which belongeth not to thee by right of purchase, else wilt thou be caught in thy transgression and suffer therefrom.

Overheard on the train. "And then as we were coming home in the street car, you know, we had to stand up. Well the car gave a dreadful lurch and the whole line of us fell down in a heap and —— —— lost her hat and we knocked down a poor man who was in our way and—oh there is one of those terrible reporters listening to everything I am saying."

The Aletheians gave a special meeting Friday evening, February 10th, to which some of the gentlemen were invited. The following program was rendered:—

Instrumental solo. - - - - -	Miss Pearce
Reading. - - - - - -	Miss Hopkins
Essay. - - - - -	Miss Brubaker
Vocal duet. - - - - -	{ Miss Brett { Miss Davis
Dream of Fair Women. - - -	Tennyson
Paper—Aletheians' Future. - -	Miss Uberne
Recitation. - - - - -	Miss Liese -
Music.	

Miss Theo. Kane gave a very pretty luncheon at her home 310 Ashland avenue, Chicago, to twenty-four of her friends Saturday, February 11. The guests were seated at four tables, each one of which represented a season. The decorations of the table representing Winter were of white hyacinths; Spring, violets; Summer, roses; and Autumn chrysanthemums. Those present from Lake Forest were Misses McCord, Eleanor McCord, Kennedy, Jeanette Kennedy, Lyon, Bennett, McWilliams, Annie McWilliams, Scott, Edna Smith and Steel. All report such a good time, and as many good things to eat. Some of the old Ferry Hall girls were present, among whom were Misses Ruth Smith, Maud Taylor, and Alice Baxter.

ACADEMY.

GAMMA SIGMA.

Gilleland was visited by his aunt last week.

John Jackson has returned from a trip to the south.

Gruenstein is now correspondent for the *Chicago Tageblatt*.

Several of the students enjoyed a sleigh-ride one evening last week.

Jaeger was called to the city Monday by his parents who were going south.

The two societies chose the new students as members last Wednesday morning.

Prof. Mendel had the misfortune to have his ears touched by Jack Frost last week.

Warner has been unable to attend his classes for some time on account of ill health.

Judson Williams has received a present in the shape of a guitar from his sister at home.

Prof. Smith explained the working of the electoral college during the chapel exercises one morning recently.

The Gamma Sigma debate was postponed for one week on account of the inability of Whitney to be present.

One of the tables at Academia "clubbed in" and had a turkey roast last Sunday. It was, indeed, good to be there.

Prof. Smith read a paper to a joint meeting of the two societies last Wednesday. Subject: "The Character of Achilles."

A Sunday evening prayer meeting has been organized by the dormitory boys. The first meeting was held in Hatch's room.

Several of the Academy students have been in the city applying for positions as guides at the Fair. Few, if any, will be successful.

Hudson, who fell from a moving train last term, while going to his home at Benton, thereby sustaining severe injuries, is just able to leave his bed.

There seems to be a weekly exodus from Mitchell Hall on account of the members smoking. Smoke less or be more careful about detection.

Gruenstein has appeared wearing a large pair of blue glasses, having been ordered to do so by his physician, who informed him he was suffering from "pink eye."

The two societies will, in the near future, give some kind of an entertainment. They are at present making an effort to secure a distinguished lecturer from Chicago. A more definite announcement will be made later.

The first and second form cads have reorganized their ball nine by the election of Erskine as captain. Capt. Erskine will at once put his men in active training, hoping to be able to meet any team, of the same size, in the west when the season opens.

The sympathy of the students is extended to Whitney, whose mother died at her home in Waukegan last Tuesday evening. Although long an invalid, she was thought to have nearly recovered from her sickness, and her death was sudden and unexpected.

Prof. and Mrs. Smith gave the students a sleigh-ride last Friday evening. The party left the chapel at 7 o'clock, returning to the house of Prof. Smith, where refreshments were served. There was a large attendance, and a pleasant time was enjoyed by all.

ATHLETICS.

The committee on athletic exhibition as appointed by the president of the Athletic association: Rossiter, Rice and A. A. Hopkins.

Champaign denies that she ever applied for admission into the Western College Foot Ball Association. She wisely advises editors of college papers to make sure of a fact before publishing it.

The Board of Directors of the Athletic Association met last Monday evening and decided to hold a special meeting Monday, Feb. 20th, in order to hear the reports of the various committees that have been appointed.

The management of the ball team is going to make an effort to secure the use of the gymnasium on those days not taken up by the academy classes. Under those circumstances the prospects of base ball would seem brighter.

There is a movement on foot to cast the University of Minnesota out of the Western College League. The reason alleged is that the taveling expenses are too high. This would virtually shut Minnesota out from all athletic contests.

The committees on Field Day should spare no pains to make the Field Day in the spring a success. Track athletics have come to be recognized here in the past two years and it only needs the coöperation of the students to bring that branch of athletics to a high standard. Many have signified their willingness to train and it is to be hoped that some amateur record will be lowered.

It is certainly time for the annual February meeting of the Northwestern College League to take place. The secretary should send out notices at once to the different colleges. It is conjectured that many interesting points will be brought out at this meeting and it is feared by some that the days of the league are numbered. Nothing definite can be said, however, but it is to be hoped that the friendly relation heretofore existing will be kept up.

ALUMNI.

Keyes Becker, '89, has returned from Odgen, Utah, to Elgin, Ill.

E. F. Dodge, '91, of Chicago, spent Sunday, Feb. 5th, at H. C. Durand's.

J. E. Smith, '91, has moved from Oskosh, Wis., to Minneapolis, Minn.

G. W. Wright, '92, of Chicago, was in town a short time on Monday, Feb. 6th.

G. W. King, '92, of Joliet, has been a guest of W. D. McNary for the past week.

Herbert Manchester, ex-'93, is training for short-stop on the Chicago University team.

Grant Stroh, '89, writes from Del Norte, Col., that the weather is like summer, and that one can sit out of doors in perfect comfort.

Dame Rumor has it that George Horton Steele, '91, is, or that is, has, or at least is about to be—but we desist. At any rate we heartily congratulate the young lady.

Of our Chicago Alumni the following favored us with their presence last Sunday: W. E. Danforth, '91; W. H. Hummiston, '91; Aubrey Warren, '92, and E. S. Chaffer, '92.

EXCHANGES

Chess is becoming quite a fad among college students. Cornell recently met to organize a chess club.

Dr. A. W. Ringland, of Duluth, Minn., was recently inaugurated as President of Macalaster College.

Prof. Owen has presented the Wisconsin University with 1,000 volumes of standard French literature.

According to the N. Y. *Herald*, we find that the latest sport is equestrian foot ball, which was inaugurated last December by Clarence Robbins, an expert polo player. There is no kicking for a goal, and tackling is subjected to modifications. Good horsemanship is very essential, as a poor mount destroys the fine points of the game.

THE STENTOR.

VOLUME VI. FEBRUARY 21, 1893. NUMBER 18.

PUBLISHED EVERY WEEK
BY THE
Lake Forest University Stentor Publishing Co.

BOARD OF EDITORS.

F. C. SHARON, '93...............Managing Editor
R. H. CROZIER, '93..............Business Manager
N. H. BURDICK, '93 }
S. B. HOPKINS, '93 } ....Locals
L. N. ROSSITER, '93..........Alumni and Personal
B. R. MACHATTON, '95.................Advertising

ASSOCIATE EDITORS.

HARRY GOODMAN, '94..............Athletic Editor
FOREST GRANT, '96...................Staff Artist
DAVID FALES, '96..........................Town

Terms—$1.50 per year. Single Copies—10c

————ADDRESS————
STENTOR PUBLISHING COMPANY,
LAKE FOREST, : : ILLINOIS.

Entered at the P. O. at Lake Forest, Ill., as second-class matter.

WHAT are you going to do about a debate with Beloit? Don't you think you owe it to your college to support the scheme?

PLAGIARISM AMONG COLLEGE JOURNALS.

If there is one thing smaller and more despisable than anything else in college journalism it is the constant stealing of news and giving it forth as original. This practice is becoming very prevalent in some college papers and the college press in general should cry out against it. A college journal is limited as to news and when an editor discovers or suggests something new for a change it is but simple justice that his paper should be given this credit. We notice numerous college papers publish items and verse which we have seen elsewhere without so much as an *Ex.* after them. Naturally the conclusion of the reader is that they are original. Plagiarism is regarded in an extremely bad light in general literature, and the plagiarist is severely dealt with. In college journalism however it is practiced with the utmost boldness. Of course it is only certain papers that will do this, but why should it be silently allowed even to a few? We would like to hear from our brother editors on this subject.

WHAT ARE WE COMING TO?

There is a great deal said in college papers about the "wonderful college men," "the energetic college boys," "the bright wide-awake youths," and other pet phrases. But with all this we must admit that if the future generation now in college sleeps through life or tumbles through it as aimlessly as the average student does in college may heaven protect this unfortunate land! Remember we say the *average* student. It is in college as in life in one respect, a very few have to do the leading, but college is unlike the outside world in this; the rest do not do their parts or give the leaders support. They sit calmly by and say to the leaders "If you succeed we will come in for a share of the praise, if you fail count us out. In either case its too much trouble for us to do anything." If something is suggested the mass says, "go ahead and do it youself." If some one actually does go ahead and do something himself, then the great majority say "he is getting too much power," and down he goes by unanimous vote. College life is extremely enjoyable and is a wonderful teacher, but we should think that those students who have absolutely *nothing* to do would become tired of living. There is no use trying to carry anything through which looks to improvement when there is so much enthusiasm (?) displayed.

WHAT HAS BECAME OF THE LEAGUE?

Has the Western College Base Ball League died a natural death without even a struggle or are the colleges composing it still patiently waiting for the Secretary's notification? This college association is quite an old institution. It has been the means of promoting Western athletics to a great degree and is the oldest of all Western college leagues. It should not be allowed to die in this, the coming year of college base ball. Northwestern certainly made more money, or rather lost less, in the smaller league last fall than in the larger, so why should she resign from the league in base ball. She seems to be rather weak in that department this year. University of Illinois and Beloit surely desire to be in a league and it is therefore to their interests to take steps with us toward keeping the present league on its feet.

Affairs have been conducted in a very slip-shod manner for some time and a complete reorganization should take place. Who is the secretary of the league, and what is the reason for not calling a meeting? What is the athletic association here thinking of when it does not make some investigation and demand *that pennant* that our ball team won last Spring. There is a lamentable lack of base ball enthusiasm here as compared with foot ball. Let the foot ball team lose every game and it is petted and talked about and excused till you can hear nothing else, but let the base ball team win a game, or a series of games, and it is accepted as an ordinary matter, and even the Faculty think that such an unprecedented thing as winning the base ball pennant ought to be prevented a second time at all hazards. We are sorry to admit that the league seems in a rather mixed condition and that it behooves us to take the initiatory step in waking it up if we care anything for the pennant. If it is of no value, of course we may as well relapse into our comatose condition.

BELOIT IS ANXIOUS TO CONTEST.

LET US DO OUR PART.

The communication below speaks for itself. Beloit college having seen our editorial on an inter-collegiate debate is very anxious for a debate with representatives from Lake Forest. Here is the gauntlet thrown down to us. What are we going to do? We must not back down. Let us, for the sake of the college and ourselves, wake up and choose our debaters. Shall the debaters be chosen by the societies or classes? Which ever is decided upon should be decided quickly. Here is a chance to prove we have something here besides athletics.

BELOIT COLLEGE.

BELOIT, WIS., Feb. 14th 1893.
MR.F.C.SHARON, *Managing Editor Stentor*

DEAR SIR:—In a recent issue of the STEN-TOR you speak editorially in favor of an inter-collegiate debate between Lake Forest and Evanston or Beloit. I write down to learn if their is enough interest in the University to realize such a plan as you suggest. At Beloit we have for some time thought favorably of in-tercollegiate debating, and I feel certain that if Lake Forest enters into the project, Beloit will respond. Personally I feel that the two institutions ought to touch on other than simply athletic interests. Our western college ought by no means to let the old-fashioned debating society die; and this plan will tend to infuse new life into them if I mistake not.

What is to be done ought to be done quickly. The debate ought not to be latter than May 1st on account of the athletic season. It is not yet too late to arrange a contest. It seems to me that as timely questions as could be dis-cussed would be the proposed change in elect-ing U. S. Senators, some phase of the immi-gration problem, or an educational qualification in the requirements of citizenship. Shall we have three or two debaters on a side?

The matter will be discussed at the meeting of the Archaean Union next Saturday. If you could reply before that date, we could take clearer action at that meeting.

I hope that your suggestion is carried out. One of our two college societies has already informally expressed approval of the plan, and I am sure that as far as Beloit is concerned the debate may be a reality.

Very truly yours,
ARTHUR E. FRASER.

CHESS AS A PASTIME.

In the issue of the STENTOR for January 17th. appears an article entitled "Chess: An Historical Sketch," written by an expert at the game. The present intention is to throw to-gether a few general facts concerning the game which it is hoped will be of some interest both to beginners in the art, and to those who do not play the game.

Chess is a purely mental game with abso-lutely no element of chance in it. Whist calls, for skill, but in a different way. It is a skill of memory. It is not always a "battle to the strong" and the winner does not always owe his victory to superior adeptness.

Billards is a game of pure skill, it is true but it is a skill of the eye and the hand, there-fore must take rank below chess. The game of checkers in the nearest approach to chess in being an analytical science which calls for an acute mind for its mastery.

The number of combinations possible on the chess-board gives to chess its superiority over all other games as a science. There are thirty-two men engaged in this bloodless combat, sixteen on a side. There are six different methods of moving these men, depending both on the man and his position. The board is divided into sixty-four squares. A few figures may serve to give some idea of the infinity of the combinations possible. It has been esti-mated that, there being twenty possible moves to open the game, the number of possible ways of playing the first four moves on each side is 318,979,564,000 and that if one were to play one set a minute it would take 600,000 years to go through them all. Try another. After the first four moves on each side there is a choice of thirty ways of playing the next six moves. By combination, it has been estimated, the number of ways of playing the first ten moves on each side is 169,518,829,100,544,000,000,-000,000,000! If the population of the whole world be taken at 1,483 millions it would take, at the rate of one move a minute, every man, woman and child playing, something like 217 billions of years to go through them all. When it is remembered that games average, on a conservative estimate, thirty-five moves on each side the claim of superiority may seem to have some justification.

These varied combinations afford a means of training and developing the analytical and logical faculties of the mind which cannot elsewhere be found. In Austrian schools this fact has been recognized and chess is now a part of the regular curriculum. Chess calls for mental gymnastics and is to the mind what the gymnasium is to the body.

It has been argued, and it would seem not without reason, by some of the great masters in the science, that chess serves to prolong the lives of those who are devoted to it. It is said that statistics show that the average life of chess players is higher than that of any other class of men.

The game is very fascinating and when one once learns to play, one is never satisfied until one becomes proficient in the game. Unlike other games, as much may be learned by studying the combinations alone, as by playing with an adversary. This statement needs to be taken with caution, for certainly one can never become an adept by solitary study, but with the aid of a good text book much valuable knowledge of the game as well as amusement may be obtained which cannot be gotten in regular games.

To be a congenial player never become angry when by some mistake on your part your adversary gains an advantage. When you touch a piece always move it and, under no circumstances whatsoever, take a move back when once made, no matter what it may cost you. Always keep cool. Accept defeat in a manly way and never disparage your adversary's skill by telling him how he won the game through some blunder on your part. If you were dull enough to make the blunder and he was sharp enough to see it, he deserves all he can make out of it.   N. H. BURDICK.

Prof. Thomas will read the paper presented to the University club last week before the Athenæn Society the coming Friday evening.

COLLEGE.

AMUSEMENTS FOR THE WEEK.
COLUMBIA—"Aristocracy."
HOOLEY'S,—Rosina Vokes.
GRAND—De Wolf Hopper in "Wang."
CHICAGO—Fanny Rice "Jolly Surprise."
McVICKER'S—Wilson Barrett.
SCHILLER—"Surrender."

Communion a week from next Sunday.

The Senior Class have petitioned the Faculty to be excused from Commencement Orations.

W. B. Smith who has been ill for some time is again able to attend classes we are happy to say.

The latest report is that Geo. T. Scofield is slowly improving and there is a good chance of his pulling through.

We notice that Ellis, '93, is a candidate for pitcher on the Amherst ball team. There are three other candidates for the same position.

Herbert Manchester, ex-'93, by winning the competitive tennis match at Chicago University the other day, becomes a member of the University team.

Dr. Hanson will deliver a lecture in the Art Institute a week from Friday evening under the auspices of the Zeta Epsilon Society. Subject—"Fools."

An athletic exhibition will soon be given in the gymnasium. Now is your time to enter. The lists will be thrown open this week and the events announced.

A lecture on "Velasquez" will be delivered in Ferry Hall chapel by Mr. Walter C. Larrned, next Saturday evening. It will be illustrated by stereoptican views.

Several of the students have been laid up the past week on account "the taking" of their vaccinations. From reports most of their arms are taking a little of everything.

The Valentine Tea given at the seminary last Tuesday evening was one of the most enjoyable affairs of the kind that Ferry Hall has ever given. Those who were so fortunate as to " stand in " told us this.

Princeton is to be represented at the World's Fair, and will occupy a space of 1,000 square feet. Among other things, a model of the campus and grounds will be exhibited. Cyrus H. McCormick '79, is one of the committee selected to take charge of affairs.

At present writing it looks as if we would have no celebration on Washington's birthday. The speaker whom the committee were after could not come. and no other speaker could be obtained. Ferry Hall will take Friday as its holiday, and between thirty and forty girls will attend Paderewski's concert in the afternoon.

The faculty have issued pamphlets containing twelve or fifteen pages, descriptive of the school and town. Last year's *Annual* cuts of the buildings and Lake Forest scenes are scattered through it, and the same old paragraph commencing "Lake Forest is a suburb of Chicago, 28 miles north on the lake," ete. The booklet however is quite a neat little affair.

The University club met at Dr. McClure's last Thursday evening and listened to a paper on "The College as Distinct from the University," by Prof. Thomas. The paper is the same one that was read before the Presbyterian ministers in Chicago, and is an admirable presentation of the present theory of education. After the paper a general discussion took place in which a large majority of the Faculty agreed heartily with Prof. Thomas.

The Senior Class of the College gave a "progressive jinks" party to the Sem. Seniors last Thursday evening at which W. D. McNary won the head prize and E. L. Jones, the "booby." The party was given in the Sem. gymnasium which had been very prettily decorated by the young ladies of the class.

Some of those who did not attend had very good excuses, but others had a bad attack of "sore-head."

The Chess Club has just closed its very successful tournament in which J. A. Linn won first place and A. B. Burdick second. The averages are given below:

		PLAYED.	WON.	LOST.	PER CT.
1.	J. A. Linn	36	35½	½	.986
2.	A. B. Burdick	37	25	12	.675
3.	G. L. Wi:son	38	25	13	.658
4.	N. H. Burdick	31	18	13	.580
5.	E. H. McNeal	39	22	17	.564
6.	C. G. Smith	38	21	17	.552
7.	Prof. Dudley	25	13½	11½	.540
8.	Dr. Seeley	35	18½	16½	.528
9.	S. B. Hopkins	27	11	16	.407
10.	W. E. Ruston	35	14	21	.400
11.	L. N. Rossiter	39	13½	25½	.346
12.	F. C. Rogers	36	7	29	.194
13.	C. W. Sherman	39	6	33	.154

TOWN TOPICS.

Miss Nellie Holt leaves this week for the South.

Mr. Step, of Edinburgh, is visiting Prof. Walter Smith.

The Misses Annie and Julia Day, and Miss Isham visited last week with Mrs. Frank Farwell.

Mrs. Glen Wood has been elected to Mr. Wood's place in the Waifs' Mission, and in that capacity now goes daily to Chicago.

It is rumored that Mr. H. C. Durand has bought the lot just west of Rev. Mr. Nichol's residence and may put up a handsome business block.

Miss Lucy Rumsey leaves Thursday for Del Norte, Colo., to visit her sister, Mrs. Grant Stroh. Miss Rumsey will be gone about six weeks.

Mr. and Mrs. J. H. Dwight were called to Evanston, on Wednesday morning, Feb. 15, by the very sudden death of Mr. Dwight's brother, Mr. Chas. Dwight.

The STENTOR is happy to report that Rev. Dr. Nichols is able to be out again. Sunday morning Dr. Nichols went to church for the first time since last October.

Mr. S. R. Taber's Scotch Collie, "Robin," was shot last Wednesday by some miscreant. A reward of $25 has been offered by Mr. Taber for the exposure of the offender.

Rev. A. C. Zenos preached Sunday evening at the church. Prof. Zenos, until 1887, held the chair of Greek at Lake Forest, and now is Professor of Church History at McCormick Theological Seminary.

The ladies of the town met last Thursday afternoon at the Art Institute for the purpose of organizing a social club. A room in the Art Institute building will be furnished and utilized as the society's headquarters.

Mr. and Mrs. H. C. Durand and Mrs. Shirley V. Martin leave Thursday for the south to be gone two or three months. They will also visit Jamaica. Mr. Durand's genial face will be missed about the college grounds.

A small company was invited to Mrs. Stanley's Saturday evening to listen to Prof. Jack's paper, "The Philosophy of Tennyson." Afterwards the audience remained to an informal reception, when light refreshment was served.

Perhaps the most interesting meeting of the Art Club this year was held at the house of Mr. Chapin, Friday evening, when Mr. Wm. L. Tomlins delivered a lecture on "The Music of the Fair." The enthusiastic manner of Mr. Tomlins is very attractive; but inasmuch as Mr. Tomlins himself has in great part not only conceived but even carried out the vast preparations for music at the Fair, the lecture, permeated as it was by his enthusiasm, and his entire absorption in his ideas, could not fail to intensely interest the listeners. Afterwards Mr. Tomlins improvised on a reed organ, conveyed from Chicago for the occasion, and brought music from that usually soulless instrument.

FERRY HALL

Friday evening, Feb. 10th, Mrs. Locy gave us a very pleasant talk on "Making the Best of Ourselves."

Miss Margaret Conger went home Friday' the tenth, to spend Sunday, but has extended her visit a week.

Miss Eloise Bronson, who was unable to return earlier in the term, on account of sickness at home, is again with us.

Miss Hallie Hall, '92, has been quite seriously ill, but we are glad to learn that the doctors pronounce her out of danger.

Miss Mildred Lyon went home Wednesday last to act as bridesmaid at the wedding of her sister, which took place Thursday evening.

Miss Dora Cressineth, who has been ill for some time, will not be able to attend classes this term. The sympathy of '93 is with her.

One of the Sems emphatically announces her intention of giving up slang, thus,—" Girls I am going to stop using slang. Honest Injun I am."

The F. H. correspondent wishes to state that the F. H. notes are sent in Friday morning. Often entertainments or items of news come in later, which must necessarily be left over until the next number.

Miss Bessie Sutton, '88, is at her home in Lake Linden, Mich. She has a private kindergarten class, and is very successful in the work. Miss Sue Flack, also '88, is engaged in the same work at her home, Quincy, Ill.

Thursday evening the College Seniors gave a "Progressive Jenks" party in the F. H. gymnasium for the Sem Seniors. The gym. was prettily decorated. Refreshments were served and all had a glorious good time.

Tuesday evening the Seniors of Ferry Hall with a few friends, celebrated St. Valentine's Day by having a few of the young gentlemen over to tea. Mrs. Seeley presided at one end of the long table, and Dr. Seeley did the honors at the other end. Each person was favored with one or more valentines, which (laying his modesty aside) he was obliged to read at the close of the meal. Through the kindness of Mrs. Seeley the entire company was permitted to enjoy the German entertainment afterward.

Tuesday evening occurred what is known to us as " Deutsche-Abend." A goodly number of guests were present, and the following program was carried out in the chapel :

Chor-Mignon	*Himmel*
Die Deutsche Klasse.	
Vortrag — Der Zigennerbube . .	*Geitel*
Grace Cloes.	
Vortrag " Geduld "	*Spilta*
Ethel Warner.	
Volkslieder . { " Die Auserwahlte " { " Frohe Botschaft "	
Vortrag, " Kinder Gottesdienst " . .	*Gerok*
Sadie Davis.	
Vortrag, " Der Sanger " . . .	*Goethe*
Louise Conger.	
Klavier Dienst, " Geburtstag Musik " .	*Bohm*
Frl. Ripley and Lizer.	
Vortrag . " Des deutschen Knaben Tischgebet "	
Sue Huntoon.	
Vortrag . " Des Fremden Kindes heiliger Christ "	
Lita Stoddard.	
Vortrag, " Mozart "	*Mosenthal*
Frl. Lizer, mit Klavierbegleitung von Prof. Eager.	
Solo . . . . . " Selbstgewahlt "	
Frau Hester.	
Chor . . . . " Die Wacht am Rhein "	

Refreshments were then served in the parlors, and each guest received a German valentine. The parlors were very prettily decorated in the German colors, and the German classes are to be congratulated on their success.

ACADEMY.

GAMMA SIGMA.

Levering has been visiting at home the past week.

Creswell's father has been visiting him the last few days.

Ask Hall how to press trousers, also the very latest style.

Breckenridge read an essay before the Cæsar class last Tuesday.

Fales and Jackson visited the Gamma Sigma society Wednesday.

Kimball spent Saturday and Sunday at his home in Milwaukee.

The principal of the Morgan Park school visited the classes last Tuesday.

As spring approaches the crop of mustaches begins to appear. All kinds and colors are to be seen.

Dr. McClure attended the prayer meeting last Tuesday evening. Mr. Angus led the meeting.

The executive committees of the two societies held a meeting at Mr. Durand's one evening last week.

Some of the students were invited to tea at Ferry Hall last Tuesday afternoon. A very pleasant time is reported.

The faculty asked the students to suggest names to whom pamphlets of the university should be sent, one morning last week.

M. H. Baker won the preliminary essay in the Tri Kappa society last Wednesday. His subject was " The Influence of Poetry."

Prin. Smith remarked upon the leading characteristics of the life of Lincoln, during chapel exercises last Monday. His talk was very interesting.

The hour of assembling for "doing time" on Saturday afternoon has been changed from 2 o'clock to 1:30 in order to give the Master time for needed exercise.

Quite a number received invitations to a reception given by the Seminary German class last Tuesday evening. Those who attended report a pleasant evening.

Hall, Hanant, and Roberts were the Gamma Sigma contestants in debate last Wednesday, Roberts being successful. Profs. Smith, Bridgman and NcNeil acted as judges.

A certain member of the dormitory has found two hair pins. Owners may have the same by proving ownership to property and rewarding the finder with a smile.

Although the study of animal life naturally belongs to the sciences, a language master made this remark to his class: "A pony is a dead translator, a jackass a live one."

Richards has been appointed a member of the committee having charge of the Athletic exhibition. He informs us arrangements will soon be made and a program published naming the various contests and what prizes, if any, will be given.

In honor of the anniversary of the birth of Abraham Lincoln the Academy classes were dismissed last Monday afternoon. Some of the students spent the time in looking up biographies of other statesmen hoping to obtain one or more holidays in the future.

As no catalogue has as yet been published, the Faculty have decided to send out pamphlets giving brief outline of the course of study and containing pictures of the Presidents house, the present Academy dormitory, and the new buildings. The pictures of the latter, however, are not very good.

LONGING.

When life is as gay as gay can be
  And joy is joined with fun,
Truly happy could I be
  Without my darling one?

When life's as sad as 'tis today
  And clouds are o'er its sun,
Through trouble could I grope my way
  Without my darling one?

No matter what my life may see
  Of joy, or pain, or fun,
Ah, life would not be life to me
  Without my darling one.
                    Iowa Unit.

MY WISH.

Many men have wished for riches,
  While for power some hearts yearn;
Beauty many a mind bewitches,
  With wisdom numbers turn.
But I do not ask for great things,
  A little boon my soul would please;
It is only that my trousers
  May not bag so at the knees.
                    Lehigh Burr.

THE EDITOR'S FINANCES.

Lives of poor men oft remind us
  Honest toil won't stand a chance;
The more we work there grows behind us
  Bigger patches on our pants;
On our pants once new and glossy,
  Now are stripes of different hue,
And because subscribers linger
  And won't pay us what is due.
Then let all be up and doing,
  Send your mite, however small,
Or when the snows of winter strike us
  We shall have no pants at all.

"What is wetter than a girl with a waterfall on her head, a cataract in her eye, a lake in her cheek, a spring in her knee and pumps on her feet?"

Answer—"A girl with a notion (an ocean) in her head."

AN EXPERIMENT.

No rose, I swear,
  E'er bloomed so fair
As this one in the north wind bleak.
  Your open eyes
  Denote surprise,—
The rose is on my lady's cheek.

  When snowflakes press
  Their chill caress,
Its petals daintier shades will take ;
  Perhaps if I
  The same should try
I could yet fairer colors make.

THE STENTOR.

VOLUME VI.   FEBRUARY 28, 1893.   NUMBER 19.

PUBLISHED EVERY WEEK
BY THE

Lake Forest University Stentor Publishing Co.

BOARD OF EDITORS.

F. C. SHARON, '93................Managing Editor
R. H. CROZIER, '93..............Business Manager
N. H. BURDICK, '93 }
S. B. HOPKINS, '93 } ....Locals
L. N. ROSSITER, '93..........Alumni and Personal
B. R. MacHATTON, '95.................Advertising

ASSOCIATE EDITORS.

HARRY GOODMAN, '94.............,....Athletic Editor
FOREST GRANT, '96.....................Staff Artist
DAVID FALES, '96...........................Town

Terms—$1.50 per year. Single Copies—10c

———ADDRESS———

STENTOR PUBLISHING COMPANY,

LAKE FOREST, : : ILLINOIS.

Entered at the P. O. at Lake Forest, Ill., as second-class matter.

We present with this issue a very good likeness of the new president, a person in whom all Lake Forest is intensely interested.

THE NEW CATALOGUE.

The Catalogue committee have been waiting for the new president to be chosen. Now that he is a living reality, that committee will immediately publish the catalogue and have it ready for the spring term. It has been all ready for some time. It has been kept back simply for the approval of the new president. It will be essentially the same as all other books of the same nature.

HONOR TO OUR ACTING PRESIDENT.

All honor and praise to our acting President, Dr. McClure. Through all this critical time he has worked unceasingly for the good of the University and his efforts have been well rewarded. Everything has receiveh his most careful consideration, and the personal interest he has shown has been much appreciated by the boys. No one is so sincerely and genuinely loved by the students as is Dr. McClure, and it is with grateful hearts that we acknowledge our indebtedness and tender our heartfelt thanks. Surely with such a president as Dr. Coulter, and such a pastor as Dr. McClure, the students are doubly blessed.

MAKE ARRANGEMENTS FOR A GRAND RECEPTION.

It is not definitely known yet when Dr. Coulter will be inaugurated but it is not to early to begin to arrange for his reception. It should be the heartiest reception possible; every townsman and every student should turn out to do him honor. If he comes before commencement, arrangements should be made on a grand scale because this is no every day affair and President Coulter is no every day president by any means. On the students' part a committee should be chosen to co-operate with the Faculty in anything they recommend in regard to the reception. If he does not come till commencement then this should be made the grandest and most imposing commencement ever held in Lake Forest.. At any rate we should hustle ourselves and see that Dr. Coulter when he comes is enthusiastically received.

WE CONGRATULATE OURSELVES.

Get out your tin horns and make a joyful noise: throw open wide your throttle and "whoop her up." And why this unseemly racket? Because forsooth a new president has been chosen and will soon be among us. Something for which we have been waiting for a long time, something we have been looking forward to and which is now a reality; someone to lead us that we may be proud of. So why shouldn't we yell? Almost a year ago Dr. Roberts resigned the presidency and accepted the secretaryship of Home Missions in New York. Since then we have been without a head. The Faculty and acting president have done admirably considering their position, but still we have felt the neccesity of a permanent head. But now that we are assured of a president, and a good one at that, we cannot but feel joyful, and have the highest hopes for our dear old Alma Mater. Our new president, Dr. Coulter, is a hustler in every sense of the word, and we congratulate ourselves heartily in being so fortunate.

THE NEW PRESIDENT.

Certainly no man will ever receive a more enthusiastic reception or be accorded a heartier support than will President Coulter when he arrives. He comes in an especially auspicious and at the same time critical period. Auspicious because the students are enthusiastic for a new president and especially for Dr. Coulter, and because the University is in such a prosperous condition. Critical, because of the threatened absorption by Chicago University and the doubt as to whether we can withstand so powerful a rival. That Dr. Coulter is pre-eminently the man for the place there is not the slightest doubt. Dr. Jordan, now president of Leland Stanford University, said that he thought he had raised Indiana State University to the highest notch possible but Dr. Coulter raised it still higher. He has quickly hoisted that school; he will be a power in this one. This marks a new epoch in the history of Lake Forest University. From this time on Lake Forest goes steadily forward until she takes her stand foremost among western colleges. She has lately taken great strides in athletics and her scholarship has always been her pride. She has only needed a hustling president to bring things to a focus and now that she has him, nothing can prevent her taking a proud place in the college world. Therefore all hail to our new president, our epoch-maker, Dr. Coulter.

Yesterday's *Tribune* announced that President Harrison would, in all probability, deliver lectures on law in the new Chicago University. He does not care to go to Leland Stanford. In this way he can retain his home in Indianapolis,

AT LAST A PRESIDENT

DR. JOHN M. COULTER CHOSEN YESTERDAY.

THE BEST MAN FOR THE PLACE AND EVERY-
ONE REJOICES.

Yesterday, Monday the 27th, at 2 o'clock, the trustees of Lake Forest University met in the Sherman House, Chicago, and formally elected John M. Coulter, Ph. D., LL. D., president of the university.

Since Dr. Roberts resigned, almost a year ago, the trustees, aided by the faculty, have ransacked the country to find a man to take his place. Many have been suggested and many have been considered, but few seemed to fill the bill. When it was discovered last fall that perhaps Dr. Coulter, of the State University of Indiana, would accept, steps were immediately taken to secure him. Dr. McClure was given almost absolute power to act. How well he has succeeded is easily to be seen. Dr. Coulter was offered a professorship in Chicago University, but would not accept. However it was currently reported that he was going there. It has been known to many since last December that as soon as he could get the appropriations for the State University, through the Indiana Legislature, he would resign and come to Lake Forest. Last Thursday, the 23d, the appropriations went through and Dr. Coulter immediately wrote Dr. McClure stating the fact and saying the trustees could go ahead with his formal election. He also stated that as soon as elected he wished to meet the committee on catalogue and also the trustees. That he means business is an assured fact.

It is not known yet when he will take charge of affairs. The president's house is at present occupied by academy students, which, however, they will vacate as soon as the new academy is finished. This will probably be opened at the beginning of the spring term. Neither is it known what change of policy will take place or whether any will be made.

Those who know him say he has a wonderful grasp of the situation here and undoubtedly he will hurry things forward so that by commencement there will be something to announce which will gladden the hearts of Lake Forest's friends. Dr. Coulter visited here during the winter vacation and all who met him were strongly impressed with the man. He has that personal magnetism which is so essential in a college president.

It has been thought best by the trustees to give Dr. Coulter almost absolute control so that he may arrange the courses and place the faculty as it seems best to him. Until something more definite is determined upon, we must patiently wait.

A SKETCH OF THE LIFE AND WORK OF DR. COULTER.

John Merle Coulter is the eldest of the two sons of Moses and Cora Coulter, two zealous Presbyterian missionaries. He was born November 20, 1851, at Ningpo, China. When only a little more than a year old, his father died, and the mother returned with her two sons to this country. They took up their residence at Hanover, Indiana, where the boyhood of our subject was largely spent. At the age of thirteen, he entered Hanover College, founded by his grandfather, Dr. J. F. Crowe, from which institution he graduated in 1870. The autumn after his graduation he went to Logansport, Indiana, where he remained until the spring of 1872, teaching in the Presbyterian Seminary of that place. This position he resigned, to accept that of botanist of the Hayden Geological Survey. During the season of '72 he was with the Hayden party exploring the now famous, but then unknown, Yellowstone country, and what is now the National Park. This was the first party to bring back anything like an authentic account of that most wonderful region, and the story of their experiences sounds like a romance. The season following, the summer of 1873, was spent exploring the mountains of Colorado, and making large collections of their characteristic plants. The winters of '72 and '73 were spent in Washington, D. C., naming and describing the plants collected during the previous seasons. In his report to the Government, he showed, to some of the older botanists, what possibilities there were in the young man of twenty-two. It was partly through this report that he attracted the attention and enlisted the sympathies and friendship of the late Dr. Asa Gray, and the bonds were only broken by the death of that great and kind man.

January 1, 1874, he was married to Miss Georgie Gaylord, of Delphi, Indiana and immediately afterwards went to Hanover College as professor of Latin. Two years later he was transferred to the chair of Natural Sciences, a possition much more to his taste.

While at Hanover, in November, 1875, he founded the *Botanical Gazette*. At first it was but a four page sheet, devoted, as its name indicates, to the one subject of botany. At that time the field of exclusively botanical journalism was nearly a vacant one. There had been founded two years before, in New York, a similar journal, but all the other periodical literature was to be found in departments of scientific journals, where too often botany is made to play a very secondary part. For seven years he associated with him, in its publication, his brother, M. S. Coulter, now of Purdue University. In 1883 the associate editors became Dr. J. C. Arthur, now of Purdue, and Professor Charles R. Barnes, now of the University of Wisconsin. The editors have been continually enlarging and improving the *Gazette* until now it is a twenty-four page journal, and in its line, stands, without a doubt, second to none, either of American or foreign journals. It is to be found in the hands of every working botanist, and many of the amateurs of this country, and, as its foreign correspondents, contains many of the most noted names known to botany of to-day.

In 1879 he was elected to the Rose Professorship of Geology and Natural History in Wabash College, and entered upon his duties

in the fall of that year. He raised the course in botany there and increased the herbarium of the college until now it is numbered among the three or four largest in the United States.

In 1884 the State University of Indiana, the State University of Missouri, and Hanover, his Alma Mater, conferred upon him the degree of Doctor of Philosophy.

In 1887 he was president of the Indiana Academy of Science, and his address of that year was a splendid setting forth of the great truths of evolution as manifested in plants. He has been an active member of the American Association for the Advancement of Science for a number of years, and is now secretary of the biological section of that body.

During the summers of '79 and '80 he was at Harvard University as an assistant in the summer schools of that institution.

During 1890-'91 he was twice called to Washington, D. C., by the Government botanist to assist, as an expert, in identifying and publishing a large collection of plants from the new and interesting locality of south-western Texas.

As a lecturer he has a wide reputation, as is shown by the many demands upon his time for such purposes. His scientific lectures have in them many facts of interest which may be understood by the popular audience, while his popular lectures cannot fail to entertain and instruct the man of science.

In May, 1891, he accepted the presidency of Indiana State University, which position he has held up to the present. Since he has been there he has raised that institution even above the standard of Dr. Jordan, now of Leland Stanford. He was offered the professorship of botany in the New University of Chicago, but preferred the presidency of Lake Forest University. He is also a lecturer in the University Extension Course. In addition to his duties as a professor, and his many engagements as a lecturer, he has written and published quite a number of works, the most important of which are as follows:

1. Report of Plants of Yellowstone Country.

, 2. Synopsis of Plants of Colorado.

3. Botanical Gazette, Vols. I.—XVII.

4. Catalogue of plants of Jefferson County, Indiana.

5. Catalogue of Indiana plants, 1891.

6. Manual of Rocky Mountain Botany.

7. Origin of Indiana Plants.

8. Revision of North American Hyperi. caceae.

9. Synopsis of North American Pines.

10. Handbook of Plant Dissection.

11. Evolution of the Plant Kingdom.

12. Revision of North American Umbelli. ferae.

13. Revision of Gray's Manual of Botany.

14. Revision of North American Corna. ceae.

15. List of plants from S. W. Texas with descriptions.

16, Manual of Texan Botany.

17. Numerous papers before A. A. A. S.

PRAISE FROM ALL SIDES.

OPINIONS OF VARIOUS EDUCATORS AND OF THE FACULTY.

If a man can be judged by what is said of him, President Coulter certainly stands high in the world. Without exception the highest praise is accorded to him by men who know whereof they speak, and praise coming from such men is worthy of consideration. Below we give letters written during the past year before Mr. Coulter was called, and also the opinions of the Faculty on the man and the benefit to the school.

Extract from a letter written by Dr. Jordan, of Leland Stanford University:

When I left Indiana State University the trustees of that institution requested that I should find my successor. I could find no better man in the country for the place than Dr. Coulter. He has filled the place splendidly and has raised that institution as no one thought it could be raised. He is a man of broad cul. ture, and not only is the greatest botanist we have bu one of the greatest educators of the present day. I would most heartily recommend him to you.

Very sincerely,
DAVID S. JORDAN.

397 N. PENN ST., INDIANAPOLIS, May 10, 1892.

MY DEAR BROTHER,—President Coulter is a man of earnest Christian spirit; he is a man of high, as well as broad, scholarship—and he has a wide acquaintance with educational methods. So I answer three of your questions very emphatically in the affirmative. His first year at the State University has been a marked success in administration as well as other respects. He was by all odds the most popular professor at Wabash before he was called to the State University. I very much doubt whether Dr. Coulter would leave Bloomington for Lake Forest. Rather than lose him the trustees would, I believe, add considerably to his salary. As I am on the committee of Wabash Trustees that has been for a year seeking a successor to Pres. Tuttle, I can sympathize with you in your work.

Very sincerely,
W. L. HAINES.

LAKE FOREST, Aug. 17, 1892.

I have heard considerable this summer, from reliable sources, regarding President J. M. Coulter, of the University of Indiana. He has many of the qualifications that are desirable in the President for Lake Forest University.

He is an educator.

He has had successful experience as a college president.

He is spoken of by those who know him as a man possessing business qualifications, and as being especially fitted to move men.

He has large influence among members of the Legislature, and is able to secure from them large appropriations for the cause of education in his state.

I am reliably informed that he makes a very good appearance in public educational assemblies, and can make a good off-hand speech.

I should judge from what I have heard of his popularity with students, both at Wabash College and the University of Indiana, that he has a large share of what we call personal magnetism.

I contribute these points, although they are mostly second-hand information, because they come from men in whose judgment I have confidence.

Very sincerely yours,
WM. A. LOCY.

President Harper, of Chicago University, says: "He is undoubtedly the greatest botanist of the day and one of our best educators."

Professor Locy is very enthusiastic over Dr.

Coulter, and says: "It is not the fact of his being a great botanist that should be brought out.
The great point is that he is such a magnificent
educator. He is a man of such broadness of
education, and is such a deep thinker on the
advancement of education that it seems a great
privilege for us to get him. And then he has
had large experience in teaching and in college
work, and after all there is nothing like experience. He is not a minister, and that is in his
favor for a college president, because it is a
profession in itself and one must devote himself
entirely to it. If any one can raise Lake Forest he can ,and I look for it to be raised to the
top notch."

Dr. McClure regards him as pre-eminently
the man for the place, thoroughly independent
and one who will always have Lake Forest's
best interests at heart. He already shows a
grasp of the situation which is astonishing.

Prof. Dawson says: "He is the broadest man
that could have been secured. Men usually
begin to narrow as they grow older, but he
seems to grow broader in intellect and feeling
every day."

Prof. McNeil says: "I have barely met him,
but he impresses me as an exceedingly strong
man, and certainly we heard nothing but praise
of him."

From a former student at Wabash:

From a student's standpoint no happier choice for
the president's chair could be made than the election
of Dr. Coulter.

Outside the classroom he is accessible to every student, while in his laboratory and study he is ever
found to be the pleasantest of gentlemen and the students' best friend.

As a professor he approximates the students' ideal.
He possesses the art of enthusing the student with his
work and of getting the maximum amount of work
out of a student, and it will be found that the Doctor
envelopes the drone in few smiles.

As a president he stands the peer of the best. In
him are equally displayed the qualities of an instructor,
an executive and a financier.

To say that he is "popular" among the students is
stating a fact most mildly. And in bringing Dr. Coulter to Lake Forest we gain more—we gain Mrs.
Coulter. Only a personal acquaintance with her can

lead to any appreciation of her pure, inspiring personal
character.

What Dr. Coulter was to scientific research in the
students' labratory, Mrs. Coulter was to moral inspiration in the students' Sabbath school class and her
Saturday "At Home."

Again we say that we believe no selection conld have
been happier, from the student's view, than Dr. Coulter's.   C.

BOOK REVIEWS.

" The Bible and English Prose Style" is a
book of selections and comments, edited with
an introduction by Albert S. Cook, professor
of the English language in Yale University.
The introduction, sixteen pages in length, contains an earnest plea of the recognition of the
English Bible as "an active force in English
literature for over twelve hundred years," a
thorough presentation of the ways in which
the Bible has been appropriated by English
writers, and an endeavor to find out why this
appropriation has been made and exactly what
has been appropriated.

Direct quotation, with a striking example
from Dickens, " Sidney Carton;" allusion,
illustrated from Matthew Arnold; and a
"*plastic* influence"—a permeation, as it were
—resulting in a style like that of Bunyan, are
the ways in which the Bible has made itself
felt in our literature from Caedmon to the
present time. And that which it has been
communicating all this time in this plastic way
may be comprehended in the single term,
"noble naturalness;" that quality through
which it appeals the whole man—"calls up a
grateful echo in the heart of every man"—to
which is added an accent of dignity and elevation. Familiar passages from Judges and 2
Chron. are quoted to illustrate this quality,
and around these are grouped quotations from
various authors of note, some of which are
very like the Scriptural passages, while others
only remotely suggest them, and still others
are their exact opposite, both in style and
spirit.

The second part, forty-four pages, consists
of " Illustrative comments " from such authors

as Matthew Arnold, Ruskin, Cardinal Newman, Chateaubriand, Renan and others, each
selection illustrating or supporting some view
advanced by Prof. Cook in his introduction.
They are admirably chosen and well arranged
to emphasize the points made by the editor.

In the third part are sixty-one pages of
" Biblical selections " from Exodus to Revela-
tions, passages designed to present clearly that
" noble naturalness " and that constructive
style for which the English Scriptures are remarkable.

ALL THE WORLD'S A STAGE AND ALL THE PEOPLE PLAYERS.

This is true in a sense, but on the evening of
March 17th the stage will be confined to the
Art Institute and the players will be members
of the Athenæan society, who will present an
amusing farce-comedy entitled " The Nervous
Man." The play has been in rehearsal for
several weeks, and will be presented as originally performed by the same company 1,000
nights in Alaska. As the 1,000th night was rather chilly in that sunny clime the company
has kindly consented to stop at Lake Forest on
its way to Africa. After the play a grand
ministrel show will be given in which the latest
and most popular jokes of the day will be heard.
The costuming and stage setting will be true to
life. Don't fail to secure tickets. More anon.

The lecture desired for Washington's birthday failed to materialize. Instead members of
the Athenæan society gave their Ferry Hall
friends a sleigh ride to Waukegan, leaving
ing Lake Forest at 1.30 p. m., and returning
at 6 p. m. The usual amount of fun and frolic
was indulged in and all had a good time.

The petition to the heirs of Gov. Bross asking that the income from the ten year lecture
fund, established by his will, be used yearly in
securing a course of lectures was read before
the students after chapel Thursday morning
prior to its circulation for signatures.

COLLEGE.

" The Nervous Man and the Man of Nerve."

The Zeta Epsilon society presents a lecture
on " Fools " March 3.

French, the druggist, puts up prescriptions
carefully and promptly.

For anything in the line of jewellery go to
Buck the Waukegan jeweler.

Don't forget the date, March 17, of the play,
" The Nervous Man and the Man of Nerve."

A full line of spring styles in gent's furnishing goods can be had at Schuster's 66 Adams
street,

It is said that for the 500 positions as guides
at the World's Fair there have been 700 applications.

The Zeta Epsilon Glee club gave a concert
at the Jefferson Park Presbyterian church Friday evening.

What's everybody's business is nobody's
business is true. What's nobody's business is
everybody's business is truer.

Vaccination has been very popular during
the last two weeks. Nearly all the boys have
been more or less ill in consequence of it.

Chauncey Thomas. '96, has resigned his college course to accept a position in the Mines
and Mining Department of the World's Fair.

Such a long season of sleighing as the present
is unprecedented within the memory of the oldest inhabitant. [This coming from our local is
not to be denied.]

At last the presidential position is settled. Professor Coulter, of Indiana State University, has accepted the call to the chair. For particulars see elsewhere in the STENTOR.

Walter Larned presented his illustrated lecture, "Velasquez," to the students of the University at Ferry chapel Saturday evening. It is a very interesting as well as profitable paper.

Prof. Baldwin of the Toronto University has been offered a professorship in Psychology in Princeton University. He has not yet decided whether he will accept or not.

Wait
    For the
        New play entitled
"The Nervous Man and the Man of Nerve," March 17.

The World's Fair Class is very anxious to inaugurate a new custom in Lake Forest by the omission of Commencement orations. The matter is at present in the hands of a committee of the Faculty for action.

The college reading room is not intended as a loafing place for cads. The academy has two reading rooms of its own upon which college students never think of intruding. Why should academy students monopolize the periodicals of the college reading room to the exclusion of its legitimate occupants?

The next event of importance in local chess circles is the evening to be spent with the Chicago Chess club. The date has not as yet been fixed. All the contestants in the late tournament whose per. cent is above 500 will have an opportunity to visit Chicago upon this occasion.

Rev. Mr. N. D. Hillis, of Evanston, delivered a lecture last evening in Ferry Hall Chapel on "Ruskin." The lecture was a masterpiece and was enjoyed by townspeople and students alike. Mr. Hillis is an alumnus of Lake Forest and one of whom she is very proud.

Prof. M. Bross Thomas very kindly consented to read his paper, "A Plea for the College," before the members of the Athenæan society Friday evening. It was thoroughly enjoyed.

TOWN TOPICS.

Mr. and Mrs. Chapin leave soon for Marietta, Ga.

Mr. and Mrs. Giles will leave soon for Tallahassee, Florida to be away several weeks.

The Young Ladies' Musical circle held its second meeting at Mrs. J. F. Rumsey's February 23d. This club meets every third week and its purpose is to find the thought underlying the music studied. The composers studied so far are Schubert, Schumann, and Chopin. The program given last Thursday is as follows:

Introductory paper,	- - - -	Miss Steel
Schubert,	- Songs, - -	Miss Hofer
	a. "The Wanderer."	
	b. Mignon.	
	c. "Impatience."	
	d. "My Sweet Repose."	
Schubert,	Piano solo, -	Mrs. J. F. Rumsey
	a. Impromptu. Op. 90, No. 3.	
	b. Impromptu. Op. 149, No. 2.	
	c. Momen's Musicals. Op. 94, No. 3.	
Schubert,	- Songs, -	-- Miss Pratt
	a. "Wandering."	
	b. "Whither."	
	c. "The Inquirer."	
Chopin,	Piano solo,	Miss Harriet Durand
	Twelfth Nocturne.	
Schumann,	- Piano Solo,	Miss Sizer.
	a. Trammerei.	
	b. Romanza Marsche.	
Schumann,	- Songs,	Miss Hofer.
	a. "Der Nussbaum."	
	b. "Im Walde."	
	c. "In My Garden."	

The next meeting is at Mrs. Warner's

After March 1st the Gamma Sigma Society will again have its regular programme. So far, this term, the contests have taken up the time of the society.

FERRY HALL.

Miss Theo Kane spent Sunday with Miss McWilliams.

Miss Julia Brown has been ill for the past few days.

Miss Nona Phelps attended a reception at Evanston on Feb. 22nd.

Be it known that Miss L—— devotes four hours a week to *Art*.

Miss Phillipps, of Evanston, spent Sunday, the ninteenth, with Miss Somerville.

Miss Dora Creswell is in Michigan. From latest reports she is improving in health.

One of the Sems. announces the startling fact that she is threatened with *"ammonia."*

Mrs. Teetshorn, of Green Bay, Wis., spent Feb. 22nd with her sister, Miss Somerville.

The Misses Wiser, of Chicago, spent Sunday with Miss Bennett and Miss Lyon.

Miss Emma Gilchrist, so well-known to many of us as "Dick," is this year a senior at Cornell.

It is rumored that Miss Ada Barker will not return next term. California has proven too pleasant.

To Miss Robinson, who has returned from the East, where she was summoned by the sickness and death of her mother, we extend our sincerest sympathy.

We feel very grateful to Mr. Larned for the fine lecture on "Velasquez," which he delivered Saturday evening in the chapel.

A fancy dress dance was given in the Gym. Friday eve in honor of the guests. Music was furnished by Valisi's orchestra.

Miss Mame Harker, who was one of us last year, and was the guest of Miss Lydia Yertson Wednesday and Thursday, is taking a course in Kindergarten in Chicago.

We hope to be able in the next number to give a fuller account of the interesting paper given by Mrs. Smith Friday evening.

Rumor says that the engagement of Miss Bessie Buell, '90, to Mr. Harry Patterson, of Chicago, is announced. Miss Buell is at present visiting Mrs. Wm. Dinsmore, of Bloomington.

On Wednesday, the twenty-second, no opportunity for having a good time was lost. Sleighing parties were out morning and afternoon. Fort Sheridan and Waukegan were visited, and everyone said they had a first-rate time. In the evening Miss Watson gave a candy-pull in the gymnasium to a number of her friends, when we had the sweetest time of all.

When a young man, the same Saturday evening, sends his card to five different young ladies, does he in the least expect No. 5 is coming down? If he had heard the remarks he would know that we don't do that way, wouldn't he, girls? [When a young man puts on his "best bib and tucker," and breaks his neck over a mile of ice to get to the Sem., does he go simply for the exquisite pleasure of sending up his card once and then sliding home on his ear? If they could see the blue atmosphere outside they wouldn't say so, would they, boys?—ED.]

President Angell, of Ann Arbor, says: "I consider him one of the best, if not best, educator in the West. He is by all odds the best botanist in the country."

Dr. Seeley says: "One of the strongest men we could possibly have found. Prominent as an educator, he has had an experience in the work, which is always the best of recommendations. His coming augurs well for the University."

Dr. Thomas says: "Reports say that he is a hustler, and that is what we want. He also believes in the college and will champion its cause."

ACADEMY.

GAMMA SIGMA.

Several of the students spent last week's holiday in the city.

A number of the day students were sleighing Tuesday evening.

The Sunday evening prayer meeting is now held in the chapel.

Wells was in Wankegan last Wednesday having some dental work done.

Judson Williams visited relatives in Chicago last Tuesday and Wednesday.

The Academy will be well represented in the coming gymnasium exhibition.

The father and mother of Mrs. Burnap are visiting the latter at Mitchell Hall.

A new student was nearly drowned in the swimming pool one day last week.

The gymnasium classes which heretofore have met Thursday now meet on Tuesday.

The book store was closed several days last week on account of the illness of Rice, the proprietor.

Nearly one third of the cads were sleighing last Wednesday afternoon. A pleasant time is reported by all.

Rogers is around on crutches on account of a sprained ankle which he got while exercising in the gymnasium.

The many friends of Hughit will be sorry to learn that he has left school with the intention of not returning.

At a recent joint meeting of the executive committees of the two societies, Flint was elected chairman and Yaggy secretary. These committees make the arrangements for the coming contest.

A rumor that we were to have no holiday on Washington's birthday resulted in a mass meeting of the students last Monday. A committee was appointed to interview Prof. Smith and ask him in the name of George Washington to dismiss classes on Wednesday. The request was granted and the students made happy.

UNANIMOUSLY ELECTED.

CHICAGO, Feb. 27, 1893.—Special.—John M. Coulter was unanimously elected president of Lake Forest University by the Board of Trustees to-day. Fifteen members of the Board met in Parlor M. Sherman House at 2 o'clock. Those present were as follows: C. B. Farwell, Jacob Bridler, Arthur Orr, Dr. E. L. Holmes, L. W. Yaggy, N. D. Hillis, E. J. Warner, W. C. Larned, Dr. McClure, Dr. Herrick Johnson, Amzi Benedict, Cyrus H McCormick, Wm. Blair, George M. Bogue, H. N. Hibbard. A great deal of enthusiasm was manifested.

"The Contributor's Club," recently started in Chicago, has among its most prominent members several Lake Forest people. We notice the names of Mr. and Mrs. Hobart Chatfield-Taylor, Mr. and Mrs. S. R. Taber, Mr. and Mrs. Jesse L. Moss, Mr. and Mrs. Walter C. Larned, and Mr. Dell Smith. The first number of the *Contributors Magazine* contains a poem by Mrs. Moss "To a Bachelor;" a short story by Hobart Chatfield-Taylor, a tragedy in circus life, entitled "Only a Clown;" and a clever picture of a fashionable dinner party entitled "The Lost Art of Conversation," by Walter C. Larned. These are Lake Forest's contributions.

While some of the boys were skating on the lake last Wednesday one of them, Taylor by name, had the misfortune to fall in the water and become wet. [Strange fact.]

Prin. Smith inspected the rooms of the dormitory one day last week. He undoubtedly came to the conclusion that everyone has original ideas about the manner of keeping a room.

$125.00 REWARD.

The person that shot and killed my collie, Robin, on Saturday evening, February 11th, rendered himself liable to both criminal and civil prosecution—that is, to an action for violating a statute of the State of Illinois and an ordinance of the City of Lake Forest, the punishment for which are fines not exceeding $200.00 and also to a civil action for damages for destroying property of great value.

I will pay $25.00 to any one that will furnish me with the name of such person and with proof of his having done the shooting: and, if either of the above kinds of prosecution results successfully, I will pay such informant the additional sum of $100.00.

S. R. TABER.

P. O. Box 13, Lake Forest, Feb. 18th, 1893.

THE STENTOR.

VOLUME VI.   MARCH 7, 1893.   NUMBER 20.

PUBLISHED EVERY WEEK
BY THE
LakeForestUniversityStentorPublishingCo.

BOARD OF EDITORS.

F. C. SHARON, '93................Managing Editor
R. H. CROZIER, '93:.............Business Manager
N. H. BURDICK, '93 }
S. B. HOPKINS, '93 } ....Local*
L. N. ROSSITER, '93..........Alumni and Personal
B. R. MACHATTON, '95.................Advertising

ASSOCIATE EDITORS.

HARRY GOODMAN, '94·..............Athletic Editor
FOREST GRANT, '96.....................Staff Artist
DAVID FALES, '96...........................Town

Terms—$1.50 per year. Single Copies—10c

——ADDRESS——

STENTOR PUBLISHING COMPANY,

LAKE FOREST, : : ILLINOIS.

Entered at the P. O. at Lake Forest, Ill., as second-class matter.

As we are now under new regime we hereby retract everything we have said derogatory to Mr. Cleveland. We presume he will feel immensely relieved *when* he sees this.

The last issue of the STENTOR, with the account of the new President and the picture, has been greatly praised by all, alumni, trustees, townspeople and students. Numerous trustees and townspeople have ordered large numbers and the issue has been entirely exhausted. The board has been seriously considering the advisability of printing the matter in condensed form in another issue, together with the half-tone cut. The demand seems to warrant such a course. The cut is the finest half-tone that is made and is well worth preserving.

PRESIDENT HARRISON SOLVES THE QUESTION.

The question "What shall an ex-President do" has at last been answered by President Harrison. It has seemed for many decades as if there was nothing for an ex-President to do; as if when he had reached the highest point, he must then drop completely out of sight.

But President Harrison has broken away from old customs and does not intend to forever bury himself and live on his reputation. He has accepted the position of law lecturer in Leland Stanford University and will give fortunate students of that university the benefit of his magnificent experience and knowledge of both international and municipal law. His salary will be about $15,000, and has he not adopted the manly course? He has occupied the highest position his nation could give and has done his best for her politically.

Now he turns to her education and who knows but what he may rise as high as an educator? There is always something more for a man to do, no matter how high he has gone, and

President Harrison is certainly show-ing the right spirit in attempting to prove it.

A NORTHWESTERN OCCURRENCE.

Recently the students at Northwest-ern rose in arms against the professor in Greek of that institution because of long lessons or hard work, it matters not which. They made a formal pro-test before the said professor and he promised to remedy the matter. So far, the students were all right. But at this juncture some bright minds composed some doggerel verses reflecting on the professor and spread them over the blackboards of the recitation room. The verses were also sent to the Chi-cago papers and have caused quite a commotion at the University. Now, this is not as it should be. No matter what the professor had done that is no way to right the matter. It was an un-gentlemanly act to say the least. Stu-dents seem to forget at times that there is at least courtesy due to their supe-riors. We have had an example here of such conduct and every one with a spark of manhood in him will agree that it was an outrageous persecution. This thing of writing verses on a man, of jeering him and taunting him, espe-cially one's superior, would not be tol-erated in any one but a student. And why is a student considered such a sanctified person? The sentiment at Northwestern ought to be against such proceedings. The men should stand up for their rights and do it in a firm, manly way, but when it comes to puerile acts they should effectually sit on them.

THE SENIORS MUST WRITE.

It is a melancholy fact that we are forced to relate, but we must do it. The Faculty have decided that the Seniors must write commencement orations. The other provisions of the bill as passed are as follows: All these ora-tions must be handed in for criticism and then six of these will be chosen for delivery on commencement day. Of these six persons the salutatorian and valedictorian will constitute two and the other four will be chosen: 1st, as regards scholarship; 2nd, on the thought in the oration; 3d, in accord-ance with the judgment of the pro-fessor in oratory. Of course, the result is not exactly what we desired, but there's no use crying over spilled milk. There are two points, however, that are bothering some of the class.

First, if the scholarship is taken into account how will the best orators get on, as it is an acknowledged fact that the best scholars of the class are not always the best orators.

Second, if the thought in the orations and the judgment of the professor in the oratory count for a great deal, where will the students who have stood at the top all the four years, but who are not orators, where will they get recognition? However close the race may be for the salutatory and valedic-tory, still there are a number who have always stood exceedingly well, although not at the very top. Still, if some of these got on for their scholarship, the best oratory may not be represented. It will be a hard question to decide in all probability and we do not envy the judges their business.

THE COLLEGE GRADUATE.

Not long since the college graduate was the exception among public men; now he is the rule. Not many years ago it was the self-made man who stood out before the people, the man who had no education to speak of, but native ability and shrewdness. To be a business man then was to know nothing outside of pure business; a college man was not expected to enter business.

Now, how are things changed. Look, for instance, at President Cleveland's cabinet. The administration is to be a business administration and the men forming the cabinet are *business* men. Yet, seven out of the eight members are college graduates. Does not that speak better for the college than volumes?

It certainly refutes the point occasionally advanced that colleges make theorists. Those men who are naturally so shrewd and successful, think how much more they might have been if they had had college training!

The American college is characteristic. Its object is not the mere accumulation of book-lore. Its object is to give a broad scholarship, a broad culture, to raise a man's ideals, to give him a clear understanding of what life is, so that he may be fitted for a business life, a professional life, anything he desires to take up. It is not narrowing and the true college man is not the theorist or dreamer.

So when we look around us and see not only the professions, but the *business life* of the nation being filled by college men, we cannot but feel that the noble mission of the college is receiving its reward and that the world is becoming more enlightened and truer because of it.

COMMUNICATION.

Thursday, March 2, 1893.

To the Editors of The Stentor:

DEAR SIRS—In the STENTOR issue of Feb. 28, a local article appeared reflecting much discredit upon the fellows in the Academy.

Believing that the writer of the article was ignorant of the true facts in the case we ask you in justice to the Academy to publish this letter and acknowledge its truth.

The inference that Academy students are *loafers* we pass as unworthy of attention, but the question of our right to enjoy the 'Varsity reading room we wish to establish once and for all.

Last fall the college representatives came among us asking subscriptions for these very periodicals. Willingly and cheerfully we responded and when we had paid our money our right to use the reading room was established equal to the right of the College men.

Trusting in your courtesy to treat us as gentlemen and in your honor to do us justice,

We are,

THE ACADEMY,
per Committee
N. U. FLINT,
L. G. BOURNIQUE,
G. U. HEINEMAN.

Owing to the hurry incident to the presidential issue of the STENTOR the item mentioned above escaped our notice until too late to cut it and it was with great regret that we found it in. It has been our purpose to preserve the unity of the academy and college and such an occurrence is merely an oversight.

HARD TO PLEASE.

It seems to be quite in order at present to abuse the Columbian postage stamps. The press, daily and weekly, humorous and serious, seems to have decided to wage war against them until they are removed from circulation. But this is not all. A joint resolution has been proposed in the United States senate by Senator Wolcott which will prohibit the sale of the stamps, if it is concurred in.

This movement is hard to understand in view of the fact that no one is compelled to buy a Columbian stamp if he would prefer a "pygmy." Both issues can be had at all offices. All objections to a stamp would seem to be invalid unless it were the only kind to be obtained. But it might not be out of place to consider some of the points raised against the new stamps just as if the above argument could not be used in their favor.

An editorial in the *Illustrated American* speaks of the color of the two cent stamp as "a dim blur of faded feathers, streaked with rudimentary rays of blue!" Such a delightful description of a beautiful shade of maroon— called in John Wanamaker's circular a purple maroon—is not often met with; it is to be hoped the author will favor us with humorous descriptions of other colors as rapidly as he can concoct them; they are extremely amusing.

We have heard the series crsticised because "Columbus in sight of land" is beardless, while he is adorned with a full beard in "landing." Perhaps the critics would like to have the masterpieces by Wm. H. Powell and Vanderlyn, from which the engravings were made, "removed from circulation" because inconsistent?

In conclusion, the argument most used is the most easily answerable of all. "Lickiness" is the word used in the *Illustrated American*. "The glutinous substance that is spread in trituration over the stamp is not, as all the world knows, a delectable composition." Certainly it is not, nor ought such an increase of of "lickable" area to be tolerated—if one had to lick the stamp. But learn to use a wet sponge in a glass holder if you are a business man and write many letters, learn to lick the *envelope* if you write few, and then allow us to use the beautiful Columbian stamps the rest of the year in peace.

OUR PRESIDENT ACCEPTS.

Although not yet officially announced, Dr. Coulter writes that he will accept the call to the presidency of Lake Forest University. He has written to know whether the trustees have accepted his conditions and upon their taking this action he will formally take the presidential chair. It is expected that he will be upon the ground the first of next term to assume the duties of his office.

COLLEGE.

AMUSEMENTS FOR THE WEEK.

COLUMBIA—"Aristocracy."
HOOLEY'S—"Joseph."
GRAND—"Ensign."
CHICAGO—Francis Wilson and Company, "The Lion Tamer."
McVICKER'S—"The White Squadron."
SCHILLER—"The Masked Ball."

Electives *must* be handed in this week.

Y. M. C. A. annual election to-night.

Prepatory service was held Wednesday evening.

Buck, the Waukegan jeweler, repairs watches.

"The Nervous Man and the Man of Nerve," March 17.

Buy your gymnasium shoes and suits of Ruston, College Hall.

Go to French, the druggist, for anything in the line of toilet articles.

Dr. Coulter, our new president, will soon visit Lake Forest on business.

The senior class intend to be a little original in their class day exercises this year.

Since the chess tournament closed the various members have been solacing themselves with private matches.

March 15 has been definitely fixed as the date when the University Chess club will meet the Chicago chess club.

Mrs. Coulter is very active in foreign missionary work and the ladies expect a very valuable addition to their circle.

The exams. will soon be upon us. Let the students take some action in regard to "cribbing." This vice is not common but it should be frozen out, root and branch.

Dr. Henson, of Chicago, lectured before a fair audience last Friday evening on "Fools." The discourse was a happy alloy of humor and wisdom and was thoroughly enjoyed by those present. Both the Athenæan and Zeta Epsilon societies adjourned their regular programs for the lecture.

TOWN TOPICS.

The U. of M. Ministrels are gaining laurels wherever they go.

The Ann Arbor-Madison debate takes place March 31 in Ann Arbor.

Mrs. Granger Farwell entertained a few young people at her home, Monday evening, Feb. 27.

Prof. Hillis' lecture last Monday evening was enjoyed by all. Many say it was the best heard here this year.

A children's party in honor of Miss Bertha Durand was given at the residence of Calvin Durand Friday evening.

Miss Helen Williams, of Chicago, who spent the summer of '91 in Lake Forest, was recently presented to Queen Victoria.

There will be a mortgage sale at the Dent livery stables next Friday, on a first mortgage of $350, held by J. R. Dady, of Waukegan.

U. of M. *Daily* says President Coulter, of Indiana State University, will accept the chair in botany in Chicago University. A little slow, brother.

Mr. L. C. Platt has been building a new dwelling on the site of the one which was burned last fall. The house was to be under roof by the end of last week.

The Senior elective Latin class has begun the study of a new method of familiarizing the student with the Latin syntax. They are very favorably impressed with it.

The Tuesday evening prayer-meeting was led by C. S. Davies. The subject was "The Student's Private Devotions." It was a very pleasant and profitable meeting.

Mrs. F. E. Hinckley was in Lake Forest for a short time Friday, looking over her summer residence. Mr. and Mrs. Hinckley and family will come to Lake Forest for the summer the last of this month.

The paving of Deerpath and Illinois avenues will be recommenced at the first approach of warmer weather. The materials are on the ground, and it is expected that the work will be speedily completed.

The following books have been added to the library during the past week. Bagehot's works, five volumes, sold at cost to advertise the Travelers' Insurance Co., of Hartford, Conn.; Index of General Literature, W. A. Fletcher, Riverside edition.

The Senior class has been learning some things about the popular heroes, Daniel Webster and Henry Clay, that tend to show that the gentlemen were not as great statesmen as many people suppose. For example, if a foolish blunder cost Clay the presidency, it was not because he was too great.

The jury of awards for the fifth annual Black and White exhibition of the Chicago Society of Artists, in its disposition of prizes for the best exhibits, awarded the first prize to Miss Ellen Benedict, of Lake Forest. The prize was the Ferris prize of $50, offered by W. J. Ferris for the best work in black and white.

Last Sunday was Communion. Dr. A. C. Haven was installed as elder and Henry Colvin Durand as deacon. There were received into full membership Mr. and Mrs. Fales and family, Mr. and Mrs. Frank Rumsey and family, Mrs. Wells, and David Jones by letter and Miss Polly Fales and Miss Mary Giles by confession of faith.

ATHLETICS.

University of Michigan has ten candidates for pitcher, all of them said to be first-class.

Leland Stanford played her first game of ball for the season Feb. 22, against the Reliance club of Oakland. Stanford won by 6–1.

"Bobby" Carruthers who played such excellent ball in the National League last year is to train Champaign ball team for the coming season.

Thirty or forty men chosen from the general practice candidates for the Mott Haven team will represent Harvard in the indoor games March 11.

The Williams base ball team began training about two weeks ago. They practice an hour each day in the gymnasium. A second nine and the four class teams are expected to furnish many available players.

The entertainment committee of the Athletic Association will soon be able to announce something definite. These entertainments are given but once a year and everyone in the college, academy and seminary should turn out and show their loyalty to the cause of Athletics.

F. W. Griffith, '95, has been chosen captain of the Northwestern University base ball team. Griffith, it will be remembered, was the prodigy whom Capt. Anson selected to pitch against the Clevelands last year and who made

a very creditable showing against that team. He is generally conceded to be among the best college pitchers of the country and Northwestern is to be congratulated in having such a phenomenon.

FERRY HALL.

Prof. Eager took dinner Saturday with Paderewski.

Miss Lizzie Williams has had a present of a banjo recently.

Dr. and Mrs. Seeley contemplate a southern trip during the spring vacation.

The parlors are to be refurnished, a welcome and much-needed improvement.

The friends of Miss Ruth Smith, '92, were glad to have her with them Sunday, the 5th.

The girls wish some one would render Mother Nature a little assistance in cleaning off the Sem. walk.

Miss Lena Scott went to her home in Lake Side Saturday. She will not resume her studies till next term.

Several of the college girls were favored with invitations to the reception at McCormick Seminary on March 3d.

Our Sunday evening chapel services are always very pleasant, but Feb. 26th we had the rare treat of Mrs. Hester's presence.

It is not often we have the privilege of hearing such a lecture as that on "Rushin," given by Dr. Hillis, of Evanston, last week Monday.

On Saturday, Feb. 25th, Miss Gilbert gave a sleigh-ride in honor of her friend, Miss Gertrude Lewis, of Chicago. The party went to Fort Sheridan.

March 1st—College wit at the Sem., 1st person to college girl—"Well, it is not very lion-like overhead." College girl—"No, but it's *lie on* the sidewalk below."

Ferry Hall was honored on Wednesday with visit its first by a bridal party,—Mr. and Mrs.

Elvadore Faucher, of Cleveland, Ohio. They were guests of Miss Lyon, the bride's sister.

Miss Nora Phelps is president of the recently-organized banjo club. The members are Misses Clark and Phelps, 1st. banjo; Misses Keener and Brett, 2nd; banjo; Miss Urvis, mandoline; Miss Messenger, harp; Misses McRea and Parmenter, guitar; Miss Ella McCord, banjorine.

Mrs. Smith, in her talk to us Friday evening, Feb. 24th, on "Our Environments, Spiritual and Material," apologized, saying when she came to take up the subject she felt her incompetency to deal with it as it should be dealt with. The way in which the paper was received showed that no such apology was needed.

ACADEMY.

Harvey was visited by his mother recently.

Ernest Woelful was visited by his sisters last week.

Wells visited relatives in the city last Saturday and Sunday.

Heinemann has returned from a recent visit to his home in Wausau, Wis.

Quite a number attended the lecture by Dr. Henson at the art building Friday evening.

The Tri Kappa society now has its regular programme at the usual hour on Wednesday.

Everyone is pleased to learn that at last we have a president. We are anxiously awaiting his arrival.

A communication from Editor Sharon to the academy students was read sn chapel last Friday morning.

· The dormitory boys will in the near future have a banquet "to drive dull care away" and renew an interest in life.

Those who attended the lecture at Ferry Hall last Monday night report it the best that has been given here this year.

Everyone is warned to keep away from the new buildings until further notice as the painters now have possession of them.

A roomer in the president's house has been unfortunate enough to have some money taken from his room by persons unknown.

A recitation in the geometry class was recently made in this manner: "Now this here line here equals that there line there."

Roberts conducted the prayer meeting last Tuesday evening, a number of others taking part. It was a very interesting meeting.

The absence of the masters in dormitory one evening last week gave the students an opportunity to give the cad yell in the halls which they did with a will.

The Gamma Sigma prelimnary contest in essay took place in the college chapel last Wednesday. There were only two contestants, Harvey and Vincent, the former winning the contest.

There will be three base ball teams in the Academy this year. The dormitory nine, the Mitchell Hall nine and the Academy nine. They will begin active practice as soon as the weather will permit.

The library has been materially strengthened by several additions to it. Mr. W. H. Hugit has contributed several volumes· Gunn & Co., the publishers, have donated the works of Shakespeare, and Mr. Brearly has given a sum of money to be used for the purchase of new books.

ALUMNI.

G. W. Wrigle, '92, visited friends Monday morning.

H. E. House, ex '94, was here over Sunday, Feb. 26th.

B. M. Linnell '89, of Chicago, was in town Sunday, Feb. 26th,

·L. E. Zimmerman '92, and F. Y. Radecke, ex '95, were here last Thursday evening.

8   THE STENTOR.

Miss Clara Hall, who was last year a Ferry Hall girl, is now attending Chicago University.

E. .G. Wood '92, of Woodstock, Ill., spent the early part of last week with his parents here.

Miss Lucia Sickels '91 is studying music in Indianapolis. Recently she took part in a large recital given in that city.

Rev. Thomas E. Barr, a Lake Forest Alumnus, was made the recepient of some elegant presents by the Y. M. C. A. of Kalamazoo, Mich.

The STENTOR is always glad to hear from the Universities Alumni, and it will consider it one of the highest favors if all the members of the alumni will write from time to time to the alumni editor giving him any note of interest concerning themselves or others who once attended the F. U.

A PORTRAIT.

A slim young girl, in lilac quaintly dressed;
  A mammoth bonnet, lilac like the gown,
  Hangs from her arm by wide, white strings,
    the crown
Wreathed around with lilac blooms, and on
    her breast
A cluster; lips still smiling at some jest
  Just uttered, while the gay, gray eyes half
    frown
  Upon the lips' conceit; hair, wind blown,
    brown
Where shadows stray, gold where the sunbeams rest.

Ah! lilac lady, step from your gold frame,
Between that starched old Bishop and the dame,
  In awe-inspiring ruff. We'll brave their ire
    And trip a minuet. You will not?—Fie!
  Those mocking lips half make me wish
    that I,
  Her grandson, might have been my own
    grand- sire.

Trinity Tablet.

SONG.

Nature felt the charm of Beauty
  On a time.
Used his varied arts to woo her,
Brought the birds and flowers to sue her,
Vowed a lasting springtime to her;
  Hearts a-rhyme.

Beauty wed her ardent suitor
  On a moon:
And the Earth burst forth a-singing,
· Came the gods their tributes bringing,
And the air with shouts was ringing.
  Love is born!
      Williams Weekly.

I sat me down and thought profound;
  This maxim wise I drew;
  It's easier far to like a girl,
    Than make a girl like you.—*Ex.*

Where is the man who has not said
At evening when he went to bed,
I'll waken with the crowing cock
And get to work at five o'clock?

Where is he, who rather late,
Crawls out of bed, not more than eight;
That has not thought, with fond regard,
'Its better not to work too hard?—*Ex.*

At Princeton no student will be allowed to bring a watch into the rooms at the coming examinations.

The new Yale Infirmary has just been opened. It will accommodate about forty patients.

The Berkeleyan is a new weekly from the University of California. It is an interesting paper.

The Editors of the *Castalian*, Ann Arbor's annual, have our sympathy. All their cuts to the number of fifty or more, said to be unusually fine, were destroyed by fire in Boston where they had been sent for printing. They have therefore abandoned the Annual.

THE STENTOR.

VOLUME VI.   MARCH 14, 1893.   NUMBER 21.

PUBLISHED EVERY. WEEK
BY THE

Lake Forest University Stentor Publishing Co.

BOARD OF EDITORS.

F. C. SHARON, '93................Managing Editor
R. H. CROZIER, '93..............Business Manager
N. H. BURDICK, '93 }......................Locals
S. B. HOPKINS, '93 }
L. N. ROSSITER, '93.........,...Alumni and Personal
B. R. MacHATTON, '95................Advertising

ASSOCIATE EDITORS.

HARRY GOODMAN, '94..............Athletic Editor
FOREST GRANT, '96....................Staff Artist
DAVID FALES, '96...........................Town

Terms—$1.50 per year. Single Copies—10c

————ADDRESS————

STENTOR PUBLISHING COMPANY,

LAKE FOREST,   :   :   ILLINOIS.

Entered at the P. O. at Lake Forest, Ill., as second-class matter.

The position of college journalists and editorial writers has changed within the last few years. The great increase both in the number and ability of college journals is one of the best signs of the times. What is now most needed in our college journalism is a higher dignity—a dignity that will not condescend to lower itself with the view of making capital thereby.

At Princeton suspension over the students in examinations is abolished. All that is required is a signed statement by the student at the close of the examination saying that he has received no assistance. It works well. The spirit of honor among the men has been found to be so high that the penalty of cribbing is ostracism. No man would think of taking advantage of the absence of the instructor.

Scarcely a more encouraging sign of sturdy and exalted manliness has been noted recently in educational life. It might be expected of a man having the benefits of a supposedly ennobling culture. This confidence in student manliness is justified. If collegiate education doesn't make honorable men it is a failure.

Dr. Arnold, of Rugby, said that the difference in boys was not in genius, but in energy. When the fullness of the idea dawns upon us, we are surprised at its truthfulness. We have been waiting to develop into geniuses before we do something great. We might take account of stock and conclude that we haven't made any high reaches because we lacked in energy. A man with lots of brains and little energy is like a magnificently built engine without any steam in it.

"Half the world rides through life on the shoulders of the other half,"—a truism which might be applied to our immediate college life, as well as to the world at large. There are always a *few* men in college who do all of the hustling; the others stand by and act as critics. Perhaps the appellation of. critic is too dignified—the plain and simple, but most expressive word, *kicker*, would be more to the point. The more work a man does in college the more he will be asked to do. When there is any extra work to be done in the class room, the professor asks the man who does the hardest and most conscientious work in his daily recitations. It is so in everything that pertains to college life. If there is anything to be done in the cause of athletics or society work, the old standbys are called out and put to work. This should not be. These hustlers will leave some time, and we want to have experienced men to take their places. Let us have some of the new blood infused into our college work in all of its departments, and above all, let us crush out this spirit of petty criticism.

SOCIETY SPIRIT.

It was only a few months ago that the Faculty were considering the advisability of suspending several members of the sophomore class for hazing. Hazing, when carried to excess, is not a good thing. It should be punished. But there is one good thing about hazing. It is open and above board. You know the man who ducked you. But there is an element creeping into our college life that is neither open and above board nor can the men who compose this element be dealt with by the Faculty. This hydra-headed, diabolical monster that is fast making itself a home in our college life is society spirit.

A healthy and honest rivalry between two literary societies is to be commended, but when this rivalry degenerates into a *rabid contention* for everything in sight, it makes one think of two curs fighting over a bone.

It not only makes our college course unpleasant, but it utterly crushes out all true college spirit. The cry becomes "Society first—college second."

· It is a well-known fact to men in both societies that this selfish spirit is fostered by the minority, but the minority in this case, contrary to the usual order of things, rule.

In all the walks of life it will be found that there are always a few despicable, underhanded people who are never satisfied until they have created dissension.

When the literary societies meet on common ground, let good fellowship prevail and let everything be done for the good of the college as a whole.

Let us do away with this babyish hostility. If we like a fellow in the other society — *tell him so*. Life is too short and friends too few to live without giving the evidence in words or acts that we revere character and native worth.

It is true that this feeling has reached such a pitch that it may have spent itself and will now die a natural death. But lest this may not be the case, let the classes of the next year create such a sentiment as will crush out this existing spirit and make it give way to a noble and manly spirit of college fellowship.

—Anon.

PRESIDENT COULTER MAKES A FLYING VISIT.

President Coulter made a short visit to Lake Forest last Friday, arriving on the noon train and leaving at ·10 o'clock that evening. His formal letter of acceptance was received not long since and this visit was a purely business trip.

He met the Faculty at 4 o'clock at Dr. Mc-Clure's and discussed his plans with them. It is gratifying to know that he has *very definite* plans, knows just what he wants and how to get it.

He believes that the college is the main_spring of this institution around which the other departments should be grouped. He thought it best not to be presented to the students this time, as he did not feel fully prepared and had so short a time to stay. At present it looks as if President Coulter would not be able to take charge before the middle of next term. We copy the following from the *Indianapolis News* of March 1st:

"President Coulter, of the Indiana State University, is much sought after. One day we hear that Chicago University, which seems to want every best man in sight, has offered him a professor's chair; the next day comes the definite announcement that the trustees of Lake Forest University have elected him president of that admirable and progressive institution. Some time ago word came from Chicago that the latter position was to be offered to President Coulter, so the election by the trustees is not a complete surprise. There cannot be much doubt in the nature of things that President Coulter will accept one or the other of these very flattering offers. We should presume that his choice would be Lake Forest, where he would be at the head of an independent institution with established reputation and bright prospects. There he would have a chance to build up a great college and allied schools, in accordance with his own theories of education; while at Chicago he would be master only of a department. His departure will be a serious loss to Indiana. But the State universities cannot expect to retain men in the face of offers from endowed institutions, until the State adopts a policy of greater liberality. It cannot be otherwise than humiliating to a man engaged in the work of higher education to have to fight with the Legislature for every appropriation of money for necessary purposes that the institution over which he presides receives. And when money is voted, it is often given grudgingly and with the air that it is a dole and not one of the most necessary expenses of the State."

AN IMPORTANT INNOVATION.

The Faculty at its last meeting decided to introduce 8 o'clock recitations next term to a limited extent. As it is at present, it is almost impossible to find enough hours for the regular and elective work without introducing either 1 o'clock hours or 8 o'clock hours. In the spring term the days are usually warm and long so that the students will not notice the earliness of the 8 o'clock recitation as they would in the other terms. One feels much brighter early in the morning than late in the day, and it will be a satisfaction to get through early. The Faculty intends putting in as few of these hours as possible. "Eight o'clocks" have hitherto been optional, but have never been seriously objected to. The STENTOR feels that it is a good thing and hails the new plan with pleasure. It ought to materially aid the ball team. If enough of the candidates could have "eight o'clocks" they could have an extra afternoon hour for practice.

Lake Forest won the Illinois State Oratorical contest, Wooster the Ohio contest, Beloit the Wisconsin, University of Colorado the Colorado, Kansas Normal the Kansas, and Parsons College the Iowa. The final contest is held at Columbus, Ohio, May 5th.

LAKE FOREST'S COLLEGE MEN.

The STENTOR has prepared a list of college graduates, resident in Lake Forest, together with the colleges and universities represented and as far as possible the classes and fraternities. Necessarily the list is neither complete nor perfect, but it is hoped that, such as it is, it may prove of some interest.

As the STENTOR has the list the summary by colleges is as follows:

Yale 10, Lake Forest 6, Williams 5, Amherst 5, Chicago University (old) 3, Oberlin 2, Harvard 2, Edinburgh 2, University of Michigan 2, Syracuse 1, Weslyan 1, Northwestern College 1, Heidelberg 1, Hamilton 1, Dartmouth 1.

Following is the list:

J. Frank Rumsey, Chicago.
E. S. Skinner, Oberlin.
Dr. A. C. Haven, '77, Psi Upsilon, Syracuse.
Hiram Stanley, Lake Forest.
Granger Farwell, Yale.
Rev. Mr. Nichols, '34, Amherst.
M. S. Scudder, Phi Nu Theta, Weslyan.
E. F. Chapin, Harvard.
Walter C. Larned, Harvard.
L. W. Yaggy, Northwestern College.
Scott Durand, '89, Kappa Alpha, Williams.
Harry Durand, '89, Chi Psi, Amherst.
Chas. Holt, '74, Kappa Alpha, Williams.
Ed. Wells, '89, Lake Forest.
F. C. Farwell, Psi Upsilon, Yale.
J. V. Farwell, Jr, Psi Upsilon, Yale.
Walter Farwell, Psi Upsilon, Yale.
Arthur Farwell, Psi Upsilon, Yale.
H. N. Tuttle, Yale.
Dr. McClure, '70, Psi Upsilon, Yale.
Prof. Stuart, Edinburgh University.
Prof. Bridgeman, '80, Delta Kappa Epsilon, Yale.
Prof. Locy, '80, Delta Upsilon, University of Michigan.
Dr. Seeley, Heidelberg.
Prof. Thomas, Williams.
Prof. Stevens, Beta Theta Pi, University of Michigan.
Prof. Dawson, Swarthmore.
Prof. Harper, Oberlin and Johns Hopkins.
Prof. Halsey, Beta Theta Pi, Chicago.
Prof. Burnap, Psi Upsilon, Chicago.

E. J. Learned, '81, Kappa Psi, Amherst.
Henry J. Durand, '89, Amherst.
Principal Smith, Delta Kappa Epsilon, Amherst.
Dudley Winston, Delta Kappa Epsilon, Yale.
Hobart Chatfield-Taylor, Alpha Delta Theta, Cornell.
Traverse Wells, Alpha Delta Phi, Dartmouth.
Prof. A. E. Jack, Lake Forest.
Prof. David Williams, '92, Williams.
E. G. Wood, '92, Williams.
Fred. Skinner, '92, Lake Forest.
Ned. Pratt, '92, Lake Forest.
A. C. Wenban, Lake Forest.
Prof. Walter Smith, Edinburgh.
Prof. Booth, Yale.
Prof. Morris, Hamilton.

Any additions or corrections to the above will be thankfully received and due attention given to them by the STENTOR.

COLLEGE.

AMUSEMENTS FOR THE WEEK.

COLUMBIA—"Aristocracy."
HOOLEY'S—James O'Neill in "Fontenelle."
GRAND—"Ensign."
CHICAGO—Francis Wilson and Company, "The Lion Tamer."
McVICKER'S—"Blue Jeans."
SCHILLER—"The Masked Ball."

Vacation next week.

Electives must be in this term.

Prof. Halsey offers to the seniors an elective study of the Civil War, the material to be taken from the original sources—government reports, etc. The work is to be a continuation of the American politics of the present term. This is the only elective he offers to seniors.

President Coulter made a short call on the University faculty Friday. His next visit will be to the students.

The College societies attended the Nu Beta Kappa open meeting in Ferry chapel Friday evening. All were pleasantly entertained. The tableaux showed much taste and pains in their preparation and reflected much credit on the young ladies.

The officers of the Athenæan society for the spring term are: President, R. H. Crozier; Vice-President, E. H. McNeal; Secretary, W. B. Smith; Treasurer, E. U. Graff; Critic S. B. Hopkins; Seargeant-at Arms, B. R. MacHatton.

Next Friday evening is the date for "The Nervous Man and the Man of Nerve." They will both be there with their full company. Don't fail to see them. Much time and pains have been spent in the preparation of this comedy. A ministrel show by home talent will follow the play and will furnish fun and frolic for frisky folk. Many new and never before heard jokes and jibes will be sprung. Songs and music will not be lacking. The aim will be to furnish an evening's entertainment which will excel anything before attempted in this line by the students.

Be sure you have a "date" when you go to the Sem. If you don't you may be left. Only one card from the same individual will be received the same evening. This is a new rule announced a week since.

The students under the care of the Board of Education were made happy by the receipt of their checks one day last week.

The catalogues will probably be out by the first of May.

"The Humor of France," translated by Elizabeth Lee, published by Scribners; "French Humorists," by Walter Besant, published by Roberts Bros.; and "References for Literary Workers,' a work of special interest to debaters, by Henry Watson, published by A. C. McClurg, have just been added to the library.

In chosing the orators from the senior class for Commencement, scholarship is taken account of only in the cases of the Valedictorian and the Salutatorian. In the four other cases thought and style of delivery alone are made the basis of selection.

The snow has gone.

A praise service under the auspices of the missionary societies was held at the church at 3:30 Sunday afternoon. A special collection will be taken for reimbursing the missionary fund.

Fine stationery, tablets, memorandum and account books. Inks, pens and pencils, at French's drug store.

Buck, the Waukegan jeweler, wants the college boys to trade with him. All kinds of repairing at reasonable prices.

TOWN TOPICS.

At a recent meeting of the Board of Directors of the Associated Press, Mr. Melville A. Stone was elected to succeed Mr. Wm. Henry Smith. Mr. Delavan Smith was re-elected to the office of secretary.

The Art Club met last Tuesday at the house of Mr. I. P. Rumsey. Major Jenney read a paper on "The Architecture of the Fair," and afterwards gave a ruuning commentary on stereopticon views of the Fair buildings. Maj. Jenney is himself the architect of the Horticultural building, and is well acquainted with the inner motives and designs of the Directors; therefore his lecture, ornamented by his charming manner, was very enjoyable and full of interest. Music was furnished by the Lotus Quartette.

The city and town elections will soon take place. There will be a special election for the town of Shields, March 28th. The regular town election takes place April 4th. The city election for mayor and minor offices, will come off on April 11th. Nomination papers must be in by the 24th of this month.

There was a boys' party at Blair Lodge Monday afternoon, March 13th, at which a prestidigitateur from Chicago amused the boys.

The Annual Union Meeting of the Missionary Societies of the Church was held Sunday afternoon in the Church Chapel.

ATHLETICS.

At the regular meeting of the Board of Directors of the Athletic Association, the report of the Entertainment Committee was accepted and it was decided to give a war song concert on a grand scale. It is intended to give this concert about the last of April. Men from both of the Literary societies in the college and a strong contingent from the Academy will take part. The chorus will probably be composed of one hundred voices. Mr. Root, the composer of many of our patriotic songs will be on hand with his quartet. Mr. N. D. Pratt has kindly consented to devote his time to the training of the chorus. Under Mr. Pratt's able leadership, our war song concert cannot fail to be a gigantic success.

The field day and gymnasium committees are actively at work getting their men in shape for the spring events. The success of these events will depend on the enthusiasm manifested by the students. We have some record-breakers in our midst. Encourage them,—they are working for the glory of the university.

FERRY HALL.

Mr. Messenger spent Friday evening with his sister Miss Mable.

Miss Traverse and Miss Smith spent Saturday with Miss Edna Smith.

Miss McIntosh spent Sunday in Chicago, at the home of Miss Glenrose Bell.

The Seniors enjoyed the reception given Wednesday afternoon by Dr. and Mrs. McClure to the Academy boys.

College Girl—" Are'nt those Indian clubs heavy?"

" No, they are pound clubs."

College Girl—"Mine are only sixteen ounce."

Miss Idell Houghton of Spokane Falls, who was a Ferry Hall girl in '90, is contemplating returning to continue her study of music.

Miss Maude Taylor of Chicago spent Saturday with Miss Jeanette Kennedy.

Dr. and Mrs. Seeley, Prof. Eager, Mrs. Hester, Miss Ripley and Miss Sizer were very pleasantly entertained at the home of Mr. and Mrs. Yaggy, Monday evening.

Miss Whitely of Evanston spent Saturday with Miss Norton.

We would advise a certain cad to read " Hiawatha," to prevent his speaking of Cupid as one of the characters.

Friday evening the Nu Beta Kappa society gave an open meeting, Music was furnished by Miss Messenger and Miss Gilbert, and after a recitation by Miss Jeanette Kennedy, tableux were given. On that evening "Nancy" resolved to resign her position as stage manager.

Miss Mabel Gilson is able to resume her studies at the college.

Miss Rhena Obene has been ill for some days past.

The Aletheians are indebted to the Nu Beta Kappas for a very pleasant evening, March 10th.

Miss Edna Hays visited friends in the city on Sunday last.

Miss Mabel Parker was favored with a visit from her father, March 16th.

ACADEMY.

Nichols arrayed himself in a spring suit one morning last week but it was so attractive his natural modesty caused him to lay it aside, after wearing it about fifteen minutes, for the conventional black one. Henceforth he will probably not get quite so far in advance of the season.

A quartette without a name, being yet in its infancy, rendered a selection in place of regular chapel exercises last Thursday morning. Messrs. Dudley, Fales, Harvey and Yaggy compose the quartette.

It has at last been definitely settled that we will move into the new buildings at the beginning of the new term. A vote of the students developed the fact that nearly as many are willing to remain where they are for the remainder of the year as those who wish to move.

Prof. Burnap gave the Iliad class a dinner at the Leland hotel in Chicago last Saturday. It was the result of a dispute between himself and a member of the class in regard to a construction. We hope he will extend his hospitality to his other classes.

At the request of Prof. Stuart, Prof. Palmer read a paper before one of the College Latin classes last Monday.

Joeger was in Waukegan last Wednesday having some dental work done.

Hatch had a cousin from the city visiting him Sunday, March 5th,

A recent addition to the Academy membership, Eppinger by name, had the misfortune to be immersed with a pitcher of ice water one evening last week while he was in such a position that unfortunately he could not pull a gun. We hope he entoyed his initiation.

Dr. and Mrs. McClure very kindly received the Academy and Faculty and Ferry Hall Seniors last Wednesday afternoon from four to six. Owing to the inclemency of the weather the attendance was not as large as it otherwise would have been, but those who went passed a most delightful afternoon.

It is rumored that Roberts firmly established himself in the good graces of the Ferry Hall seniors last Wednesday afternoon. We congratulate him upon his good fortune and the ladies upon their making such a worthy acquaintance.

We are always glad to receive items of interest about the Academy from students or faculty. It is our aim to make these notes of interest to any of the many friends of the Academy who may chance to read them.

Flint, Yaggy, Durand, and Bournique will take part in the Athenæan entertainment to be given March 17.

A number of the students attended the recital of Padereweski at the Auditorium last Wednesday afternoon.

We neglacted to mention, last week, among the other gifts to the library the one of Rev, Dr. Hillis, of Evanston.

COLLEGE VERSE.

A HINT.

" Your figure petite is ever so sweet,
And there's certainly no getting 'round it."
Her adorer was scared, and hence unprepared,
For her question meant more than she hardly
    dared,
But she coyly found voice to propound it:
"So my figure petite is ever so sweet?
And you're—*quite*—sure, there's no getting
    'round it?"—*Amherst Student.*

A NEW YEAR'S POEM.

Here's the postman with the bills—
    New Year's bills.
With a world of merriment my soul their coming fills.
    All around they sprinkle, sprinkle,
      A gloom like that of night,
    While the postman's keys they tinkle
    And his eyes they fairly twinkle
      With ironical delight,
    As he comes, comes, comes,
    Till the neighbors think us chums,
And to my great tribulation, my letter box he
    fills
    With the bills, bills, bills, bills,
      Bills, bills, bills,
While I'm moaning and I'm groaning at the bills
      —*Columbia Spectator.*

The Durand Art Institute,

Friday Night, March 17th,

**First Presentation here of a New
and Original American Comedy,**

The Nervous Man and The Man of Nerve,

By the Members of the

Athenaean Literary Society

of Lake Forest College.

Between the Acts, Music will be furnished by the Banjo and Guitar Clubs.

The Entertainment to conclude with an

Old Time Minstrel Show,

In which the Athenaean Society will be assisted by the

Chicago North Shore Quartette.

SCALE OF PRICES.

Parquette and Dress Circle,	75 Cents.
Parquette Circle, first five rows,	50 "
Balance of Parquette Circle,	35

Theatre parties from Highland Park and Lake Forest have already written for reserved spaces.

The Sale of Reserved Seats will begin Wednesday, 15th.

B. R. MᴀCHATTON, Business Manager.

THE STENTOR.

VOLUME VI. APRIL 11, 1893. NUMBER 22.

PUBLISHED EVERY WEEK
BY THE
Lake Forest University Stentor Publishing Co.

BOARD OF EDITORS.

B. R. MacHatton, '95.............Managing Editor
Forest Grant, '96......Ass't Mgr. Ed. and Athletic
Harry Goodman, '94.............Business Manager
A. B. Burdick, '95
J. H. Jones, '96 ....Locals
David Fales, Jr., '96
A. O. Jackson, '96.............Alumni and Personal
W. B. Smith, '94.........................Exchange
J. A. McGaughey, '95 ....Advertising

Terms—$1.50 per year. Single Copies—10c

————ADDRESS————
STENTOR PUBLISHING COMPANY,
LAKE FOREST,   :   :   ILLINOIS.

Entered at the P. O. at Lake Forest, Ill., as second-class matter.

In accordance with the custom of eastern college journals, a new board of editors has been substituted. The present board of editors make their greeting to the public with this issue, and promise to keep the character of the STENTOR up to its former standard. It is intended by the management to devote more space to literary work, and with that end in view we have asked several of the most prominent men and women in Lake Forest to contribute articles from time to time. These articles will always be on subjects connected with student life.

———

Not long ago a gentleman who is something of an authority on musical matters visited chapel. After coming out, said he: "Your students here all sing and they sing well, except that they drag and lack somewhat in spirit." Singing is a good habit. If in College we practice it in chapel and elsewhere, there will be more sunshine in our souls in after-life. The man who sings is not apt to develop into a very bad man. Music and wickedness are seldom found consorting together in a human heart.

———

One of the societies gave a farce comedy and a minstrel show recently. Are such things of much benefit? It was a pessimist who asked this question. Of course such efforts are beneficial, and that, too, aside from the few paltry dollars made. They help to keep the wheels of life and laughter going 'ronnd. Every student who took part gained an experience that will stand him in good stead some day. He was obliged to think, to plan, and to use tact and judgement outside of the ordinary routine. It is no small undertaking to produce such an entertainment. But it is worth all that it costs, because it saves the student life from lethargy.

———

In another place attention has been called to prizes recently offered to the students of the Academy for literary work. It certainly must be very gratifying to the students and faculty of this department to know that their work is being recognized to such an extent. It is generally conceded that Lake Forest has the best working preparatory school in the northwest. Students who have graduated from our Academy have taken enviable positions, both in point of scholarship and social standing at the most prominent eastern colleges. Much praise is due to the present Academy faculty. A high scholarship is only attained through the efforts and instruction of *educators*. The College congratulates the Academy.

The STENTOR is glad to hear that Dr. Coulter is for carrying out the college idea first and foremost. The Indianapolis *News* in an editorial March 25th says:

"President Coulter of Bloomington, will soon be President Coulter of Lake Forest. While we regret exceedingly the loss of President Coulter 'to Indiana and to the State University, we still congratulate him on his new field of effort; and we congratulate Lake Forest on securing so able and so progressive a man. The state universities are not yet the most attractive institutions for educators of 'light and leading.' Lobbying with a legislature for money necessary to carry on the university's work is distracting and distasteful to men whose thoughts are intent on the higher problems of education and on the furtherance of science. Endowed institutions with progressive boards of trustees offer the greatest attractions to men who wish to make their mark in educational work.

"President Coulter takes up the work at Lake Forest at an auspicious time in the history of that institution. The hard and often discouraging foundation work has been done. The need and place for the college have been demonstrated. It is just ready to be made one of the solid and influential colleges of the central west. The institution is identified with the Presbyterian church, but it is not and never has been narrowly sectarian. The faculty is strong in teaching ability and in sound educational ideals.

"Dr. Coulter's idea, which is also the idea of the acting president, Dr. McClure, and of the whole board of trustees, is to make Lake Forest a strong, high grade college. The scheme of study will be brought up to the standard and scope of the best Eastern colleges. It will seek to win success by deserving success. Dr. Coulter will take with him to his new home the best wishes of hosts of Indiana admirers, who believe that he will rise level to every demand that Lake Forest shall make upon him."

The College has been lifted up to a high plane by able hands in the past, but just such a strong hand as Dr. Coulter possesses is needed to lift her up to a more lofty height. Some changes will be made in the curriculum and each department will be strengthened according to its needs. There should be congratulation all around that the College idea is no more to languish under the shadow of an ungainly university scheme.

THE SHORT STORY IN FICTION.

The short story is becoming the taking form of fiction. Long sermons, long articles and long stories are incompatible with the swiftness of life in 1893. College journals up with the times are making a feature of short bits of fiction. The columns of the STENTOR might easily be graced more often with interesting short stories if the students would assay this field. The student could scarcely find a line of study for his semi-leisure minutes that would yield him a richer harvest. All great projects are first imagined, then carried out. The successful orators, writers of whatever sort, generals and even business men have been men of imagination. It is a faculty capable of cultivation too often neglected. The short story calls it into play. Have you not in your lifetime somewhere met with a character that was unique? There is your chance for a short story. Take this man or woman you have met, this odd one, and weave about him or her a little story. When you take your pencil and begin to write you will be surprised at the suggestions your imagination will offer. A good rule to follow is to let the action of your story illustrate the phases of character you wish to bring out. For instance, if the person about whom you will write was a brutal man, have him perform some brutal act in your story. Don't try to draw his picture by simply saying that he was brutal with a long string of adjectives. The short story must be crowded with action. If you haven't taken a fall out of the short story try it. The STENTOR would gladly print a series under the caption: "Their First Short Stories." Send them in and your names will not appear unless you wish. A short story usually has from 800 to 1,200 words in it.

THE DRAMA IN SCHOOLS AND COLLEGES.

A college man reading Hamlet's question to Polonius, and the reply: " My lord, you played once in the University, you say?" " That I did, my lord; and was accounted a good actor. I did enact Julius Cæsar. I was killed i' the capitol,"—is very likely to think that the old courtier must have alluded to the practices of some literary society of those days. The recent venture of one of our college societies gives us a good occasion for glancing at the history of the drama in its connection with schools and colleges.

In French schools and colleges as far back as '1315' dramas were enacted in public, on saint's days by students. In Germany there was a similar practice. At Cambridge and Oxford the practice of acting plays was very ancient, and continued to be an important feature of university life down to the time of Cromwell. At Trinity College, Cambridge, there was a special officer appointed from among the Masters of Arts whose business it was to superintend the classical comedies and tragedies that were acted in the great hall. There were similar officers at Oxford. On these occasions, the heads of the colleges and the most eminent doctors were present.

No doubt the attention paid to the drama in schools and colleges at this time was excessive. Parents send their children to school for a different object. The old condition of things is not likely to return, but a partial revival of the old customs might be made extremely beneficial. Capability and love of play-acting are almost universal among college students. Why not make this taste useful, so that not only recreation shall come of it, but training and valuable knowledge as well? The best part of our old literature is in dramatic form, never intended to be read, but to be seen and heard. It would be possible to construct entire acts from some of these old plays. Some of the speeches in this old literature are soul-stirring. A study of them would refine the mind of the student and the public acting of the pieces would acquaint the people with the works of genius. The Greek drama has been claiming the attention of the Sophomore Class. It might be well to make a practical use of the knowledge gained. A classical presentation of some of Aeschylus' or Sopocles' plays would be instructive and elevating. Inferior pieces should, of course, receive no consideration.

OUR BASE BALL PROSPECTS.

In spite of the excellence of last year's ball team, a comparison drawn between it and the prospective team of this year need not dishearten the most skeptical. It is true we have lost many good men, but it is safe to say that their places will be quite satisfactorily filled. Let us look for a moment at the material we have at hand, and knowing the respective merits of the men, some opinion of our chances on the diamond can be formed. That much of last year's success was due to the pitching and captaining of Ellis no one will deny, and to fill his place is no easy matter. But Capt. McNary is a ball player of many years experience, and his thorough acquaintance with the game will count a great deal toward accomplishing good results. He will most likely occupy his old position behind the bat. Lewis is a pitcher of much promise. He has speed, good curves and can be depended upon to use his judgment. Sharon at first base needs no introduction. Everyone is acquainted with his matchless game, and although a trifle slow at times his long reach makes up in a great measure for this defect. He is one of the very few strong batters that Lake Forest can boast. Second base is a disputed point. Heretofore it has always been ably guarded, and Capt. McNary must exercise his judgment in selecting a man for the place, in order that this year shall be no exception. In his gym. practice Kimball led one to expect great things of him at short stop, but it is clearly shown that playing on a dirt diamond is something quite different from a hard wood floor. He lacks snap and is a weak thrower. If he expects to play on the team he must improve considerably. Curry will fill Dewey's shoes at third base very nicely. His play is sharp and accurate, and what is of vast importance, he is a hard and conscientious worker. Grant, Hayner and Durand in left, center and left respectively complete the list. Grant and Hayner are two of last years champions, and both did excellent work with the stick, especially Hayner.

Durand is a new hand, and nothing can be said of his batting abilities, but he is a sure catch in the outfield.

With such a team as I have mentioned, considering the names of Gilliland, F. C. Rogers, J. Rogers, Jaeger, Forbes, Mc Donald, Nash and Sherman for the vacant positions we can maintain our standing. The chief point wherein we are weak is batting, and it always has been a weak point. Special attention must be paid this year to the development of a good batting team. It will be noticed perhaps that a few of those who practiced faithfully in the gym. last winter are not mentioned in the above list. Let it be understood that, as far as the writer knows, this is not the team for the coming year, but merely *his* opinion of what it should be. Complaints have been made that the management is violating its agreement by placing men on the team who did no work in the gym. The team is not yet selected, and everyone still has a chance for a position. But work in the gym. is not the only thing; a man's playing abilities must enter into the consideration. Some men can practice for years and then not know the rudiments of the game, and such must not expect a place on the team. These petty grievances and secret conferences condemning the management are most discouraging. Let's have done with them and not lose sight of the fact that we are trying to select a ball team to represent Lake Forest University and not a few individuals attending it.

But the greatest difficulty all our athletic teams have to contend with is the finance question. The expense of running a successful ball team is large, and this nightmare will continue to haunt us until the finances are put on a firm and systematic basis. Too much dependence is placed on the town people. Their kindness in subscribing so liberally is taken advantage of, and we rely too little on our own efforts. But how remedy it? The writer of the present article feels some hesitation in proposing any scheme, as the one suggested by him last year met with so little favor. The question can be solved, and let each one think of some good plan. It is a matter that concerns us *all*, and until we have unanimity we will proceed in the same manner as formerly, ending every season in debt. Let us begin anew; lay aside all society and partisan feeling, and let everyone consider it his duty to work for the further advancement of athletics in Lake Forest.—*H. G.* '94.

THE AMHERST GLEE CLUB CONCERT.

The social event of the Spring term so far was the Amherst College Glee Club concert last Thursday evening in the Durand Art Institute. The Glee and Banjo clubs, numbering thirty members, arrived at 4 p. m., and were driven to the residence of Mr. Calvin Durand where a reception was given them from 4 to 5:30. Mrs. Durand was assisted in receiving by Miss Platt and Miss Steel. The boys were entertained by the townspeople and seemed to enjoy themselves thoroughly. At 8:30 in the Durand Institute the clubs gave the following program.

PROGRAM.
PART I.
Glees: Song to Alma Mater,   *Prof. F. J. Genung*
     Old Amherst, - - - - *Amherst*
Normandie March, - - - - *Armstrong*
     THE BANJO CLUB.
Glees: Now to the Dance, - - - *Clark*
     Maid of Phillipopolin
     Bedalia, Jane McCann, - - *Connolly*
     SOLO BY MR. SMITH.
Airs from "The Sphinx," - - *Thompson*
     THE BANJO CLUB.
Glees: Selected, - - - -
     THE OCTETTE.
From "The Fencing Master," - *DeKoven*
The Best People - - - *Whitehouse*
     SOLO BY MR. PORTER.
PART II.
Selected, - - - - -
     MR CANE AND MR. GRANT.
Glees; The College Widow, { *Words by H. W.* / *Boynton, '91 Arr.* / *by O. A. Merrill,'91*
     SOLO BY MR. FRENCH.
Hey Diddle Diddle, - - - *Geibel*
She Had to Decline, - - - *Furst*
     SOLO BY MR. OLMSTEAD.
Potpourri { Steamboat Dance, / Darkey's Awakening } *Arr. by W. A. Cole.*
     THE BANJO CLUB.
Amherst Medley, - - - *F. S. Hyde,'83*
     THE GLEE CLUB.

The Glee Club showed carefully trained voices and sang well, "The Best People" and "She Had to Decline," being among the best. The Banjo Club was excellent. There are few better. The "Steamboat Dance" was especially attractive but all their music was splendid. The concert was given under the management of Mr. Harry Durand who is an Alumnus of Amherst and it was owing to his efforts that Lake Forest was given such a treat. The Clubs were greeted by one of the largest and most fashionable audiences the Art Institute has ever held and the whole affair was a decided success.

COLLEGE.

AMUSEMENTS FOR THE WEEK.
COLUMBIA—"Country Circus."
HOOLEY'S—Modjeska.
GRAND—Mr. Richard Mansfield.
CHICAGO—"A Society Fad."
McVICKER'S—"The Black Crook."
SCHILLER—"Gloriana."

George H. Steel spent Easter Sunday in Lake Forest with his sister.

The highly ornamental protections from the blasts of winter have disappeared from College Hall for a six month.

Dr. and Mrs. Seeley have returned from their Southern trip and report it a very enjoyable one.

T. M. Hopkins, Harris, and McGaughey will not return to school this term, we are sorry to state.

April 2nd was Easter Sunday and Dr. Mc Clure preached two splendid sermons appropriate to the day. The music and beautiful floral decorations given by Mr. and Mrs. Cobb added much to the service. In the morning the annual collection for the Hospital Bed Fund was received, and amounted to $726.95.

At a meeting of the Oratorical Association called by Pres. Henry, May 18th was decided upon for the contest. May 18th is not very far away, and real work of preparation cannot be begun too soon.

The Freshman–Sophomore preliminary 'tens' have commenced work under Prof. Booth. April 24th will be Freshman evening, and May 5th Sophomore. The place has not yet been decided. Following are the contestants:

Freshman—Messrs. Coolige, Hopkins, Jones, McGaughey, Rogers, Sherman. Misses Brown, Hopkins, Kenaga, McClenahan.

Sophomores—Messrs. Burdick, Graff, Henry, Lewis, MacHatton, Vance. Misses Davies, Hays, Phelps, Steel.

The Academy contest takes place April 21st. The contest this year promises to be an exciting one, both societies have fine timber, and those who would win realize that it must be by work. In no department of Lake Forest does the contest enthusiasm reach so high a pitch as in the Academy, and there is no intention to let the interest flag.

As a proof that the college man does not lack in enterprise and business ability, we would call your attention to the advertisement of Messrs. Skinner & Erskine. They have designed and have had executed a very beautiful souvenir spoon. For further particulars read their display advertisement.

Buck, the Waukegan jeweler, will fit you out in watches, diamonds, and all sorts of jewelry.

Prof. Eager will give a complimentary violin and piano recital, assisted by Mr. Edmund Knoll and Mrs. Marie Hester on Friday evening, April 14th, at Ferry Hall Chapel.

Woolsey has been under the weather for a few days but is improving.

Dr. French has everything in the line of perfumes. Call and inspect his goods.

F. Grant, ex-'96, spent Easter Sunday at home, in Stevens Point, Wis.

The class of '96 held the first meeting of the term last Wednesday for the purpose of electing officers. After a hot discussion on constitutional questions, the class managed to elect the following officers: J. H. Jones, president; Miss Kenaga, vice-president; Miss Linnell, secretary and treasurer; D. H. Jackson, sergeant at arms.

The steam-heat apparatus seems to be as unreliable as ever. On some of the warm spring days it keeps working at a winter pace: and when finally it realizes that the weather is warm and begins to calm down, colder temperature arrives and students suffer another extreme. This variable climate seems to be too much for the steam heat.

The ball grounds have once more become the center of interest. Every afternoon students singly, in groups, in uniform or in some undescribable costume can be seen moving toward the field. Enthusiasm runs deep, and the nine is already a reality.

The present weather has been very auspicious for tennis. The grounds have already been rolled once, and will soon be in condition to use. There will be a meeting of the Tennis Association soon, and if any one wants to become a member and so to have the privilege of using the courts, let him pay 50 cents to the treasurer, G. T. B. Davis, '94. There has been talk of getting up a tournament this spring, for there is abundant talent both in College and Academy.

B. M. Linnell, '89, is now an assistant in the Clinic Department of the Presbyterian Hospital.

Sartell Prentice has been in town for a few days.

The officers of the Zeta Epsilon Society for the spring term are as follows: President, A. P. Bourns; vice-president, W. B. Hunt; secretary, E. A. Drake; treasurer, J. H. Rice; critic, A. F. Waldo; sergeant, J. M. Vance.

Those of the students who spent their vacation in Lake Forest report the dullest time in years. Application was made for the use of the gymnasium during the vacation, and was granted on condition that the students pay three dollars for the cleaning up which would be necessary at the end of the week. Saturday, however, the building was locked, and for the rest of the time the boys were obliged to do without their exercise.

"Cat" tried to jump off the noon train the other day. He succeeded, but says he will go on up to Milwaukee next time.

The Glee and Banjo Clubs of the Zeta Epsilon Literary Society returned Wednesday, April 8, from their annual Spring tour. The following towns were visited: Galesburg, Peoria, Monmouth, Kewanee, Woodhull, Hanover, Galena and Mt. Carrol. A very pleasant trip is reported by all of the members.

"Redda" has not yet returned from his vacation, but we hope soon to look upon his beaming countenance once more.

C. H. Royce, formerly of the Academy, spent a few days during the vacation visiting old friends in Lake Forest.

Most of the young gentlemen who called at Ferry Hall upon April 1st found it necessary to make their exit through the parlor window. Someone had fastened the door.

Messrs. Rossiter, '93 and Parish, '95 spent several days last week on a hunting trip.

A mass meeting of the students was called for last Fricay evening in the college chapel in the welfare of the Athletic Association. Prof. Bridgman called the meeting to order and Mr. Pratt then laid before the fellows his plan for a war song concert to be given in the middle of May. The affair gives promise of being even better than those given in former years which is indeed saying a great deal. Our local talent will be assisted by the Messrs. Hubbard and Root also Major Nevins, of Chicago. The popular North Shore quartet also will render several selections. Systematic practice for the concert will begin this week and will be carried on regularly.

Upon the evening of Friday, March 17th the Athenæan Society presented a sparkling comedy entitled " The Nervous Man and The Man of Nerve " upon the stage of Durand Art Institute. Theatre parties were given by Mrs. Dwight, Mrs. Fales and Mrs. Durand, besides parties from Waukegan, Ft. Sheridan and Highland Park—in fine, it was the grandest of the galaxy of social events which so pre-eminently characterized the term just passed. The play was rewritten and locally adapted by Mr. Danforth, '91, and to his dramatic ability and energy the unprecedented success of the enterprise was in a large degree due. Mr. Sharon, Mr. Danforth and Mr. Goodman carried the most difficult roles in perfect style and might easily have been taken for " old stagers." Mr. Grant, THE STENTOR artist, prepared three full sets of scenery, each of which elicited much praise for their beauty and perfection of execution.

THE CAST.

Aspen, a Nervous Man,................F. C. Sharon
McShane, a Man of Nerve,..........W. E. Danforth
Mr. Vivian, a Country Squire,......B. R. MacHatton
Emily, His Daughter, Engaged to Aspen,....
................................E. H. MacNeal
Biggs, Valet to Aspen,................S. B. Hopkins
Dr. Oxyde, Physician,......................D. Fales
Capt. Burnish,......:...................R. H. Crozier
Mrs. Leech,............................H. Goodman
Mr. Lounge..............................J. A. Linn
Clackett, Landlord ....W. D. McNary
Waiters, Sheriffs, Servants, etc.

TOWN TOPICS.

Mrs. J. H. Dwight, with her daughters, Misses Mary and Florence, has been east for two weeks.

Mr. N. B. W. Galway is again about after a four week's confinement with pleurisy.

The funeral service of Mr. H. I. Cobb's little child was conducted by Dr. McClure, Tuesday moring, April 4, in Chicago. The funeral party came in a special car to Lake Forest, where the burial took place.

Mrs. Calhoun has lately been visiting with her daughter, Mrs. Moss. Mrs. Calhoun has for 28 years been a missionary in Beirut, Syria, and goes out this year to Africa for work among the Zu.us. Mrs. Moss gave a dinner for Mrs. Calhoun, and Mrs. McClure an afternoon tea in her honor.

The new pavement, while much superior to our customary muddy streets, has yet proved to be imperfect and unsatisfactory in many respects. Along each side, over the line where the drainage pipes were laid, the blocks have sunk from 6 to 8 inches. It is not known whether this new kind of foundation, sand and slag, is an experiment or not; however that may be, such foundation has evidently proved to be a failure.

Capt. Townsend has taken a contract for building the Japanese Jurikshas to be used at the World's Fair. A large quantity of bamboo has been carried to the building in the rear of Capt. Townsend's house, and there the work will be carried on.

FERRY HALL

An unusually large number of the girls were present at chapel Wednesday, March 29th. Will Doctor grant the same privilege this term as last?

We regret to say that Mrs. Seeley has been quite ill the past week with tonsilitis.

Prof. Stuart has the class in English Literature this term.

Miss Bessie McWilliams, who was unable on account of illness to resume her studies the first af the term, is with us again.

April first passed quietly, with the exception of some confusion regarding callers.

It is evident that the College girls had a pleasant vacation, because it took them so long to get back.

We are glad to welcome as a new student Miss Martin of Omaha, Neb.

Those young ladies who were able to attend the reception given the Amherst Glee Club, by Mrs. Calvin Durand, had much to tell the less favored ones. The stormy evening for the concert kept none at home, in fact, "every cloud has its silver lining." It was a fine evening to lose one's way.

The last paper in the etiquette serie ranged by Mrs. Seeley, for the pleasure and benefit of the girls, was given Friday evening by Mrs. Halsey. The subject, "Education and the Home," was one of especial interest to the girls.

The new furniture for the parlors has come, and we feel grateful indeed to those who, with their work and all that which is the senior's inheritance, have thought of and given time and strength to the carrying out of this plan.

All are glad to welcome Miss Creswell back after her long illness.

Word has come announcing the marriage of Miss Grace Humphrey, who attended College last time.

Miss Elizabeth Williams spent the spring vacation in Sterling, Ill.

Miss McGaughey has become a resident of Ferry Hall.

Miss Laura Hickok will not return to College this term because of the health of her father.

The Senior College ladies are excused from the duties of the Aletheian Society for the remaining days of their college course. It makes one feel rather melancholy to realize that the time has come to step aside and let the younger ones come in.

The officers of the Aletheian Society for the coming term are as follows:—

President,	-	-	Miss Bruebaker
Vice-Pres.,	-	-	Miss Oberne
Secretary,	-	-	Miss Phelps
Treasurer,	-	-	Miss Hopkins
Critic,	-	-	Miss Hays
Sergeant-at-Arms,	-		Miss Brown
Program Committee,	-	{	Miss Kenaga Miss Davies

ACADEMY.

Baseball and spring seem to have come together.

Society spirit is beginning to wake up in anticipation of the coming contest.

Breckenridge, Rice, Kennedy, Bodle, have not returned this term. They will be greatly missed.

"The gang" were introducing several uninitiated members to the mysteries of their order last week by what is known as the pumping process.

Those of the Academy who are fortunate enough to be members of the Sabbath school class of Mr. Wells were very agreeably entertained by him at a dinner Thursday evening, March 30th.

The dormitory baseball team has been organized, with Gilleland, captain, Graham, manager, Roberts, treasurer. Jaeger and Gilleland will constitute the battery. They hope to play some of the College class teams.

The Academy have organized for baseball by the election of Rogers, captain, Forbes, manager. Mr. Durand, who was offered the position of captain, declined from lack of time. Durand will probably pitch; the catcher having not as yet been decided upon. Several games will be arranged for in the near future.

Prof. Burnap, on the last Saturday evening of last term, gave the Mitchell Hall boys a spread in honor of the anniversary of his birth. One of the features of the evening was Keith's becoming intoxicated on a glass of manufactured cider which, in order to save expenses, the Prof. himself had made. There is talk of having the authorities investigate to see whether he enjoys the benefit of having a government permit.

Hall suffered a very painful accident last Wednesday evening by being thrown from a horse. He was mounting near the barber shop, and had not become seated in the saddle when one of those irrepressible small boys, who are always around when they are not wanted, cracked a whip which frightened the animal and caused it to jump to one side, throwing Hall to the ground. He sustained an injured spine and internal injuries and will be unable to be around for a week at least.

The many friends of the Academy will be delighted to learn that two new annual prizes have been offered by two gentlemen who have always been friends of the Academy. The first is a gold medal offered by Dr. Haven for the best written and best delivered commencement oration, by a member of the Senior Class. The other is a fifty dollar prize offered by Mr. A. C. McNeill, a graduate of Lake Forest University for the best literary production by an Academy student. Two things will be required, first, an examination will be held upon some poem, second, a critique upon some literary character must be written by the contestants which will be submitted to judges who will judge it according to its thought and expression. The poem selected for examination this year is Arnold's "Sohrab and Rustum" and the critique must be written upon the character "Dinah Morris" in Geo. Elliot's "Adam Bede." The examination will be held about May 15 and the critique must be handed in by June 1st. The one having the highest examination mark and the best critique will receive a first prize of thirty-five dollars. The one having the second highest mark will receive a second prize of fifteen dollars. It will be known as the Mary Humes prize in honor of Mr. McNeill's wife. There will probably be about fifteen or twenty contestants this year.

On Tuesday evening, March 21st, the dormitory boys of the Academy gave a banquet as a farewell to what has served them so long as a dining hall, and which is remembered by every graduate and member of the Academy as Academia.

Royce, a former Academy student, from Oconto, Wis., was around shaking hands with old friends at the beginning of the term.

HAVE YOU SEEN IT?

WHAT?

A NEW, PRETTY AND UNIQUE SOUVENIR OF LAKE FOREST

THE LAKE FOREST SOUVENIR SPOON . . . .

No one, who has an interest in Lake Forest should be without it.   A solid Silver Spoon, gold bowl, with view of church.   Exact size of cut. Sent to any address on receipt of price, $3.00.

Drop us a postal and we will call on you.

R. V. ERSKINE,
F. M. SKINNER,   LAKE FOREST

THE STENTOR.

VOLUME VI. APRIL 18, 1893. NUMBER 23.

PUBLISHED EVERY WEEK
BY THE
Lake Forest University Stentor Publishing Co.

Terms—$1.50 per year. Single Copies—10c

———ADDRESS———
STENTOR PUBLISHING COMPANY,
LAKE FOREST, : : ILLINOIS.

Entered at the P. O. at Lake Forest, Ill., as second-class matter.

The pages and columns of THE STEN-
TOR are always open to the alumni and
friends of the college. Communications of interest and for the welfare of
the college will be gladly received and
printed. A college paper furnishes the
best means for discussion of college
topics, for reforming present evils and
preserving the good.

———

Our respected and beloved seniors
will soon be out in the cold world. Will
they discover that they have been living
in a hot-house for some years? "Out
in the cold world, out in the streets" is
different from being snugly ensconced in
a college dormitory. Our seniors are
all of them persons of sound common
sense, and they are accordingly prepared for the difficulties. It takes a
stout heart and a stiff upper lip to realize the ideals we have raised before
ourselves in these college days.

———

"The nature and place of the college
in our educational system," is the title
of an article written by our Professor
Thomas. No further introduction is
necessary. Suffice it to say that the
subject is one in which the professor
himself is deeply interested, and he has
written exactly what he feels. THE
STENTOR is glad to have the opportunity
of giving to its readers such an able and
instructive article.

———

Some people have brain-fag and some
suffer from mental laziness. Brain-fag
is a legitimate ailment resulting from
over-work. Few college students are
troubled with brain-fag. Many of them
are afflicted with mental laziness. They
dream life away. They seldom think
real hard. It is not that they haven't
good brains, but it tires them to think.
How absurd! And yet you can find
such men and women all about you. If
you don't use your brains, you might
as well be a horse or an ox or a saw-
buck. The only remedy for mental
laziness is to shake one's self out of it.
Are you troubled with it?

A COLUMBIAN LIBERTY BELL.

It has been determined to create a Columbian Liberty Bell to be placed by the lovers of liberty and peace in the most appropriate place in the coming World's Exhibition at Chicago. After the close of the Exhibition this bell will pass from place to place throughout the world as a missionary of freedom, coming first to the capital of the nation.

This Columbian Liberty Bell is under the care of the National Society of the Daughters of the American Revolution, of which Mrs. Abby Farwell Ferry is a member. THE STENTOR has been asked by Mrs. Ferry to place this matter before the students.

In creating the bell it is desired that the largest number of persons possible shall have a part in it. For this reason small contributions from many persons are to be asked for, rather than large contributions from a few. They are to be of two kinds:

First: Material that can be made a part of the bell.

Second: Of money with which to pay for the bell. Each student is asked to contribute one cent towards this bell. Boxes will be placed in the College, Academy, and Ferry Halls, and the boys and girls can drop their pennies in and do something towards creating a Columbian Liberty Bell. The boxes will be left in the halls for a few days only, as the money must be sent at once. The contributions will be sent with the compliments of Lake Forest University.

THE NATURE AND PLACE OF THE COLLEGE IN OUR EDUCATIONAL SYSTEM.

I have been asked to state briefly the characteristics which distinguish the college from the university. The only difference of opinion is as to the nature of this distinction. Some maintain that it is merely one of scope. They hold that the college is simply a smaller university, and that the university is simply a larger college. Many of our most prominent educators, however, recognize a distinction in ends and consequently in method and use of means. They ground the necessity for this distinction in the nature and needs of the student during the period of his college course. The college stands midway between academy and university. It receives young men and women who are still undeveloped. Consequently its aim is not primarily to impart information, but to evoke disciplined power. It seeks to teach the student how to know, and the use of what he knows in securing what is best in life. Its end, therefore, is both intellectual and ethical. It would produce mental and moral character. It does not ignore special capacities and tastes; but it attempts primarily and mainly to develope those which are common to all. Not the individual man, nor the average man, but the *generic* man does it supremely regard. Thus, it would give to each one a broad and symmetrical culture. It would widen the intellectual and ethical outlook; strengthen and enlarge the intellectual and ethical sympathies; awaken and purify intellectual and ethical enthusiasms, and intensify and direct intellectual and ethical forces. Having done this, it has prepared the individual for a supreme devotion to a specific pursuit, as well as guarded him against that narrowness and inability to grasp the real nature and relationships of such pursuit which a too early entrance on it inevitably entails. For, as an eminent specialist said to me only the other day: "The man who confines himself to one field and knows little or nothing of other fields, does not really understand his own." The college, however, may, to some extent, introduce the student to a special field, but to do so is not its primary intention.

In order to develope in each one the essential elements of mental and moral power the college uses two educational means. The first of these consists of certain *selected* studies. All studies are not alike and equally adapted to secure a rounded culture. This has been recognized ever since men began to consider educational ends and means. No one better states it than Bacon: "History," said he, "makes men wise; poets witty; the mathematics subtle; natural philosophy deep; moral, grave; logic and rhetoric, able to contend,— nay, there is no stond or impediment in the wit but may be wrought out by fit studies." The college, therefore, chooses just those specific studies which, within the time to which its course is limited, will best awaken and train the essential faculties. And as these are manifold, its course of study must, to a certain extent, be manifold. It must be restricted to neither man nor man's environment. It must include somewhat of both. But the end to be reached

requires that man and his higher nature and relationships shall enter more largely into the course of study than his lower nature and the material forces and conditions in the midst of which he is at present placed. "Know thyself," in the Socratic sense, is still a maxim of high wisdom and importance, and such knowledge is still the best means by which the best education is not only attained but attainable.

The second means is the teacher. If a special educating power lies in the thing taught, much more does it lie in the one who teaches. The subject may develope power, but the enthusiasm, which is the most essential and vital element of power, is mainly quickened and sustained by the teacher's personality. Hence, the college is, or should be, careful to have men of high and vigorous intellectual and moral character. Those colleges whose faculties have been largely composed of such men have most markedly attained the real end of education.

This being the end, and these the means, the method which the college mainly adopts is that of required rather than elective courses. Once the colleges allowed no election. Within the past twenty-five years, however, there have been great changes in this respect Thoughtful educators, however, are beginning to question whether such changes have not reached their proper limit. All agree that, to some extent, in the last years of the college course election should be allowed. This secures, in some degree, in its right place, the recognition of the individual taste and capacity. If, however, all studies are made elective, this destroys at once and entirely the distinction between college and university. For the underlying idea of the university is that the individual is alone regarded. He is to be allowed to follow his bent and choose what will best minister to that. Thorough, even exhaustive, knowledge of the special subject is the end in view. Courses of study are so multiplied that the student may have wide choice, and so arranged and enlarged that he may devote his entire time to one or, at most, two immediately related. Freedom of choice is therefore essential to the university; without it specialization to the extent to which the university carries it could not exist.

If, however, the aim of the college is not to make specialists but to give a rounded culture, it cannot leave the choice of studies wholly to the student. To do this is to assume that he knows clearly, and will choose, whatever will best minister not only to his wishes but his needs. This assumption, however, is contrary to the fact. Wishes and needs do not coincide. The ordinary college student does not know what special exercises are best fitted to symmetrically develop his physical nature. Much less does he know what are best fitted to develop symmetrically his intellectual and moral natures. The college curriculum must therefore continue to consist to a considerable extent of required studies. To introduce altogether at this stage of the students educational career entire freedom of choice as to what he shall study is to ignore the real end which the college seeks and to mistake the means and method best fitted to attain that end.

The need of the college can never pass away. It fills an essential place in our educational system. All cannot be specialists. It is not important that all should be. Complete mastery of one subject by some is indeed greatly to be desired. In this way alone can investigation be effctually carried on, and the frontiers of human knowledge be enlarged. But at the basis of such mastery as this, and aside from it, we need an increasing class of broadly educated men and women, who know the functions, character and claims of their higher natures, and the intellectual, moral and religious forces which are most immediately related to these, and so most stimulative and directive of them. Such a class is the spiritual leaven of society. Out of it will come those who will best solve social problems, work deliverance from social evils, and secure the highest social welfare, just because they have not so confined themselves to one field of study with its limited point of view that they have lost sympathetic contact with the complex spiritual forces and needs which belong to human society and to it alone.

M. Bross Thomas.

An interesting feature of the fraternity exhibit of the World's Fair will be the contribution of the Kappa Alpha Theta of Palo Alto. The display consists of four transparencies representing views of the university buildings and grounds.

Many of the exchanges complain of a general lack of interest in literary society work this term. The students of the University of Iowa are overcoming this lethargy by holding union meetings. Two or more societies joining together occasionally produces a wholesome effect on all concerned. A healthy rivalry is thus stimulated, while the barriers of self-conceit and prejudice, too common in college societies, are broken down.

COLLEGE.

CALENDAR.

Junior Reception given in honor of the Seniors, April 27.

Freshman Contest in Declamation, April 28.
Contest of the Academy societies, May 2.
Sophomore Contest in Declamation, May 5.
Oratorical Association Contest, May 23.
Annual Senior Reception, May 26.
Academy Commencement Exercises, June 9.
Annual Academy Reception, June 10.
Annual Concert at Ferry Hall, June 12.
Freshman Sophomore Prize Speaking, June 12.
Commencement Exercises of Ferry Hall, June 13.
Senior Class Day, June 13.
Junior Contest in Oratory, June 13.
College Commencement Exercises, June 14.
Alumni Banquet, June 14.
President's Reception, June 14.

The Junior and Senior orations are limited to 1200 words.

Last Friday gave Lake Forest people quite a taste of winter.

E. H. McNeal, '95, returned last week to resume his studies.

Base-balls, tennis balls and other athletic goods on hand, W. E. Ruston.

J. H. Jones was the victim of a slight attack of the grippe for several days last week.

J. A. Linn, who has been detained in Chicago by weak eyes, came back to us last Thursday.

G. L. Wilson will not return to Lake Forest this term. He has secured employment in Chicago for the summer months.

The Sophomore Latin Class give one hour a week to the study of Roman Literature. The subject is made specially interesting by Prof. Stuart's frequent lectures.

The date of the Annual Contest of the Oratorical Association for the choice of a speaker to represent Lake Forest in the State Contest has been changed from May 18 to May 23.

The officers of the Junior Class for the ensuing term are: President, H. L. Bird; Vice-President, Miss Pierce; Secretary and Treasurer, T. Marshal; Sergeant, W. Gibson.

Robert Mercer, the carpenter who was run over by the Green Bay express on the 8th inst., is improving slowly, and at present the chances are in favor of his ultimate recovery.

Those of the Junior and Senior classes who are members of the special class in Shakespeare, under Prof. Morris, went to the city Wednesday to see Modjeska in "As You Like It."

The officers of the Sophomore Class for the spring term are as follows: Pres., E. H. McNeal; Vice-Pres., F. S. Mellen; Secy., Miss Edna Hayes, Treasurer, Dean Lewis; Sergeant, E. U. Graff. Dean Lewis was also elected base-ball captain, and a committee was appointed to confer with committee from the other classes, concerning the formation of a class league.

The Tennis Association at its meeting elected the following officers: — G. T. B. Davis, President; E. V. Graff, Vice-President; C. A. Coolidge, Secretary; W. S. Keyes, Treasurer. Flint, Ruston, and Bird were appointed a committee for a tournament, which will take place this spring. The tennis courts are already being put to good use, and it is evident there will be an exciting tournament.

Prof. Swing of Chicago delivered his popular lecture upon "The Place of the Novel in Literature," at the Art Institute Building last Tuesday evening. The lecture was given under the auspices of the Art Club, who kindly issued a general invitation. Prof. Swing's definition of the novel is especially worthy of notice: "The novel is that part of the world's literature which is ornamented by womanhood." The Zeta Epsilon Glee Club sang.

At the annual election of the Lawn Tennis Association, held Wednesday afternoon, the following officers were chosen: Pres., G. T. B. Davis; Vice-Pres., E. U. Graff; Secy., C. A. Coolidge; Treas., W. W. Keyes.

In spite of the heroic efforts of the Trustees and their assistant engineer, the old college dormitory is slowly disintegrating and falling into ruin. Last week students on the second floor were alarmed by a great crash in the hall, a large section of the ceiling had fallen and had just missed a poor freshman, who then aud there declared that he "wasn't even going to room in that building." Thus in many ways does the old ruin declare its age.

TOWN TOPICS.

Mr. C. K. Giles and family have returned from Florida.

Prof. and Mrs. Hale, of Chicago University, spent Sunday with Mr. Chapin.

Mrs. J. H. Dwight returned last week from the East. Miss Mary Dwight will remain at Ogontz School for the rest of this term.

Miss Lucy Rumsey will return from Del Norte about the middle of May. Her sister, Mrs. Stroh, will probably return with her.

The Musical Circle meets this week at the home of Mrs. I. P. Rumsey. The Circle has the music of modern composers this week.

The rehearsals for the War Concert take place every Monday night at Mr. Pratt's. The fellows have a hearty genial time with Mr. Pratt, and the rehearsals are well attended.

It is reported that there will be special World's Fair trains this summer from Waukegan to Jackson Park. If such a scheme be carried out trains will leave Waukegan in the morning, running south to North Evanston, where they will branch off to the south-west, and finally around the city to the Grand Terminal station at the Fair Grounds.

Those of the college who went to the recital at Ferry Hall last Friday enjoyed it very much. The numbers were al: well appreciated. Prof. Eager's playing especially pleasing them. The only point which marred the evening was the deplorable carelessness and selfishness with which persons in the rear of the room kept talking. Such actions are not only unseemly in themselves, but they are very disagreeable to others who are trying to listen.

At the last meeting of the city council it was decided to extend the road which now runs in front of Ferry Hall down to the south boundary of the city; this means that there will be about a mile of new street to make, on which it will be possible to nearly reach the heart of the Fort Sheridan post. The council also passed an electric light ordinance, permitting poles and wires to be put up; this, however, does not mean that we will have electric light immediately. The persons interested in the movement have yet decided upon nothing definite.

ATHLETICS.

THE EVANSTON GAME.

The ball season was opened at Evanston on the 15th by a game between Northwestern and Lake Forest. The team left on the noon train with much hope of playing a strong and close game, but a very decisive defeat was the reward in waiting. As is usual at this time of year the team is playing a very poor game of ball. Yet when a look is taken at the men who composed the nine placed before the graduate team from Evanston, it will surprise none to read the score. As has been said before, there are but four old men in use, consequently owing to the inexperience of the new men the opening game was expected to be one in which the team in general would show up in a badly rattled condition. It is well nigh useless to give a detailed account of the game which was characterized by the heavy batting of N. W. U. The long hits of Griffith were a brilliant feature, while his pitching, though strong at times, was only fair. Poor throwing and ragged work, especially in left field, told the same old story on Lake Forest. However, when the teams of previous years are taken into consideration, there is no cause for discouragement. Every position. on the nine is well-filled, and every man is willing to work, which is more than some of the late teams can boast. The only fact which remains to be emphasized is that the defeat be used for the future welfare of the men. The weak points are now apparent, and can be remedied only with hard and more systematic practice.

The score:

LAKE FOREST.

		R.	B. H.	P. O.	A.	E.
Grant	l f	0	0	1	0	3
Sharon	1	0	0	8	0	0
Hayner	c f	1	1	1	0	1
Lewis	p	1	1	1	2	2
McNary	c	1	0	4	0	0
Durand	r f	0	0	0	0	0
Curry	3	0	0	2	1	1
Nash	2	0	0	0	2	1
Gilliland	s s	0	0	1	5	4
Totals		3	2	18	10	12

NORTHWESTERN.

		R.	B. H.	P. O.	A.	E.
Hendricks	l f	3	3	0	0	0
Shepherd	1	3	2	7	0	0
Maclay	s s	3	1	0	1	0
Griffith	p	5	4	0	2	0
McWilliams	3	2	0	1	0	1
Noyes	2	1	2	0	3	0
Cooling	2	1	1	1	0	0
McClusky	l f	2	2	0	0	0
Short	r f	2	1	0	1	0
Heywood	c	1	1	10	1	0
Snell	c	0	0	3	1	0
Totals		23	17	21	9	1

Earned Runs—Northwestern 2. Two base hits—Shepherd (2), Noyes. Three base hits—Griffith (2). Home run—Griffith. Sacrifice hit—McWilliams. Stolen bases—Grant (2), Sharon, Hayner, Lewis, Curry, Maclay, Noyes (2), Short, Heywood (2). Struck out—by Lewis 3, by Griffith 12. Bases on balls—by Lewis 3. by Griffith 7. Passed balls—Heywood 4, Snell 4, McNary 1. Wild pitches—Griffith 2. Umpire, Chapin. Scorer, Lewis. Time, 2 hrs.

NOTES ON THE GAME.

Capt. McNary has handled the men well and will make the team play ball before long. A study of each position would help him.

Lewis pitched a remarkably cool-headed game in face of the heavy batting and such

support. He should take especially good care in controlling the ball and also of short infield hits. It must be kept in mind that "bunting" has been reduced to a scientific standpoint, and in consequence a thorough preparation on the part of the pitchers and third basemen would certainly be a move in the right direction.

Nash's play at second was a disappointment. He failed to cover any of his allotted ground. His play was too near the bag twice, allowing men to reach first on easy hits, which he did not attempt to field.

The work on Saturday proved conclusively that this year ought not to witness a repetition of the custom practiced in former years of neglecting the out-fielders. Difficult and regular work must be given them.

The batting was of course weak. Each man should learn that the first requisite is that the batter never step back from the plate when the ball is delivered.

Curry and Gilleland were somewhat rattled, nevertheless both played well. They are willing and earnest, and are the most promising of any on the team.

As a whole, the team should put more life in its work. The play is painfully slow at present.

FERRY HALL.

There is a suggestion of LaGrippe in the air.

April promises to continue a month of social events.

Miss Elizabeth Williams had a visit from her father on Sunday, Apr. 9.

Work in the gymnasium has given place to long walks under the new rule, which requires an hour's walk daily.

A number of young people enjoyed a delightfully informal party at the home of Miss Pratt on Saturday evening.

Miss Anna Lord has our sincere sympathy in the death of her mother, which occurred at Evanston Saturday morning.

The "paw" and "maw" of the senior college girls celebrated the fourth anniversary of their wedding, Friday evening, April 15, in Aletheian Hall.

It is evident that conversation between seniors and juniors is at present somewhat strained although we have not heard that they are unfriendly.

The members of Mrs. Malloy's Art Class are doing work upon a scale that is constantly broadening. They contemplate sketching out of doors this term.

We appreciate the kindnes of the Art Institute in giving us the advantage of Prof. Swing's lecture and regret that the weather was not more in our favor.

Several pieces of furniture have been placed in the parlors this week. The Junior class are to be complimented upon their unique selection. It is at least a cozy piece of furniture, and—beware young man.

We are happy in congratulating Miss Barnum and Miss Gerry upon having won the honors of the class of '93. At the Senior class meeting on Monday afternoon Miss Barnum was elected valedictorian and Miss Gerry salutatorian.

There has been some discussion in regard to dividing the Nu Beta Kappa society next year and with the help of some of the Faculty raise the standard of work. We hope this idea will materialize or at least one quite as good, for even the most earnest worker needs some strong incentive in order that the best results may be attained.

We are indebted to Prof. Eager for the delightful program which follows:

PROGRAM.

Suite—(No. III in G Major, - - *Franz Ries*
Mr. Emanuel Knoll and Mr. Geo. Eugene Eager.
Gavotte - - - - *Ambrose Thomas*
From the opera of "Mignon"
Mrs. Marie Hester.
a.—Romanze - - - *August Wilhelmj*
b.—Mazourka - - - - *Alex. Zarzycki*
Mr. Emanuel Knoll.

a.—Air de Ballet - - - - - *Moszkowski*
b.—Gigue - - - - - *Bachmann*
Mr. Geo. Eugene Eager.
Sonate for Violin and Piano - - *Edward Grieg*
Mr. Emanuel Knoll and
Mr. Geo. Eugene Eager.

Prof. Eager, Mrs. Hester and Miss Ripley are well known here. There is no need to sing their praise. The violinist, Mr. Emanuel Knoll of the Thomas Orchestra gave us music whose charm a silent and attentive audience most effectually proved. We thank Prof. Eager for his kindness to us in giving us this recital.

ACADEMY.

Tennis is a prime favorite as an out-door sport with those who do not play base ball.

Prof. Swing and Dr. Thomas Hall of Chicago act as judges on the Academy Contest.

Jo. Anderson left Monday for a two week's trip through Kansas and Texas on business and pleasure.

Geo. Rice spent last Sunday with his brother and friends. He is now on the road in the employ of a Chicago firm.

G. N. Heineman was in Milwaukee last Tuesday evening attending a society event and renewing old acquaintanceships.

The new officers of the Tri Kappa Society delivered inaugural addresses at their meeting last Wednesday. The Gamma Sigma's had their usual programme.

Those who attended Prof. Swing's lecture last Tuesday evening were more than repaid for their trouble and enjoyed a genuine treat. It is hoped he may come again.

A number of the boys are either receiving their old wheels from home, or are purchasing new ones since the weather has become pleasant enough to permit of their use.

Prof. Williams was visited by his father last Saturday and Sunday. He greatly enjoyed a "water scrap" between the members of the East and West ends of the dormitory on Saturday evening, so it is said.

The Glee Club has resumed its weekly meetings on Wednesday evening, and is busily engaged preparing music for the coming contest. It is becoming quite talented under the efficient management of Prof. Dudley.

The date for the contest has at last been definitely fixed for May 2nd. The joint committee is making necessary arrangements for it. It promises to be the closest and most exciting one the Academy has ever known.

The reported appearance of the crinoline was a subject of much humorous discussion among the Academy boys last week. Every one is now watching for it to see how large it is and how much it improves the appearance of the owner.

Hayner now has charge of gymnastics in place of Mr. Everett. Out-door exercises will be substituted for work in the gym., and ball teams and foot ball teams are being organized. There will also be running and cycling. All are compelled to take some kind of exercise except the seniors.

During the absence of the dormitory masters Saturday evening, April the 8th, the members of the East and West ends put on their old clothes and had a "water scrap." In the height of the evening's enjoyment, Prof. Smith very unexpectedly gave the boys a call and incidentally a lecture. Promises of better conduct in the future were the result.

Those of the students who are not directly interested in baseball had a scrub game of football last Saturday afternoon. During the game Ed. Wells, who was playing guard, had his arm dislocated at the elbow. Dr. Haven was called to replace it. Although it was a very painful accident he was fortunate in that it did not result more seriously.

EXCHANGES.

ANTICIPATION.

The girl who says she'll never wed
  Because she fears no man will suit her,
Has got a fancy in her head
  That perhaps the question won't be put her.
            —Exchange.

IN BASE BALL.

"Will you drop into my mitten?"
  Said the fielder to the fly,
"No I thank you," said the spheroid
  As he passed the fielder by.

"My skin is very tender
  And your mitten's hard and tough,
And though I fear you may object
  I think I'll use a muff."

A recent number of the U. of M. Daily contains a letter from Prof. Kelsey, who is now traveling in Northern Africa. The Professor gives a very interesting account of the French excavations of the Roman remains at Zambesi and Linigad.

In the *Church Friend* for April appears a beautiful poem, written by Rev. G. D. Heuver of Milwaukee, in memory of his wife, Martha Post Heuver, who died on the 25th of March. We sympathize with Rev. Heuver in his severe loss.

The term examination farce is the recognized evil of our present educational system. Educators universally realize that it is such, and are longing for some one to take the initiative in doing away with it. In the junior and senior grades of the University of Chicago it is optional with the instructors whether they examine their classes or not. This is a step in the right direction, but why make it optional at all? While there are many arguments against the system, there is only one which seems to be in its favor. It is claimed that the review preceding the examination is necessary to give the student a thorough and comprehensive view of the subject. Could not the same review be made without winding up with the "Comedy of Errors?"

HAVE YOU SEEN IT?

WHAT?

THE STENTOR.

VOLUME VI.   APRIL 25, 1893.   NUMBER 24.

PUBLISHED EVERY WEEK
BY THE
Lake Forest University Stentor Publishing Co.

BOARD OF EDITORS.

B. R. MACHATTON, '95.............Managing Editor
FOREST GRANT, '96 ......Ass't Mgr. Ed. and Athletic
HARRY GOODMAN, '94.............Business Manager
A. B. BURDICK, '95 }
J. H. JONES, '96   }....................Locals
DAVID FALES, JR., '96 }
A. O. JACKSON, '96.............Alumni and Personal
W. B. SMITH, '94........................Exchange
J. A. McGAUGHEY, '95.................Advertising

Terms—$1.50 per year.   Single Copies—10c

————ADDRESS————

STENTOR PUBLISHING COMPANY,

LAKE FOREST,   :   :   ILLINOIS.

Entered at the P. O. at Lake Forest, Ill., as second-class matter.

Delinquent subscribers are very cordially invited to call on the business manager at their earliest convenience. .

———

THE STENTOR will from this time on contain a World's Fair Department, in which not an exhaustive account of the doings and exhibits at the Fair will be set forth, but a few notes of interest and unique and remarkable objects to be seen. This department will from time be filled with a sight-seers remarks, written by a special STENTOR reporter. It is hoped that the department will prove of interest to the readers of the STENTOR.

Steps should be taken at once to put the grounds surrounding the Art Hall in shape before Commencement. It is a disgrace to the University and an insult to the donor of this magnificent building to allow it to stand as it now does surrounded by heaps of rubbish and piles of dirt and stone. The STENTOR would suggest that this rubbish be hauled away,—that grass should be given a chance to grow and that a bridge be thrown across the ravine. Imagine taking your mother over to the Art Hall during Commencement Day and having to help her climb over the rocks and the pyramids of dirt scattered over the grounds. On the other hand should the three suggestions of the STENTOR be received favorably and acted upon at once, you could walk by a short and most picturesque route over a rustic bridge and point with pride to a beautiful building situated in the midst of a natural park. Green grass and flowers, beautiful trees and rustic bridges will do wonders toward improving property.

———

The STENTOR, through the columns of "Town Topics," has frequently called attention to the fact that the block paving which has recently been laid is utterly unfit for a town like Lake Forest. It might have been made durable if it had been laid properly, but there has been a total disregard of practability and fitness in its construction. It seems almost Providential that by laying only a part of it last fall the town has been given an opportunity of recognizing the failure of the experiment. It is at this point the STENTOR reiterates its warning and, like Demosthenes of old calls out to " Act while there is time!" Otherwise the pavement will be laid and the chance for making good the mistake will have slipped away. It is absurdity and folly to claim that pavement with sand foundation is stable and durable. If the rains of an unusually mild and propitious spring have been sufficient to essentially spoil the road in several places, what would have been the result of floods like those of last spring? It seems that more or less repairing is necessary after every rain storm. Does this appear consistent? Are the people of Lake Forest paying $60,000 and more for an ostensibly fine pavement, and then obliged to pay the customary tax for road repairing and improvement in addition? No. Lake Forest expected a good system of roads, but to get them the town must wake up and realize the danger of disappointment. The STENTOR is supported in its opinion by the majority of the leading gentlemen of Lake Forest, who have learned the defects and wish to remedy them.

A COMMUNICATION:

It would be well for some of us to know "how to attend a classical concert."

It is not supposed that all present at these entertainments understand or appreciate the music, but one naturally expects that young ladies and gentlemen who have spent all their days in a civilized country to have some idea of what is expected of an audience.

It is annoying, to say the least, to a musician, who has spent years of labor in his art, to hear, while rendering some beautiful composition, a buzz of voices (even if it is in the back of the room).

These whispers have become so accomplished that they crescendo and diminuendo with the music.

They will probably study dynamics, so as to accompany the musician with more ease and intelligence.

These concert talkers not only disturb the performers, but those in the audience who understand music and would like to hear a note now and then.

MABEL MESSENGER,
For THE STENTOR.

[THE STENTOR received the above communication too late for insertion in the last issue. Concert-talkers are a species of humanity who have no regard for the feelings or interest of anyone but themselves. There is nothing so indicative of the lady or gentleman as a strict regard for the feelings of others.—ED.]

A COMMUNICATION.

THE APPROACHING FIELD DAY.

It is now generally understood that the date for the coming Field Day has been set for Wednesday afternoon, May 3, but in view of several important facts the majority of the students believe that the committee has been unwise in the choice. The committee claim that the faculty do not wish an interruption in school work, and as the academy students have Wednesday afternoon off, that date must be taken. Such a decision is manifestly unfair, because the college and seminary departments will be given a half-days relaxation from recitation, while the poor academy student will not receive any time off. Also the Annual Academy Contest will take place the night previous and of necessity all those who attend will be excited and tired, and will consequently be unable to compete the next day with the requisite snap and vigor.

A fact which will prove that a *half*-day will not give time enough for the successful running off of the events is: there are seventeen events on the program, and many of the boys will desire to compete in two or more of these, and they cannot do so without proper resting periods between these events; to be more explicit, the short distance runners will have to run in the 100 yd. dash preliminaries, the winners of these will have to compete in the 100 yd. finals, and then later in the 220 yd. dash, and probably in other events. The same men will probably be in both the mile and the half-mile runs. Now proper resting periods cannot be given when the events are all jumbled and crushed into half a day. The committee, therefore, should demand a whole day, and should choose Thursday as the day, and if properly approached the faculty would probably accede.

The committee also have announced their intention of throwing the contests open to the professional departments in Chicago, but this also appears unwise and premature. In tha first place the committee cannot do this lawfully without the permission of the Athletic Association which they have not and cannot obtain. In the second place this action is in direct opposition to the precedent established here. Again it is in direct opposition to the new rule adopted by Yale, Princeton and other eastern colleges who after twenty or more years of experience have passed a law which prohibits all members of the professional departments from participating in *any branch whatsoever* of University athletics, as it has been found that these departments injure and degrade college and amateur athletics and tend toward the importation of the professional. In this connection it might truthfully be stated that L. F. U's past experience goes to prove this, as year before last the baseball team was nearly ruined and did not win a single game under the captaincy and pitching of a professional department man, and foot ball has also been seriously affected. Another fact is that most of the professional department men are professional athletes and, though in each individual case this may not be absolutely proven, yet it will make our undergraduate athletes liable to suspension and expulsion from all amateur contests for the rest of their natural lives.

In regard to the proposed giving of books as prizes it can well be said that the average prize taker would regard mud pies or saw horses with as much esteem as books. None of them can be worn as a medal can, none of them can bear a suitable inscription as a medal does. All of them are common, are beggarly cheap, can be purchased anywhere and by anybody, and gives the owner no distinction.

—*R. '93.*

INTERESTING FACTS ABOUT DISTINGUISHED LAKE FOREST MEN.

At a concert of the Cornell clubs in Minneapolis the other night I told a University of Minnesota fraternity man that I was from Lake Forest. He said, "Where's that?" nothing more. I remembered the Chicago man in Jerusalem who wanted to cable home. The operator could not be made to understand when Chicago was. Finally, with the clutching motion of a drowning man, he asked if it were near St. Louis. To my chagrin I had to locate Lake Forest near Northwestern. The man had actually never heard of you.

I went over to his frat. house and spun until I am sure the impressions concerning our college and university, which must have originated years before Dr. Robert's administration, were changed for new ones.

The Forester and Herbert Baker's view of Lake Forest are mighty useful instruments in ocular surgery. And just my fortune, B. Fay Mills and J. Wilbur Chapman were here. I pointed to them as samples of Lake Forest men. "If Mills and Chapman come from Lake Forest, it is a great college," they argue.

It is a source of pride that our college alumni list is headed by B. Fay Mills. He and his college chum are honored in their work above most men. Even now Boston must wait two years for Mr. Mills. Dr. Chapman is engaged until the summer of 1894, and can accept only one of many calls.

In June, 1890, the STENTOR obtained a $7.50 cut of Mr. Mills from Dr. Talmage's paper for $2, and printed it with a sketch of his life. In January, 1891, it was republished with additional mention. The *Forester* will tell you how these men joined and successively presided over the " Old Athenæan," and how when a disturbance arose in 1878, this David and Jonathan pair were " the leading spirits among the revolutionists." They were once pastors in neighboring towns, and now each is an evangelist.

B. Fay Mills was born the son of a minister at Rahway, thirty-six years ago. He attended Hamilton and lectures at Carlton College. He is a Delta Upsilon. He preached his first sermon at Granite Fall, Minnesota, April 29, 1877, was ordained February, 8, 1878. His methods as a pastor were evangelistic. His first efforts in that line distinctively were at Middlebury, Vt., while stationed at Rutland.

Mr. Mills is short, except when addressing an audience. His face is smooth, complexion light. The lines of his mouth in repose indicate firmness. He is not what the world calls handsome, but nevertheless he is beautiful. He has very pleasant, winning ways, yet is a general from the ground up.

Dr. Chapman is a friend of President Coulter; is an Indianian, thirty four years of age. He studied at Lake Forest, Oberlin, and Lane Seminary. Was the head of Dutch churches at Schuylerville, and Albany, N.Y., and in 1889 became the pastor of Bethany church, (Wanamaker's) at Philadelphia. October 10, 1892, he gave up worldly ambition and entered the field as an evangelist.

Dr. Chapman is tall, dark, handsome, prepossessing, married, at times wears glasses. He appears more like the cultivated club man, and of the two is the theologian, so Mr. Mills declares. His manner is pleasing. He is a magnetic speaker, has a sympathetic voice, and perhaps wins souls more through the heart, as his friend does through the brain.

Both men carefully watch the growth of Lake Forest, and remember Prof. Halsey. They both feel the weight of men's souls, and are both given up body and will to their master.

Of Mr. Mills' success as an evangelist Dr. Chapman says: " It is largely due to his superb system. He is a great organizer. In his preaching it is his straightforwardness that seems to tell the most." For himself Dr. Chapman says: " I have two lines—first, I devote myself to the quickening of the church and church members: following that I preach for sinners, choosing the plainest possible words. I press immediate decision, but not by undue excitement, sensationalism, or claptrap." Mr. Mills says of the secret of Dr. Chapman's power: It is spiritual magnetism, if I may use that term. You hear him talk for a few minutes and imagine he is not saying very much, but after awhile his words impress you with power. The Spirit is with him."

The " Mills Meetings " are over, the visible results are wonderful. Audiences as large as nine and ten thousand gathered to hear the sermons, often many were turned away, yet the objectionable excitement of " revivals " was entirely absent. Analysis does not show the power of the sermons over the people. For instance, Dr. Chapman with test in hand will very unassumingly begin a sermon. The opening remarks may seem tame, but the listener will soon notice that his attention is involuntarily held, that the eyes of all are intent upon the speaker. A pathetic story is used to illustrate, then there are many weeping women and men. Yet when the opportunity is given one wonders at the number who rise to their feet. This is especially true of Mr. Mill's address.

It is supposed that considering the size of the city such immense audiences have never gathered in the world for divine worship as in this "Gibraltar of religion." In regard to the relative advantage of drawing people by evangelistic services, or by "a godless choir singing heathen music in an unknown tongue," Mr. Mills says: "More people attend where they are continually asked to come to Christ than where they are not." "Real evangelistic preaching will draw better than oratorical pyrotechnics." He also proved by personal demonstration in one audience from among the pastors present that converts made at revivals are the "stickers."

Dr. Capman could assist here for a time only. Mr. Mills was the leader. The movement to call them began in 1889. Mr. Mills was here some weeks previous to his arrival for work. He also studied the map carefully and was thoroughly acquainted with the city. He says that the unity of the churches is the great lever toward the great results that are attained; that "we could accomplish nothing without the power and co-operation of the press behind us." One hundred and eight churches united in the preparation for this coming. The Christians were aroused and eager for the work. The choir had been formed, and the usher band of 600 and more trained according to Mr. Mills' methods. Extensive advertising had been done. The expenses of the campaign had been met. Every detail was complete. The ground was ready.

The evangelist began meetings in the southern and northern parts of the city for those districts only, then a week was devoted to the other two districts. As a climax, mass meetings for the entire city were held two weeks in the exposition building. There were daily morning sermons down town at ten o'clock, a noon prayermeeting for business men, a

woman's noon meeting and a prayermeeting conducted by them in the afternooon. There were preaching services every afternoon and evening, except Saturday, the rest day. There were special services for Sunday school teachers, non-church members, for mothers, boys, young people, for men only. There was one all night prayer meeting, and one mid-week sabbath. On that day cottage and church prayer meetings were held all over the city early in the morning. Over three hundred and fifty of the business houses were closed, demonstrating strongly the interest among business men.

The meetings were after one general plan. The large choir under the direction of Mr. Mills' leadership sang for an opening half hour. A minister prayed. More singing with the congregation, scripture reading, announcements, and sermon, preceded perhaps by a solo from the evangelist's musician. The sermon was immediately followed by the appeal to begin Christian life. While the choir sang, the ushers and assistants passed cards for the name, address, and church preference of those desiring to sign them. Following the benediction came the after meeting, to which a special invitation had been given, a short talk, another appeal, another card passing, and dispersal. The assistant, Mr. Ralph Gillam, takes the non-preference cards and follows them up. The appeals to sinners are not hurried, they are calmly given, addressed to the intellect and better nature of the people, and are ended at the right moment; hundreds answer them at each meeting.

From the time Mr. Mills reaches the platform he is the head and brain, the spiritual dynamo of the meeting. Everything must move just as he directs through messengers, and it does under pain of instant rebuke. Natural ability and experience have fitted him to be the leader. There is not space to give even an outline of the system of ushering, assisting, baby checking, messenger service, and general direction. But the man himself is so thoroughly in earnest that it is contagious, and in all ever avoids that which would seem to place the honor of the servant above that of his master. With the preparation for his coming, the complete system, and Mr. Mills' earnestness something has to give way. You may go to his first meeting unsympathetic, you will go again, and within five weeks' time will be thorougly won over.

Mr. Mills impresses one as being a man of new ideas, yet old ideas rejuvenated. A feeling steals over the listener that Mr. Mills is saying just what he would think if he thought it himself, or his conscience had not been smeared with the dust of disuse. Furthermore the hearer's inner self keeps repeating "that's so" as the sermon is unfolded. He never proclaims his denomination, but is sound of doctrine. At one meeting clergymen of various sects arose and publicly declared their belief in everything they had just heard taught in a sermon on the "Unpardonable Sin." Mr. Mills does not force his doctrinal opinions on anyone and when a reporter in his first interview asked his idea of eternal future punishment he said: "Life is too short and eternity is too long to consider that thing; we will all know soon enough."

Dr. Gray, of the *Interior*, says: "B. Fay Mills is originating and quoting epigrams. 'An ounce of mother is worth a pound of clergy,' he quotes from the Spanish. One of his own is, "It does not take a great man to be a Christian, but it takes all there is of him."

He also says, "Suffer the little children," and says it often. "Revival meetings are not the consummation, but the beginning." "If I were to be a pastor again I should like to be the pastor of a church where they baptized people as soon as they were saved." "I do not approve of the average Sunday paper. I never have anything to do with them, and I think the world could get along without them." I have not seen the inside of a theatre for sixteen years. I have known hundreds of men and women who have been ruined by them, but I never heard of any one's being helped." "I believe in teetotalism."

Mr. Mills' text to new converts is Isaiah 50:7. Here are four principles he gives: "It is never right to do wrong." (Mr. Mills is said to never use the street cars on Sunday.) Don't do anything you are in doubt about." "If meat make thy brother to offend, eat no flesh while the world standeth lest ye make thy brother to offend." Surrender first, get light afterwards."

Dr. Chapman is now in Eau Claire. Mr. Mills is in Milwaukee, and from there goes to St. Paul. A Chicago paper states that they will both be in that city for four weeks during the Columbian Exhibition (as Mr. McAllister would say).

—*J. E. S.* '90.

THE IDLER.

As our readers may have noticed we haven't "idled" for some time. We never "idle" in winter. That time is given up to deep ponderings on the "whichness of the hitherto," and wondering when "this blamed weather will let up." But "in the spring," you know, "a young man's fawncies" get the better of him, so once more we can be found "idling" at the old stand; office hours 8 A. M. to 9 P. M., when the Sem. doors close (excuse us, one of the fellows who knows says they close at 9:30. Pardon our ignorance). It is wonderful what a sense of contentment steals over one when the beautiful balmy spring weather begins to burst forth. (N.B. At present writing it is snowing, with prospects of a blizzard.) So, with the return of spring and its companions, our muse again sings—slightly off the key however.

*
* *

But, speaking of the weather and looking over the sick-list in the college, we are constrained to ask if you, dear reader, were ever ill. If so, were you ever ill in college? If you have not been, shake hands with yourself and graduate as soon as possible for fear you will be. We were there once. (Pardon us if we speak sadly. This balmy (?) spring weather has a depressing effect.) When one is sick in college he muses thusly the first day: "Well, this is great. Get out of four straights. I'll get over this just in time to blow around to that party to-morrow night. Wonder if any of the 'fels' want a game of cinch." Then the fellows drop in and "haven't time for a game," but say "there's an impromptu dance for to-night." Invalid's face falls. "Doc says you can't go out for a week." More face falling. More fellows drop in. "Sorry you can't go to the party to-morrow, old boy-" By this time the invalid's visage is terrible to behold. "Say, by the way, old man, Blank is going to take your girl to the concert next week. He's banking on your being sick that long." Actual profanity from the sick man. Then everyone scatters and goes to recitation, and he is left alone with the picture of two "shows" and a concert, including that "chump" Blank. He decides to write to the girl and tell her not to accept Blank's invitation. Then he remembers that that would be the very thing that would make her accept. Then he thinks he will write and tell her to accept Blank's invitation, and what a nice fellow he is. But then with the sweet inconsistency of her nature she *will* accept and tell him afterwards that she did it

to please him. So he groans inwardly and decides not to write. That night everyone goes to the dance. The last man to go sits on the foot of his bed, and in the darkness regales him with stories of people who have died while everyone is gone. Then that man jumps up, says he must hustle or he'll miss the first dance, and is gone. The invalid lies there in the darkness and imagines he is already defunct, and is being talked of "as a good youth." He drops into a troubled sleep, and dreams that he is a pall bearer at his own funeral, and watches Blank waltzing around the church with his best girl while the band plays "Annie Murphy" and the organ chimes in with "Maggie Rooney's Home." The next day when dinner is brought up he finds he can't eat pie, as the Doctor has expressly forbidden anything like it. Accordingly, well-meaning friends send in pies, cakes, candy and dessert. The Doctor says, "Be content with milk." Again the fellows drop in. "Say, old swipes, how do you feel? Too bad you can't eat that pie." "That's what, old boy. Say, what are you going to do with all that stuff anyway? Help ourselves did you say? Well, I guess so. Come on fellows." And the good people who send in the "goodies" imagine that the invalid's stomach is made of India rubber. "Well, good night, have to get ready for the concert. Hope you get better." And so it goes. It's delightful being sick. When you are ill every social event that has been on the tapis for months is sure to come during your week. You might just as well accept your fate and think over your faults and mistakes. We believe that if some men didn't get sick occasionally they would imagine they were faultless.   S.

WORLD'S FAIR ITEMS,

The longest and largest single block of stone in the world will be exhibited by a Wisconsin stone company. The stone is over 115 feet in length, which is 8 feet longer than the obelisk in Central Park, New York.

The largest and finest locomotive to be exhibited will probably be one of English make, which recently was installed at Jackson Park. This engine is unique in that each of its two driving wheels are operated by a different cylinder, instead of by one.

The Cunard Steamship Company will illustrate the growth and development of its line by a fleet of full-rigged models built on the scale of one-quarter inch to the foot. These models have been in preparation for a year past at the company's Liverpool yards. In fact, the list of lines exhibiting models is almost unlimited. There will also be exhibits by nations showing the development in war ships, docks, harbors, and everything pertaining to the sea. There will be enough models of war ships to exactly reproduce the Naval Review at New York in miniature.

COLLEGE.

L. F. U. CALENDAR.
Junior Reception given in honor of the Seniors, April 27.
Freshmen Contest in Declamation, April 28.
Contest of the Academy Societies, May 2.
Sophomore Contest in Declamation, May 5.
Oratorical Association Contest, May 23.
Annual Senior Reception, May 26.
Academy Commencement Exercises, June 9.
Annual Academy Reception, June 10.
Annual Concert at Ferry Hall, June 12.
Freshmen-Sophomore Prize Speaking, June 12.
Commencement Exercises at Ferry Hall, June 13.
Senior Class Day, June 13.
Junior Contest in Oratory, June 13.
College Commencement Exercises, June 14.
Alumni Banquet, June 14.
President's Reception. June 14.

Invitations are out for the Annual Junior Reception.

The senior examinations begin three weeks from to-morrow.

Present indications point to a repetition of last year's spring.

Prof. Dawson was unable to attend his classes the early part of last week.

Mr. Linn has been quite ill for several days past. Mr. McNary has also been confined to his room.

The Freshmen have elected D. H. Jackson captain of the base ball team, and M. Woolsey manager. Ninety-six will be ahead if the other classes do not hasten.

The morning after the Evanston ball game a notice appeared upon the college bulletin board, requesting all who had never seen a base ball game to report for practice.

The old cisterns back of the college have been filled up, and a very pretty lawn has been started, to take the place of the old coal-sheds, which were such an eye-sore last year.

The friends and members of the Athenæan Society were very pleasantly entertained by Mrs. Fales, at her home, last Tuesday evening. Mr. Larned read an interesting paper on Millet.

The students, under the leadership of Mr. Pratt, are practicing regularly for the War Song Concert which is to be given in a few weeks for the benefit of the Athletic Association.

The trustees of the Lake Forest Church have published the financial report of the congregation for the year ending April 2d. The summaries are as follows:—For the Home Field, $4,978; for the Foreign Field, $2,936; for Congregational Expenses, $6,247; making the total amount raised, for all purposes, $14,163.

The Sophomore Greek Class are making a study of the plays of Sophocles, with the aid of a metrical English translation. In this way the class gets a more general knowledge of the Greek drama, and, at the same time, get enough practice in the actual work of translation that they will not lose their knowledge of the Greek language.

Last Tuesday evening State Secretary Burt, of the Y. M. C. A., talked to the students of the College and Academy upon the annual summer school at Lake Geneva. It will be remembered by old students that Lake Forest has usually been quite well represented since the scheme was started. Last year Illinois was the banner state as regards the number of students who represented it. Of the colleges in this state Lake Forest sent the largest delegation.

The attention of the students is called to the ruling made by the Lawn Tennis Association with regard to the use of the tennis courts. The court nearest the gymnasium is for the exclusive use of the Academy boys. No one but the college students may use the other two courts, except when said courts are vacant and no one from the college wishes to play upon them. The rule requiring the wearing of tennis shoes upon the courts has been disregarded to such an extent that one of the courts is unfit for use.

Among the recent additions to the library are the following: On Truth: a Systematic Inquiry, by St. George Minart; the entire set of Lessing's Works, consisting of six volumes; English Wayfaring Life in the Middle Ages by J. J. Jusserand; Life of Leigh Hunt, by Cosma Monkhouse; Life of Hume, in two volumes, by John Hill Burton; Matthew Arnold's Poetical Works, McMillan & Co.'s edition; Charles O'Malley, the Irish Dragoon, by Charles Lever; Ordeal of Richard Feverel, by George Meredith; The Works of Fielding, in seven volumes.

Saturday, May 3, has been chosen by the committee for our Annual Field Day. Some think that a regular school day ought to be given up to an event of this character, which is of interest to all parts of the university. Following are the events of the day:

100 yd. dash.	Running broad jump.
220 yd. dash.	Standing broad jump.
440 yd. dash.	Running high jump.
880 yd. dash.	Throwing base ball.
Mile run.	Kicking foot ball.
120 yd. hurdle race.	Three-legged race.
Mile walk.	Wheelbarrow race.
Putting the shot.	Throwing the hammer.

Relay or class race.

TOWN TOPICS.

H. C. Durand and family have returned from their southern trip.

Mr. and Mrs. A. M. Day have returned, and are now living at their home in Lake Forest.

Mr. Aldrich has bought the lot east of Mr. Chapin's house from Mr. Chapin.

Mr. F. E. Hinckley and family will soon return to Lake Forest for the summer.

Dr. Edgar Reading, one of the founders of Lake Forest, died last Tuesday at his residence in Chicago. Dr. Reading was a member of the land company which originally bought the then untouched land of Lake Forest, and which converted its 1,300 acres into a large park for the university.

There does not seem to be the usual activity in house renting this spring. While nearly as many houses have already been rented as there were at the corresponding time last spring, the proportion is smaller on account of the new houses erected. The decrease in proportion is attributed by some to the rent, which is generally fixed higher than last year. The following houses have already been rented for the summer: Mrs. Humphrey's to Mr. Hannah; Mr. Wells' to Mr. Cremer; Prof. Locy's to Mr. Wm. H. Smith; Mrs. Sawyer's to Mr. Fitzhugh; Mr. Bowen's to Mr. Byron Smith; Mrs. Ralston's to Mr. Crosby; Prof. Thomas' and Prof. Stevens' houses have also been rented. Mr. Rainey's, Mr. Larned's, Mr. Yaggy's and Mr. Blackler's houses are for rent.

ATHLETICS.

With the recent election of the officers of the Tennis Association, a new impetus seems to have been given this favored sport. The courts, which just now are not in the best of condition, are used at every available time by large numbers of enthusiasts. Among those most promising we have noticed Messrs. Marcotte, Bournique, Davis, Flint, Fales and

Davies. A tournament is being worked up and should not be lost sight of. This bevy of players, together with other local talent, can certainly make things interesting for some time.

We have heard many complaints among the students of late regarding the foot-ball practice that has been taken up by many on the field near the college. The general opinion is that it will injure the base ball spirit. We are all aware that base ball has no strong hold among the fellows, and that all the material available is needed to make a successful nine. While the foot ball practice in itself is a good thing and would be commended providing our college were larger, yet in the present state of affairs it seems quite expedient that the old rule, "foot ball in the fall and base ball in the spring," be adhered to.

Capt. McNary has been suffering from a severe cold during the past week, so that he has been unable to take charge of the team. This fact, together with the unfavorable weather, has caused practice to be suspended and served to make things look rather dubious regarding the coming games. No matter how badly the respective mem' ers of the track and ball teams need exercise, they ought to avoid practice in cold, raw weather, and particularly in the rain. This was tried several times during last week, and on the following day the lame joints and sore muscles were thought to be the result of over-exerci-e. To any member of an athletic team a cold caught in a muscle is very liable to become a permanent injury. Our athletes cannot be too careful in regard to this fact.

FERRY HALL.

Miss Alice Keener is ill.

Miss Edna Hays is very ill with measles.

The Ferry Hall teachers entertained the University club Thursday evening.

Miss Lyon has been the victim of La Grippe for a few days.

Misses Bessie and Kitty Adams were guests of their sisters Apr. 14th.

Miss Clemens, of Chicago, spent Sunday, April 16th with Miss Brett.

Miss Garrett, of Chicago, was a guest of Miss Keener on Sunday last.

Dr. Hays, of Albion, Ind. is here in attendance on his daughter, Miss Edna.

Lovers of tennis are very glad of the new rule which admits of their playing at any time after noon.

A larger number than usual are looking forward to the exemption this term. A good incentive to study.

A few of the teachers enjoyed the musicale given at the home of Miss Minnie Rumsey Thursday afternoon.

The Misses Conger, Smith and Thompson gave a feast on Tuesday evening in honor of Miss Louise and Miss Margaret Conger.

The spread given by the Misses Adams on Friday evening, Apr. 14th was fine. A great many noted people were present and the refreshments were especially enjoyed.

Those doing fourth year work now have a class organization with the following officers: President, Miss Louise Conger; Vice-President, Catherine Parker; Secretary, Miss Stoddard; Treasurer, Miss Vera Scott.

Miss Norten entertained her friends in an unusually pleasant manner Tuesday evening. Mrs. Hester sang after which Mrs. Emerson talked in the most informal and interesting fashion on travels in Greece. Light refreshments followed music by Miss Orvis and Miss Messinger.

Prof. Eager has received the appointment of director of A. B. Chase and Co's piano exhibit at the Exposition. This is a recognition of merit as musician of which we at Lake Forest have a right to be proud. Probably no piano exhibitors at the Fair will be represented by so talented a performer and the firm are to be congratulated upon the wisdom of their choice.

WHAT THE GIRLS THINK OF CRINOLINE.

We cannot favor both crinoline and co-education.

The Sems. should advocate crinoline for it facilitates walking. What say the youths now, shall we wear it?

Our grandmothers wore crinoline. No one questioned their good common sense. Why should they doubt ours?

—*E. & E.*

During the spring vacation Mother Fashion took a little trip out to L. F. and since then the girls have been—well to say the least a little stiff.

The gentlemen will have to invent a new walk if the skirts get much bigger else how can they take a lady's arm without crushing her crinoline.

Certainly an extra board will have to be added to the side-walks in Lake Forest if two Sems. wearing crinolines must take their daily constitutional together.

We feel that day by day we are nearing the cricis—when crinoline shall put in its *full* appearance. We dread it but must submit to the inevitable, for Fashion having once come into power has since reigned supreme.

Crinoline or not Crinoline, that is the question, which is agitating so many feminine minds, as well as the masculine intellect. But girls, you might as well adopt it now, as you will come to it sooner or later—for Crinoline will conquer.

To the Editor:

Since Crinoine has come in, it is noticed with dismay, that it is now impossible for a young gentleman to break into the ranks as each Sem. occupies the space formerly enough for three.

Sorrowfully,

A SEM.

ACADEMY.

A number of the students were visiting the college societies last Friday evening.

The continued rainy weather has made outdoor exercise impossible the past week.

Ed. Yaggy has been confined to his home the past few days threatened with tonsilitis.

Mrs. Smith and children will leave Wednesday morning for the South to remain until next Saturday.

On the authority of one of the members we are able to state that we will not move into the new buildings this term.

The faculty have been quit lenient in regard to restric-ions this term, for which the students most heartily return thanks.

Erskine's ball team were to have played a game with a town nine last Saturday, but were preۿented by stormy weather.

Someone, inclined to be humorous, posted a list on the bulletin board of a ba l nine, in which Prof. Mendel played second base, Havant first, and Gruenstein short stop. They were billed to appear in tights.

The following are the members and their respective positions of the Academy ball team, subject to future changes: Rogers, catcher; Laughlin, pitcher; Rheinhart, first base; Kimball, second base; McDonald, third base; Gilleland, short stop; Jaeger, left field; Durand, center field; Heineman, right field; substitutes, Rheingaus and Forbes.

For the benefit of former members of the Academy, who may wish to attend the coming contest, we again state that it will take place Tuesday evening, May 2nd. Following are the contestants:

DECLAMATION.

GAMMA SIGMA.	TRI KAPPA.
Lyman Bournique	B. S. Cutler.
G. N. Heineman	C. E. Durand.

ESSAY.

T. W. Harvey	M. S. Baker.

DEBATE.

"Are labor unions a detriment to the best interest of the country?"

Neg.	*Aff.*
R. L. Roberts	A. Cooker.

EXCHANGES.

TO MY PIPE.

A cloud of smoke will soon begin
To soften all the harsh world's din;
A subtle vein beyond which lies
All darkened days and saddened skies.
And gloomy realms of fretful sin.
Within the smoke, white-hued and thin,
Dame Fortune wears almost a grin,
While upward to the ceiling flies,
    A cloud of smoke.

Nirvana must be close akin
To that rare state a pipe can win;
You see the melting clouds arise,
Quite hushed are earthly sounds and sighs,
All earthly cares will vanish in
    A cloud of smoke.
       — *Williams Weekly.*

Table board is always a perplexing question, but especially with students. The varied experiences and inconvenience of boarding halls and clubs connected with educational institutions are phenomenal. But the students of the University of Chicago say that with them "patience has ceased to be a virtue." Cheer up, fellows, you have the sympathy of the college world.

"The great problem that I have to deal with," said the keeper of the imbecile asylum, "is to find some occupation for the people under my charge."

"Why not set them inventing college yells?" asked the visitor.—*Buffalo Ex.*

The students of the University of Wisconsin are to be congratulated upon their new athletic grounds. It was mainly due to their appeal to the Legislature that the appropriation of $25,000 for the purchase of the grounds was granted.

"Knox will be represented at the World's Fair by about thirty young men who will act in the semi-official capacity of chair-rollers."—*Exchange.*

A youth upon the campus stood,
    A window on the third floor eyeing,
A fair form draped in white above
    Was listening to his sighing.
He whistled softly, gently, low,
    The echo quickly dying,
And then response was made, you know,
    Which sent his heart a-flying.
       —*Exchange.*

THE AMERICAN GIRL.

She knows no Latin, she knows no Greek,
But the purest American she can speak;
She knows the uses of her and she
And the proper places of I and me;
She doesn't use big words to tell
A story, although she can use them well;
In short she's a girl without pretense:
With an ample supply of common sense.
And I'd rather have her any day
Than the girl who can parley voo frong say.

Freshman yell:
       Rah—rah—rix
       Mamma's chicks
       We'll hatch out
       In '96.   —*H. S. Herald.*

In a class scrap between '95 and '96 of Berkeley, thirty Freshmen tied up twenty-five Sophs and took their photos.

    "J stands for Junior,
      Of whom it is said,
      The Freshes so green
      By the noses are led.
    "F stands for Freshman,
      And green though he be,
      To Sophs and to Seniors
      He ne'er bends the knee."
       —*Exchange.*

A thoughtful citizen has suggested that if slates be hung in the vestibules of churches where young ladies could register their names on entering, it would save a good many young men from incurring the danger of taking cold by standing about the open door waiting till church is out to see if their best girl is there.
       —*Business Collegian.*

THE STENTOR.

VOLUME VI.   MAY 2, 1893.   NUMBER 25.

PUBLISHED EVERY WEEK

BY THE

Lake Forest University Stentor Publishing Co.

BOARD OF EDITORS.

B. R. MacHatton, '95.............Managing Editor
Forest Grant, '96 ......Ass't Mgr. Ed. and Athletic
Harry Goodman, '94.............Business Manager
A. B. Burdick, '95
J. H. Jones, '96   · ..../............ ....Locals
David Fales, Jr., '96
W. B. Smith, '94 ....Alumni and Exchange
R. G. McKinnie, '97 ....Academy
Miss Tena Kennedy, ...Ferry Hall
J. A. McGaughey, '95 ....Advertising

Terms—$1.50 per year. Single Copies—10c

————ADDRESS————

STENTOR PUBLISHING COMPANY,

LAKE FOREST,   :   :   ILLINOIS.

Entered at the P. O. at Lake Forest, Ill., as second-class matter.

TO OUR ALUMNI.

This column has been sadly neglected for some unaccountable reason. The present management of THE STENTOR are firm believers in the fact that one of the purposes of a college paper should be not only to keep the alumni posted in regard to what is going on in their *alma mater,* but to acquaint them, where it is possible, with the whereabout and occupation of their classmates. We believe that Lake Forest college can justly lay claim to the possession of some of the most distinguished men in the west among its alumni. Viewed from the standpoint of reputation, the alumni constitute the wealth of a college. The personal character, the public influence, the loyalty and enthusiasm of its alumni

belong to the earnings of a college quite as much as the interest on its endowments.

Beginning with the next issue THE STENTOR will give you a full page of interesting facts.

———

We make no apologies for another editorial on that time-worn, oft written-upon subject of the College Paper. Until some radical reform is made we will keep harping on this subject.

The purposes which the ideal college paper should accomplish are numerous. First and foremost the college paper should be *representative.* It should voice the sentiment of the entire student body and not any particular party or class. Anything which contracts the sphere of action and influence in a college paper has a tendency to make its supporters narrow-minded. We certainly believe that a college paper is the best advertising medium for the college which it represents. Parents debating where to send their son get a clearer idea of the moral, intellectual and social condition of the college life by looking over the files of its paper than by wading through a large catalogue of names. But, in order to be a good advertising medium, the college paper must be the exponent of the whole mass of students.

The insincerity and duplicity of the outside-world journalism is so manifest that one needs only to pick up two of our morning papers, representing different factions, and one becomes convinced that journalism has become merely the voice and echo of party.

Is there not a little too much of this party spirit, this one-horse representation, creeping into our college papers?

TO THOSE WHO GATHER WILD FLOWERS.

May a lover of wild flowers address through these columns a few words to those readers who from time to time go to the ravines to gather their treasures?

Few places, even among the mountains, are as rich in native flora as our beautiful Lake Forest. When thirty years ago this spot was chosen for a seat of Learning, Natures' lavish hand was seen throughout the length of these ravines, from side to side of these spreading groves. What do we see now? Not only the removal of trees and wild growth necessary for the erection of buildings and laying out of grounds, but alas! evidences of inexcusable vandalism, where jealous guardianship should have watched over the beauties of field and ravine.

Even within the last four or five years some of us have noted with dismay the gradual dis. appearance from parts of the ravines around the campus of some of the most delicate wild flowers and ferns. They have been either uprooted by careless gatherers, or hoed and burned up by unenlightened workingmen, or gradually discouraged in their growth by indiscriminate clearing away of underbrush in the name of "improvement." Look at some of the so-called "cleared up" ravines. Instead of an exquisite net-work of leaf and twig, with a plentitude of low-growing flowers and ferns nestling under such protection, we find naked tree trunks (if indeed *they* are spared), scraped or blackened earth, and in mid-summer a rank growth of weeds. That some who have been indirectly responsible for such blunders are having their eyes opened is manifest, but much injnry is still being done.

It is, however, to the flower-gatherers, and to those who love these treasures, that I now beg to say an earnest word. Let us be careful how we cull them! Do not pick every blossom from a single Hepatica root, pick them in a way to avoid strain on the roots themselves, do not tread on the plant while gathering blooms

from another. Do not break branches ruthlessly, either in gathering their blossoms or in moving about. On the edges of ravines I frequently find mutilated shrubs trying to tell by means of a few straggling twigs their sweet story of Beauty, their former symmetry destroyed by careless hands.

Strengthen the things that remain. Nature is shy of harsh treatment. Silently and inevitably she shrinks away from vandal man, only by much gentle coaxing to be enticed back again to her old-time haunts. At this moment I see two flower-gatherers with a basket descending into the ravine I love dearest. When I go down after their departure I shall perhaps find evidences of a carelessness *wholly useless*.

What New York state is doing for her injured forests, what the city of Hartford, Conn., had to do for her little trailing fern, we are not likely to do here for our vanishing wild flowers, viz.: establish laws for their protection and punish all offenders. "Behold, I show you a more excellent way." Guard each beauty jealously, love it with an affection that is inconsistent with mutilation and destruction. Bushels of wild flowers can be gathered without inflicting injury on land, tree, shrub or plant.

Who will respond to these words?

ONE WHO LOVES WILD FLOWERS.

THE RAMBLER.

Did you ever notice the cosmopolitan character of the university sphere?

It is a veritable microcosm—in it is found every disposition, every nationality, every color. The learned professor and his anti-podal, hollow-pated dude, the perfect mannered preceptress and the faithful disciple *de mode*.

See yonder distinguished looking gentleman with the high forehead, immaculate suit of Parisian importation and withal an intellectual mien—That is our president? No indeed. You mistake character; he is our most important and highly exalted curator.

In the University faculty is found great wisdom some of which is garnered from the intellectual granaries of Europe, the Orient and Hawaii while it is said that the greater part is brought to the University by Freshmen and as the Senior carries none away the members of the faculty are furnished with a never ceasing supply of knowledge.

This leisure loving rover approaching is a psychological authority, by the depths of whose reason one is convinced, much against his better self, that there is no matter, that he does not exist and that the stately " co-ed " upon whom he has showered floral confusions and unpaid-for confections is an illusion. This philosopher's tall, handsome Scotch companion is an astronomer who nightly sits at the eye piece of the mythical Yerkes' telescope and pours into the ears of his " electives," who have been enjoying the enchanting evening strolling, a most vivid description of an unruly cloud. The third member of the trio is a German biologist; his mission is to lecture upon the superiority of the gymnasium, the native swordsman and pretzel and incidentally to discover for you invisible yet undeniable traces of the continuity of protoplasm.

Let us drop in at the Historical Club.

That ermine locked sage buried betwixt the mammoth sheep covers of an ancient book is our far famed professor of Hellenic dialects who is just about to discover that Homer was not written by Homer but by Homer jr. as a memorial to the deceased Homer.

In the second alcove are seated Herr Füller and Monsieur Parlez Vous. They are comparing, or contrasting rather the " California " with the " Rhein," the American cook with the French *chef*, the continental opera with the American music and at last come to a " defend " when the accomodating librarian accidentally dropped a life of Napoleon between them.

If the faculty is diversified in its origin and function the student body is more so—that is in its origin, for the student's function is as yet an unsolved enigma.

The student's world is unique—it is a life lived for four years and suddenly ended by the roll of the " real" world's musketry upon Commencement eve.

Yonder group of cringing lads are Freshmen. They are somewhat crest-fallen—inflated crests at that—because they met correction at the hands of those lords of the earth, the Sophomores, because they chose to hold class meetings and class canes—to attend receptions unchaperoned and to call upon newly arrived fairer students who are by all rights of comity the peculiar property of the Sophomore.

The second group is composed of Sophs. whose importance is depicted upon every brow, whose cigarettes picturesquely and properly project from daintily gloved digits, while the latest walking sticks are propelled through the surrounding ether in that truly indescribable Sophomoric style.

That Junior seated beside his chosen fairy has tired of hazing, athletics and study and has betaken himself to the sterner task of practically conjugating the Banquo-vision, like verb amo— with varying degrees of success.

Upon the steps of University Hall have gathered the Seniors. Each has a more direful tale of Fresh-Soph-Junior adventure to relate than his predecessor. Each tells the other of his prospects—those with bright ones to accept congratulations and those with less brilliant ones to elicit the sympathy of comrades in misery. Each consumes the last cigars purchased from the farewell allowance and each casts aside his tears and dignity as the rumor gains credence that the president neglected to place the remaining freezer in the burglar proof vault.

Time fails us to mention in this college world the special students: specials in German and botany specials, Irish specials and special policeman, specials in ethics, and inethical specials, specials in foot-ball and Seminary specials, specials in debt and specials in bon-fires, specials in love and special—pencil's broken.

In the foot-ball match between England and Scotland, England won by a score of 5 to 2. 30,000 persons witnessed the game.

COLLEGE.

L. F. U. CALENDAR.

Sophomore Contest in Declamaticn, May 5.
Oratorical Association Contest, May 23.
Annual Senior Reception, May 26.
Academy Commencement Exercises, June 9.
Annual Academy Reception, June 10.
Annual Concert at Ferry Hall, June 12.
Freshmen-Sophomore Prize Speaking, June 12.
Commencement Exercises at Ferry Hall, June 13.
Senior Class Day, June 13.
Junior Contest in Oratory, Jnne 13.
College Commencement Exercises, June 14.
Alumni Banquet, June 14.
President's Reception. June 14.

Mr. Linn is recuperating at the Hull house in Chicago.

The Sophomore contest this year promises to be of special interest.

Tennis and base. balls always on hand, also other athletic supplies.—W. E. Rustin.

Gamma Sigma, Tri Kappa, Freshmen and Sophomore colors are very numerous this week.

Rev. N. D. Hillis, of Evanston, visited several of the class rooms of the college last Thursday.

The subject of the last Y. M. C. A. meeting was " Betraying Christ." N. H. Burdick was leader.

Those who wished to visit Chicago on May 1st had to " cut " recitations.. We did not get a holiday.

Mr. McNary went to Milwaukee Saturday where he will remain until he gets over his present illness.

Mrs. Jones, of Clinton, Iowa, arrived Wednesday evening to take care of her son who is still suffering from the grippe.

All entries for field day were in by last Friday. Each contestant is required to deposit twenty-five cents for the first event he enters and ten cents for each succeeding one.

A half-holiday was granted by the Faculty for field day, which takes place to-morrow. On account of there already being one holiday granted the holiday for the Fair opeinng was refused.

Special attention is called to the article of the STENTOR by " One who loves the wild flowers." The warning given and the suggestions to " those who gather wild flowers," are indeed timely and well worth the notice of everyone who loves Lake Forest.

The Faculty announced last Wednesday that all who wished to take positions at the World's Fair could do so and could make arrangements to take their examinations any time during examination week. A half holiday was also granted for the field day exercises of May 3rd.

During the late rain visitations there has been a continual puddle of rain in the upper floor of the college dormitory under the skylight. Anyone passing along the hall is very liable to an anonymous ducking, for which he can either thank the weather or preferably the trustees.

On Monday noon of last week, the 12:10 train left a little group of unfortunates at various distances from the station, as it began to wend its tortuous way to the city of the World's Fair—about ten minutes too soon. So the disappointed suburbanites sat down to wait three quarters of an hour for the slowest train but one on the road.

Tennis players should bear in mind the rule that a court can be held only one hour when others are waiting to play. This rule has several times been broken. Another important rule is that a player can only play on that court to which he is assigned, unless there is an unoccupied place in another court. The following is a list of the persons who have been assigned to the several courts. It be will noticed that the 3rd court, (the one next to the gymnasium), is assigned chiefly to use of Academy students.

FIRST COURT.	SECOND COURT.	THIRD COURT.
MacHatton.	Bird.	Thornton.
McKee.	Ruston.	Kilgour.
Henry.	Chaffee.	Cross.
Prof. Jack.	Curry.	Franklin.
Graff.	Davis.	Vincent.
Levering.	Sharon.	Nichols.
Keith.	H. F. Jones.	Keyes.
Coolidge.	Rogers.	Reid.
Parish.	Linn.	Newcomb.
Lewis.	Drake.	Baker.
	Dorah.	Hamil.
	Fales.	Brearly.
		Bournique.

The Annual Freshman preliminary in declamation took place in the Art Institute on Friday evening. Notwithstanding the threatening weather the house was filled to its utmost capacity. The stage decorations were extremely tasteful and received much favorable comment. The programs, painted in green on white paper, and tied with green and white ribbons were quite unique in their way. The " closing exercises " were rather tame in comparison with those of the former classes. The faculty forbade all demonstrations, even going so far as to forbid the singing of the class song. The declamations on the program were all especially well rendered. The musical number, a harp selection by Miss Messinger was most heartily received. The judges were Messrs. E. S. Wells, Wm. Henry Smith and E. S. Skinner. They chose the following five for the final contest: Julia D. Brown, Louise M. Hopkins, Katharine J. Kenaga. Olive T. McClenahan, and Clayton W. Sherman The program, as rendered, follows:

PROGRAM.

Wat Tyler's Address to the King. - - Southey
Clayton W. Sherman.
The Legend Beautiful, - - - - Lonfellow
Katharine J. Kenaga.
Harp—Romance, - - - - - Schuecker
· Miss Messenger.
Crime its own Director, - - - - Webster
Clarence A. Coolidge.

The Painter of Seville, - - - - Wilson
Louise M. Hopkins.
MUSIC.
Hannibal on the Alps. - - - - - Swan
Olive F. McClenahan,
The March of the Mind, - - - - Bard
Frank C. Rogers,
The River, - - - - - - - -
Julia D. Brown.
MUSIC.
Decision of Judges.
Gradu diversa, una via..

TOWN TOPICS.

The Art Institute met last Tuesday at the home of Mr. Amzi Benedict. Dr. Haven read an interesting paper.

Mrs. E. F. Chapin has charge of the Illinois exhibit of the Association of Collegiate Alumnæ for the World's Fair.

Mrs. Ralston gave a dinner Friday evening to a party of young people. Covers were laid for eight. The company afterward attended the Freshman Contest at the Art Institute.

Mr. Frank Hall and family will return this week to Lake Forest. Mr. Hall will make Lake Forest his permanent residence. Prof. Stuart will, for the present, live with his family at Academia.

Lake Foresters will be glad to learn that there is to be a new means of communication with Chicago. Thursday of last week the Grand Central Railway Company was incorporated at Springfield, one of the promoters being Mr. J. V. Farwell, of Lake Forest. The railroad will be operated by electricity. In addition to other roads, a branch will be run up the north shore to Waukegan, starting at some point on the north side. The advantages of another railroad are evident; but the advantages of this road will exceed everybody's fondest hope. It is said that the trains will run seventy miles an hour. Not only will trains be faster, but they will be more frequent than those to which Lake Forest has been accustomed for so many years, while, at the same time, rates of travel, freight and express will be cheaper. Lake Forest may truly be satisfied if such a road materializes.

WORLD'S FAIR ITEMS.

The World's Fair has indeed been aptly named " The Eighth Wonder of the World." The spectacle which at present commands the attention of the whole world, which brings the Moslem far from the country of sacred Mecca, and, most remarkable of all, causes the devout Hindu to step from his holy native land and traverse the sea, such a spectacle is, indeed, worthy to rank with Diana's great temple, the Pharos at Alexandria, or the ancient Pyramids by the Nile. The same thought might be said of any of the main buildings, which in themselves are wonders of art and architecture.

As the special STENTOR reporter stepped through the side entrance of the Manufactures Building one rainy day last week, his first impression was one of immensity. Here, under one roof, was the life and the business of a city. The roar and the bustle was worthy of a great city. On every side were buildings of innumerable varieties. Wagons and trucks were rolling over the floor, and through the middle of the building a switch engine kept puffing and working.

The reporter was, however, suddenly awakened from the reverie on immensity by a "plunk" on the upper side of his hat, which nearly broke it in. Looking up, he discovered away up near the regions of the roof a solitary drop of rain water dropping right toward his face. So he stepped aside to wait for the drop to fall, which struck this time a puddle in the floor, which had been slowly accumulating at the rate of two drops a minute for about two weeks.

In taking a general view of the building, the first object that strikes the eye is the clock tower in the center, which is nearly 100 feet in height, yet seems small. This, when completed, will have under it soda fountains and a candy booth.

Around it rose up obelisks and columns of various designs, the whole group together forming a fit focus of interest. Below, however, was a scene of confusion. Workmen were hustling and scrambling among the tangled mass of unopened exhibits. The exhibits were packed carefully in wooden boxes, bearing a poster marked with a large hand with the flag of the nation from which it came.

At one place a group of men was seen pulling at a rope, which in a graceful curve reached up and up, until lost to sight. The reporter, by close inspection, made out what he supposed was a man on a rafter near the roof, but what the man was doing was beyond the power of sight.

The STENTOR correspondent passed on, carefully avoiding puddles of water, and pausing here and there to remark upon points of interest. On the whole, comparatively few booths with their exhibits were completed. On inquiring of a prepossessed Austrian what a certain gateway of iron represented, the special reporter was rebuffed with the unaccountably gruff reply: "Nicht speak English."

On a door near by, evidently the foreman's headquarters, the notice: " Positively no beer sold here." Probably the surliness of the Austrian accounted for.

The Japanese were the first to have their exhibit completed. The booth of Japan is typical; of massive wooden architecture, and of gaudy colors. The whole is surmounted by that levable bird, which, to an American, is indefinable—a development of Japanese imagination. It might be denominated a dragon, but a dragon has four feet and a pair of wings. This wonderful object had a full complement of feathers, but only two feet.

One original stove firm had erected as a booth a huge cooking stove, nearly 30 feet high, which might well roast a Cyclops' shaggy sheep, or indeed his whole flock.

The reporter now left the confusion of the Manufactures Building, and began to turn his steps homeward. He stopped for a minute at the Japanese Village on the Midway Plaisance. The Japanese were, unhappily, absent, kept in their hotel by the inclement weather. Their houses, however, were there, in the shape of a rectangle, with the main gate in the middle of one side. On either side of the main gate was a tiny box of a house, made of bamboo and matting. Here were the police stations. From the ceiling of one hung a large wooden fish, reaching to the ground. The fish was hollow, and when beaten gave forth a resounding, rounded tone, not harsh, but penetrating. When the guard beats it, the whole town comes running, knowing that danger of some sort is on hand—fire, tiger, or enemy. This exhibit is made by a Holland trading company, to introduce Japanese commerce into the U. S. The STENTOR representative, having determined to come again when the Japanese were home, hurried off to his train, and was soon back in Chicago, although but shortly before in Austria, England, far away Java, and almost every other country. Such is the wonder of the World's Fair.

FERRY HALL.

Where *are* the serenaders?

"It rains and the wind is never weary."

'Tis grip that makes our heads go round.

Dancing in the Gym. seems to lag as spring comes on.

Coffee was served in Miss Bennett's room Wednesday evening to a few of her friends.

Miss Grace Minty, of Minneapolis, spent two days this last week with Miss Florence Slayton.

Miss Walter Larned has generously added to the parlors by giving us a handsome picture on a large ebony easel.

Misses Edna Smith, Ina Scott, Mildred Lyon, Conger, Orvis, and Nightingale, were among the girls missed over Sunday.

Mrs. Seely received word Thursday evening of the extreme illness of her mother. Mrs. Seeley has the heartiest sympathy of the girls in her trouble.

Miss Nellie Dillin has gone home to attend the wedding of her sister, Miss Cora, who was Ferry Hall girl last year. She takes with her the best wishes of us all for the happiness of the future Mrs. Watts.

Doctor Seely has very kindly allowed us to have one of the pianos in the parlor. So often now, between six-thirty and study hour, one can hear "sweet music in our drawing rooms," and we even have the good fortune at times to persuade Prof. Eager to make that piano talk to us as only he can; then the girls sing or play, and altogether the hour is a very pleasant and refreshing one.

Excitement ran high over here the other night, and all on account of woman's most unconscious enemy the mouse. About two o'clock in the morning room 238 echoed and re-echoed with the cries of frightened maids. "The awful thing ran right across my pillow!" "Oh, I shudder when I think it is still in the room!" and like exclamations were distinguishable. Peace was finally restored, and the first streaks of dawn fell upon a poor little chip-munk curled up in the corner.

Friday evening, April 21st, at the suggestion of Miss Norten, the girls entertained themselves in a way that has been quite neglected in Ferry Hall this year. Three or four light charades were given on the stage in the gym. by some twenty girls, in the acting of which it was well proven that, though undeveloped, there is considerable talent among the girls for this sort of thing. It would be well to do it oftener, for it not only helps the girl who acts to be self-contained and graceful, but it sharpens the wits of the audience to guess her well planned subterfuges.

Thursday evening Ferry Hall doors were opened for one of the swellest events of the season. The Juniors gave a reception and banquet in honor of the Seniors. At nine o'clock, after a pleasant hour of gossip (?) the company turned to the dining room, where a very pretty sight greeted them. In the middle of the room was a centre table upon which flowers, bon bons, and class colors were arranged, grouped around this were sixteen smaller tables at which the guests were seated. One of the fire places at the end of the room was decorated in purple and white, the colors of '93, with the class flower and ribbons; tne other represented the class of '94 with the marguerites and ribbons of yellow and white. The banquet was served by Kinsley. At the close, Miss Clark, as toast master, announced responses to the following toasts: "The relation between Seniors and the University," Dr. McClure. "The relation between Seniors and Ferry Hall," Dr. Seeley. "The Senior Class as I have found it," Miss McWilliams. "The Senior Class in relation to the Junior Class." Miss Brinkman.

ACADEMY.

T. W. Harvey was confined to his room with eye troubles a few days last week.

Those who formerly composed the Caesar Class have purchased a bust of Caesar which will be placed in the Latin room.

Jaeger was in the city Wednesday, meeting his parents on their return trip from the South, where they have been spending the winter.

The ball teams of Erskine and Kline played a match game last Tuesday afternoon, the score resulting 20 to 6 in favor of the former.

Since the reorganization of the Field Day Committee, Messrs. Richards and Harvey have been appointed as members from the Academy.

A large number of the students attended the Freshman contest last Friday evening. It was voted a disappointment, as no war-like spirit between '95 and '96 manifested itself.

It is said the Academy societies greatly disturb the College classes by their noisy exit from the College Chapel. As it has been done through thoughtlessness heretofore, it will of course be stopped in the future.

The Anabasis Class will purchase a bust of Xenophon to adorn their class-room. The names of the members of the class will be placed upon it, that future generations may know who were the donors, and who their worthy predecessors.

The ball game between the Sophomores and the Academy last Friday evening resulted in a Waterloo for the Academy. The Cads did as well as could be expected for their first game, pitcher Laughlin's arm not being in shape and Jaeger having not as yet returned to his "old-time form."

Someone with the shape of "The Black Crook" and a face as dark as the night was wandering around the dormitory last Thursday evening. Going to the President's house he demanded money, but "Wild Bill" appeared with a six-shooter of the latest pattern, and sent the stranger away empty handed.

Last Thursday evening one of the tables at Mitchell Hall raised a mutual benefit fund, and with the proceeds purchased a spread. Six courses were served, and mirth, pleasure and plenty reigned supreme. The following were present: Baker, Cutler, Wiley, Fred Smith, Lamberton, Heineman, Kilgour, Rice, Thornton, Prof. Jack.

The Field Day Committee report about twenty entries from the Academy for the various prizes. This shows an interest in athletics, as no effort has been made to get the boys out until within the last week. Had there been someone to work among the boys earlier no doubt a great deal of systematic training would have been done.

At a special meeting of the faculty Monday morning their former action was rescinded and a holiday was granted to the students. The announcement, however, was made too late to allow the students to get into the city in time to see anything of the exercises.

THE STENTOR.

VOLUME VI.   MAY 9, 1893.   NUMBER 26.

CAVOUR.

By Addison A. Hopkins, of Lake Forest University.

BIOGRAPHICAL.

Addison A. Hopkins was born April 17, 1868, at Bloomington, Ind. Mr. Hopkins has always been an earnest student of oratory and debate. He took his preparatory course at the Denver High School and his freshman year at Denver University. At both of these schools he was always successful in public debates. In 1890 Mr. Hopkins entered the Sophomore Class of Lake Forest University. Since that time his record as a public speaker and orator has been noteworthy. In June, 1891, he won the second prize in the Freshman-Sophomore declamation contest.

Last May he received the appointment from the college contest to represent Lake Forest in the State Contest which met at Champaign Oct. 6th. He was there chosen to represent Illinois in the Inter-State Oratorical Contest.

THE ORATION.

Delivered at the Inter-State Oratorical Contest at Columbus, Ohio, taking first prize.

JUDGES.

THOUGHT AND COMPOSITION.

Dr. Carl W. Belser, University of Michigan.
Dr. T. C. Chamberlain, University of Colorado.
Pres. Chas. F. Thwing, Western Reserve University.

DELIVERY.

Rev. R. J. A. Ronthaler, Indianapolis.
Pres. S. F. Neff, Neff College of Oratory, Philadelphia.
Judge D. F. Pugh, Columbus.

In 451, when Attila, King of the Huns, laid waste all Italy with a devastation that gained him the title of "The Scourge of God," the power and grandeur of ancient Rome had vanished forever. The mighty empire, brought forth under most auspicious circumstances, maintaining its intregity and nationality for ten centuries, overcoming nations, dethroning kings, and bearing its ensigns to every part of the known world, was at last so weakened by vice and corruption that she became an easy prey to the advancing hordes of her conqueror.

Althoug Venice, Genoa, Florence and Rome figured prominently in the great dramas of the Middle Ages, the Italian nation was no more. Possessing no power, having no leader, ground under the iron heel of relentless tyrants, bought and sold by intriguing dynasties, torn and dismembered by petty conquerors, Italy lay for centuries beneath a galling yoke, hopeless, motionless and benumbed. Years rolled on, but brought no help nor hope to Italy. Her roads, deeply furrowed by the chariot wheels of a hundred triumphs, lay covered with ruins. The centuries known as the Middle Ages passed away, but Italy still lay prostrate. The Seventeenth Century beheld the monarchies of Western Europe rise to the zenith of their strength. The Eighteenth smiled upon the islands of the North. But when the Nineteenth, with its spirit of freedom, was ushered in, the shackles of slavery fell clanging to the ground and the tyranical yoke of Italy was rent asunder. Her day of revolution was fast approaching. The time when she was to be aroused from her miserable, hopeless condition was at hand.

There appeared a man of the ancient Roman race, to which proud lineage he not only did honor, but gave additional lustre. He was silent, wise, faithful, not easily moved from his purpose, always armed with infallible logic, a faithful friend, a terrible, irreconcilable enemy and more inclined to actions than to words. Fondly cherishing the hope of a united nation, (of which former patriots had only dreamed,) he stepped forward with the political sagacity of a tried statesman to bring about the desired result. Imprisoned when a youth for declaring in favor of liberty, rising from obscurity to the position of Prime Minister, he counseled kings, commanded generals, aroused patriots, and finally regenerated entire Italy and bound her together under a national constitution. That man was Camillo Bensi di Cavour.

Italy was divided among the Hapsburgs and Bourbons. The Emperor of Austria held Lombardy and Venice. Other members of the Austrian House contended over Parma, Tuscany and Modena, while the Bourbons held sway over Naples and Sicily. The little republic of San Marino, looking sadly over the waters of the Adriatic, was all that was left to remind Italy of her former grandeur and independence. Indeed, the Italians were nothing more than slaves under the Austrian lash. Twenty millions of human beings, gifted with ardent, noble natures, similar in social life, speaking the same language, animated by the same glorious records of their ancestors, were held as vassals by rulers who were strangers to their institutions.

Such was the political condition of Italy when Count Cavour appeared before his countrymen as a patriot of one idea—*the unification of Italy*. Difficult as were the perplexing problems he was called to solve, he unhesitatingly accepted them as a God-given mission. Believing that political revolutions, to be permanent must be inaugurated by moral reforms, he began with his pen, condemning the oppressive tyranny of Austria and demanding for his country, a government, a chamber and a constitution. Hissed by the populace, opposed by the aristocracy, misunderstood by the Cabinet, having at times only the king in his favor, with cool judgment he stood firm to his principles and conquered by the indomitable power of his genius.

On the 19th of April, 1859, Austria dispatched an ultimatum to Piedmont demanding recognition or war. Cavour unhesitatingly chose the latter. To array a small and poorly equipped province of four millions against a powerful nation of forty would be defeat and ruin. Cavour, thoroughly acquainted with the relations existing between European nations,

saw the only chance for Italy. To make an attack on Austria was to encounter the whole German Empire. Cavour, with a shrewdness seldom equalled, fanned to a flame the long existing, but ill-concealed hatred between France and Germany. He convinced Napoleon III. that by an alliance with Italy an opportunity would be given to strike a blow at his deadly enemy. The alliance was formed. The French-Italian army met the Austrians at Magenta and answered the ultimatum with a glorious victory. Napoleon counted it a victory for France. But Italy and the world saw that the Austrian power was broken and Italian unity was not far distant.

Cavour's fame was won. He was no longer an unpopular minister, hissed and jeered by the throng. Henceforth his history was the history of Italy. His name passed from lip to lip. His enemies became his ardent admirers and friends. " Viva l'Italia!" "Cavour the Liberator!" were re-echoed and reverberated from the Alps to Etna. All Europe beheld in wonder the brilliant success of a man swayed by lofty sentiments, influenced by strong convictions, and urged to duty by the masterful principles of liberty and independence.

Although the name of our Statesman had become illustrious at the beginning of his great work, it was soon to be shadowed and defamed by merciless accusations of impetuous, short-sighted opponents. The ultimatum had been answered, yet the Austrians remained strongly entrenched in the Valley of Po with a Bourbon army threatening in the south, Russia and Prussia hostile and nothing expected from neutral England. France alone remained friendly. For services rendered she demanded the cession of Nice and Savoy, which would straighten her southeastern boundary and add to her domain two cities which were almost entirely French. To refuse this demand at such a time, to the only friend and ally of Italy, would have ruined every hope of regeneration and unity. Yet Cavour hesitated. Why did he hesitate? If he refused to sign the treaty he would loose the support of France, the only power in Europe that was friendly to Italian unity. If he signed it he would encounter the calumny and abuse of Garibaldi and his followers. Garibaldi was a native of Nice, and if Nice were signed away he would be a foreigner. Cavour loved that noble general and patriot as Italy loved him. Will he sacrifice this love to save his country? Will Cavour, the only man who realizes Italy's awful danger forsake her now? Will he abandon that noble struggle for which he has so long contended because of the slander and opprobrium which awaited him? By no means. Having laid himself upon the altar of his country he did not reserve fame, friendship or popularity. He rose to the heroic sublimity of personal sacrifice and self-abnegation, signed the treaty, and Italy was saved.

The storm of discontent which followed was overwhelming. It descended upon that one man like an Alpine avalanche. The events which transpired in the Chamber were most thrilling. General Garibaldi, aroused to madness by the signing away of his native city, poured forth a volley of invectives which was fired by a passionate spirit as uncontrollable as it was generous. Our hero in the midst of this storm maintained the calm, dignified, immovable, magnanimous bearing which only the noblest can command. And yet his spirit, under that upbraiding attack, seemed crushed. From that time forth he seldom smiled. He was hated by one he loved. But as the black clouds of that storm passed away, his untarnished fame beamed forth in all the brightness of its orignal splendor, like a jewel in the crown of Italy brightened by its rubbing.

The work of this man was herculean. Rising at four in the morning he seldom retired until twelve at night. That slight form, with its spirit flashing from dark, deep set eyes, could be seen hurrying from office to office, giving orders, dictating messages, equipping volunteers, directing operations on the field, and at the same time inspiring the despondent and rousing the lukewarm to rally round the standard of regenerated Italy. Although his ardent spirit seemed ceaseless in its activity, the

strength of the body in which it dwelt was almost spent. Upon the 2nd of June, 1861, the day appointed by the government for the celebration of the grand achievement of Italian unity, amid the public rejoicings of a happy people, Cavour returned home to die. Never was rejoicing turned more suddenly into mourning. Never did Italy at the bier of a hero give vent to such deep feelings of sorrow or shed such bitter tears as at the tomb of her liberator. A wail of grief arose from the midst of an afflicted people as the form of their beloved patriot was laid in the grave.

Search the records of the mighty Roman Empire for a soldier, celebrated it may be in heroic song, who has done so much for Italy! What man in the mighty past ever toiled against such opposition? Sulla conquered foreign enemies, but Sulla passed to his throne of power through streets crimsoned with the blood of his friends. Nero found Rome of brick and left it of marble, but Nero was a bloodthirsty tyrant. Cicero could advocate a cause with mastering eloquence, but Cicero's motives were selfish and personal. Cæsar, the greatest Roman that ever lived, conquered Gaul, amassed great fortunes in Spain, and ruled the empire justly. But, controlled by an unbridled ambition, Cæsar was slain by the hand of conspirators, " and there were none so poor to do him reverence." Cavour lived for his country; labored for one grand idea; was urged on to duty by one pure motive. Never desiring power, he sacrificed property, fame, reputation, ambition, life, upon his country's altar, and died beloved and lamented by a regenerated, united, powerful nation.

The announcements of the Lake Geneva Students' Conference this summer have come out, and it is hoped that a large number may go from L. F. The opportunities this summer are unusually advantageous, and the terms are very low. Last year Lake Forest had the honor of being the banner college, sending more students in proportion to its members than any other college. The conference is from Friday, June 23, to Sunday, July 2.

PUBLISHED EVERY WEEK
BY THE

LakeForestUniversityStentorPublishingCo.

BOARD OF EDITORS.

B. R. MacHatton, '95............Managing Editor
Forest Grant, '96 ......Ass't Mgr. Ed. and Athletic
Harry Goodman, '94............Business Manager
A. B. Burdick, '95   ⎫
J. H. Jones, '96   ⎬ ....Locals
David Fales, Jr., '96 ⎭
W. B. Smith, '94 .... Alumni and Exchange
R. G. McKinnie, '97 .... Academy
Miss Tena Kennedy, ... Ferry Hall
J. A. McGaughey, '95 .... Advertising

Terms—$1.50 per year. Single Copies—10c

————Address————

STENTOR PUBLISHING COMPANY,

LAKE FOREST, : : ILLINOIS.

Entered at the P. O. at Lake Forest, Ill., as second-class matter.

LAKE FOREST WINS THE INTER-STATE ORATORICAL CONTEST.

ADDISON A. HOPKINS THE CHAMPION.

The prize orators from Wisconsin, Iowa, Nebraska, Missouri, Colorado, Minnesota, Indiana, Kansas, Ohio and Illinois met to do battle for the Oratorical Championship at Columbus, Ohio, the night of May 5th. Illinois came out on top of the heap, and to Lake Forest University, with Mr. Hopkins as her representative, belongs the credit of Illinois' victory.

It can easily be seen by the tabulated result given below that the contest was close and exciting. Our orator won by the narrow margin of five points. The Stentor, figuratively speaking, shakes hands with Mr. Hopkins, and predicts for him a great future. Below is given the result of the markings:

JUDGES. ON THOUGHT.	Ill.	Wis.	Ohio	Ind.	Kan.	Iowa	Minn.	Neb.	Miss.	Mo.
C. F. Thwing.........	3	5	1	7	4	2	9	8	10	6
C. W. Belser.........	3	7	9	2	1	5	4	10	8	6
T. C. Chamberlain....	4	7	8	1	2	5	3	6	9	10

ON DELIVERY.										
S. F. Neff	1	2	3	4	6	9	10	5	7	8
J. A. Ronthaler.......	3	2	1	9	10	4	5	6	7	8
D. F. Pugh...........	4	1	3	7	10	9	8	5	2	6
Total	18	24	25	30	33	34	39	40	43	44

In the final reckoning above, the least count gives first place.

What was the secret of Mr. Hopkins' success? It might truly be said that he has all of the qualifications of the ideal orator, but the real secret of his success lies in that simple word, *work*. It took energy to win that contest. We have it from his own lips that his victory was the result of four years' hard and earnest work. One may be brilliant, may have all the qualifications which go to make up the successful well-equipped man, but to be successful one must have an untiring energy. Work, work—success never comes to drones.

THE ORATORICAL CONTEST.
(Special to The Stentor)

Columbus, O., May 5th.

The oratorical contest at Columbus brought together over a thousand bright and jovial college students from ten different States of the Union.

Their headquarters were made at the Neil House, where the lobbies were filled at all hours of the day and night. Some trouble was had in securing judges on delivery, but by Thursday afternoon all arrangements were completed. The contest was held in the Grand Opera House. The large building was filled to its fullest capacity with an enthusiastic and appreciative audience. The contest was close and exciting. The program was interesting from the beginning to the close.

It clearly demonstrated the fact that college oratory was of a very high order, and the efforts of each year were raising the standard higher and higher. As each orator stepped forward and delivered his speech it was evident that the contest would be won on a narrow margin.

It can be fairly said that there were but two poorly written orations on the program. The efforts of Mr. Kimball, of Wisconsin, and Jones, of Ohio, were grand, their subjects being interesting and eloquent; their style of delivery was oratorical and powerful, and they presented a very fine appearance on the rostrum. Their weak points were in their voices, which showed huskiness and lack of training. It would be no disgrace or dishonor to occupy a low position in the list of college orators that met in contest at Columbus.

The decision of the judges was not rendered until the late hour of 12:30. After the large audience had dispersed the students met again in the banquet hall of the Normandie. Here an elaborate spread was enjoyed until the small hour of 3:15, when the intellectual feast of toasts from the delegates of the ten states, began. The responses were bright and spicy. The Ohio delegate gave an elaborate account of the greatness of Ohio and of Ohio's great men. While Colorado's representative surpassed himself and every one who ever came from Colorado in narrating startling and extravagant stories. The banquet broke up at the early hour of 4:45 A. M., which brought to a close the greatest college event of the year.

THE ACADEMY CONTEST.

The annual contest between the Tri Kappa and Gamma Sigma societies of the Academy took place Tuesday evening, May 2nd. The contests in the past have always been exciting, but, owing to the apparent eveness in the abilities of the declamers and debaters, more interest than usual was manifested in this one, and the Art Institute held one of the largest audiences that has assembled to witness any of Lake Forest's entertainments during the present school year.

The committee on decorations made a pleasant variation from the manner in which the hall has always been decorated at previous contests, and, instead of using the colors of the societies, used the Academy colors, orange and black, which made a very pleasing effect hanging in loops at the back of the stage,

along the sides of the assembly rooms, and from pillar to pillar in the entrance hall. The pillars at either side of the entrance were also wrapt with the Academy colors.

Flowers were tastefully arranged at the sides and back of the stage, materially adding to the appearance of the hall.

The large audience was composed of the cultured of Chicago and Lake Forest. Principal Smith presided, Dr. McClure occupying a seat at his right.

The exercises opened with prayer by Dr. Clure.

Tomaso's Mandolin Orchestra, of Chicago, then rendered a musical selection, after which the essays were delivered, Mr. Baker coming first, followed by Mr. Harvey. The latter surpassed the former in thought and expression, and also in delivery. Both essays were remarkable for Academy students, and surpassed any that have ever been presented by the societies.

After music by the orchestra, the declamations were rendered, Mr. Cutler speaking first, following him Mr. Heineman, he in turn being followed by Mr. Durand, Mr. Bournique coming last on the program. Each and every contestant delivered his selection remarkably well, and to those who are not experienced in this line of work it would indeed have been hard to tell who the winners would be. To illustrate how close the race was for first prize we have but to quote the markings of the three highest contestants, all of which fell between 87 and 89 per cent, and also the fact that Messrs. Bournique and Durand tied for first place, the latter winning only on account of his having a higher average per cent.

Mr. Cutler's declamation, although not taking a prize, is deserving of mention. It was a fine piece of work and showed ability. Mr. Cutler has a graceful presence and an easy manner on the stage.

The debate showed careful preparation. Mr. Cooke had the affirmative and acquitted himself in a most creditable manner. His delivery was good and he had his points well in hand. Mr. Roberts supported the negative. He had an excellent debate, but his delivery was not as graceful as Mr. Cooke's.

When the decision of the judges was announced each society cheered lustily whenever it obtained an honor, but when the Tri Kappa's knew that they had won a majority of the honors and the banquet, a deafening and ear-splitting yell, which can only be likened unto the savage war whoop of a band of Apache Indians, took a hasty flight towards the rafters and echoed and re-echoed throughout the building.

Principal Smith, when asked to give his opinion of the contest replied, "It was in my opinion the closest and hardest fought contest I have ever witnessed between the two societies. While the Tri Kappas won, the Gamma Sigmas acquitted themselves nobly and showed a marked improvement over the last two contests. They really gained victory in defeat, as from their remarkably fine showing they can take renewed courage and go in and win the next one."

President Flint of the Tri Kappas was highly elated. "We won," he said, "simply from the fact that we worked incessantly day and night. No stone was left unturned to accomplish our purpose, and—we won."

President Graham of the Gamma Sigma society said, "While we may feel pretty sore at present, we are not disheartened, but will buckle on our armor for the fight next year, and prepare for it at once. We gave them a close chase, and hope by work and perseverance to make it closer a year hence."

COMMUNICATION.

Editor of Stentor:

In the *Red and Black* of April 28 appeared an article in which I was quoted as saying "that the only difference between Mr. Bethels oration on Cavour and mine was the last part of the title." This was a mistatement. I did say that some portions of his oration were similar to some of my own, which is true. But the article in the *Red and Black* conveys a wrong impression. I do not, nor I have not accused Mr. Bethel of any unfairness. If such an impression has been made I hope it will be corrected.   A. A. HOPKINS.

WORLD'S FAIR ITEMS.

Through a compositor's error, the word "Japanese" was used in place of "Javanese" in the "Items" of last week, thus making it appear that there was a Japanese exhibit on the Midway Plaisance, and that it was operated by a Dutch Trading Co. The national Japanese exhibit is on the north end of the wooded isle, and is conducted through the ruling of the Japanese legislature. There the observer may see the temple, or Hooden, and if he had been looking there about four months ago he would have seen the nimble Japanese workmen in their variegated, many-colored native dress working at the building. The temple, situated as it is in the greenwood and filled with costly relics and treasures of the Mikado, forms one of the most attractive foreign exhibits in the grounds. As a curiosity of laborious, painstaking and elaborate detail alone, it is worth careful scrutiny.

In the catalogue of big things at the Fair, three immense American flags are surely worthy of recognition. Their great size will not be noticeable in comparison with surrounding objects, but they are large enough when seen near at hand; each stripe is over three feet in width, while the bunting has been made extra strong. Even then it is expected they will wear out in two or three months. One of the flags will be on a pole in front of the Administration building, another near the Government building, and a third in front of the Art Hall.

The poles on which they are hung will probably gain the attention of but few. They are, however, quite remarkable for their size and perfectness. The State of Washington offered the Fair Commissioners all the pine flag-poles they wanted, and these are the tallest of the nineteen which the Commissioners accepted. They are single sticks of fir nearly 150 feet high, without a flaw. If they were not so perfect they would not be able to sustain the weight of the crowns. These crowns are, as a rule, large gilded eagles, but on the three poles in front of the Administration building, models of the three ships of Columbus have been perched. Such flag-poles would, in a country town, long be objects of admiration and pride, but to the great part of the crowds they will not be worth more than a glance. Such is the overflowing abundance and satiety of sights at Jackson Park.

COLLEGE.

L. F. U. CALENDAR.

Oratorical Association Contest, May 23.
Annual Senior Reception, May 26.
Academy Commencement Exercises, June 9.
Annual Academy Reception, June 10.
Annual Concert at Ferry Hall, June 12.
Freshmen-Sophomore Prize Speaking, June 12.
Commencement Exercises at Ferry Hall, June 13.
Senior Class Day, June 13.
Junior Contest in Oratory, June 13.
College Commencement Exercises, June 14.
Alumni Banquet, June 14.
President's Reception. June 14.

Many of the students spent "opening" day in Chicago.

We came very near having a pleasant day for Field Day.

'96 was strictly "in it" on Field Day. They took seven first and six second prizes.

Prof. Stuart very kindly excused the Sophomore Latin class from recitation on Field Day.

Charles Thom, '95, returned last Wednesday and expects to finish the term at Lake Forest.

Remember that you can buy Birch beer, Orange cider, Ho Ko, etc., in the college building.

The Academy societies were more closely matched this year than they have ever been before.

The subject of the Y. M. C. A. meeting for Tuesday evening was "City Missions." A. F. Waldo was leader.

Too little interest is manifested in track athletics. We have several first class runners and plenty of undeveloped material. Lake Forest is sadly in need of an outdoor running track of some description, and the only way she will ever get it will be for the students to take the matter in hand and rush it through.

J. J. Johnson, a former member of '93, has returned to Lake Forest with the intention of finishing his college course.

Those who are interested in declamation and oratory will find a first class article in the May number of *Werners Voice*, entitled "A helpful condition in vocalizing."

At a special meeting of the Faculty Friday afternoon it was decided to hold the Commencement exercises on Thursday, June 15, in order that Dr. Coulter might attend. At that time the valedictorian and salutatorian of the class will deliver their orations. On Monday the six who have received the highest marks on the thought and composition of their oration will compete for the McClure medal.

The annual Field Day events came off last Wednesday afternoon. The following are the events with winners and records. One hundred yards dash, D. H. Jackson, time 10 4-5; running broad jump, Bourns, 17 feet 8 inches; mile walk, Hunt, time 8:43 2-5; half mile run, Rossiter, time 2:23 1-5; standing broad jump, D. H. Jackson, 9 feet 4 inches; 220 yd. dash, D. H. Jackson, time 2:23 1-5; punting foot ball, Marcotte, 118½ feet; 120 yd. hurdle, D. H. Jackson, time 20 seconds; mile run, Rossiter, time 5:25; 440 yds. dash, A. O. Jackson, 60 3-5 seconds; base-ball throw, Gilleland, 285¾ feet; putting shot, Woolsey, 31⅓ feet; running high jump, Sherman, record 4 feet 10 inches; class relay race, won by the Junior class.

Our representative at Columbus, A. A. Hopkins, took first prize at the inter-state contest. J. H. Kimball, of Beloit, Wisconsin, took second, and M. J. Jones, of Wooster, Ohio, took third. The judges on thought and composition were Dr. C. N. Belser of the University of Colorado, Dr. T. C. Chamberlain of the University of Chicago, and President Charles F. Thwing of the Western Reserve University. The judges on delivery were the Rev. J. A. Routhaber of Indianapolis, President Challis of the School of Oratory, Philadelphia, and the Rev. Washington Gladden of Columbus. The

oratorical program was as follows: Missouri—
"National Perils," W. J. Williamson, William
Jewell College. Kansas—" The Philosophy
of Reform," W. C. Coleman, Kansas State
Normal. Illinois—" Cavour," A. A. Hopkins,
Lake Forest University. Indiana—" The Im-
migrant and the Republic," Hugh H. Hadly,
De Pauw University. Ohio—" The Greatness
of Personality," Myron J. Jones, University of
Wooster. Minnesota — " Wendell Phillips,"
Charles S. Patler, Minnesota State University.
Iowa—" Webster and the Constitution," F. A.
Heizer, Parsons College. Colorado—" The
Poet's Mission, Frank W. Woods, Colorado
College. Nebraska—" Patriotism and Bro-
therhood," Thomas E. Wing, State University.
Wisconsin—" The Judgments of History," J.
H. Kimball, Beloit College. After the contest
an elaborate banquet was given, at which toasts
were responded to by representatives of the
several states contesting and by some of the
distinguished guests present. The STENTOR
extends most hearty congratulations to Mr.
Hopkins, and also thanks him for the honor he
has conferred upon Lake Forest by his victory.

The Sophomore contest which occurred last
Friday evening was a success in every sense of
the word. Every speaker showed good,
honest, systematic work, and did honor to the
careful training of Prof. Booth. The following contestants were chosen by the judges to
represent '95 in the June contest: Burdick,
Graff, Henry, Lewis, and MacHatton. Following is the program of the evening:—

PROGRAM.

Music,	- - - - -	Selected
	Mr. Greienstein.	
William Tell,	- - - - -	Anon.
	Ellis U. Graff.	
The Missouri Compromise not a True Peace,		Beecher
	Abigail Davies.	
The Results of the American War	-	- Fox
	Edward E. Vance.	
Music,	- - - - -	Selected
	Class Quartette.	
Selected: " Last Days of Pompeii,"	-	Lytton
	Albert E. Burdick.	
Mrs. O'Toole and the Conductor,	-	- Anon
	Nona Phelps	

Liberty and Union,	- - - -	Webster
	Burtis R. MacHatton.	
Music,	- - - - -	Selected
	Miss June Brett.	
Idols,	- - - - -	Phillips
	E. U. Henry.	
Hand Car 412,	- - - - -	Heard
	Dean Lewis.	
A Legend of Cologne,	- -	Bret Harte
	Edna Hays.	
	Class Song.	
	Decision of Judges.	

While the judges were out the class octette
sang the class song, which was one of the best
ever given in Lake Forest. A representation
of the different classes was given by some of
the boys of '95, Mr. Mellen representing '93,
Mr. Hayner, '94, Mr. Parish, '95, and Mr. Mc-
Neal, '96. Mr. Smith acted as instructor. A
great deal of amusement was gained and the
awkward interim was very agreeably filled in.

TOWN TOPICS.

Sartell Prentice spent Sunday at the home
of Mr. Day.

Miss Garrett is visiting with Miss Florence
Durand.

Miss Dixon, of Westerly, R. I., is staying
with Mrs. McClure.

Miss Mary Roberts is now visiting Mrs.
Larned at Blair Lodge.

Mrs. Shirley V. Martin has returned to
Lake Forest from her trip South.

Mr. F. C. Aldrich is building a two-story
addition on the rear of his house.

Mr. Watson and Mr. Fauntleroy acted as
judges for the field day events last week.

Mr. Thomas Hall staid at Mr. Yoggy's last
Tuesday night, having come up to act as judge
on the Academy contest.

Mr. Alex has moved into his house on
Westminster Ave., which for some time has
been undergoing repairs. A roomy addition
has been built on, and the house has been improved in every way.

The water works on Westminster Ave. are being extended from the front of Mr. Fales' house to Mr. Warner's.

Mr. and Mrs. Cramer and family will come to Lake Forest for the summer, the first part of the week. They will occupy Mr. Well's house for the season.

Next Friday evening Lake Forest will have the opportunity of listening to Rev. J. G. Paton, who for thirty years has been missionary among the savages of the New Hebrides.

FERRY HALL.

Oh to be a Senior!

And still the parlors grow in beauty.

Miss May Stowell was present at the Sophomore contest.

Miss Theo Kane has given a piano lamp to the parlors.

Miss Kenaga enjoyed a visit from her mother and sisters April 29th.

Miss Holmes, a cousin of Miss Julia Brown, attended the Freshman contest.

Miss Grace Brubaker will graduate with the Senior Class of the Seminary in June.

How natural it seems to have it rain while we were on the ball grounds Wednesday.

Mrs. Seeley has our sincerest sympathy in her recent sorrow, the death of her mother.

Miss Hallie Hall, well-known among us, spent Sunday with her old room-mate, Miss Lyon.

Mrs. Hester was obliged to give up her classes Friday and submit to the universal foe, La Grippe.

The Misses Maud Taylor, Abbie Platt, Hallie Hall and Grace Taylor, all old girls, were guests at Ferry Hall last week.

The Senior classes of the Academy and of Ferry Hall were charmingly entertained at the home of Mrs. Reid Thursday evening.

The Misses Creswell, McCumber and Beatrice Taylor attended the commencement exercises of McCormick Seminary, May 4th.

We are very sorry that we are to lose from among us Miss Georgia Bennett. Her recent illness has made her unable to continue work this spring.

Prof. Clement, known in Lake Forest, and but recently of Ann Arbor, has accepted the position of instructor of ancient languages at the University of Idaho.

The Faculty have so arranged it that the four Wednesdays in May may be taken up by the girls to visit the Fair grounds. Several teachers will hold themselves in readiness each Wednesday to chaperone different parties. But those who remain in Ferry Hall will continue the regular classes on those days.

It was the good fortune of the Ferry Hall STENTOR correspondent to make one of the five thousand people at the B. Fay Mills meeting in the Milwaukee Exposition building April 30. The meetings are being conducted in the manner mentioned in THE STENTOR article April 25. One could not fail to be impressed at sight of such an audience sitting so quietly that the slightest sound might be heard, and truly Lake Forest should not only be proud but very happy at the result of Mr. Mills' work.

It was thought by the Faculty that a few informal talks on Art would be of advantage to those of us who have had no opportunity to study the history of Art as yet, or to become acquainted with its best examples, and that a mere outline of what had been done in the Art world would assist us to understand the treasures which we all expect to see in the Columbian Exposition. Accordingly Miss Robinson gave the first talk Tuesday evening on English Art, covering in outline the progress of English art from Hogarth's time to our own. Dr. Seeley followed on Thursday evening with sketches of German Art, dividing it into three periods for convenience—the art before Durer, work of Durer himself, and the modern school. Of the latter he read us some interesting notes of his own, written after frequent visits to the Gallery in Berlin. We are promised two next week—one from Mrs. Mallory on the Art of Holland, and one from Miss Norton on French Art. We greatly appreciate this kindness to us on the part of the Faculty.

ACADEMY.

The Cad team expect to play the Freshmen ball team in the near future.

The banquet for the winning society in the recent contest will in all probability occur next Friday evening.

Arthur Reid entertained the Senior Academy and Seminary classes and a few others last Thursday evening.

Since the contest the members of the faculty are giving longer lessons. Thus Cad life is always varied and interesting.

Newcomb's father visited him a few days last week. He made a very pleasant talk after chapel exercises Wednesday morning.

Warner has sufficiently recovered from his recent illness to again be able to enter school. His southern trip was very benificial to him.

Chandler was visited by his father last week. He is one of the oldest of the Academy students, having attended about the beginning of the civil war.

Sanford, a former Academy student and member of the Tri Kappa Society, attended the contest and spoke in a reminiscent way of the Academy in days gone by.

The Academy team played Highland Park Military School last Saturday, winning by the score of twenty-one to twenty. The last half of the ninth inning, which belonged to the Cad, was not played, and would probably have increased the score in their favor.

ALUMNI.

E. S. Chaffee, '92, and W. F. Love, '91, came over from McCormick to attend the Academy contest.

McCloud, '92, visited Lake Forest friends Tuesday and Wednesday of last week.

Billy Sanford, of Academy fame, was here to enjoy the Academy contest and the Field Day sports. His old friends say that he is the same old Billy.

Bert Conkil is engaged in missionary work in Mexico.

N. B. W. Galley, ex-'91, also graduated from McCormick.

Wilson Aul has won the McCormick Senior scholarship of $600.

Jos. Sutton, '91, has been licensed to preach the Presbyterian faith.

Dave McAlister graduated from McCormick last Thursday evening.

J. J. Johnson, ex-'93, will engage in S. S. work during the summer.

H. H. Davis, '91, is sporting a natty uniform and wheeling stout corpulent invalids about the Fair grounds.

Geo. W. Wright, '92, will insure people's lives on week days, and on Sunday he will try to persuade men to insure themselves.

Keyes Becker, '89, is one of the editors of the *Ram's Horn*. He is also doing valuable work on the *Inter Ocean* in his inimitable style.

G. W. Ellis, ex-'93, is making an honorable record for himself on the Amherst ball team. He has the best wishes of his many friends at Lake Forest.

Rev. S. F. Vance, '85, who has been preaching in the neighborhood of Chippewa Falls, was here last week visiting his brothers. He expects to spend some time abroad, perhaps in Germany.

'91. W. E. Danforth is back at his old haunts on the *Tribune*. He is acting as assistant to the city editor on the *Tribune's* World's Fair Bureau. He was a member of the Press Committee that went down into Indiana to meet the old Liberty Bell on its way to Chicago.

W. F. Lewis, '90, now attending Princeton Theological Seminary, won the Carter prize on a Hebrew exegesis of an assigned passage in the old text. The subject assigned this year was the Hebrew prophecy of Obadiah. Mr. Lewis has received and accepted a call to the Rodney Street Presbyterian Church, of Wilmington, Delaware. This church has a membership of 300. Mr. Lewis is certainly doing his share towards keeping up the reputation of Lake Forest's Alumni.

THE STENTOR.

VOLUME VI.　　　　　　MAY 16, 1893.　　　　　　NUMBER 27.

PUBLISHED EVERY WEEK

BY THE

Lake Forest University Stentor Publishing Co.

BOARD OF EDITORS.

B. R. MacHatton, '95............Managing Editor
Forest Grant, '96 ,......Ass't Mgr. Ed. and Athletic
Harry Goodman, '94.............Business Manager
A. B. Burdick, '95　}
J. H. Jones, '96　　}....................Locals
David Fales, Jr., '96 }
W. B. Smith, '94 ....Alumni and Exchange
R. G. McKinnie, '97 ....Academy
Miss Tena Kennedy, ...Ferry Hall
J. A. McGaughey, '95 ....Advertising

Terms—$1.50 per year. Single Copies—10c

————ADDRESS————

STENTOR PUBLISHING COMPANY,

LAKE FOREST, : : ILLINOIS.

Entered at the P. O. at Lake Forest, Ill., as second-class matter.

A mule can kick, but it takes brains and energy to carry an enterprise to success. Don't be a mule.

*_

It is not safe to judge the sweetness of a girl's disposition by a pleasant and agreeable little chat in the Ferry Hall parlors. Just watch her sometime when Madame or the Doctor takes away one or two of her privileges.

*_

Somewhere there is a city with sun-lit castles that rest on gold-lined clouds, and the land is the land of Hopes and Dreams. Most of us devote considerable time in drawing the plans and arranging the architectural designs for the building of these castles in this land. One division of the city is devoted to the Things We Mean To Do. We mean to be better men and women after a while. We mean to study

harder next year. We mean to settle down to earnestness of purpose in the near future. Once there was a man who died and went up to the city of hopes and dreams. When he came to take an inventory he found that his only eternal possessions consisted of the Things He Had Meant To Do.

*_

There is not an accomplishment more enchanting, nor one which adds more dignity and grace to a woman then a broad and liberal education. Whatever share of beauty she may be possessed of, whether she may have the tinge of Hebe on her cheek, vying in color with the damask rose, and breath as fragrant—whether she may be able to discourse sweet music and play Chopin's funeral march in a way to make one weep, still, unless she is endowed with a good, liberal education, all her personal charms and *luxurious* accomplishments will not count for much. A higher education gives a tone and character, a conversational power to woman. The whole list of female accomplishments are in their kind essential to the beauty and grandeur which go to make up the ideal woman. But that which has been justly esteemed by writers as the chief excellence in woman is a liberal education.

*_

Greeley once said: "Of all horned animals, deliver me from the college student." A rather strong assertion and probably prompted by prejudice. But remember, Mr. Greeley, that all college students are not alike. There is the man fresh from receiving his diploma who fondly imagines that the eyes of the world are upon him. He feels big, and has no fear whatever of his future career. He has only to say that he is a college man and he will be immediately received as the junior member of some law firm or business house. My friend, the world is looking for *men* not college graduates. Paste that in your hat when you go out to apply for your position in life. But by far the greater number of college students graduate with a feeling of humility and a willingness to undertake the smallest things. This is the right spirit. A four years course in college does not constitute an education. It is hardly a beginning.

Socrates was a wise man, he may even have gone slightly beyond the average college student in his research and reasoning, yet Socrates said, " There is *one* thing. I know, and that is, that I know nothing."

***

Charles Dudley Warner, speaking of the higher education for women, says: "Anxiety is exhibited in many quarters about women who are striving for the higher education usually given to college students. What is it for? What will they do with it? What will they become? The professions are already full; even that of teaching, the least desirable, will eventually, at the rate of supply, be overcrowded. There are more women now who write than there are who can read discriminatingly.

"Why urge so many into the higher education, the college training for which they will have, if the world goes on marrying, and baking, and sweeping, and keeping domestic establishments running, so little use? The question might be briefly answered, to make them women. In detail it might be added, to make them more interesting women, better company for themselves and others, fuller of resources for a life alone or a family life, with an intelligent appreciation of what is going on in the world.

"To improve the tone of society is excuse enough for the higher education, even if it were not desirable that typewriters should be intelligent. And beyond the needs of society, can it be doubted that if all the mothers of this generation were educated, capable or rightly directing the intellectual development of young minds, the next generation would show a marked improvement over the present?

"The disappointment about this education arises from misplaced expectations. It isn't the office of education to upset society, but to make it better. The professions can absorb a limited number only. Society needs an unlimited number of highly intelligent persons."

DR. PATON INTERVIEWED.

A FEW REMARKS FROM THE GREAT MISSIONARY.

THIS HIS FIRST VISIT TO AMERICA.

If simplicity is greatness, Dr. Paton is one of the greatest men of the century. In this hurrying age, such simplicity seems almost quaint; but no other personal attribute than this one which Dr. Paton possesses could accomplish such marvelous results among the childish and ignorant savages of the South Sea. A STENTOR representative, therefore, who had the opportunity both of dining and conversing with him, felt greatly favored. Everything Dr. Paton said was sincere and from the heart. His conversation was, therefore, distinct; there was no doubt as to its meaning.

WHAT HE THOUGHT OF AMERICA.

To a rather ambiguous question as to what he thought of America, Dr. Paton had but one answer. He saw the question in but one light. " I found America," he said, " much better than I expected. There is much more piety here than I thought there would be. We have very bad specimens from America in our islands; the traders, who bring the cursed rum. In some of our islands every native is a devout spiritual Christian; but the traders are bringing in great evils. Yes, there is a great work to be done there."

WHY HE IS HERE.

That is why I am here. I want young men. I am praying for young men who will come and tell our people of the Gospel. I had a very encouraging talk with one young man this afternoon. He seemed very much in earnest. I pray that the Lord will give us that young man." Such was the oneness and intensity of Dr. Paton's purpose. There was to him no thought of anything else.

NO TIME FOR THE FAIR.

When asked if he expected to see the Fair, he replied, as if the Fair were but a matter of curiosity or sight-seeing: "I will not have any time for the Fair. I drove through the grounds last September with Mrs. Paton, and gained a general idea of the Exposition. No, I will have no time to see it." Such is the way in which he looked at the Fair. There are greater, more important objects to be attained.

HIS MEETING WITH MOODY.

On the subject of Mr. Moody he was very enthusiastic. "Yes, I have met Mr. Moody. One day a man came rushing up to me, and catching my hand, he shook it very hard, and said: 'I'm Moody.' I asked him if he was Mr. Moody the Evangelist. 'Yes,' he said, 'I'm Moody. I want you to come and address my colleges.' 'Yes,' I answered, 'by the Lord's will I will speak to your colleges.' 'No, no, no,' he said, 'not by the Lord's will. Of course it is the Lord's will, but it is your will that will take you to my students.' Yes, Mr. Moody is very abrupt. Mr. Moody is a good man." Then Dr. Paton added, with a touch of humour: "but although it was the Lord's will I did not have the opportunity of peaking to his colleges."

THE CANNIBAL'S METHOD OF HEALING.

Are you troubled by the climate of the New Hebrides, Dr. Paton? "No, we soon become accustomed to the climate. Fever and ague is prevalent there, but we have our quinine. It is much harder for the natives. When one of them is ill and is shaking with chills, they lay him flat on the floor. Then the whole town comes in and sits down all about him, from his head to his feet, and fan him with big leaves." The natives are not yet very civilized then? "They are not as far advanced as the American in the way of civilization. But spiritually they are better. You sing here in the Missionary Hymn:

"Where every prospect pleases
And only man is vile."

But we sing there

"Where every prospect pleases,
Not even man is vile."

Thus ended the talk with Dr. Paton, a talk which the THE STENTOR representative will remember for a long time; so full of life, so hearty, so simple, so intense, so tactful, such a man could not fail in whatever he attempts.

D.F. '96

COLLEGE.

L. F. U. CALENDAR.

Reception to Mr. Hopkins, May 16.
Tri Kappa Banquet, May 18.
Promenade Concert, May 19.
Oratorical Association Contest, May 23.
Annual Senior Reception, May 26.
Academy Commencement Exercises, June 9.
Annual Academy Reception, June 10.
Annual Concert at Ferry Hall, June 12.
Freshmen-Sophomore Prize Speaking, June 12.
Commencement Exercises at Ferry Hall, June 13.
Junior Contest in Oratory, June 13.
Senior Class Day, June 14.
College Commencement Exercises, June 14.
Alumni Banquet, June 15.
President's Reception. June 15.

Our readers will notice several material changes in the University Calendar.

Last Tuesday morning the Sophomore Latin Class read the whole of *Heanton Timorumenos* at one sitting.

Dr. Herrick Johnson, one of the trustees of the University, visited several of the class rooms last Thursday.

The subject of the last Y. M. C. A. prayer meeting was "Love Your Enemies." R. H. Crozier, '93, was leader.

We may have an epidemic of hydrophobia. Eleven dogs were bitten by a mad dog one day last week. Every dog in town should be muzzled.

There is another new rule at Ferry Hall. The young ladies of the college cannot go walking with the boys these beautiful evenings. (?)

Workmen have been busy during the last week in converting the wilderness in front of the Art Hall into what will become, in time, a beautiful lawn.

We are pleased to announce that Mr. Jones, '95, who has been sick with typhoid fever, is much improved, and we may hope to see him among us very soon.

At a mass meeting of the students, held Wednesday morning, it was decided to tender to Mr. Hopkins a reception in honor of his victory at Columbus. The following committee of management was appointed: H. Marcotte, chairman; Miss Williams, '93; H. Goodman, '94; E. U. Henry, '95; and D. Fales, 96.

The Seniors, at a meeting held last week, decided that they would hold no contest this year for the McClure gold medal, but asked unanimously that it might be given to Mr. A. A. Hopkins. It was also decided to hold the class day exercises Wednesday evening of commencement week instead of Tuesday after‑noon.

The examination schedule for the Senior Class has been posted. It is as follows: May 18, (9) American Literature; (2) Botany, Geology, Mathematics; May 19, (9) History of Philosophy; (2) Latin Shakespeare; May 22, (9) American History; (2) Kant; May 23, (9) Biblical; (2) Pedagogic; May 24, (9) Greek, Philosophy of Religion.

Among the recent additions to the library are the following: Goethe's Works, in ten volumes; Lessing's Works, in two volumes; Notes on the Life and Friendships of Whittier, by Mrs. James T. Fields; Essays on German Literature, by H. H. Boyesen; The Modern Novel, by Marian Crawford; Society in the Elizabethan Age, by Hubert Hall.

The leveling and improving of the Art Institute grounds is a pleasing sight to those who for over a year have looked out upon old bricks and clay. The work has been supervised by Mr. H. C. Durand himself, and will soon be finished. Mr. Durand said that there will be a gradual slope down on the sides of the building toward the street, thus setting it up and making it more prominent.

A very interesting, but decidedly one-sided, game of base ball was played between the Freshman and Sophomore classes on Monday, the 8th. Of course '95 won, but everyone was surprised at the score. It was as follows:

'95—2　3　0　0　4　3—12
'96—2　0　0　0　0　1— 3

Following are the totals as reported by the official scorer, Mr. Linn:

	A.B.	R.	B.H.	S.H.	P.O.	A.	E.	S.B.	S.O.	B.B.
'95—	25	12	6	2	18	5	8	5	6	5
'96—	21	3	2	0	10	9	9	4	2	2

Earned runs, '95, 2; '96, 0. Two base hits, Mellen, '95; A. O. Jackson, '96. Home run, Nash, '95. Double play, Jackson-Hunt, '96. Triple play, Fales-Rogers-Jackson, '96. Hit by pitched ball, Woolsey, '96; Hayner, '95. Passed balls, Rogers, '96, 9. Wild pitch, Fales, '96, 3.

The Freshman team was outplayed from the start, although they showed much good material for a first-class class team. The principal features of the game were Hunt's batting and the fielding of Vance, '96.

The Seniors have at last formed a ball team. At least, we should judge so by the following notice:

"The following Seniors will report for practice immediately after service next Sunday: McNary, c.; Marcotte, 3d b.; Daran, s. s.; Hopkins, A. A., 2d b.; Linn, l. f.; Dysart, r. f.; Chaffee, c. f.; Rossiter, sub.; McKee, surgeon; Jones, chaplain; Burdick, (R) usher; Crozier, bat carrier; Grove, 'cop'; Davies, water shagger; Hopkins, S. B., official yeller.

"By order of captain,
"T. C. Sharon.
"Schedule committee,
"Miss Marshall,
"Miss Taylor.
"Manager,
"Miss Williams."

The special STENTOR reporter who interviewed Mr. Sharon was informed that, owing to the new rule which moved the pitcher's box back to second base, the Senior Class had decided to dispense with the unimportant position of pitcher, and allow Mr. Hopkins to play second and at the same time act as pitcher.

TOWN TOPICS.

Mrs. Shearer is visiting with her mother, Mrs. Joseph Durand.

Miss Ada Rainey has returned home after a year at school in Boston.

Mrs. Sydney Taber was visited last Friday by her parents, Mr. and Mrs. Cox, and her sisters, the Misses Cox.

The symphony and concert given Monday night by the children of the Alcott School was very interesting. The children were favored with a good audience, which was greatly pleased by the performance.

The work of paving has at last been renewed and Lake Forest will soon see the rest of the pavement laid. Excavation was also begun last week for the macadam pavement west of the track. Macadam will be laid from the subway under the track at Illinois Ave. to the north end of the depot, and from there east to Mr. Scudder's corner.

One day last week a stray dog went mad and began to fly around in a lively fashion. Before the dog could be captured, it had bitten or otherwise wounded twenty-two other dogs. An order has been issued by City Marshal Healy that these dogs must either be destroyed, muzzled or confined by the 18th of this month, otherwise they will be shot by his order.

FERRY HALL.

We both enjoyed and appreciated the Cad serenade.

Mrs. Creswell visited her daughters Sunday May 7th.

We are quite looking forward to next Friday evening.

Miss Steel spent a few days of last week at her home in Dixon.

Mi Beta was postponed Friday evening in order that the girls might have the benefit of Mr. Paton's talk.

Miss Royce was the guest of Miss Maeumke last week, and Miss Mary Watson spent Sunday with Miss Pate.

The Seniors had a double pleasure Friday in spending the afternoon at Dr. McClure's and meeting Rev. J. G. Paton.

Were it not for the excitement attendant upon each visit midnight episodes with chipmukns would be very welcome.

Miss Robinson and Miss Norten chaperoned a party of the girls in to the Fair Wednesday. They spent a part of the day very satisfactorily examining pictures.

The girls renewed their childhood-days the other evening by playing such games as "crack-the-whip," "drop-the-handkerchief," and so forth. A certain uncomfortable stiffness the next day reminded them that they were growing old.

Mrs. Malloy's paper on the Art and Artists of Holland on Tuesday evening made the third of the series. It brought before us very plainly the ideal Dutch peasant life and, also, the pretty marine views for which their country is famous. Miss Norten's paper followed on Thursday evening on French Art, and made the fourth and last of the course. It was a charming review, giving a very good outline of the work and character of the French masters and the schools to which they belonged.

FACES

FROM AN OLD PHOTOGRAPH ALBUM IN FERRY HALL.

It was recently my good fortune to observe an unusually heterogeneous company of people. Here a group of young girls, but recently graduated, were, I fancied, talking of the moment when the essay had to be delivered, of their gowns, flowers, class-day, and—well you know of what girls talk. A tall yellow-haired girl was standing near them, so that her profile only was revealed, but I knew that her lips were red and her eyes were blue; a bright looking young man was at her right and at the left were two girl friends, their heads bent low as they discussed some girlish plan. One of them was pretty; the other, a girl of simple manner and dress, I had heard of as an artist, a story teller, something of a a musician, and an adept with the needle.

From them I turned to a queer little professor in a very tall silk hat. He was talking, methinks, in a very learned manner, of biology, and I wondered how such a little man could know so much. Ah! Professor, I wonder if any of your pupils will ever impress me with their vast knowledge.

I next gave a passing glance to a girl in green, with an angelic look upon her face; I fear, however, that the expression was assumed and that she was posing— for I have been told that she studied Delsarte. As I moved my head to obtain a better view of a young man with a fine strong face who, I thought, would one day make for himself a reputation as an orator, I was attracted by two pretty girls laughing and talking together; they had beautiful eyes and pretty pink cheeks, but in their gay mood I could not judge them fairly, so gave a few moments to the contemplation of three dashing looking college fellows, whom I concluded, were freshmen, and, for the present, above everything else, they liked pretty girls and good times.

A tall man, with a slightly foreign air, next attracted my attention. He wore a fur trimmed coat and frowned a bit, but, as I looked at his mouth and eyes, I thought that if naughty boys burned barrels and girls broke rules he would forgive them if they said that they were sorry and would not do it again.

I could not help smiling at four of the dearest of baby faces, laughing in sympathy with the merry crowd of boys and girls ready for a sleigh ride. Then, too, there was the jolly Professor (of music) beaming upon all of us from his superior height. I noticed how pretty the dark haired girl looked in the fluffy white gown standing near the sergeant in his uniform of blue and gold.

With only a passing thought for the girl in the tennis gown, and for many people old and young, pretty and plain, I was obliged to go away from the interesting, though mute assemblage, found in a Ferry Hall photograph rack.

COMMUNICATION.

Editor of Stentor:

The college girls were summoned to the office last Wednesday morning and were informed of the following facts: That in all probability they will return to Ferry Hall next year, and will be expected to pay the regulation Seminary rates, viz: three hundred and ninety-five dollars per year; certain restrictions will be imposed on them at the beginning of the fall term; and that they will desist from having gentlemen company, except on nights of calling and entertainments, for the remaining time of the present school year. While the college girls appreciate the kindness that has been shown them by Ferry Hall authorities, and realize the difficulty which their freedom causes among those who are under rules, still they have individual rights to be respected, and they have no intention of obeying any more rules, with exception of house rules, than those to which the college boys are subjected. Unless some action is taken whereby the college girls will have a building of their own by next fall, very few will return.

THE PROMENADE CONCERT.

All of the students are looking forward to next Friday evening in anticipation of an exceedingly happy time at the promenade concert given by the Athletic association. For several months the entertainment committee have had this affair under consideration and now that the time is nearing they are exerting every effort in the way of extensive decorations to make the evening as pleasant as possible. They are to be congratulated especially for holding the concert in the gymnasium. Every body likes this building, it being particularly adopted for promenades because of its brilliancy. Tomaso's mandolin orchestra will be another strong attraction. During the evening, by way of variety, Miss Florence Stuart will give an exhibition of club swinging, while several of the boys will perform on the apparatus. Tickets at fifty cents apiece will be on sale Tuesday and it is sincerely hoped that everybody in Lake Forest will turn out and help Athletics for the last time this year.

ACADEMY.

But a few weeks and then—vacation.

Ernest Woelful was at home last week attending the wedding of his sister.

The yearly affliction still retains its " grippe " upon us, nearly all succumbing to it.

The regular weekly faculty meeting will hereafter be held on Thursday afternoon.

The Academy base-ball nine will meet the Highland Park Military school team on the home grounds next Friday afternoon at 4 o'clock.

The program has been arranged so that former Saturday morning recitations now come on Wednesday afternoon, giving those who may may wish to take advantage of the opportunity of a whole day of each week for visiting the Fair.

The Academy Glee Club, accompanied by a stringed orchestra, seranaded the Seminary last Thursday evening. A number of selections were rendered and apparently heartily received, one or two young ladies going so far as to hammer the steam pipes in order to show their appreciation.

On Thursday afternoon will occur the examination in " Sohrab and Rustum " of those who wish to compete for the McNeil prize. The critique is to be handed in by the first of June. It is to be hoped there will be a large number of competitors in order to show a just appreciation of such a large gift by a generous donor.

Those of the senior class are working hard on their final orations, it being but a short time until commencement. The class of '93 is very proficient in this line, many reporting their ability to write an oration in a single evening. This leaves them ample time to attend to their social duties and hold their pleasant little conferences in the ravinés.

There is a boy in the Cad whose name is Condon. There is a bull dog in the town whose owner is Calvin Durand. The boy has a a sore leg, the dog has a large piece of a pair of fashionable pants. It happened in this way. Condon, who makes periodical visits to the sem, when he had crossed the bridge by the gym., argued that as the spring fever had made such inroads into his physical constitution he would for the time being forget the old adage " the longest way around is the surest way home," and take the short cut through Mr. Durand's back yard. But the bull dog thought otherwise. With a stern expression upon his face and fire flashing from his eye he made a rush for Condon and caught him in the calf of the leg. Then the bull dog chewed and Condon yelled. Finally Condon succeeded in gaining his liberty, then he literally took to " tall timber " and climbed a tree as smooth and straight as a telegraph pole. After the dog had guarded the tree for some time and Condon had yelled enough to wake the sleepers of the distant cemetery, some one kindly came out and led the dog away and Condon limped home a sadder but wiser boy.

ATHLETIC.

The Annual Field Day of the Western Inter Collegiate Athletic Association, held at Champaign on the 12th, managed to be a success notwithstanding the poor weather, which came on unfortunately at the wrong time. There was a large number of contestants present: North-Western University, Purdue, Rose Polytechnic, College of Christian Brothers and the University of Illinois sending the strongest teams.

Grinnell and Iowa College, the other two members of the Association, had their men on the ground but were prevented from contesting because of their delay in making entries. The poor weather caused much disappointment among those interested, as it was expected that many of the records of the Association would be broken. As it was six records were lowered, among these being the mile run, which our representative, L. N. Rossiter, won, lowering the record by six seconds. The *Chicago Inter-Ocean* speaks of his performance as the feature of the meet His record is now 4.45¾. A. O. and D. H.

Jackson, the other representatives of Lake Forest, did good work, the former taking third in the 440 yards dash. The Association, of which A. O. Jackson is now vice-president, will hold its meet next year in St. Louis, on the last Friday in May, at which time the College of Christian Brothers will entertain the contestants.

The following is a brief summary of the day's events:

The colleges contesting are denoted by the following abbreviations: Northwestern University, of Evanston, Ill., "N. W. U."; Lake Forest University, of Lake Forest, "L. F. U."; Purdue University, of Lafayette, Ind., "P. U."; Rose Polytechnic Institute, of Terre Haute, "R. P."; College of Christian Brothers, of St. Louis, "C. C. B."; University of Illinois, by "U. of I."

One mile run, won by L. N. Rossiter, L. F. U. Time, 4:54¾.

One hundred yard dash, won by Weedman, U. of I. Best time, 10¾ seconds.

Running high jump, won by Clark, U. of I. Height, 5 feet, 7½ inches.

One hundred and twenty yard hurdle, won by Clark, U. of I. Time, 17¾ seconds.

Running broad jump, won by Weedman, U. of I. Distance, 19 feet.

Two hundred and twenty yard hurdle, won by Clark, U. of I. Time 25 seconds.

Throwing sixteen-pound hammer, won by Sullivan, C. C. B. Distance, 87 feet 3 inches.

Pole vault, won by Culver, N. W. U. Height, 9 feet 9½ inches.

Four hundred aud forty yard dash, won by Lewis, U. of I. Time, 57 seconds.

Two hundred and twenty yard dash, won by Culver, N. W. U, Time, 25 seconds.

One mile walk, won by Evans, U. of I. Time, 8:07.

Putting sixteen-pound shot, won by Tozier, C. C. B. Distance 35 feet 1 inch.

Two mile bicycle race, won by Haley, U. of I. Time, 7:09.

One-half mile run, won by Orr, U. of I. Time, 2:12¾.

EXCHANGES.

ADVICE TO THE POET.

When you write a merry jest
   Cut it short;
It will be too long at best
   Cut it short;
Life is brief and full of care;
Editors don't like to swear;
Treat your poem like your hair;
   Cut it short.—*Illini.*

The Pen-Cornell boat-race will be rowed on Lake Minnetonka in July.

Attendance at recitation is optional at Harvard, Ann Arbor, Cornell and Johns Hopkins.

In England one man in 5,000 attends college; in the United States one in 2,000; in Scotland one in 615, and in Germany one in 213.—*Ex.*

So long as we have a university open to women as well as men, and to both on the same terms there should be just as good provision made for the neccessary physical training of the one as of the other.—*Detroit Free Press.*

The leading universities of the country in order of wealth are: Harvard, $10,000,000; Columbia, Cornell, Chicago, Yale and Johns Hopkins or Princeton. England with 94 universities has 2,723 more professors and 51,814 more sudents than the 360 universities and colleges in the United States. The revenues of Oxford and Cambridge represent a capital of about $75,000,000. The university of Leipsic is worth nearly $20,000,000.—*The College Fraternity.*

We hope our northern athletes will heed the following gentle criticism: Southern colleges are conspicuously free from the barbarous and brutal customs which have been so freely introduced in the great athletic contests in our northern institutions. Owing to their exceptional advantages they have far surpassed their southern friends in the scientific development of the popular college games, but in achieving this standard of excellence they have suffered a marked depreciation in the code of morals.—*Univ. of South Mag.*

·THE STENTOR.

VOLUME VI. MAY 23, 1893. NUMBER 28.

PUBLISHED EVERY WEEK

BY THE

LakeForestUniversityStentorPublishingCo.

BOARD OF EDITORS.

B. R. MacHatton, '95.............Managing Editor
Forest Grant, '96 ......Ass't Mgr. Ed. and Athletic
Harry Goodman, '94.............Business Manager
A. B. Burdick, '95
J. H. Jones, '96 ....Locals
David Fales, Jr., '96
W. B. Smith, '94 ....Alumni and Exchange
R. G. McKinnie, '97 ....Academy
Miss Tena Kennedy, ...Ferry Hall
J. A. McGaughey, '95 ....Advertising

Terms—$1.50 per year. Single Copies—10c

————ADDRESS————

STENTOR PUBLISHING COMPANY,

LAKE FOREST, : : ILLINOIS.

Entered at the P. O. at Lake Forest, Ill., as second-class matter.

THE ONE PAPER QUESTION.

In a recent number of our esteemed contemporary, *The Red and Black,* an article appeared on the advisability of conducting but one college paper next year. A proposition to combine The Stentor and *The Red and Black* under a new name was made.

The Stentor is most thoroughly in favor of a coalition of the two papers. Such a coalition would do away with much of the ill-feeling which now.exists between the two literary societies and " The long expected era of good feeling " would indeed appear.

If the two papers could combine into one bi-weekly having for its name The Lake Forest Stentor, and having equal representation on its editorial board from both literary societies, we believe that not only a new era of good feeling would dawn but also a *long expected era of good college journalism* might begin to appear on the horizon.

The Stentor, speaking not as the organ of any society or party, but as the old and tried Lake Forest paper of seven years past, is jealous of its name. We are asked to give up the name " The Stentor "—a paper that is known as one of the standard papers in western college journalism, a paper that has the prestige of the Lake Forest people and the alumni of this college. The Stentor also has a large advertising list. Under a new name this important feature would have to be worked up anew. The Stentor would suggest that a joint committee from the two societies meet at once. Writing editorials on the subject is not the method to be pursued if anything is to be accomplished. Let a meeting and a full discussion of the subject be held at once.

***

This spring has witnessed a decline in athletics which is so painfully evident that attention must be called to the fact for the sake of the future welfare of the different 'varsity teams. Our standard was raised very high last year by the base ball team, and naturally it was expected that this fact would have much influence on the work of the team this spring, but on the contrary the work so far has been much worse. We seem to have reached the climax in '92. It has been argued that our college is outclassed, therefore playing against great odds, and as we are compelled to play with large colleges of our educational standard, knowing that there is little show of winning, the tendency is toward discouragement. This, on the face of it, is a weak argument. Since it is only by forgetting the winning prospects and by overcoming these difficulties that strength is obtained and progress made. The question now before us all is "What can be done to better our athletics next year?"

* *

We wish that it were possible to give to our readers a full account of the toast to " The College," delivered by Professor Halsey at the Tri Kappa banquet last Friday evening. In it there were many things said which, although not particularly new, yet they fell with particular force because of the sincerity with which they were presented by the speaker. The idea that Lake Forest in the outside world and even among her Alumni has no recognized place among other colleges was, we are glad to say, corrected. However, it can be said with a great deal of truth that this impression is so prevalent among the students that many are being deprived of the pleasure of their college course, while among those preparing for college the same opinion exists to such an extent that many have signified their intention of attending school elsewhere. Professor Halsey showed plainly that the idea is a false one, only existing among a few, and being largely due to ignorance of the educational matters of the country.

THE IDLER.

Not long since we went out on a wandering tour, and without apparently knowing where we were bound, suddenly came out of our trance, and found ourself on the " Sem." bridge. (We always chronicle unusual facts). By the way, aren't these glorious nights for wandering—by yourself, of course, since the new rule? But, as we stated, we disovered ourself on the Sem. bridge, apparently bound for the Sem., though we could discover no reason. It was a beautiful night. The moon seemed to hang in the heavens like a huge yellow ball. The frogs held high carnival in the stream beneath, and a gentle breeze soughed through the trees. But if the breeze soughed, *we* actually suffered, for at the precise moment, when our thoughts were most deeply engaged

in pondering the "whichness of the hitherto," a long · quivering· note broke through the atmosphere. It was followed by several more notes of a similar character, and more of a dissimilar character, and these "characters" meeting formed a conglomeration called "Down on the Mississippi floating." We breathed easier. It was only a college serenade. We used to assist in those musical slaughters, but "we haven't for a long time now." As we listened we couldn't help wondering if this serenade would be carried on in the orthodox · way. There were the usual groups at the windows, the usual applause (the poor girls get so desperate they applaud any noise), the usual songs, the usual scraps as to "what shall we sing next?" and—then we waited with bated breath. Would it come? Would this crowd dare to leave it out? Ah, no! "There she blows." Listen! "Farewell, farewell, my own true love." We are so overcome that we can but hasten up and join in the chorus. And what would a Lake Forest serenade be without that song. Absolutely nothing. At least that is the way the boys view it. The girls think differently. The college youth seems to be possessed with a desire to eternally bid farewell to his own true love. It isn't essential that he possess one. He singles out some window, and wiggles his voice up to it with all the concentrated emotion of weeks. No matter how the other songs have gone, everybody yells "farewell" with a will, knowing they will see these same young ladies next day they persist in bidding them adieu in the most heartrending manner, as if they were all going to be suspended soon. It is very doleful. A stranger would be melted to tears no doubt, but Lake Forest audiences have ceased melting. They say it doesn't pay. If they melted every time the song was sung, they would be no more than grease spots at the present. When that solemn line commencing "I'd murmur soft when dying" is reached, everyone imagines the thought will not be appreciated, so the murmur becomes a roar—and, for dying men, a decidedly healthy yell. But, strange to say, the song is always welcome. Why? Because it is the invariable signal of the ending of the serenade. To sing another song after that would be gross sacrilege. In the aforesaid evening these poor fellows bid their loves a lasting farewell, and a brief silence ensued. The following conversation was then overheard. "Say, did you swipe that bottle of olives?" "Well, I should rather say so. What do you take me for?" "Great scott, I thought you fellows weren't going to yell 'farewell' long enough. We barely got those oranges in time." Another youth now joined the throng. "You fellows may say that 'Farewell' is not a good song, but I tell you the racket you made over it enabled us to get *this*, all hunkidori." And we recognized in the moonlight A GREAT, BLUE, GASOLINE BARREL. Thus is a sentimental song made to serve a purpose.

THE BANQUET

GIVEN BY MR. HOLT IN HONOR OF THE WINNING SOCIETY.

Last Thursday evening the Tri Kappa Society was banqueted by Mr. Holt in honor of its recent victory in the Academy contest.

This, like the contest, is an annual affair, and is given to the society making the highest average percentage in the contest.

It was held in the dining-hall of Academia, the scene of so many enjoyable events and happy gatherings, where man meets man as brother meets brother. The hall was brilliantly lighted, the gas jets being trimmed in the colors of the society—maroon and orange. Part of the pillars were also decked with the same, the others were trimmed with the colors of the Academy. Patriotism and ornamentation were combined by hanging a large flag with the words "Lake Forest Academy" upon it, on the west side of the hall.

Owing to the large number of guests the tables were arranged in the form of a hollow square around the walls of the room, and in the center of the square was placed the piano, also tastefully covered with the Academy and Society colors. Around this, rows of flowers were set one above the other, making a very pretty effect.

The only thing which occurred to mar the pleasure of the evening was the inability of Professor Burnap, who was to have acted as toast master, to be present on account of the severe illness of his wife. However, this difficulty was overcome and the position very acceptably filled by the president of the society, Mr. Flint. Not only the present members of the society were present, but also those were invited who were formerly members of the society, also the members of the College and Academy faculties, and the president of the Gamma Sigma society and those who were the Gamma Sigma contestants.

After the banquet proper, or rather after "the feed," a brief recess was taken, then all reassembled to hear the toasts which were appropriate to the occasion. The toast, "Our Society," was responded to by Mr. Cooke on behalf of the Tri Kappas, and by Mr. Graham on behalf of the Gamma Sigma society. Owing to the absence of Dr. McClure, Prof. Halsey, dean of the Faculty, responded on behalf of the University Faculty to the toast, "The College."

The programme closed with the Cad yell given with a will, and then the Society proceeded to the Seminary and displayed fireworks consisting of sky-rockets, red and blue fire, and so forth. This closed the evening's entertainment, and the gathering broke up tired but happy.

The following is the program in detail:

Old Tri Kappa,	-	-	- A. Cooke
Fools,	-	-	- B. S. Cutler
Gamma Sigma,	-	-	- J. C. Graham
The Academy,	-	-	Prof. W. F. Palmer
Visions,	-	-	- J. S. Laughlin
Reminiscences,	-	-	- E. H. McNeal
The College,	-	-	Prof. J. J. Halsey

WORLD'S FAIR ITEMS.

Major Jeuney, the architect of the Horticultural building, has said that the view from the dome of the Administration building is the finest view on the grounds. " It is the only way," he said, " to receive a first impression. The Board intended that every visitor should start on his sight-seeing with the Administration building. That is the key to the whole fair." It should indeed be the first aim of every visitor of the Fair to ascend that dome and simply look, it may be for five minutes, or for hours. They will be well repaid. The STENTOR will not attempt to describe the beauty and magnificence of the scene. It cannot. But one of the thoughts which came to the correspondent as he leaned on the lime shattered railing, and crunched bits of plaster under his feet, " was, " What would that person think, who, knowing nothing of the Fair, even having never heard of it, should in some magical way be set down in that dome, or under the columns of the Peristyle? If, notwihstanding the efforts of Major Handy and his Publicity and Promotion Bureau, such a person could exist, what would be his feelings, what wonder, what confusion! How dumb-founded he would be! It would be Fairy land, a dream, or some imaginary city! Where was he? " There was a gondola of Venice! But that immense mass of architecture was not Venetian. Those columns are Ionic! But these people are not Athenians."

LIVELY PAINTERS.

In the midst of the stranger's consternation, the STENTOR's reporter was distracted by the painters over the tall entrance to Electricity Hall. Five o'clock had just rung and these painters were most zealous in putting away their brushes. But how were they to get down? No ladder was to be seen, there was not the customary swinging platform which painters use. But the artisans did not long leave room

for doubt. The first one to prepare himself quickly swung out upon a rope which reached over one hundred feet straight down, and sliding down with seemingly no tearing of hands or of trousers was soon on solid ground. The rest followed, hurrying one after the other like monkeys, and soon all were quietly walking home, as if nothing unusual had happened.

" OLD GLORY " WELL CARED FOR.

At five o'clock also the great flag began slowly to drop from the top of its pole. It took three men to care for the flag. The first laid out a great sheet, while the other two laid the flag on it and folded it up as carefully as one would a napkin. But at this point the STENTOR's representative had to leave, and he was soon bumping home in an Illinois Central freight car, one with seating attachments, however. The view from the dome had been at once instructive and interesting. It indeed is the best way to drink in the spirit of the buildings and scenery of the Grand Court.

D. F., '96.

COMMUNICATION.

Of late there has been considerable shooting on the campus by some of the Academy students. Song-birds, squirrels, etc., have been destroyed seemingly for no other reason than from mere wanton sport. Several song thrushes have been found dead in the last three days. It was evident that they had been shot. Do the students not know that shooting is prohibited on the campus? Further, there is a state (as well as a city law) fixing a fine of five dollars for every song-bird and squirrel killed. There was a time when the rule prohibiting Academy students from using fire arms during the school terms was enforced, but it is now apparently a dead letter. This wanton shooting is not done by genuine sportsmen. Any manly sportsman would scorn to kill birds in the nesting season. If the Academy authorities do not stop this abuse, the townspeople should take steps to punish the offenders.

R. V.

COLLEGE.

L. F. U. CALENDAR.
Oratorical Association Contest, May 23.
Ball Game:—U. of Chi. vs. L. F. U.
Annual Senior Reception, May 26.
Academy Commencement Exercises, June 9.
Annual Academy Reception, June 10.
Annual Concert at Ferry Hall, June 12.
Freshmen-Sophomore Prize Speaking, June 12.
Commencement Exercises at Ferry Hall, June 13.
Junior Contest in Oratory, June 13.
Senior Class Day, June 14.
College Commencement Exercises, June 14.
Alumni Banquet, June 15.
President's Reception. June 15.

Pleasant weather at last.

Rogers, '96, was ill several days last week.

Regular examinations will probably begin Monday, June 5.

The hand ball and tennis courts have become very popular during the last week.

Miss Violet Phillips, of Elmwood, Illinois, attended the reception given to Mr. Hopkins.

Professor M. Bross Thomas preached at the Presbyterian church, morning and evening last Sunday.

Sunday evening, May 14, Dr. McClure gave his views on revision and the Briggs case in a very interesting way.

Arrangements have been made for a ball game between Chicago University and Lake Forest, for Wednesday the 17th.

Mr. E. H. McNeal left school Monday, in order to accept the position of Cashier of the Clam Bank, on the World's Fair grounds.

Those who are shooting song birds in and around Lake Forest are reminded that they are liable, by the state law to a fine of five dollars for each bird destroyed.

J. H. Jones, who has been sick for several weeks with the grippe, followed by typhoid fever, returned to his home in Clinton, Iowa, accompanied by his mother, last Wednesday.

A symphony and concert was given by the children of Alcott School, Monday, May 10, at the Art Institute building. The proceeds go to the children's sanitarium at the World's Fair grounds.

After the promenade Friday evening, the mandolin orchestra was persuaded to serenade the Seminary. The serenade was pronounced by the girls, " Fine, perfectly grand. We could listen nearly all night to music like that." The young ladies seemed to infer that for *some* serenades they did not care to stay awake all night.

The police have been the object of much criticism by the citizens because of a serious mistake made last week while carrying out the Mayor's order. After the order to destroy all unmuzzled dogs had come into force, it seems that the first canine to suffer was found after death to be wearing the required muzzle.

The Athletic Association still remains in debt notwithstanding the repleated efforts of the Entertainment Committee last Friday evening. The Promenade given was a success in every way except from a financial standpoint. We are at a loss to account for the small attendance. However it must be kept in mind that the debts of the association are to be paid and the fellows in refusing to pay them in a pleasant way are simply forcing the officers to adopt some measures which may not be so satisfactory to the majority.

The faculty meeting last Thursday must have been quite interesting. Partial Seminary rules had been placed upon the young ladies of the college. The young ladies resisted such an infringent on their rights and presented their case before the college faculty. The faculty decided that although they might be restricted from receiving callers in the Seminary parlors on any other than the regular calling evening, they could not be restricted from going walking with the young gentlemen. However the faculty advised moderation.

The reception given in honor of Mr. Hopkins last Thursday evening was, in every way, a success. The auditorium of the Art Hall was decorated with shrubs and cut flowers, so that it presented a very pleasing appearance. About three hundred guests were present. Prof. Halsey, as dean of the Faculty, made the address of welcome to Mr. Hopkins, congratulating him, in the name of the University, for his success as an orator and thanking him for the honor he had conferred upon his Alma Mater by his victory. Mr. Hopkins responded in a few well chosen sentences, expressing his gratitude for the efforts made by the faculty and students to show their appreciation of his success. Everyone reported a pleasant evening.

TOWN TOPICS.

Miss Florence Dwight gave a party to about twenty young people last Friday evening.

Prof. Thomas preached at the Presbyterian Church last Sunday morning and evening.

Mrs. Rhea, Mr. Foster Rhea and Mrs. Dulles are now in Lake Forest, visiting with the Reids.

Mrs. Burrell is visiting her mother, Mrs. Benedict. Mr. Sydney Benedict spent Sunday in Lake Forest.

Mr. and Mrs. Charles Scribner and Miss Sherman, of New York, are visiting with Mrs. Larned at Blair Lodge.

Mrs. Grant Stroh and Miss Lucy. Rumsey have returned from Del Norte, Colo. Mrs. Stroh will remain in Lake Forest for a month.

The Art Institute will hold a musicale Tuesday night at the house of Mr. Larned. Miss Sherman will sing and the Max Bendix string quartette will play. This is the last meeting of the Art Institute this year.

Last Thursday night several of the residents of Lake Forest were awakened by an unearthly yelling about half-past eleven. It was only the overflow of spirit which naturally comes after a banquet; a few Academy students who wanted to make a noise. Such noise had not been complained of but, a racket at that unreasonable hour seemed to the good burghers of Lake Forest a little too much, and several were heard asking what the noise was for and who made it. Let the Academy students, and indeed all students, be careful when they make their noise.

FERRY HALL.

The girls report a delightful time .Friday evening.

We of Ferry Hall are happy in congratulating Mr. Hopkins upon his numerous honors.

A beautiful copy of the Sistine Madonna has been purchased by the fourth year class for the parlors.

The severe illness of a friend has made it necessary for Miss Nightingale to be out of school for several days.

There is some talk, in fact it has almost been decided, to change the present Y. W. C. A. into a Christian Endeavor Society.

Mrs. Hester was obliged to give up her work at Ferry Hall this week owing to the illness of Dr. Hester at their home in the city.

Miss Conger learned this week of the sudden death of a friend, at Baraboo, Wisconsin. Miss Conger will be in Baraboo for a few days.

We would like to suggest the more frequent use of the Gym. for entertainments given by the students, as it is large enough for most purposes as well as suitable in other ways.

Last week Professor Eager was introduced by his friend, Baron von Fraetsch, at the home of Mr. George Pullman, where he entertained a great many distinguished guests, people from Chicago and abroad.

> "No voice in the chambers,
> No sound in the hall;
> Sleep and oblivion
> Reigns over all!"

And then the most beautiful serenade. Many thanks to whom it may be due.

ACADEMY.

Hand ball has become a favorite game lately.

The warm weather makes studying rather irksome these days.

Lamberton's brother has been visiting him the last few days. He was an Academy student some years since, and can tell entertainingly "how we used to make it lively for the masters."

The east and west ends of the dormitory expect to play a match game of ball in a few days.

The students sympathize with Prof. and Mrs. Burnap in the severe illness of the latter. We hope for her speedy recovery.

How may the faculty establish themselves in the good graces of the boys? By allowing them an extra half-hour in the evening.

Erskine's nine now have brilliant uniforms with which to adorn themselves. The prominent feature is bright red and blue black stockings.

Nearly everyone is making arrangements to tarry long enough in the "White City" at the close of school to see the many sights contained therein.

We would like to suggest a game of ball between the Senior Class and the Faculty. It would be interesting from start to finish. Profs. Burnap and Williams would make a good battery for the Faculty; Prof. Mendel could "hold down" first all right, especially if he stood on it; Prof. Dudley could play second; Prof. Smith third; Prof. Jack short stop; and Prof. Palmer in all probability could handle all the field alone. Come out and show your athletic ability.

Following are the officers of the senior class:

President and Class Jester, - - N. W. Flint
Vice-President, - - - - - A. S. Reed
Lord High Scribe, - - - - F. C. Vincent
Chancellor of Exchequer, - - R. L. Roberts
Envoy Extraordinary Minister Pleno- } M. K. Baker
  potentiary to Seminary, - - }
Director of Cuisine, - - - - E. C. Yaggy
Chaplain, - - - - - T. W. Harvey
Class Poet, - - - - - - F. C. Ritchey
Class Historian, - - - - W. R. Cheever
Class Sport, - - - - - G. M. Wells
Attendant of Hoodoo, - - - F. B. Whitney
  Class Colors, - - Black and White
  Class Pin, - - - Hairpin

Last Friday afternoon the Dormitory and College Freshmen crossed bats on the athletic field. Jaeger was in first-class condition, and fanned out the men in one, two, three order. The game became very much one-sided, with the Freshmen on the wrong side, and when in the second innings the Dormitory hit the ball away out in left field, close to the foul line, and Umpire Linn called it a fair ball, thereby frustrating Hayner's clever little trick of picking up the ball and standing just outside the foul line to make it appear a foul, the Freshmen in true school boy style refused to continue the game. The score stood 16 to 6 in favor of the Dormitory.

Some weeks since the Seniors elected a full quota of officers, among others Hon. M. K. Baker as envoy extraordinary and minister plenopotentiary to Ferry Hall. The election had hardly become known to the public when it was announced that hereafter Dr. Seeley would permit no one to call on his "jewels." In short, he had become converted to the "high protection" theory. Mr. Baker at once journeyed to the Seminary to see what he could do to change the opinion of the doctor, and allow a resumption of society between the Academy and Seminary Seniors. He was seen last night by the STENTOR correspondent at his residence in Mitchell Hall Place, and although somewhat fatigued by his tiresome journey, he consented to a short interview. When asked what policy he tried to obtain for the future, he said: "I tried to show Dr. Seeley that his policy was entirely wrong, and that while the Academy Seniors would be the immediate losers, eventually his own seniors would sink into insignificance and lose their identity as a class. He replied that he could not think of free and unrestricted society, and so I broached to him the idea of reciprocity. It seemed to strike him favorably, and he has consented to take the matter under advisement. I have no doubt that we will eventually come to terms, as he seemed willing and anxious to do whatever he could to advance the cause of society."

ALUMNI.

A. S. Wilson, '92, is an immigrant inspector on the Chicago Board of Health.

J. H. McVay, '91, has charge of the cash carrier exhibit at the World's Fair.

L. E. Zimmerman is making large investments in South Waukegan real estate.

W. E. Pratt, '92, is now operating a flourishing manufacturing industry in Chicago.

Miss Frances Patrick, a '92 graduate from Ferry Hall, has been very ill for some time.

The thanks of the STENTOR are due to Mr. J. E. Smith, '91, for his excellent article on "Interesting facts about Lake Forest's distinguished Men," which was published April 25. We wish that more of the Alumni would contribute interesting facts about the former students of our Alma Mater. Let some one write up the women who have gone from our halls.

EXCHANGES.

What is that wild unearthly sound,
That seems as 'twere creation's knell?
It is the college boys. They've found
A new and most heart-rendering yell.—*Ex*

The senior class of Luff's college has chosen a lady as their foot-ball manager.

The dean of the medical faculty of Drake University was arrested recently, by Des Moines officials, for grave robbing.—*Illini.*

Beloit and Wisconsin have organized Camera Clubs similar to those of Cornell and Harvard and many other universities.

The authorities of Minnesota University are endeavoring to introduce the eastern custom of *working* six days a week. The students do not favor this plan.

Harvard has the largest college library in the country. There are 700,000 volumes to 200,000 at Yale, 136,000 at Cornell, and 133,000 at Columbia.—*Ex.*

During the summer Evanston will entertain some four hundred young ladies from Vassar, Wellesley, Smith, Cornell and other eastern schools, who are coming to see the Fair.

The Nassan Lit fears that the trustees of Princeton will prohibit the annual foot-ball match between Princeton and Yale on account of the disgraceful carousels at these games.

The appointment of Ruskin as poet laureate is a recognition of the fact, too often forgotten, that there are poets who are not verse-makers, as well as verse-makers who are not poets.—*Philadelphia Ledger.*

Several of the instructors of Iowa college have established a prize of $20 to be awarded at commencement to the athlete maintaining the highest average scholarship during the year. The candidates must be either regular members of the ball teams or win either a first or second prize in the field meet of the State Athletic association.—*Northwestern.*

The students of Yale are making preparations for presenting a play entitled "Robin Hood." Vassar will soon give the "Antigone of Sophocles," and the Harvard men are making elaborate advancement, under the supervision of Prof. Grenough, with a Latin play, "The Rhonnio of Terence."—*Round Table.*

Yale now has a hospital where students will be cared for during illness. It has thirty-two rooms, and will have trained nurses and the best infirmary equipment.—*Ex.*

Lake Forest does not want such an extensive hospital as Yale has, but we do want, and must have, some kind of accomodations for caring for students in case of sickness. The Seminary and Academy students have been well provided for, and now we of the College feel that it is our turn. Dear friends, and Alumni of Lake Forest, we ask you for a home for the College girls, and a home for the College boys.

Lake Forest has received many congratulations from the college world on account of our orator's recent victory. We would like to publish all that our friends have said of double A, but we can only find room for the following from the *Collegium Forense:*

"Mr. Hopkins' graceful bearing, in entire harmony with the treatment of his subject, won at the start the good opinion of the audience. His clear, musical voice, with its marvelous flexibility, which it retained to the end, was the strongest factor in his success. His was, perhaps, the most symetrical production of the evening—thought, composition and delivery combining to make one harmonious whole."

THE RIDDLE.

DOMUS.

I asked the man in the moon one night.
What under the sun made his face so bright.
He looked at me in amazed surprise
As he answered " Young man before I rise
I do what every man, maiden or dude
Should do after they rise for their pulchritude."

Of course the riddle was easy to guess,
And my question absurd I must confess,
For even a dunce might readily know
That he gave his complexion such a glow,
By leaving alone cosmetics and dope,
And washing his face with Cleanemup's soap.

N. B. Only 9 cents a bar at Vance Bros. grocery department.

THE STENTOR.

VOLUME VI.   MAY 31, 1893.   NUMBER 29.

PUBLISHED EVERY WEEK
BY THE
LakeForestUniversityStentorPublishingCo.

BOARD OF EDITORS.

B. R. MacHatton, '95............Managing Editor
Forest Grant, '96 ......Ass't Mgr. Ed. and Athletic
Harry Goodman, '94.............Business Manager
A. B. Burdick, '95 ⎫
J. H. Jones, '96   ⎬ ....Locals
David Fales, Jr., '96 ⎭
W. B. Smith, '94 ....Alumni and Exchange
R. G. McKinnie, '97 ....Academy
Miss Tena Kennedy, ...Ferry Hall
J. A. McGaughey, '95 ....Advertising

Terms—$1.50 per year. Single Copies—10c

————ADDRESS————
STENTOR PUBLISHING COMPANY,
LAKE FOREST,   :   :   ILLINOIS.

Entered at the P. O. at Lake Forest, Ill., as second-class matter.

ATHLETICS.

A CLOSE GAME. L. F. U. VS. CHICAGO UNIVERSITY.

The ball game last Wednesday demonstrated one thing and that is that L. F. U. has ball players and could have a winning team if the players were properly trained.

With the exception of the fourth inning our boys played as good a game as was ever seen on the home grounds.

Stagg's aggregation is one which contains but one first-class player in it, namely Stagg, the others are good second class men. The team however excelled in team work and therefore won. No balls dropped between players because the nearest ones did not understand whose ball it was and all the bases were backed up in fine style by all the available players.

The whole team backed up the third baseman and catcher and showed that they at least understood the principals of ball playing. Our boys also do not seem to understand base sliding and consequently lost much. Under the existing circumstances the teams were about evenly matched and L. F. U. should have won out.

The criticism of Chicago on our ball grounds was merited but they should understand that it is not the fault of the team.

Lake Forest has positively the worst athletic field and ball diamond in the United States and all because of the lack of interest in many of the trustees and faculty, the former of whom allowed the ball grounds to be laid out and irretrievably ruined, as they now are, by incompetent workmen. Till L. F. U. has a first class athletic field she can never be the leading college in the west in any branch whatsoever of college athletics. The game started with Lake Forest at bat and they got two runs in the first inning. Havner was sent to first on four balls. After Sharon and Lewis had been retired Goodman stepped up to the bat. He swung his club at an out shoot. There was a crack like a bucket rolling down stairs and when the ball was returned to the diamond Goodman was panting on third. He came in a moment later on a passed ball. Chicago was retired in one, two, three order on well fielded hits to the infield. In the second Rhinehardt made a base hit but did not get around and no one scored for us. Chicago got their first run in this inning by bases on balls and a sacrifice hit.

In the third Lake Forest got three runs and made the score five to one. Chicago went out without a run. The disastrous fourth inning now began. Lake Forest retired without a tally and Chicago went to bat. Prescott, the first man up was hit by a pitched ball, then came two base hits scoring one run, then three bases on balls forcing in two more. Stagg next appeared and lined out a two bagger and Nichols shortly did the same. This ended Chicago's run getting and the side was retired having made nine tallies in one inning, thus making the score 10 to 5.

In the fifth inning Stagg went behind the bat and Conover to left field while Nash went on third and Lewis into the box for Lake Forest. Till the first of the eighth neither side scored. In the eighth Nichols presented us with three bases on balls and hit one man while Stagg had a passed ball allowing one score to come in. In all we got three runs across the plate, making the score 8 to 10 in Chicago's favor. The game was stopped at this stage to allow the Chicago team to catch the train. Several of the errors on both sides were due to the roughness of the infield, which is so uneven that the correct judging of grounders is impossible. The muff by Conover of Durand's fly in the sixth was inexcusable, as was also Stagg's wild throw to second in the same inning, and the general work of Gilleland was too poor to be commented on. The score:

LAKE FOREST.

	A. B.	R.	B.	P.O.	A.	E.
Hayner....c f	3	2	1	1	0	0
Sharon 1	3	1	0	8	0	0
Lewis....3 and p	5	1	1	2	1	0
Goodman....r f	3	1	1	0	0	0
McNary....c	2	0	0	6	2	0
Durand....l f	3	0	0	1	0	0
Rhinehardt....2	3	1	1	2	2	2
Gilleland....s s	3	1	1	1	2	3
Nash....p and 3	4	1	1	0	0	0
Totals.....	30	8	6	21	7	5

CHICAGO.

	A. B.	R.	B.	P.O.	A.	E.
Pike....c f	2	1	0	0	0	0
Stagg....l f and c	4	1	3	4	1	1
Conover....c and l f	4	1	1	3	1	1
Nichols....p	5	1	1	0	3	0
Prescott....1	2	2	0	8	0	1
Adkinson....2	3	1	2	5	2	1
Webster....s s	4	1	1	0	4	0
Speer....3	3	1	0	2	0	2
McGillivray....r f	2	1	0	2	0	0
Totals.....	29	10	8	24	11	6

Lake Forest——2 0 3 0 0 0 0 3——8.
Chicago——0 1 0 9 0 0 0 *——10.

Two base hits—Stagg, Nichols. Three base hits—Goodman. Stolen bases—Hayner (3), McNary (1), Durand (1), Adkinson (2), Pike (1), Stagg (1), Conover (1), Webster (1), McGillivray (1). Bases on balls—off Nash, 10; off Nichols, 8. Hit by pitched ball—Gilleland, Prescott. Struck out—by Nash, 4; Lewis, 3; Conover, 7. Passed balls—McNary, 2; Conover, 3; Stagg, 1.

Umpire, H. Marcotte, Time, 2 hours.

NOTES ON THE GAME.

Stagg's team shows careful training. Their work is far from perfect but it is very evident that a master hand has directed their practice.

A finer lot of gentlemen than the Chicagos would be hard to find. A lack of useless kicking characterizes their game.

McNary's work behind the bat was exceptionally good. He stopped many difficult balls and saved the pitcher from the error column in more than one instance.

Nash has demonstrated that he can pitch. He has a cool head and deceptive curves. His arm is not strong but with practice he can develop into a first-class twirler.

Gilleland has a bad habit of conversing with the crowd during play. It takes his attention from the game and is the cause of a good many blunders. The captain is the only one privileged to talk during a game and then only to the umpire or his men.

On the whole we need not be ashamed of the team's work. With diligent practice from now on, they can make a creditable showing.

The Academy base ball team met the Highland Park team on the Lake Forest Athletic grounds last Saturday afternoon and defeated the visitors in a seven-inning game by the decisive score of 12 to 5. It was an ideal day for ball, the sun coming out and putting the grounds in fine condition. Jaegar and Gilleland formed the battery for the home team, and Dickson, Hubbard, and Bayless for the visitors. Hubbard caught the first four innings and pitched the last three. Jaeger was in fine condition, giving only two men bases on balls and striking out nine men. The visitors pitchers gave six men bases on balls and struck out nine men. Lake Forest made five errors, Highland Park seven. The feature of the game was a home run by Rheingaus. The visitors team was composed of perfect gentlemen with whom it is a pleasure to play, and there was an entire absence of any kicking. McNary as umpire was very satisfactory in his decisions.

WORLD'S FAIR ITEMS.

"A stitch in time saves nine." This is an old proverb, but if it had been heeded more, and if certain men had been less negligent, the World's Fair would not have been open last Sunday. Negligent is the only term that can be applied to men who might have taken steps to restrain Sunday opening, but who let the opportunity lay idle. For a clear example of the sin of omission, look at the Sunday Protection Leagues of Chicago, whose business it was to try and close the Fair Sunday. In the midst of the agitation by the dailies and in the face of the actions of the Directors and Commissioners, these "enthusiasts" were seemingly as supremely oblivious as so many sphinxes. They said they were waiting for the Government to act; but they should have known better than to wait for such a weak and incompetent official as the present District Attorney, who kept making the miserable excuses that he "didn't have time to attend to it," or "if the gates were closed the people would break in," the paltriness of which is alone able to inspire one with disgust.

At the last moment a small party of private citizens got together and took actions with a little more independent spirit. The same day, Saturday, E. F. Cragin, the head of the Sunday Societies of the country, returned to Chicago and began to work. But it was too late.

Although now the Exposition is being assailed on every side and on every conceivable point, the "stitch" was not taken "in time," and the World's Fair goes on record as being open one Sunday at least, and the Directors and Commissioners have gained for themselves the reputation of civilized, respectable law-breakers.

Of the many thousand daily newspapers in the United States, only three are openly advocating Sunday closing, of which Chicago owns one. They are as follows: The Chicago *Daily News*, the Boston *Journal*, and the New York *Mail and Express*.

THE RAMBLER.

A senior sat beside his walking stick at the Lake bluff, musing upon the vanities of life, the memories of his almost past college career, the price of Havanas, the beauties of "Canaan" and the chances of evading "his" florist upon the day following commencement.

His mind had been so trained during his four years of college life that simultaneously he waved his hand at an imaginary maiden upon the deck of a passing steamer, turned several unread pages of Exmoor description, eyed his room-mate's timepiece for the silent announcement of his daily senior vacation engagement, and outlined a plausable financial budget for his father's endorsement.

His memory was his lord upon this afternoon: all friends, save his ever faithful stick and pipe, had forsaken him, and the cycles of his short past revolved in quick succession; the enchanting phantoms of the "irrevocably gone" held high carnival in his mind.

The programme of the last dance dropped from his book, his feet unconsciously described elipses, parabolas and circles amid the encircling sunshine as he again executed the Lance Waltz with the queenly blonde—"his latest."

This dance led forward other dances, which in turn gave way to parties, receptions, the summer camp with its almost forgotten "friend," the football game, the stroll upon the beach, the summer-house, and the sigh.

Three years are reviewed in a moment. Liverymen, landlords, stewards, florists, subscription managers, college treasurers and "the boys" omnipresent in true life have been dismissed with a flourish of his stick from this afternoon's dream, and he finds himself a freshman at the portals of another college "back in eighty-nine."

How agreeable are these collegemen to a new comer! He is sought after at every turn.

A newly made friend invites him to call with him that evening upon some one of his friends. Does he go? Well, fish ordinarily go bathing, and no less usually does a somewhat flattered college freshman call—when he may. His friend, a senior, wears a mystic cross upon his vest. This pin, with its gold skull, its silently eloquent Greek letters has been the instigator of much admiration in the freshman. They call. The freshman is pleased with his reception.

Jack's—the senior has permitted the freshman to call him Jack—friend is indeed a sweet character. Her manner is *so* pleasing, her conversation so delightful; how different is she from all the friends of the past, how he envies Jack his position in a society which is graced by such a belle. Must he wait until he too is a senior, like Jack, before he may call upon her and patronize *other* freshmen? She rises: what grace! how beautiful is that stately and perfectly draped figure! She seats herself at the piano: the freshman follows—to turn the leaves, of course—listens to the sweetest strains which ever greeted human ear, looks into her deep, dreamy eyes, forgets to turn the page, recovers himself with apologies and begs a red rosebud from her raven hair.

She leans lazily against the keyboard, and tells the freshman of all the pleasures in store for him—the dances, the masquerade, the fraternity banquets; ah! now she is playing the true frat. sister to Jack. She tells him how Jack's frat. is the greatest social institution in the world, the only local chapter containing any athletes, any prizemen, and that an invitation to join is the greatest honor bestowed upon a student.

Does he consent to join? Well, yes. How could he do otherwise? Did *she* not advise it?, *She* surely would do no wrong. Out of gratitude for such a valuable service rendered, Jack, the chairman of the "spiking committee," played the only waltz he knew, while the freshman danced with Miss Elston, or, as Jack called her, "Sister Annie." What a waltz! It was a poem! How lightly she danced! The freshman circled through air. He thought he had danced before, but not until Jack refused to play "his piece" the thirteenth time could the dancers be stopped.

But the evening was forcibly closed by the warning of the town clock. "Sister Annie" asked them to call again—"You, Jack, and you, Mr. Rhoads, and come soon."

A few weeks passed, and each successive week found Mr. Rhoads—now Paul—a more frequent visitor at Sister Annie's—for Paul had joined Jack's fraternity and had also become a "brother" to "Sister Annie."

The impressions of the first evening spent at Annie's were but a *soupçon* of realities which ripened later. Paul read poetry, bought sweet confections, hired sleighs, borrowed money from his friends, dreamed and even studied his lessons with but one object before him—Annie.

The year was closing, and with it came all the festivities best known to a college town. At them all "Paul and Annie" were always seen together, and everyone, even Jack, concluded that Cupid had fixed the fatal seal.

Returning from the farewell hop, Paul presented his case with all the fervor youth could lend, and all the oratory that the winner of "Freshman" could muster. He was gaining ground; he took hope and begged that she would but permit him to wear the plain band ring which she always wore. Ah, she yields. She placed the ring upon his finger, and said: "Mind, Paul, this signifies nothing; you may have the ring forever, I am through with it." Paul resolved to let well enough alone, and so they parted.

The following day as Paul was carried homeward upon the train, he slipped the ring from his finger, and saw rudely scratched upon the inner surface, and in various styles: "J. '81," "M. R. '83," "L. '84," "B. '87," "W. W. W. '88," "F. '90," "H. L. '91" "F. H. '92." Paul then knew he had played the lover, for a year, in his turn, to a "College Widow."

Upon the outside of the ring he engraved, as best he could, "P. M. R. '93."

The senior of Lake Forest arose from his freshman past and filled his engagement with the stately blonde—not the byegone COLLEGE WIDOW.

***

The time was night. The great silvery luminary, tho' of the gentler gender, was nearing the state of intoxication. Not only was the moon dissipating, but she was tempting others. Spring was robing herself in her latest cotsume; an oriole slept in its new home for the first time, while the bat winked the other eye as he saw a couple of lovers*—no adjective is necessary—stroll through avenues of beauty and labyrinths of fragrant blossoms.

· Now, all strollers do not love, nor indeed do all lovers stroll, but these lovers both strolled and loved—all on account of that intoxicated moon.

Like all dreams, this lover's evening was drawn to a close: not from choice, to be sure, but on account of the omnipresent dispensation of causation, in this instance the cause was the revolution of Doctor's Key.

For brevity we will call the lover—the boy —Dick.

Dick stopped at University Hall in search of company townward; this was found in Stan.

They walked silently. Each dreamed of the woman who loved him best. The shade of a spreading oak enshrouded the twain. To the right ran a beautiful hedge; silence reigned with fears—such silence was it that Dick thought he heard a lemon drop, and embraced Stan. in consequence.

"Stop! Your life!" cried two score voices in unison, from behind the hedge.

A shower of meteor-like, city-street-improvement slag dropped upon the heels of the mandate—not to mention Stan.'s. Faster and faster fell the stone, louder and more loud grew the cries of the student's enemies—"the town boys." · Always a fast runner, Dick distanced himself and the bombarding missiles, and gained succor upon a neighboring veranda. Stan. fell into the hands of the foe. Stan. forgot his injuries in his delight at finding not the awful "town boys," but the never absent—upon such occasions—and true reformer Luther, behind whom stood, in battle array, the mighty David.

Dick gained the University Hall steps and his wind, to find he had been the subject of a joke. To-day he is dealing out his brother's soft drinks to his friends, and is mentally agonized by the saying: "Faint heart never won fair lady."

· * Hypothetical.

COLLEGE.

L. F. U. CALENDAR.
Ball Game—Lake View vs. L. F. U., June 3.
Academy Commencement Exercises, June 9.
Annual Academy Reception, June 10.
Annual Concert at Ferry Hall, June 12.
Freshmen-Sophomore Prize Speaking, June 12.
Commencement Exercises at Ferry Hall, June 13.
Junior Contest in Oratory, June 13.
Senior Class Day, June 14.
College Commencement Exercises, June 15.
Alumni Banquet, June 15.
President's Reception, June 15.

The Sophomores have finished analytic geometry.

The boys voted the Senior reception a decided success.

The College base ball team beat the Academy by a score of 8 to 7 last Thursday.

The Seniors are enjoying their vacation. Strolling seems to be their most popular diversion.

The numbers attending the preparatory department of the University have been materially lessened during the past week.

A good many of the boys have signified their intention give up their situations at the Fair if it is open Sundays.

W. K. Clement, a former professor in Ferry Hall and the College, has been the guest of Dr. and Mrs. Seeley for several days.

" The Idler " has freed himself from all suspicion of ever stealing a gasoline barrel at the " Sem." Those barrels are always 'red never blue.

On Saturday, June 3rd, there will be a ball game between Lake View High School and the Lake Forest team. All come and help out athletics.

The ball game Wednesday was not as good as might be expected from last year's record, but considering the many disadvantages under which the team has labored this year, it made a very creditable showing.

Prof. Bridgman gave the Sophomore Greek class a two hours talk last Monday on modern Greece and the Greek language of to-day. The talk was made doubly interesting by personal reminiscences of his journeys through Greece.

It seems to be a favorite pastime with certain youths who are old enough to know better, to go around town and smash street lamps. It certainly cannot furnish much amusement to the boys, but it causes a great deal of annoyance to the public.

Last Tuesday evening the students of the Academy and College held a joint prayer meeting in the Academy chapel. Mr. Burt, state secretary, gave an account of the State work and the summer school at Lake Geneva. Mr. Chatfield, of Evanston, told about the work at North Western.

The orators for the Junior exhibition have been chosen. Their names, together with the subjects of their orations, are given below:

Miss Pierce,   -   -   -   -   " Sincerity."
Miss Smith,   "The Mission of Charles Dickens.''
Mr. Bourns,   -   -   - "In Defence of Blaine."
Mr. Drake,   -   -   "England's Dark Blot."
Mr. Smith,   -   -   -   " W. T. Sherman."
Mr. Waldo,   -   -   -   " William Carey."

The STENTOR would like to suggest that the Tournament Committee of the Tennis Association be gotten together and arrange a tournament. Tennis players have been practising up for some time in anticipation of the tournament, but no tournament is as yet in view. The members of the committee are Flint, Ruston, and Bird.

The Lake Geneva Summer School is to be more brilliant than ever this year. The Southern summer school will adjourn for the World's Fair, thus sending students to Lake Geneva. California and the far west will be represented, that part of the country not having hitherto sent any delegates. Lake Forest this year expects to send a good number, but it is not good enough. Last year L. F. was the banner college, having more delegates in proportion to its size than any other college. But it means more work this year. If any student does not care to go let him give a little to help others.

The Oratorical Association contest of last Tuesday evening was pronounced the best in "originality of thought" and "spontaniety of expression," that has been held in Lake Forest for some time. Mr. Bourns was chosen as Lake Forest's representative at the State contest, and Mr. Bird was chosen as alternate. Following is the program:

Oration, -   -   -   - " Roger Williams."
          William B. Hunt.
Oration,   -   -   -   - " William Carey."
          Alfred F. Waldo.
Oration, -   -   - "The Uncrowned King."
          Henry L. Bird.
Oration,   -   -   - " In Defence of Blaine,"
          Arthur P. Bourns.
Oration, -   -   -   - " Ultimate America."
          Joseph Z. Johnson.

TOWN TOPICS.

Mr. Hinckley and family have come to Lake Forest for the summer.

Prof. Curry, of McCormick Theological Seminary, preached at the church last Sunday.

The Art Institute met for the last time Tuesday night at the house of Mr. Larned. The program was a Musicale. Miss Sherman, of New York, sang, and the Max Bendix String Quartette played. The musicians were delayed some time by the wreck at North Evanston, but the interval was pleasantly filled up by Mr. Larned, who in a few chosen words told the origin and history of the Art Institute. He then, inasmuch as he is to be absent in Europe for two years, resigned his position as President of the Art Institute. Mr. Larned will be much missed by the members. It is difficult to see how the Institute can get along without him.

Mr. Hannah has returned to Lake Forest for the summer. He will occupy Mrs. Humphrey's house.

Mrs. Abbie Jerry gives a Musicale Tuesday night for the benefit of Mr. Frederick Clark. Mr. Clark is to give some piano selections.

Mr. David Jones, of Chicago, has rented Mr. Yaggy's house for two years. Mr. Yaggy will in July start on a trip around the world, and will be gone about two years.

Miss Harriet Durand has returned from an extended visit in the East, spending part of the time with her sister Mabel, at Smith College; part with her sister, Mrs. Allen, at Orange, New Jersey.

FERRY HALL.

We are glad to welcome Miss Barker after such an absence.

A letter from Miss Edna Hays announces her complete recovery.

Miss Pain, of Dixon, was the guest of Miss Jean Steel over Sunday.

Miss May Stowell spent Sunday, May 28th, with Miss Alice Keener.

We enjoyed having the small sister of Miss Macomber with us for several days.

Miss Olive Cost, last year of Ferry Hall, spent Sunday with Miss Nellie Dillon.

Some of the young ladies say that by boat is a charming way in which to go to the Fair.

The Aletheian Society will give a reception to its senior members on the evening of June 2nd.

Miss Julia Brown spent Sunday, May 21st, with Miss Rena Obern, at the home of the latter in the city.

Prayer-meeting has become quite popular since it has been decided unwise for the girls to go out in the evening without any particular place to go.

The members of the present junior class feel the approaching dignity of their senior year, as they are invited to meet the faculty.

We noticed among the guests of Friday evening Miss Maud Taylor, Miss Ada Barker, Miss Glenrose Bell and Anna Walters.

The Misses Rumsey, with an informal party, Saturday evening, entertained a number of young people in honor of Miss Florence Platt and Miss Avis Paine.

Miss Martin, of the Y. W. C. A. state work, visited Ferry Hall last week, so that the society of Ferry Hall proper will henceforth be a Christian Endeavor Society.

The Senior Reception Friday evening was something that we who are not seniors feel at liberty to praise. The music and decorations were beautiful, and everyone looked happy, and if they did not have a good time there must have been some very special reason.

The music room, refreshment room, and reading room were noticeably pretty, the novel idea of using the colors of other colleges being prettily developed in the host room.

By no means the least charming part was the girls dancing "After the ball was over," and the guests had fled. The receptions of Dr. and Mrs. Seeley are always a success.

I stood near not long since and watched a young man being told that theosophy, philosophy and similar subjects were common themes of conversation among our number. His eyes may have opened with interest and they *may* have opened with astonishment. He rapidly reviewed his several calls at Ferry Hall and his encounters with the young ladies elsewhere. He could not remember ever having received any information upon those subjects or of their having been touched upon. He tried to explain that circumstances may have had something to do with his case, but reflection proved that " circumstances " ought not to have influenced every time, and growing desperate did the usual thing, let the you ladies have their own way.

ACADEMY.

The societies will probably have but one more meeting this year.

The cool weather last week had a very depressing effect on the spring fever.

A note in one of last week's papers caused no little difficulty between two members of the Academy.

A great many will not remain during Commencement exercises, preferring rather to spend the time in the city at the Fair.

There was a large exodus from the Academy last week, the faculty kindly returning some of the boys to the bosoms of their parents, others going of their own volition.

Owing to the fact that he has not time to devote to the interests of the team, Rogers has resigned the captaincy of the ball team. Jaeger has been elected to fill the vacancy.

The new buildings will be dedicated on Friday June 9th. After the exercises there will be a reception in them. If the programme is conpleted in time we will publish it in the next is-sue.

The College and Cad played ball last Thursday afternoon. The score was very close and was a matter of dispute, probably being 8 to 7 in favor of the College. No doubt another game will be played in the near future.

Prof. Smith gratified his own ambition and the ambition of the senior class to get into the Reid Hall this year by having his Virgil class recite there one recitation last week. It is the intention at present to have commencement exercises held there.

It has been decided to have a reception, as has been done annually heretofore, given by the Academy. It will be held on Saturday evening, June 10th. The following compose the committee on arrangments: Durand, Cutler, Jaeger, Bournique, Forbes.

COLLEGE VERSE.

THE "SEM." BRIDGE.

In times gone by in Venice old,
A bridge between two buildings lay,
And oft upon it drear and cold
The muffled drums the dirges play,
  'Tis called the Bridge of Sighs.

Tradition says, perhaps 'tis true,
Whatever mortal o'er it passed
Ne'er saw again the heavens blue
Nor looked upon the mountains vast,
Aye, truly, yes, and rightfully.
  'Tis called the Bridge of Sighs.

Another bridge now meets our eyes,
A bridge that is both long and wide,
And many a youth upon it sighs
With some fair maiden at his side,
And wondrous though to you 't may seem,
  'Tis also also called the Bridge of Sighs.

For when this bridge has once been passed,
And in the "Sem." the poor maid is,
The look the youth has ta'ens the last,
Hereafter loneliness is his,
Aye, truly then, and rightfully,
  'Tis called the Bridge of Sighs.
                                    —S.

To the Stentor:

I understand there is some talk of uniting the two college papers under a new name. Now, the alumni for several years back associate "THE STENTOR" with their Alma Mater. Perhaps some other name would be more apropos, but the STENTOR is now nearly six years old, and is widely known as the college paper. I do not see anything in the way of uniting again under the old name.

                                    —ALUMNUS.

[The above is the expression of one of the Alumni of the Zeta Epsilon Society.—ED.]

The recent intercollegiate oratorical contest held at Columbia, South Carolina, was won by Mr. M. D. Hardin, of Center College, Kentucky.

THE STENTOR.

VOLUME VI.   JUNE 13, 1893.   NUMBER 30.

Job secured considerable reputation for his patience, but Job never was manager of a baseball team nor tried to act as principal of a female seminary.

**

As the year draws to a close we would like to again remind those indebted to THE STENTOR that a remittance would be highly acceptable. Dunning is always disagreeable, but we trust our subscribers will appreciate the situation and address the business manager at their earliest convenience.

**

Like the sweet commencement roses that will have withered, leaving naught save a lingering perfume, the cherished school days of many of us will soon have entered into the past. There is always a sadness about these commencement seasons in spite of all that should make them glad. It is the withering of the flowers. But then like the other roses that will bloom in other fields there will be new scenes of activity, new hopes and joys. Cheer up, old man.

YET ANOTHER PAPER.

The STENTOR extends its congratulations and compliments to the editors of *The Daily Commencement Bulletin*. This paper is issued every morning during commencement week, giving a full account of the events of the day.

For downright energy, perseverance and pluck, we would commend our readers to our two young academy friends and editors, Mr. Cutler and Mr. Gruenstein.

TO THE TOWN'S PEOPLE.

Too many thanks cannot be given to the townspeople who have so liberally contributed to the Athletic Association and to other enterprises undertaken by the students. One of the chief advantages of Lake Forest College lies in the fact that its moral and social atmosphere is not surpassed in any college town whatsoever. No higher compliment than this could be paid to the people of Lake Forest.

The students of this college and its different departments will always look back with a sense of pleasure to their intercourse with the townspeople.

To use hackneyed phrases and say nice things to you is not the purpose of this editorial. We simply wish to express our sincerest appreciation and thanks for your generosity and kindness during the past year. Until next September, farewell, and a pleasant summer.

WHICH SHALL IT BE, GIRLS?

Recently, in Chicago, the representative women of the world met in congresses at the Art Palace and discussed subjects relative to the progress of womankind. Such distinguished persons as Susan B. Anthony, Julia Ward Howe, Helena Modjeska, Kate Field, "Jennie June" and others, representing nearly every branch of notable endeavor, have contributed to the grand symposium winnowings from their own experiences. What has there been in all this array of the flowers of womanhood to prove an inspiration to the sweet buds that bloom in the every-day garden of life?

Shall our dear girls strive to attain what is known as a "career" or shall they direct their thoughts toward that sacred sphere of motherhood?

The time has gone by when the world ridicules the woman who chooses a "career."

Too many women have attained the highest reaches of human endeavor and still preserved all their God-given graces for anyone to taunt the sex with the bugaboo of "mannishness."

But withal it is not proved that a sorry day would not have come when sweet maidenhood ceased to cherish as dearest of all that mellow old word "home."

The world is large and there are many kingdoms where woman may justly seek to rule, but frankly girls, is it not a sublime destiny to be crowned the queen of that large, though little dominion, "home."

THE ATHLETIC ASSOCIATION.

In another place appears the report of the Athletic Association. We would call the special attention of the students to this report, as it is very comprehensive and has some excellent suggestions for next year.

It will be seen by this report that the association is still in debt. Various reasons are given to account for this deficit. Briefly and frankly, the reason lies with the students.

Entertainments are given for the benefit of the Athletic Association, but where are the students?

A few men do all of the work. If the Athletic Association is ever to end the year in good financial condition, the fellows must get up and shake themselves.

The president of the Athletic Association recently suggested that the two literary societies be restricted to one entertainment only during the year.

This is an excellent suggestion, because if athletic interests clash with society interests, society is given the benefit of the clash and athletics suffer. The societies should be self-supporting. This idea of going around town and begging money for different society clubs is an imposition to which the townspeople should not be called upon to submit.

Let us do our work in the literary societies next year independent of any outside help. But when it comes to athletics, let the two societies as one man get up and hustle. Let each individual do his utmost for the cause of athletics. Quit begging and go to work. It's a wonder we haven't lost the respect of the townspeople.

ALL HONOR TO DR. McCLURE.

There has been a great deal written about the new president of Lake Forest University. His character aud executive ability have been justly praised.

But the man who has been silently and unselfishly working for the best interests of this institution has not received more than a passing mention. Perhaps

Dr. McClure has, for more than a year, been the acting president of this university. During that time he has worked unceasingly for the interest of

DR. McCLURE.

the reason for this is because we have always been accustomed to see our own Dr. McClure work for our interests and we take this late task of his as a matter of course.

this institution. In return for his work, he has declined all compensation, not even allowing the university to pay his railroad expenses. It is generally conceded that the pastorate of a church as large as Dr. McClure's is work enough for one man. Dr. McClure has not only fulfilled his pastoral duties, but has performed and executed most satisfactorily and acceptably to the trustees and students the numerous and important duties which pertain to the high office of the president of a university. It has been a passing wonder to his friends how he has ever been able to keep his health under the constant strain and work always incident to each one of these tasks.

We welcome to the presidency of Lake Forest University, Dr. Coulter. We give to our retiring president and beloved pastor, Dr. McClure, our sincerest and heartiest thanks for his unselfish devotion to our interests.

A COMMUNICATION.

THE FACTS IN THE CASE.

An editorial in the last issue of the *Red and Black*, relative to a union of that paper with THE STENTOR, might carry a misapprehension of facts to those unfamiliar with the history of college journals in Lake Forest University if it went unchallenged. The *Red and Black* complains because its proposition to merge THE STENTOR and the *Red and Black* into a new paper was not received favorably by those interested in THE STENTOR. The *Red and Black* claims in that proposition to have met THE STENTOR half-way. The absurdity of the claim is palpable. The sublime assumption implied in the term shalf-way is amusing, The *Red and Black* is not yet one year old. It has not quite proved that it is not the ephemeral creation of an accident, born of sore-headed feelings and nurtured by artificial methods. It has been, to speak plainly, playing a bluff game from its inception, and its fondest admirers have more than once admitted that it was started to run THE STENTOR down.

On the other hand THE STENTOR has reached its sixth volume, and is about to enter its seventh. It has reached its present position by years of hard struggles, working up by natural means, adapting itself to varying conditions; studying the needs of Lake Forest, setting up nights during these long years of hardship to make itself the paper that should fill the field and conscientiously represent the voice of Lake Forest University. The natural fruits of these efforts have been a strong and abiding constituency, and a stable advertising patronage in this vicinity, and in Chicago has been built up by ceaseless energy. THE STENTOR is known and read far and wide. It has a name that commands respect, and, what is more valuable, a name that wins among those who wish to place their ads in an old and well established newspaper. It has a firm hold on the affections of a majority of the Alumni. Contrast these essential merits of THE STENTOR with the ephemeral qualities of the *Red and Black*.

This is meeting the STENTOR half-way. Fudge and nonsense! THE STENTOR is more than willing to be reasonable and give the wandering sheep a chance to return to the fold on justifiable terms. But as for sinking the results of long years of toil into oblivion, or placing the same in the scales where they must be made to balance with a will o' the wisp existence of a few months, in order to give rise to some new order of things is asking too much in any reason. To cite an analogous case. The new *Cosmopolitan Magazine* and *Harper's Monthly Magazine* might find beneficial results attendant on an amalgamation of those two magazines, but how the Harpers people would laugh were the Cosmopolitan people to ask them to give up their name and fame in return for a similar giving up of name and fame of the Cosmopolitan people as a basis of union for starting a new magazine.

As for the assertion made in the *Red and Black's* editorial that the STENTOR asked the former paper to simply drop itself it is a barefaced falsehood. THE STENTOR made a fair and equitable proposition for union suggested by unbiased outsiders, who had only the true interests of Lake Forest journalism at heart, and the *Red and Black* has asserted itself in the face of public opinion.

[THE STENTOR received a very urgent request to print the above communication. We however acknowledge the *Red and Black* as a competitor of no mean dimensions, and would have been more than gratified to unite with our enterprising contemporary. EDS.

THE FACULTY INTERVIEWED.

The members of the faculty were interviewed by a representative of the STENTOR in regard to the consolidation of the two papers.

Prof Halsey said:—" I think it would be an excellent plan: I wish you would do it." With regard to the name he said: " I never liked the name STENTOR as a name. Being the older paper, however, its name, if either, should be retained. Don't let such a small matter as the name interfere with consolidation. It occupies too much time of too many men to run two papers.

Prof. Dawson said:—" I am heartily in favor of it. I think the young ladies should have some representation beyond a mere correspondent. I think the name STENTOR should be retained. It has established itself as the University paper."

Dr. Seeley said: " From a personal standpoint and for the good of the University I think two papers are better than one. If it is question of financial support the papers should be consolidated. I believe the name should be conceded to the STENTOR."

Prof. McNeil said:—" I think it is desirable by all means to unite the two papers if a plan of equal representation could be hit upon. The STENTOR is generally looked upon as the college paper, and although I do not particularly like the name I think it should be retained."

Prof. Thomas said:—" I am heartily in favor of the plan proposed for the consolidation of

the papers. The STENTOR is the elder paper and it is just that that name should be retained. It would to unite under a new name than not to unite at all."

Prof. Smith said:—" I think that something of that kind should be done, and that it would be well to introduce something of a literary character into the new paper. If all the students would ballot for the name a satisfactory conclusion might be reached."

Prof. Harper said:—"I am thoroughly in favor of having only one paper if any basis of agreement can be found." With regard to the name he said: "I can see that there is a great deal on either side of the argument, but should like to see the name STENTOR continued."

Prof. Locy said:—"I can see some advantages in having two papers, because of the competition it causes. Considering our numbers, and the ill-feeling which seems to be increased, I would think it advantageous to unite into one strong paper. Both papers have been splendidly managed, but to unite the forces of the two would make a first-class paper. The name seems to me to be of little importance."

Prof. Stuart said:—" Unite by all means. The STENTOR is the old stand by and is known. I don't think any objection should be raised to the use of that name. Personally, I prefer the name *Forester* for a Lake Forest paper. I consider the STENTOR better than it has ever been before since I've known it."

Prof. Morris said:—"I think the two papers should unite—Lake Forest is not large enough to support two. I think it should be more of a literary paper than either of the present sheets. I like the name *Red and Black* better than STENTOR, but think the name STENTOR should have precedence. Its six or seven years of existence have established its reputation."

Prof. Bridgman said:—"The two papers should be united by all means. I like the name STENTOR very much." Prof. Bridgman seemed to be very much interested in the matter, and suggested to the STENTOR representative a fair and equitable propoposition, which he thought would cover the existing conditions. This proposition of Prof. Bridgman was acted upon by THE STENTOR board and submitted to the editors of the *Red and Black*. It was not accepted.

Lake Forest Academy
Reid Hall

LAKE FOREST ACADEMY.

AS IT WAS AND IS.—ITS SUC-
CESSFUL PAST AND BRILLIANT
FUTURE.— THE   NEW   BUILD.
INGS.

It was back in the fifties the academy was
started in a building near where the Art institute
now stands.

There it continued until in March 1879, when
the building was burned and Academy Hall was
built where the school reopened in the following
fall.

Those were days of trials and hardships for
the Academy but contributions were liberally
given and it was placed upon a firm financial
basis. It has always been fortunate in having
trustees of good business ability as well as having a faculty at its head of good educational
qualifications who leave no stones unturned for
its welfare, making its future an assured success.

It has never been the purpose of those who
are in charge of it to make the Academy a
school noted for its large attendance but rather
for its thorough, its high standard of education,
and its religious influences and paternal care of
the youth during their attendance. To accomplish this end new and commodious buildings
have been erected at a great cost with money
contributed by some of Lake Forest's most
philanthropic citizens and in the fall of '93 these
will be occupied for the first time. Here it is
the ultimate purpose to care for the two hundred boys and surround them with all the home
comforts modern conveniences offord.

PROMINENT ALUMNI.

The alumni of the Academy are scattered
far and wide. Many who attended in its earliest days are now business men of marked
ability in Chicago and elsewhere and some of
them have boys who are now attending the
Academy. As these older ones return to look
at old familiar scenes great changes are noticed.
What was then a wild country with game
abounding in its native forests is now thickly

inhabited, its forests cleared and stately mansions erected. Its more recent members are scattered among the eastern colleges besides prominent members in the various departments of Lake Forest University.

Among the former are Pine of Ann Arbor class of '94 remembered by older students for his academy and society spirit and his debating ability. Jo Flint, now at Princeton, class of '95, well known as an athlete both here and there, having been captain of the football team and since then having played half back on the Princeton team. He is also on the staff of the daily Princetonian.

Two others known for their good work while in the Academy are Burchell and Wells. The latter has added to his reputation since entering Princeton, having taken during his Freshman year the two hundred dollar prize, given to that member of the Freshman class who shall make the highest average standing in his studies for the year. There are also many others deserving mention.

THE SOCIETIES NOT TO BE SNEERED AT.

It is unnecessary to say there are two societies in the Academy, Tri Kappa and Gamma Sigma. While under the control of the Faculy these societies are conducted by the students themselves and good work is done as shown in the annual contest considered by many the best literary event during the school year.

The prizes for the contest are given by Mr. Holt an Alumnus and warm friend of the Academy. The contests are for supremacy in declamation, debate and essay. There is also the McNeill prize of fifty dollars given to the student who shall make the highest mark in a literary work, the character of which is announced before the contest.

A GOOD EYE FOR ATHLETICS.

The Academy ranks second to none in athletics. It takes pride in its past record and future prospects. Enthusiasm in such work is always on tap and when the word is given all the money needed is cheerfully subscribed.

The football teams and base ball teams of the past year never knew defeat.

The faculty, composed of seven members, are all college bred men, the best that money will get. Chas. A. Smith, the principal, is a man well known for his sincerity of purpose, his upright character, and his polished and dignified bearing toward the students.

It can indeed be truly said that those who wish to do good preparatory work at a moderate expense with home surroundings in one of the most beautiful towns in the west can do no better than to come to Lake Forest.

REPORT OF THE ATHLETIC ASSOCIATION.

Owing to the withdrawal from college of the treasurer, the accounts of the association cunnot at present be published, though they will be published eventually. The association ends the year as it began, about $100 in debt. This is largely due to the fact that certain students have not paid subscriptions actually pledged.

The special thanks of the association are due to the citizens of Lake Forest, who have been very generous in their support, and to the gentlemen who under a pseudonym, gave a more than liberal sum. We hope that at some time such gifts may be so offered as to yield a permanent return and commemorate the giver.

The Board of Directors has met with regularity throughout the year. The vacancy caused by the resignation of Mr. Everett was filled by the election of Mr. Durand. The accounts of the treasurer, Mr. McGaughey, who left college in February, were turned over to the president. Some of the members of the Board of Directors have not been faithful in attending the meetings, but only once has the meeting wanted a quorum. It is urged that the members of the Board of Directors hold themselves responsible for the success of all athletics and be ready to serve on all occasions.

The year has been an unsuccessful one owing to three causes, lack of enthusiasm on the part of the students, financial embarassment, and, in a measure, faults of calculation on the part of the officers. These causes are inter dependent, each modifying the others. The students have shown lack of enthusiasm in put- ting their interest in the Athletic Association, second to personal or party interests, and in failing to meet their written obligations to pay subscriptions; while candidates for the teams have been careless in their training. The last is true of the foot-ball team most of all, for they at the end of an expensive season, when much had been done for them, broke training and practice repeatedly during the last two weeks, on the eve of the most important game. College sport should not tolerate this in its re- presentatives.

Financial embarassment has been caused by procrastination in the treasurer, by the failure of the college students to meet their subscriptions, and by the exceedingly heavy expenses, com- bined with small receipts of the foot ball teams. Any failure on the part of the nine to keep up its organization and its practice is excusable on the ground of absolute lack of funds and the unwillingness of the association to contract fur- ther debts. Thirdly, the Board of Directors is responsible for a very unfair division of the available funds between the various interests, though they justify themselves by the state- ment that apparently safe sources of income have failed them.

Now for the future: There is good athletic material in college. We have an energetic foot ball captain and manager elected, and we do not wish to fall behind in the awakening of interest in the game of foot ball. There will still be good material for a nine next year and the Board of Directors will take care that base ball has proper consideration, proportioned to the funds at its command. It is urged that in the line of the most successful event of the year, the Field Day, the development of indi- vidual athletics, which is most possible in a small college, be encouraged. It is suggested that if the trustees will furnish the material and proper

supervision the students shall agree to do the manual labor of putting the field in order. Ad- ditional tennis courts are much to be desired, especially if by their construction the ladies of the college can be encouraged to take more in- terest in athletics. The gymnasium needs a little more developing apparatus, in the way of chest weights and special appliances, but its beautiful interior and many conveniences ought to win every students frequent presence there.

It will be seen from the financial statements, when published that the Association is, as in former years, greatly indebted to the support of the gentlemen of the town. As long as we have so small a population and un- enclosed grounds we must depend on such support, but we are bound to make some re- turn. They must not be allowed to feel that they are paying a mere tax in residence in Lake Forest from which they get back not even amusement.

We must show by activity and by skill in the games that we appreciate their kindness, and if our games are worth seeing they will attend them and not begrudge their contribu- tions. The officers feel that they must manage to have more games in Lake Forest and that the students must take as much interest in town matters as we expect the town to take in college matters.

Every one connected with the college knows that internal bickering is more disastrous to success in athletics than constant defeat in the field. So long as the patriotic energy of the students is exhausted in party politics, no enter- prise of common advantage can prosper. The Athletic Association has been the recipient of second-rate enthusiasm and languid support, when honorable victory in the field has seemed less desirable than the triumph of trickery. If rivalry is not to be confined to the legitimate object of rivalry, the association must continue to make the best of a discouraging situation.

It is recommended:

1 That the time of Athletic Association en- tertainments be fixed at the beginning of the

year, and that all other college entertainments give them a wide berth.

2 That there be a University Glee Club whose Inteaests shall be in a degree identified with those of this Association. Such a club would be truly representative of the college and could give an annual concert in Lake Forest, half of the receipts to go to the Athletie Association.

3 In view of the fact that the Academy students are to have, in due time, separate grounds and consequently are likely to develop independent athletics of their own, they must be asked for only moderate subscriptions.

4 It is also urged that the membership fee of $1 be done away with, and that whoever pays a fixed sum, to be determined by the Board of Directors, shall be entitled to a season ticket good for all outdoor events. Respectfully,

W. R. BRIDGMAN,
President Athletic Association.

MRS. COULTER INTERVIEWED.

" If first impressions augur truth my Lake Forest life must indeed be an happy one," said Mrs. Coulter to a STENTOR representative upon the occasion of her brief visit to Lake Forest recently.

" Last night I had the pleasure of attending the meeting of the University Club and was delighted with its personnel and I had expected great things of Lake Forest people. Between showers today we have driven about the city and to say that I am more than pleased with its beauty and freshness is expressing an im pression most mildly. Surely nature has almost out done herself in displaying her aesthetic cunning, and where nature has been in error, man has, and is making correction.

A student should be happy here if anywhere with such an environment, and I am eagerly looking forward to my new home life in Lake Forest with happy anticipation."

SHE USED TO "CRIB."

Something about the girl-hood of the woman who has done more to make Grover Cleveland than any other factor in his life may be of interest to the girls. As a matter of fact Mrs. Cleveland's metamorphoses from the blithesome girlhood into that stately womanhood becoming the wife of the chief executive of a great nation is scarcely less wonderful than the remarkable development seen in the president himself.

When, as Frances Folsom, Mrs. Cleveland studied Cæsar's Commentaries in the Buffalo High School, she was neither the brightest nor the dullest girl in her class. She was a popular girl, and a great favorite with the boys. She used to "crib" her French and Latin books in the good old way. While she did not lead her classmates, she possessed remarkable intuitions, making it easy for her to grasp almost any subject. She was a society girl and loved fun and frolic.

Her engagement ring, girls, was a sapphire and a diamond. She wore it on commencement day at Wells College not so many years ago when she read her graduation essay and said good bye to school life. The next day when she was packing up to go home she was seen to wrap a cabinet photograph up in a little blue shawl. The girls said it was the picture of Grover Cleveland.

There was another romance before Grover came. We all have them. "Frankie" Folsom and "Charlie" Townsend had their's. Charlie was forgotten, but he had the satisfaction of having stolen a good many sly kisses before Grover came.

Mrs. Cleveland graduated from Wells College in 1885, took a year's trip abroad with her mother, and was married to Grover Cleveland June 2, 1886. DANFORTH

COMMENCEMENT DAYS.

DEDICATORY EXERCISES.
FERRY HALL GRADUATES.
ANNUAL CONCERT.

The golden sun of our college year is now
setting. Its irridescent rays are now sinking
into a flood of ruddy effulgence, and the season
of '93 will soon have set into the boundless
night of the present future, to be succeeded by
the morning of coming time. That portion of
the yearly sunset already accomplished has
cast a more than usual lustre about the fame of
old Lake Forest, as was evinced in the dedicatory ceremonies over those noble structures
that will form the new home of Lake Forest
Academy.

THE DEDICATORY EXERCISES OF REID HALL.

The hopes of the trustees and the expectations of the patrons of Lake Forest University
have at last been fulfilled, and the much talked
of new buildings are a reality. The dedicatory
exercises were held in Reid Hall last Friday
afternoon at 3 o'clock. The principal address
was made by Rev. Dr. Simon J. McPherson,
who, in a few well-chosen remarks, gave some
valuable ideas concerning Secondary Education.

The Doctor said that the preparatory course
meant everything to the future education of a
boy, and that whereas the high school must try
to please everybody the academy could have a
clearly defined policy to which its attendants
must either live up to or change to some other
school.

He also said that in his opinion earnest, honest, concentrated efforts on the parts of the
trustees and faculty to build up the college and
its preparatory departments would amount to
infinitely more in an educational line than trying to sustain in addition to them a number of
professional departments at a distance.

The keys were delivered to the trustees by
Arthur Reid. Immediately after the program
Mr. and Mrs. H. C. Durand received the stu-
dents and friends of the University at the
Annie Durand Cottage.

FERRY HALL EXERCISES.

Amid flowers in profusion and that delicate
air of feminine grace which makes conspicuous
the sweetness of young womanhood, the Ferry
Hall girl appeared on the Commencement platform Wednesday morning in one of the most
successful exercises ever presented by the Seminary department of the University. A bare
mention of the features of the day is as follows:

PROGRAM.

MARCH AND OVERTURE.

Salutatory with Essay—The Study of the Stars
Effie May Gerry.
Essay—Jacques Bonhomme.
Anna Johnson.
Essay—Dreams That Come True.
Margaret Mae Creswell.

MUSIC.

Essay—People I Do Not Like.
Jennette Kennedy.
Essay—The Three Great Elegies.
Jane Campbell Fraser.
Essay—Not the American Way.
Mildred Raymond Lyon.
Essay—The Eloquence of Decay.
Maud Josephine Black.

MUSIC.

Essay——The Way of the Words.
Grace Abigail Brubaker.
Essay—Is David or Goliath the Knight of the
Nineteenth Century?
Grace Louise Taylor.
Essay—Oh, Ye Simple! Understand Wisdom.
Edith Jane Smith.
Essay—Healthy Ambitions.
Mary Elizabeth McWilliams.

MUSIC.

Essay—The Other Side of the Moon.
Margaret Grace McCord.
Essay—Does Modern Aestheticism Include
High Art?
Virna Theodora Macomber.
Essay—The Sense of Proportion, with Vale-
dictory.
Alta Barnum.

MUSIC.

Address by the Principal.
Presentation of Diplomas.

FERRY HALL CONCERT.

Music and song mingled with charming dramatic selections, combined to make the Ferry Hall Concert of Tuesday afternoon one of the prettiest functions of Commencement Week. The delicate and masterly touches of the instructor's art were pleasingly apparent in every item of the program. Costumes worn by the young women were unexcelled for their dreamy loveliness. Galaxies of feminine beauty like clusters of apple blossoms contributed to the attractiveness of Ferry Chapel. The music, both vocal and instrumental, was of a high grade of excellence, and the selections were received with more than usual applause. Following is the program:

PROGRAM.

The Prophecy.,......................W. A. Croffut
Dedication Ode. Recited at the Opening of the
World's Fair, May 1, 1893.
Miss Mildred R. Lyon.
Introduction and March. Two Pianos....Hans Huber
Mr. George Eugene Eager and Miss Ripley.
It Was a Dream..................W. C. E. Seeboeck
Miss Emma Parmenter.
Rondo in A Minor..........................Mozart
Miss Lucia E. Clark.
The Courting of T'nowhead's Belle............Barrie
Miss Nellie Dillin.
Habanera, (Carmen)..........................Bizet
Miss Byrd Huddart.
"Le Favori"...............................Hummel
Miss Sizer.
Pauline Paulovna..........................Aldrich
Miss Sadie Davis.
Rondo Capriccioso..................Mendelssohn
Miss Ripley.
Recitative and Aria (Orfeo)...................Gluck
Miss Hester.
Concerto in F. Sharp Minor..............Ferd Hiller
Mr. George Eugene Eager.
Accompaniment on Second Piano by Miss Ripley.

ACADEMY COMMENCEMENT.

The Academy Commencement Exercises were held last Friday evening in Reid Hall. The orations were of a high order, and showed thought and careful composition. F. B. Whitney was salutatorian. He argued modern sciences and classics as of more benefit than ancient classics.

M. K. Baker captured the valedictory. His subject, "Universal Culture," was admirably handled and showed painstaking work.

The Haven Gold Medal was won by N. W. Flint.

The McNeil Prize was won by F. Angus, first, and B. S. Cutler, second.

PROGRAM.

PRAYER.
Music.
*Salutatory Oration—Modern versus Ancient Classics.
Fred Brown Whitney, Waukegan.
Oration—Chinese Gordon.
Nott William Flint, Chicago.
Oration—University Extension.
†Arthur Somerville Reid, Lake Forest.
Oration—Our Debt to the Past.
Frederic Carlton Ritchey, Portage, Wis.
Music.
Oration—Heroism.
Robert Lloyd Roberts, Colwyn Bay, Wales.
Oration—Decline of Oratory.
Fred Cameron Vincent, Odell.
Oration—Imagination in Literature.
George Mulford Wells, Macomb.
Music.
Oration—Home Rule.
Turlington Walker Harvey, Jr., Chicago.
Oration—Cortez.
Edward Esher Yaggy. Lake Forest.
*Valedictory Oration—Universal Culture.
Maurice Kingman Baker, Chicago.
Awarding of Marietta Humes McNeil Prize.
Awarding of Haven Gold Medal.
PRESENTATION OF DIPLOMAS.
Rev. J. G. K. McClure, Pres. Pro tem of the University.

*Second Honor.
†Excused from Speaking.
‡First Honor.

ACADEMY RECEPTION.

The Annual Academy Reception given by the students was held last Saturday evening in the Art Institute, consisting of a promenade of sixteen members. The hall was tastefully decorated with flowers and Academy colors, and the music was furnished by Tomaso's orchestra. A very pleasant evening was enjoyed by all attending.

BACCALAUREATE SUNDAY.

Sunday morning saw the church full, the number of visitors being greater than were before. Dr. McClure had for the text of his Baccalaureate Sermon, Luke ix,-56. "The son of man came not to destroy men's lives, but to save them." The subject of the sermon was, "The Emphasis on the Affirmative." "Be a positive factor," he said to the graduating classes, "Do not take more from the world than you give. Realize that you must construct, leave something behind you, not destroy."

In the evening Dr. McClure led a beautiful prayer-meeting on "Faithfulness," Prof. Halsey and others speaking. At 7:45 Dr. Carlos Martyn delivered the annual address before the Christian Associations.

THE FRESHMAN-SOPHOMORE CONTEST

Monday evening the annual Freshman-Sophomore contest took place at the Art Institute. The hall was tastefully decorated by the committee and there was a spirit of anticipation in the air as the audience gradually assembled. When at last Dr. McClure rose to offer the opening prayer the room was crowded to its utmost capacity. Quickly everything quieted and then for two hours the great audience listened attentively to the round of speakers and music. After the prayer, Miss Ripley and Miss Sizer rendered a cradle song, by Bohm, on the piano. From thence the program was as follows:

Program.

The Sultan's Sadness,................E. J. McPhelim
Julia D. Brown.
Selection from " Last Days of Pompeii,".........Lytton
Albert E. Burdick.
Address to an Old Coat....................G. L. Baker
Louise M. Hopkins.
William Tell,................................Anon
Ellis U. Graff.
MUSIC.
The Legend Beautiful,....................Longfellow
Katharine J. Kenaga
Idols,..............................Wendell Phillips
Edward U. Henry.
The Revolutionary Rising,......................Read
Olive McClanehan.
MUSIC.

Hand-Car No. 412,.......................John Heard
Dean Lewis.
Wat Tyler's Address to the King,.............Southey
Clayton W. Sherman.
The Union of the States,.............Daniel Webster
Burtis R. McHatton.
MUSIC.
Decision of Judges.

The singing of Mr. Whitehead, of Chicago, during the last three numbers, was very well received. The decision of the judges, Mr. Wm. H. Smith, Mr. Ward and Mr. Will Terry, awarded the first prize of $30 to E. U. Henry, '95, a freshman, Miss Louise Hopkins won the second prize of $20. Such was the result of the contest, '95 having won for two years. The popularity of this contest is every year increasing, and the Art Institute will no longer be large enough for it.

JUNIOR ORATORICAL CONTEST.

Tuesday night the juniors crossed swords in their Annual Oratorical Contest. Following is the program.

PRAYER.
MUSIC.
In defense of Blaine,   -   -   A. P. Bourns
England's Dark Blot,   -   - E. A. Drake
Sincerity,   -   -   -   - Grace Pierce
MUSIC.
William T. Sherman,   -   - W. B. Smith
The Mission of Charles Dickens,
Eudora Smith
William Carey,   -   -   - A. F. Waldo
MUSIC.
Decision of Judges.

CLASS DAY '93.

The senior class day exercises of the college take place Wednesday evening of this week. There will probably be the usual gibes upon, and presentations to the lower classes and faculty. '93 has always been a "hustling" class and we can safely promise our readers something entirely novel and of a startling character. The exercises are of such a nature that the class wishes to keep them secret.

COMMENCEMENT DAY.

Thursday will be the grand finale of the busy week. On that day occur graduation exercises, inauguration ceremonies, luncheon and reception.

The day will begin with the procession of students, which will form on the campus at 9.30 and march with the band to the church. The program will be as follows:

March and Overture.....................
Prayer.
Music.
Salutatory Essay,...........Annie L. Adams
Honorary Oration,.......Stephen B. Hopkins
Oration,................." Phillips Brooks."
Charles S. Davies.
Oration....................." Savonorola."
Robert H. Crozier.
Oration........." The Political Compromise."
William N. McKee.
Oration,   -
"Webster and the Compromise of 1850."
Frederic C. Sharon.
Valedictory Essay.......Rebecca E. Adams
Conferring of Degrees.

Then the usual addresses will come, Prof. Jack speaking for the alumni, Prof. Halsey for the faculty, and Dr. Herrick Johnson for the trustees. Each address will bear more or less on the inauguration.

What Dr. Herrick Johnson will communicate is of prime importance, as he tells of the actions, appropriations, etc., which occurred at the meeting of the trustees the day before.

The inauguration proper will consist in an address and the handing over the keys by Dr. McClure, and an inauguration address by Dr. Coulter.

Luncheon will be served at the Art Institute immediately after the exercises for those who have no other place to go.

In the evening Dr. and Mrs. McClure will receive at the Manse from 8 to 10 o'clock.

It is very unfortunate that the programs for commencement week have been so dilatory in coming out. It has been impossible to ascertain the program for any of the exercises more than a few hours before hand. The STENTOR has, however, managed to get a program for Commencement Day, but the final program may vary a little from that given.

COLLEGE.

Examinations were finished at 12:15 Friday.

Prof. Smith will spend a part of the summer in Nova Scotia.

Prof. Stanley will spend most of his vacation at Harbor Springs, Mich.

President Coulter led chapel for the first time Friday morning, June 2d.

L. H. Beals, of Ann Arbor, spent Sunday, the 4th, with friends in Lake Forest.

The Seniors defeated the Freshmen in baseball Wednesday afternoon by a score of 14 to 3.

The College defeated the Academy at baseball Thursday afternoon. Mr. Crozier umpired.

The young ladies seem to have the advantage over the boys of the senior class. Miss Rubie Adams is valedictorian and Miss Annie Adams is the salutatorian.

The faculty have lately discussed the question of changing the present division of the year into that of semesters. This is the plan in vogue in Ann Arbor and seems to be more satisfactory than the three-term scheme into which our school year is divided.

The engagement of Mr. N. H. Burdick and Miss Alice Conger has been announced. Mr. Burdick is a member of the class of '93 and Miss Conger is an alumnus of Ferry Hall Seminary and is at present an instructor in that institution. The STENTOR offers its heartiest congratulations.

The officers for the Athenæan Society, for the fall term of '93, are:

President,   .   .   .   C. Smith
Vice-President,   .   .   J. H. Jones

Secretary,   .   .   .   E. U. Graff
Treasurer,   .   .   .   D. H. Jackson
Critic,   .   .   .   E. H. McNeal
Sergeant,   .   .   H. C. McClanahan

The officers of the Zeta Epsilon Society for next term are as follows:

President,   .   .   .   A. F. Waldo
Vice-President,   .   .   .   E. C. Clevelad
Secretary,   .   .   .   G. T. B. Davis
Critic,   .   .   .   T. Marshall
Treasurer,   .   .   .   J. M. Vance
Sergeant, ...   Chas. Thorn

The president of our Board of Trustees, ex-Senator Farwell, has just given another example of his watchful interest in Lake Forest by securing for us a collection of rocks and ores from the Smithsonian Institute at Washington. The set numbers about seventy-five specimens and includes several of the important silver-lead ores, gold ores from California and Nevada and a series of typical ores of the base metals. The limited number of sets distributed by the Smithsonian are made up with especial reference to their use in the class-room and the college is fortunate in securing this one.

THE SENIOR.

Pity 'tis—'tis true. That is subjectively it is regarded a pity, though perhaps, aye doubtless, the students, townspeople and instructors deem it a blessing—Ninety-three is going, going—GONE.

The world is the highest, that is the lowest bidder. The class is dropped into the world's oblivion. Now, if it is thought that this class can be disposed of in such an unceremonious manner remember the past, forget not that history repeats herself, and that in this Ninety-three finds a friend.

From the time that she baffled with those mightiest of the mighty, the Sophomores, conquered the well-nigh invincible forces of the antiquity by her dashing cavalry charges, escaped the grim checkered shadows of the Waukegan Bastile and permitted the confiscated chancellor's "freezer" to escape her not, until the day when the last obligation was laid upon her in the form of a class endowment requested by "Box 149," as a "graduation fee" she has pushed victoriously forward against a tide of difficulty, opposition and prejudice to the end.

The Freshman year was fraught with hope, fear and examinations; the Sophomore period brought experience, ponies, and livery bills; the Junior season was one of joy, not unmingled with physics and psychological data, but the Senior year, ah, what a year!

Senior! what a name, what an implication it carries! It is the term applied to those who have gotten through, whether by virtue of hard study or otherwise, three years of college existence, and who are entered upon the last heat in a happy race. The chapel bell announces the start, and amidst the warm, cheerful rays of a September sun the contest begins

It is one in which receptions, the garnering in of apples and grapes, very much absent in '92, football games, class meetings, ethics and love commingle. Pleasure is the senior's byword. Pleasure is sought and found, although somewhat tarnished by the examination and the letter from home inquiring about the future profession. Now this is the spectre which ever haunts the senior. As he glides through the waltz he thinks himself a lawyer, the quadrille proves him a physician, the polka decides him to be an editor, while the Virginia reel brings to him the most sensible conclusion that he is nothing. Winter comes with its sleigh-ride, and the senior is there. Spring comes with its party and rainy night, but the senior's regrets represent him there. His vacation comes, his class day and his graduation. It is over. He is a senior no longer, a collegian no more. He goes out having conquered all that has been assigned him. He feels that his college days have not been in vain. The Ninety-three man has ever succeeded, and why should he fail when college has been abandoned. He has met much opposition and has never been overcome; he enters the race of life as he entered the college race, bent upon SUCCESS.

THE ACADEMY SENIORS.

Again has Commencement Day come and gone, and another class has separated never to meet as Academy Seniors again. It was a great class, the class of '94, and as we think of them there flits across our memory a vision of Academia, the President's House, Mitchell Hall, Waukegan girls, bums and, need I mention it, cigarettes. How liberally they construed English until, indeed, the word "bluff," by which is ordinarily designated that portion of land along the lake, meant to them only how they persuaded the Faculty to give them just what they wanted!

What large drops of intellectual sweat stood out on their noble brows as they worked over " those orations ! "

But, though they had their faults, each had his good qualities as well. There was Flint, the foot ball player—the class could never meet without him. There was Reid, the man of classics, he made his name immemorial by having it placed upon the new Chapel. There was Vincent, the noble, and pure, and good; and Roberts, whose joy and hope was in the Sem.; and Baker, who stood so high in his classes that he never knew what it was to be without privileges; and Yaggy, who loved tennis; and Flint, and the girls; and Ritchey, who made himself famous and will ever be remembered by his poetry and puns.

And now we think of Cheever, who had that quality known as nerve, and made his own way along the thoroughfare of life; and Wells, the gentlemanly sport and scientific scholar; and Whitney, with his curly locks and checked pants, and who never cared whether people looked his way or not. Then there was Harvey, a prize winner in the contest, everyone knows him.

But they are gone, and whatever faults they may have had, whatever little difficulties may have come between them and the Faculty, they will ever cherish in their memories a year of pleasure, and a class known for its hearty good fellowship.

FERRY HALL.

NU BETA KAPPA.

Our society has, for many reasons, been at a great disadvantage this year, but a committee has recently consulted with the faculty and the following, by one of the members expressing the sentiment of many of the girls, makes us hope for a better condition of things.

The question is, should Ferry Hall have two literary societies?

If we have two societies with the same work before each, would they agree and, as a conseqence, would good work be the result? or would they conflict and prove a disadvantage to the girls and Ferry Hall?

We have at present but one society, the Nu Beta Kappa, and, as a matter of course, it is the only way in which literary work is done.

About one-third of our number are enrolled as active members and but few of these have any real interest in the work and welfare of the society. We meet but once in two weeks. Every member is supposed to take part at least once a term and as much oftener as the committee see fit. Some have not taken part all year, because they regard it as an irksome duty and never think of the benefit. I have heard many men, prominent in a business, professional or literary way, say they owed their success largely to the imperative duties of their society when at college. This statement, by men who are capable of judging, ought to mean a great deal to us, for if man can attain so much from literary work, cannot woman be elevated by it also?

It has already been said the girls lack enthusiasm for their society.

Could not this difficulty be dissipated by organizing a rival society?

Would not the girls be interested in seeing their society foremost?

Have we not a natural pride in whatever we claim or what claims us? The interest of each member could not but result in good thoughtful work. Some one has said that if Nu Beta were divided it would cause contention.

The faculty could arrange that the number in each society be about equal and surely we can be ladies.

There could be *at least* forty members in each society, and what cannot forty earnest workers accomplish?

Our pride will not allow the standard of Ferry Hall to drop, as it certainly will, unless good society work is done, as to many parents this seems a thing of first importance for their daughters.

Shall it be said that we have no ability or that we do not use what we have?

No, let us have two societies, competition and good work.

AUTOBIOGRAPHY OF A WASTE BASKET.

My dear friend, were you ever a waste basket? Not a common ordinary business man's waste basket but a real pretty bamboo Ferry Hall waste basket? I have been one for two years now and although sometimes I have been made exceedingly tired by being stuffed so full and never emptied, yet on the whole I have passed an interesting and instructive life. I wonder if anything can learn as much in two short years as a Ferry Hall waste basket—especially if its mistress is popular. At those rare times when I have been empty and felt real free I have received some hard knocks.

I have been *impressed* rather unfavorably several times by being used for a foot-ball, but then the dents are *very small* because you know Ferry Hall feet—but we digress. Let me tell you a day's experience. I am supposed to be emptied on Saturday. On this particular Saturday, wonderful to relate, I was empty until evening. I was awakened from a dream of home and mother (they reside in a furniture store you know) by something hitting me in the side and hearing my mistress express herself in the following terms:

"Well, did you ever! That chump calling on me. Well, I'm not in. Tell him I'm in the city or dead, anything you like, Sarah." Then

I examine the article that so rudely awakened me and find it is the small square, engraved card of Mr.——. I have held many of these but none of them ever hit me so hard before. Having recovered from this epistle, I am made the recipient in quick succession of a cocoa can, orange peelings, Saturday's laundry paper, broken hair-pins, notes from "my dearest," in fact, everything that did not go into our memory book. I began to think that with such a conglomeration my digestion would be seriously impaired, when to my horror I received a bill from Marshall Field. It filled me so utterly that I must have wept for I heard my mistress say to her room-mate, "Why what *are* you spilling your cocoa in the waste basket for? But then you are not accountable. Did you enjoy your walk this afternoon?" I was then promiscuously stuffed with withered rose leaves from "my latest," algebra problems, French exercises, "Daily Princetonians" and empty candy boxes. When I could hold no more I was gently but firmly stepped in and almost smothered. This extra space being gained I was then enabled to hold my last precious addition. There was a dull thud as of some one trying to dislocate the lounge with one fell swoop, deep wailing and suddenly a shower of scraps of paper accompanied by a flood of tears struck me at the same time, and being overloaded I fainted. When I recovered consciousness the light was out and silence reigned. Perhaps you do not know it but a waste basket can always see better in the dark. So as the scraps of paper were on top of me and most easily discernible I began to put them together with the most startling results. Would you like to see what I saw? You shall. "Here it is: "My Ownest Dear," it began— (now what an *ownest dear* is I'm sure I don't know) I have just received a letter from my mamma and, oh how can I tell you, love, it breaks my heart to tell you, but we must part, oh we must. My papa says I am paying too much for candy and flowers and must either give up you or my new spring suit and oh, darling, much as I love you, you could not ask me to do the latter. I love you as much as ever' dearest and as soon as I get my suit I will go with you again. Until I pay my tailor, farewell, sweetest. Your Devoted,

WILLIE.

N. B. Willie has his suit but he seems to be pressing another suit now.

Thus endeth my day's work—SELAH.

THE SENIORS.

For pretty entertainments and good times the present year has never been equaled in the record of Ferry Hall social events. As students, the young ladies of the senior class have one more opportunity in which to reveal their capabilities, what they have done for us in many ways we will tell you briefly.

They began the year with a great deal of enthusiasm and interest in other people and things, and thus in making many happy were happy themselves. In the early fall they entertained the juniors in the Art Room, giving them the daintiest and prettiest spread imaginable.

A dumb concert in the gymnasium followed soon after, in which Miss Macomber, Miss Black and Miss Kennedy were marvels as musicians, and Miss Lyon's recitation and minuet have never been surpassed. Music by the class quite overwhelmed the audience.

The only wedding which took place in Ferry Hall this year was a double wedding, and occurred in the winter term. It was a chrysanthemum wedding, and beautiful in every detail. Promptly at eight o'clock the march began, and after the ceremony, which was the modification of several forms, the wedding party received in the Reading Room, after which the guests danced in the Gymnasium.

In November the young ladies entertained the faculty at afternoon tea, which all voted a great success.

The Valentine Tea, which was also German evening, was perhaps as charming with its informal and novel ideas as anything they have undertaken.

The usual Senior Reception is fresh in the minds of all, and needs no further mention.

Aside from the pleasure they have helped us to in a social way, they have been active in suggesting and assisting in all the enterprises undertaken. In the refurnishing of the parlors they gave much time and energy, and they have won the good-will of the girls in general. The class president is Miss McWilliams, its number, fourteen, its colors royal purple and white, and its flower the modest pansy.

Wednesday they had a right royal senior celebration in the way of a picnic, which was truly a picnic, and in which they were joined by the members of the senior class in the Academy.

Tuesday afternoon, June 6, being warm enough to admit of light pretty dresses, the tennis tournament was a success from an artistic standpoint as well as a means of entertainment. The grounds were filled with animated young people, and four tennis courts were in use all the afternoon. The most successful players of the twenty-five who entered were Miss Davies and Mr. Marcott.

HERE AND THERE.

The Fair this year has made some difference in the work known here as special work, as it always seems easy to put off an extra for outside things. In spite of this fact a great deal of work has been accomplished by the various classes. In the art room almost twice as much work has been done this year as there was last, and it is of a better kind and greater variety.

Circumstances have made it impossible for us to hear Miss Fleming read this year as much as we would like Rhetoricals, and the recitals are proof that she has not been idle, or the girls without interest.

We are indebted to Prof. Eager, Mrs. Hester and the Misses Ripley and Sizer for charming bits of music at different times during the year.

There is cause for regret that Mrs. Seeley's class is not going to have another display, but we will enjoy seeing Mrs. Seeley's work at the Fair.

A YEAR AT FERRY HALL.

It makes one ambitious.

It makes one unselfish.

One has become attached to Ottomans.

One has become Graffic in her descriptions.

Ferry Hall teaches most of its inmates self-reliance, a few dependence.

It has managed of late in some mysterious way to make several rather sarcastic.

A few of our dignified ——? have come to prefer windows to doors, and have a leaning toward a certain green chair.

Fine place for the blues—sure cure for conceit. Teaches self-reliance, a very important thing.

Browning is also in vogue. Taking it all in all, Ferry Hall is a pretty nice place, and we shall be right sorry to leave it.

Ferry Hall really hardens and strengthens many girls who enter it with the intention of taking proper advantage of all opportunities afforded.

When a girl leaves home for her first trial of boarding school, she little realizes what harships, temptations and disappointments await her, nor yet the benefit derived from even one year of seminary life. She gains independence, self-reliance and discovers her true worth. She finds she is fitted for some thing, and encouraged and discouraged in turn she leaves school ennobled and strengthened for the future.

AMONG THE ALUMNI.

THE CLASS OF '94.

Anna Blair has advanced to the position of teacher of elocution in Peoria High School.

Eva Bouton is a champion tennis player.

Miss Mathes is studying vocal music abroad.

Lidia Yertson mingles in the highest literary circles.

Miss McIntosh is exploring the North Pole for botany specimens.

Miss Welton has a beautiful summer residence at Roger's Park.

Miss Bird is doing splendid work as a missionary in Hunt Chow, China.

Ola Brinkman gave the welcoming address at the alumni banquet last week.

Miss Thompson's new version of "Poor Richard's Almanac" is just out.

Miss Stella Condon has written a great book on the Briggs Case. Be sure and read it.

Lucia Clark has become the wife of an inventor. She is the "lamp" of the household.

Miss Emma Parmenter is preparing her old maid's chester—er casket. She has our best wishes.

Mabel Palmer is living in independence of all, being a great discoverer in science, i. e. chemistry.

India Wilson has developed into a great Y. W. C. A. worker, being president of that society, and presiding at its meetings with dignity and grace.

May Stewart is a famous musician, owing to her early training under Prof. Eager, and reports Blanche Barnum as one of her most promising pupils.

She, who was Miss Davis, resides at Lake Forest and writes society notes for the STENTOR. Judging from her reports in that paper, the young men are kept busy in giving swell banquets and dinners—not to mention serenades—for the benefit of the "Sems."

THE ALETHEIAN SOCIETY.

In a secluded nook and in a peaceful clime dwells the Aletheian Society for the college girls.

The remark is often heard: " is there such a society as the Aletheian; I hardly ever hear its name mentioned?" For the benefit of such inquirers we affirm that there *is* such an institution, the members of which hold in honor its name and obey its rules.

Its history has been comparatively uneventful, few foes have made intrusions on its rights; hence there have been few wars to bring it into prominence. The interest in literary efforts has not been impeded by being diverted into other channels that usually threaten college sollege societies. The questions of "how can we work that girl to join *our* society," or "what scheme can we work to get ahead of *that* society," never come up among the Aletheians, for numbers come without the asking and there is no one our rights to dispute.

Let no one say they have no force because they are seldomly heard from, for they work on the principle that "the deeper the stream, the silenter."

Miss Bessie Adams at Ferry Hall.

Miss Lila Phelps is visiting her sisters.

Miss McKee is entertaining her two sisters.

Miss Florence Linnell is visiting her sister, Miss Grace.

Miss Elizabeth C. Williams, '90, has been a guest at Ferry Hall for the past week.

Miss Maltby and the Misses Smith, of Minneapolis are guests of the Misses Creswell. "One can't tell t'other Miss Smith from which."

TOWN TOPICS.

Mr. and Mrs. Yaggy and sons will shortly leave Lake Forest to travel abroad for two years. They will sail on July 18th. Mr. David A. Jones has taken the Yaggy home for this summer and next.

PUBLISHED EVERY WEEK
BY THE

Lake Forest University Stentor Publishing Co.

BOARD OF EDITORS.

B. R. MacHatton, '95.............Managing Editor
Forest Grant, '96......Ass't Mgr. Ed. and Athletic
Harry Goodman, '94.............Business Manager
A. B. Burdick, '95 ⎫
J. H. Jones, '96 ⎬ ....Locals
David Fales, Jr., '96 ⎭
W. B. Smith, '94.............Alumni and Exchange
R. G. McKinnie, '97.................Academy
Miss Tena Kennedy, ...Ferry Hall
J. A. McGaughey, '95.................Advertising

Terms—$1.50 per year. Single Copies—10c

————ADDRESS————

STENTOR PUBLISHING COMPANY,

LAKE FOREST, : : ILLINOIS.

Entered at the P. O. at Lake Forest, Ill., as second-class matter.

THE EDITOR'S EASY CHAIR.

Room 31, 2 A.M.—Snakes flying around promiscuously; said snakes represent the fag ends of thoughts which could not be worked in. The snakes are intermingled with globules of ideas for editorials.

Sporadic sprays of news for which there is no space shoot up among the snakes and globules. The foregoing is a chapter from the mind of the managing editor, as he surveys the chaotic results of his efforts to get together the commencement issue of THE STENTOR. It is in no braggadocio tone that we say that no one knows the exact psychological phenomena attendant upon presenting to the public a fair-to-middling issue of a college weekly. The experience is unique in the field of newspaper work. The managing editor of a college paper with his limited facilities, his peculiar environment incident on uncertain quantities which are liable to fail at the critical moment, finds himself at the end of the year in the midst of a hideous nightmare inadequately pictured by the opening sentences of this screed.

The moral of this little story is: If you

want to cultivate that priceless virtue, patience; if you are desirous of becoming somewhat adept as a searcher after green thoughts or a manipulator of fag ends in this big world you could not select a more suitable field for your education than the old cane seat and seldom cushioned Editor's Easy Chair.

***

Speaking in this same strain—various and sundry faces of our old loves float about in the hazy and tobacco-laden atmosphere of our sanctum. Those faces of the loves of former years mingle in strange and cogent fancies. There is the sweet face with the melancholy eyes and sadly winning smile, the ideal and the reality of which have lingered 'round our fleeting years like the memory of a beautiful and half-forgotten dream. There is the saucy, dashing face, with pouting red lips, and the flashing black eyes that erstwhile flooded our life with hopes or chased us into the sullen degredation of despair. There is the proud patrician face of the girl we admired at a distance, the memory of which still causes a cold but delicious shudder to play at cross-tag 'round about our yielding physique. There were other faces into whose soulful eyes we looked with yearnings unutterable and whose description palsies the pen and quite escapes the compass of words. They have gone—all gone into the past, and, like the ashes of a fragrant Havana, let them rest where they lie.

There is another subject that rises before us like a phantom and will not down. It is the engaged young man. This individual is a peculiar development of the *genus homo*. He lives in a little world all by himself, high above the reach of his less fortunate fellows. Dwelling in that world with him is a creature, shall we say, of his fancy, the fair ideal about which he has draped garments that lend a glamours and an enchantment unreal? It may be so, but he does not think so. He is happy. Let no serpent of Eden ingratiate its glistening folds into the sun-lit and flower-encircled gardens of his blest estate. The hard-hided and supercilious bachelor who fancies that he has played upon the heart-strings of all the beautiful heart harps he has met with only to produce an inharmonious and doleful dirge may fling his little joke at the engaged man with unsatisfactory results. The domestic man who is regaled nightly with the dulcet tones of baby and who pursues his seemingly unsatisfactory round of daily toil only that the proceeds may find a receptacle in the inevitable maw of home, may sagely shake his head at the engaged young man and assure him that things are seldom what they seem. But, taken all in all, the experience of the engaged young man is one that comes but once in a lifetime, and long may it live.